AUSCHWITZ— THE NAZI CIVILIZATION

Twenty–Three Women Prisoners' Accounts

Auschwitz Camp Administration and SS Enterprises and Workshops

Compiled, Translated and Edited
by
Lore Shelley, Ph.D.

Foreword by Yehuda Bauer, Ph.D.

UNIVERSITY
PRESS OF
AMERICA

Lanham • New York • London

Copyright © 1992 by
University Press of America®, Inc.
4720 Boston Way
Lanham, Maryland 20706

3 Henrietta Street
London WC2E 8LU England

Library of Congress Cataloging-in-Publication Data

Auschwitz—the Nazi civilization : twenty-three women
prisoners' accounts : Auschwitz camp administration and
SS enterprises and workshops / compiled, translated, and
edited by Lore Shelley ; foreword by Yehuda Bauer.
        p.   cm. — (Studies in the Shoah)
    Includes bibliographical references and index.
    1. Auschwitz (Poland : Concentration camp)
2. Holocaust, Jewish (1939–1945)—Personal narratives.

        I. Shelley, Lore, 1924–   . II. Series.
D805.P7A956   1992   940.53'18—dc20   91–41659 CIP

        ISBN 0–8191–8471–3 (cloth : alk. paper)

Die Weltgeschichte ist das Weltgericht

(Friedrich von Schiller)

To the memory of

M and M

Meta Schoeneberg-Weinberg

my mother

and

Masza Szaldajewska-Pinczewska,

my mother-in-law

both of whom were gassed in Auschwitz

Acknowledgments

I wish to express my gratitude to a number of people who helped me put this book together.

Edita Maliarova, Grete Roth and Lili Duschinsky served as coordinators for the contributors in Czechoslovakia, Dr. Marie-Elisa Cohen did the same for those in France, while Menahem Rafalowitz served in this capacity in Israel.

Hermann Langbein of the Comite International des Camps in Vienna supplied information about the SS personnel of Auschwitz.

Kazimierz Smolen, Director of the Panstwowe Muzeum Oswiecim Brzezinka, generously allowed me to copy archival material.

Linda Breder and Jan Pessl translated material written in Slovakian, Irene Miller translated from the Czech language, Mila Muller from Polish, and Miriam Silberschatz and Miriam Ofer from Hungarian.

Dr. Erich Kulka and Dr. Jacques Stroumza provided documents from the Wiener Library and from Yad Vashem. Jerry Dubin furnished the sheet music for the Auschwitz Song. And Nina and Mark Lees tirelessly and devotedly typed the manuscript.

I would like to thank Jerzy Bielecki for his permission to reprint excerpts of the story of Cyla Zacharowicz from his book *Kto Ratuje Jedno Zycie*, Ludowa Spoldzielnia Wydawnicza, 1990.

This study would not have been possible without the assistance of my husband, Sucher Shelley.

Table of Contents

Foreword

Lore Shelley's book presents us with the Auschwitz inferno from an angle that is different, and in a real sense, new. The twenty-four personal accounts in the book are not just haphazardly collected. They deal with a number of issues, and they are checked for accuracy, as far as possible, against the known development of the camps that together made up the Auschwitz complex. They try to present, basically, the female experience in the camps, and deal with both general issues that were common to all inmates, and also with gender-specific problems. Not only the victims appear in the accounts—also some of the perpetrators appear, of course through the eyes of the inmates. The perpetrators are both male and female, and some of the relationships between them, hierarchically and gender relations within the same level, contain some important insights. But the main problem of course is that of the inmates—how they lived, how they managed to survive, what were the main problems they had to confront in their struggle for bare existence.

Another new element is the fact that Lore Shelley's fascinating book deals with a number of sub-camps that were within a general area around the chief three camps of Auschwitz (Auschwitz I, the headquarters camp; Auschwitz II, Birkenau, which contained the gassing complex, the women's camp, the Gypsy camp, and the Czech families camp, among others; and Auschwitz III, Monowitz, the industrial center). It deals with agricultural experiments, with forms of industrial slavery, and details the specifics of each such sub-camp through the experiences of the victims. Nor are the testimonies one-sided within themselves. Jews and non-Jews, women from different European countries, all of them participate with their personal stories. Together, they make up a mosaic which has historical as well as psychological interest in the first degree.

We do need more such books—they deal with the problems of oral testimony in a way that enables us to approach the latter with a cross-check and verify the testimonies. In the absence of trustworthy and reliable German documentation, oral testimonies are a most important element in supplementing our knowledge, and whatever written material survived can serve not only as a reference point to the witnesses' stories, but can also be corrected by them, if there are converging testimonies in sufficient number.

Lore Shelley has made another important contribution to our knowledge of that darkest period, so far, in human history.

Yehuda Bauer
Hebrew University, Jerusalem

Preface

The tens of thousands of survivors' testimonies stand in lieu of written documentation; they are central to our knowledge. Without the survivors we are nothing. They are the link between us and the Jewish life that was destroyed; they are the testimony and the proof; they saw their fellow Jews die. We should treat them and their experiences with the utmost respect—for this, after all, is the basis of all the "lessons."

Yehuda Bauer

Auschwitz does not require any introduction. It stands for the complete negation of everything man has accomplished, achieved and created since the dawn of mankind.

More than forty-four years have elapsed since the Russian Army liberated the camp and the world caught a glimpse of what had been going on behind the electrified wires. Many events have not yet been recorded and we are trying, at the eleventh hour, to fill in some of the missing pieces of the mosaic.

After the publication of *Secretaries of Death*, the story of some of the inmates who worked in the office of the Political Section of Auschwitz, narrated by thirty-one of my co-prisoners and myself, I was approached by a number of friends who asked that I produce a similar description of other Auschwitz work details. I decided to exclude the FKL (women's camp in Birkenau), about which a vast literature exists, and to restrict the accounts to women who worked in Auschwitz. I contacted or visited more than one hundred and fifty persons in different countries and encountered, in many instances, extreme reluctance to touch upon the deeply traumatic events of the past which were often unmitigated by the passage of time. In addition, quite a number of potential contributors and actual participants passed away since the inception of the project. Thus, the compilation of stories was a truly arduous feat, but eventually, fifty-seven reports were obtained, of which twenty-four are presented in this book.

We have attempted to describe a few non-Birkenau based women's work details through eyewitness accounts. The stories are often of an extremely personal nature and contain many varied recollections, insights and reactions.

Some of the contributors focused on the pre-Holocaust period, depicting the deterioration of conditions, the narrowing of options, the seemingly inexorable course of events; some dwelled on the dehumanizing Birkenau inferno, on happenings they were ill-equipped to portray because our human vocabulary is simply devoid of adequate terms; a few attempted to tell about, or sometimes only enumerate, as many of those that had perished as they could remember, to tear them out of the anonymity of the Six Million, to give them a face, a voice and a name and to enact a sort of roll call of the dead; some concentrated on recounting simple survival, some on helping others, sabotage, resistance or solidarity among inmates; some recalled the terrible letdown of the liberation period after the initial euphoria had subsided when most of the outside world proved to be unable and unwilling to emotionally assist the survivors, so marked by their experience that total integration into everyday life was a semblance; others wrote about the post-Holocaust era, the psycho-social adjustment problems and the difficulty in coming to terms with a world that had not changed in the direction many of us in camp had idealistically hoped it would.

Some of the women are accomplished writers while others are eloquent in their inarticulateness. Each contributor was unrestricted as to contents, emphasis, structure or format of her story and I tried to preserve the uniqueness of every memoir in terms of style, expression and terminology, refraining similarly from value judgments, comments, assessments or corrections.

The contributors are a widely heterogeneous group with regard to age, education, religious background, occupation, nationality, political and ideological outlook, lifestyle, affiliation and other characteristics, comprising Jewish women from various European countries—now dispersed over four continents, former political prisoners as well as one Jehovah's Witness. Even in Auschwitz their experiences were vastly different. Some worked in offices, others in agriculture, sewing or laundry workshops, camp hospitals or grain warehouses. However, all of them were fortunate enough that, eventually, they managed to fulfill—however inadequately—at least the lowest level of Maslow's hierarchy of needs. Otherwise, they would not be here to tell their stories.

The accounts offer different points of view and perspectives which frequently pertain to the same occurrence—almost in Rashomon fashion. At the same time, they complement, corroborate and resemble each other closely, describing identical atrocities and identical horrors. They lend credence to some scholars' belief that "eventually a consensus version of Holocaust history may emerge from these personal accounts" (Hartman). Hopefully, they forever disprove some academic historians' narrow view that survivor memoirs can never serve as primary material for history.

Introduction

The concentration camp of Auschwitz was formed in May 1940 in the vicinity of the Polish town of Oswiecim, located in the Voivodeship of Cracow, 60 km. west of Cracow and 30 km. south-east of Kattowitz.

It became the largest concentration camp in the German system comprising approximately 135,168 inmates at one time according to a document smuggled out of camp by the Resistance movement on August 22, 1944: Auschwitz I had 15,971 male prisoners; Auschwitz II had 19,424 male prisoners, 39,234 female prisoners and 30,000 unregistered Hungarian Jews in transit, while Auschwitz III had 30,539 male prisoners (Czech, 1989, p. 860).

Auschwitz had been designated by Himmler as the stage for the execution of the "Final Solution" of the Jewish problem. After the cessation of the killing centers working under the code name of Operation Reinhardt, i.e., Treblinka, Sobibor and Belzec, and the discontinuation of Majdanek and Chelmno, Auschwitz became a gigantic death factory.

It is estimated that approximately 1.6 million people died in Auschwitz, about 1,350,000 of them were Jews. Of these, it is believed that about 1,345,000 were gassed (1,323,000 of them Jews) while about 255,000 found their death through hunger, disease, work, torture, shootings, hanging, phenol injections and pseudo-medical experiments (Bauer, 1989, p. 7).

In Auschwitz more persons were killed than anywhere ever before at one place on this planet. That's why the term Auschwitz became a symbol for men's organized inhumanity toward their fellow-men.

Auschwitz had been purposefully planned as a place where prisoners were exterminated. The work and living conditions in camp were such that a young, strong and healthy person had the chance of surviving from a few weeks to about a few months, provided he or she was not selected for the gas chambers, did not fall ill, did not have an accident, was not experimented on and did not attract the attention of a prison functionary or an SS man. Nevertheless, there were survivors and the women in this volume are all survivors. What accounted for this survival? Three Polish researchers, Jagoda, Klodzinski and Maslowski, asked former Auschwitz prisoners, most of them Polish political prisoners, in 1974/75 the reason for their survival. They came up with a number of factors believed by them to have been responsible for their outlasting the camp:

Psycho-physical ability to resist (inurement of body and mind) was named by 65.5%; 60.6% cited attitudes which had a positive influence on survival (such as belief in survival, religiosity, closeness to relatives, trust in the ultimate victory of good over evil, even a desire for revenge); 59.4% reported the help received from co-prisoners; 55.6% listed heightened self-preservation instincts, presentiment and instinctive avoidance of danger, slyness, spontaneous willingness of risk-taking and good adaptation to camp conditions; 36.3% stated work conditions favorable for survival; 33.7% mentioned chance; 25.6% knowledge of German; 17% referred to medical help received or other factors.

The editor investigated attitudes of Jewish Holocaust survivors in 1981, and obtained the following self-reported reasons for survival:

- 73.8% believed that chance (also termed "luck", "destiny", "miracle" or "coincidence") was the principal ingredient responsible for survival, agreeing with two well-known survivors:

    "Even Solzhenitsyn...would not have survived if he had not been set free by those who rule the Gulag Archipelago."
    (Bettelheim, 1979 pp. 287–288)

    "For Lustig, survival or death was more often a matter of chance than of choice."
    (Sherwin, 1979 p. 27)

- 49.5% of the respondents believed faith enabled them to survive the camp.
- 26.8% stated that coping skills helped them to survive.
- 26% asserted that friends assisted them in surviving.

Additional factors mentioned were: the will to survive, special capabilities, youth, survival for some purpose, resistance, type of work in camp, and psychological removal.

Most of the participants of this volume lived outside the main camp, isolated from their fellow-prisoners and survived precisely because their living and working conditions were atypical for Auschwitz and incomparably better than those of the women in Birkenau. Quite a number of them belonged to the resistance movement in camp. A few of them succeeded in saving human lives and others were able to smuggle out information about Auschwitz to the Polish underground which was transmitted to the government in exile and broadcast by the BBC in London.

Finally, I would like to point out that this book contains accounts of survivors about their personal Auschwitz experiences; it does not comprise an overall vision of their camp universe (the make-up of the SS-state, the geography of the camp, the camp structure, the SS-murderers, etc.). It has been said that the Holocaust is not one story but many, not one history, but rather six million or more case studies. To truly comprehend these dark years, we would need nothing less than to trace the individual experience of every survivor. Thus abandoning the general view of the anyway too gigantic whole in favor of an essential detail establishes the right of the individual not to be overlooked and conforms to John Ruskin's view of obtaining the facts right from the source: "The only history worth reading is that written at the time of which it treats, the history of what was done and seen, heard out of the mouths of the men who did and saw."

PART ONE

Office Work Squads of the Stabsgebaeude Camp Offices

Administratively, Auschwitz concentration camp was under the authority of the Central Office of Economy and Administration, Section D (SS-Wirtschafts Verwaltungshauptamt, Antsgruppe D) and was structured similarly.

I—Command Post (Kommandantur)

The camp commandant was in charge of the concentration camp and was responsible for all problems connected with the camp. He was also the chief of the garrison, the director of all enterprises belonging to the SS (such as DAW, DEST, etc.) and located within the confines of the camp.

II—Political Section (Politische Abteilung)

An SS officer of the Gestapo in Kattowitz was in charge of this section. It kept the personal files of the prisoners, corresponded with the Central Security Office of the Reich (Reichssicherheitshauptamt—RSHA) and with the centers of the Secret State Police (Gestapo) and the Criminal Police (Kripo) that sent prisoners to the camp. They received new transports; were in charge of camp security (fight against the inmate resistance movement); of interrogations during which the prisoners were horribly tortured and which often ended with the inmate's death; of the civil registry and of the administration of the crematoria. The Erkennungsdienst (photographic service) also belonged to this section.

III-Camp Management (Schutzhaftlagerfuehrung)

The most important duty of this section was the direct administration of the concentration camp. The section chief made reports about the number of prisoners, was in charge of interior camp order, participated in the execution of corporal punishment and assisted at executions. He was assisted by Rapportfuehrers and Blockfuehrers.

IIIa—Manpower Section (Arbeitseinsatz)

The head of this section was in charge of employment for all prisoners, exploitation of manpower, work schedules, formation of work squads (Arbeitskommandos), etc. He was assisted in his task by Arbeitsdienst-men (noncommissioned officers) and sentries, SS-garrison members who guarded the prisoners during their work. This section also kept books about the monetary compensation the different enterprises had to pay to the camp for the labor performed by the prisoners.

IV—Administration (Verwaltung)

This section was in charge of all assets of the camp. It was subdivided into several departments, for example, administration of prisoner belongings, cash and all storage facilities, including the ones where the goods were kept that had been stolen from the victims.

V—Physician of the Garrison (Standortarzt)

The physician-in-chief was in charge of all health problems and was responsible for the control of sanitary and hygienic conditions. He was the head of the garrison doctors (Truppenaerzte), the camp physicians (Lageraerzte) and the auxiliary personnel, i.e., the SS-orderlies (Sanitaetsdienstgrade or SDG).

VI—Administration of the SS Sections (Truppenbetreuung)

This section was in charge of instruction for the SS.

CHAPTER 1

Command Post

(*Kommandantur* — Section I)

The concentration camp was led by the camp commandant, who was responsible for all of the problems connected with the concentration camp, above all for guaranteeing full security. At the same time, he occupied the function of chief of the garrison (Standortaeltester) and of director of all enterprises in the Auschwitz area (Interessengebiet) belonging to the SS, such as, for example DAW (Deutsche Ausruestungswerke, the German Armaments Works) and DEST (Deutsche Erd- und Steinwerke, the German Mineral and Stone Works).

The first commandant of Auschwitz was Obersturmbannfueher Rudolf Hoess (May 1940-November 1943), the second was Obersturmbannfuehrer Arthur Liebehenschel (November 1943-May 1944), and the third and last was Sturmbannfuehrer Richard Baer.

In November 1943 Auschwitz was subdivided into three separate camps: Auschwitz I (Auschwitz proper), Auschwitz II (Birkenau) and Auschwitz III (Monowitz and other satellite camps). Each camp had its own commandant.

Shoshana Heymann (née Susanna Rosenthal)
Jerusalem (Israel)

I was born on March 3, 1925 in Essen (Ruhr) as the oldest of two children of Hanny and Sally Rosenthal. My
family belonged to the upper middle class. We owned
two stores in the major business district of Essen. My
mother, whose maiden name was Weinberg, had an orthodox upbringing in a little village called Huemmling
while my father, who came from Ruedesheim (on the
Rhine) had been raised in a liberal way. We kept a kosher household and followed the traditions of Judaism.

Unfortunately, my father died when I was nine
years old, and my mother continued to take care of both business enterprises with
two of her sisters who had always lived with us. At the end of 1937, we were com-
pelled to give up everything.

I attended the Jewish elementary school and was prevented from going on to
high school because of the Nuernberg Laws.[1] I, therefore, completed only the
eight mandatory grades offered by the Volksschule. Through some business connections, my mother managed to enroll me in a private commercial school where I
was able to take a course in shorthand and typing in the summer of 1939, without
receiving credit or obtaining a certificate of completion.

For a number of years, I had been a member of Maccabi Hatzair,[2] a Zionist
youth movement, which is why I decided to go on Hachshara (preparation for emigrating to Palestine) to Havelberg at the end of 1939 or the beginning of 1940. In
1941, most of the smaller Hachshara locations were liquidated and I came to Neuendorf near Fuerstenwalde (Spree).

In April 1943, we were transported to the Grosse Hamburger Strasse in Berlin in order to be deported to Auschwitz. We arrived in Birkenau on Hitler's birthday, i.e., on April 20, 1943.[3] My prison number was 41983.

The single, overriding thought in the inferno which I recall was the determination of the active Neuendorf group of girls, even the non-Zionist ones, to attempt to stay together. In the beginning, we were in quarantine, then in the herbal
work detail and later in the Weisskaeppchen. Meanwhile, some of the Neuendorf
women were transferred to the Stabsgebaeude.

At our arrival in Birkenau, I had reported my skills as a shorthand-typist. One
evening, during roll-call, they were looking for secretaries. Lore Weinberg and I
(and perhaps a third one) were selected from a large crowd (I do not remember
any more how many there had been). Anyway, the following day we were taken to
the Stabsgebaeude.

After a few days I was sent to the Kommandantur (the commandant's office)
to work in the personnel department. The adjutant of camp commandant Hoess, I
believe his name was Zoller (he was limping like Goebbels), tested my shorthand

and typing skills. He most probably was satisfied because I remained in the work squad. My boss was Unterscharfuehrer Herpel, who could not understand why I was in Auschwitz since I had not committed any crime. He also did not want to believe that I was Jewish. I did not look Jewish, behaved like his children and spoke the same language, only, perhaps, a little better. It did not fit into the picture. He had been indoctrinated for so long and all his beliefs and concepts were shaken. He was not so young anymore, had children my age and treated me like a little girl. Later, he brought me lunch every day in his canteen and stood guard while I was eating so that nobody would notice.

Well, I worked in the personnel department of the SS. Every morning I had to check and correct the list of SS men on duty in the room of the head of the section, Stabscharfuehrer Detlev Nebbe. Afterward, I had to keep the sick list in the SS-Revier. In addition, I had to take care of the correspondence from the RSHA (Kaltenbrunner) and WVHA[4] (Pohl). When Adolf Eichmann[5] visited Auschwitz, he noticed me at the Kommandantur. Since I did not look "Jewish," he tried to convince me that somebody in my family must be "Aryan," if not my parents, then my grandparents. He asked me to let him know and promised that he would personally take care of my transfer to Ravensbrueck. I told him that my parents as well as all of my grandparents were Jewish and this settled the matter. Two other women prisoners worked together with me in the Kommandantur, Lilli (married name after the war was Angress) and Alma Weiss. Lilli came from Berlin and Alma from Muenchen. Both of them worked in different rooms with different SS men.

The three of us later received additional rations once a week from the prison kitchen in the men's camp, such as bread, margarine and also possibly ersatz jam. We were not allowed to take these food items to the Stabsgebauede, but because of them I could give my portions in the block to the other girls of our Neuendorf group. Anyway, we did stick together and helped each other, especially spiritually. Our madricha (youth leader) was together with us in the Stabsgebaeude and every Friday night we celebrated Oneg Shabbat. We remembered the Jewish holidays and did fast on Yom Kippur. On Hannukka we lit candles; one of us always had to stand guard until the lights burned down.

In the summer of 1943, I fell ill with malaria. At first I was in the sick room at the Stabsgebaeude. A few days later, some other girls and I were transferred to the KB (Krankenbau-Revier) in Birkenau. One of the girls was Slovakian and knew the Slovakian KB physician. Thanks to her, we were registered as influenza cases, and the physician secretly gave us chinine (quinine). When there were selections, they announced, "Those from the Stabsgebaeude remain in their beds." So we were spared. After a short while, we were returned to the Stabsgebaeude.

Through a chavera of our Neuendorf group who worked on the Trockenboden (drying the laundry) and had connections with a kapo, I received chinine. In addition, I obtained the medication from an inmate of the SS Revier, whose name I have forgotten. My Unterscharfuehrer knew that I had malaria, but helped me as much as he could to overcome the attacks. Whenever I had a shivering fit, I did not work at all, and he took care that nobody else noticed it. However, I was able to somewhat control the attacks with the help of chinine.

Around the end of 1943, Hoess was replaced as commandant by Liebehenschel. I do not remember too much about him, only that he attempted to improve conditions in the camp. He was not too successful, because only six months later he was replaced by Richard Baer who became commandant of Auschwitz. Baer's first act was to replace us three Jewesses with Non-Jewish German prisoners. We had to initiate our replacements. But the three new prisoners did not know shorthand or typing and were eventually replaced by civilian workers.

I then joined the Political Section. At first I wrote interrogations for the Gestapo of Kattowitz for about six to eight weeks. Afterward, I became secretary of Pery Broad, who worked at that time, toward the end of 1944, with Wilhelm Boger. Elfi Spandau was Boger's secretary. Boger was the interrogator-in-chief of the Political Section and the horror of Auschwitz, even for the SS.

I do not remember exactly what kind of reports I typed, most probably not too many because the Russians were approaching, and it looked as if the war was drawing to an end. The SS tried to destroy as much incriminating evidence as possible. For many weeks we had to burn documents. Broad was—an exception is not the correct term—he actually did not fit into the framework of the SS. He was intelligent, had studied, spoke foreign languages and loved literature and music, particularly those pieces that were forbidden. Nevertheless, he was an enthusiastic Nazi. He was friendly and polite to us. I do not know whether he pitied us because he was certain that we would not leave Auschwitz alive. We knew too much about the gigantic machinery of destruction.

And then there were rumors that Auschwitz would be evacuated. On January 17, 1945, we did not go to work any more. On January 18, the infamous death march began. So much has been written about it that I don't want to dwell on it. Our group of girls from Neuendorf tried to stay together as much as possible. We came to Ravensbrueck and from there to Malchow. At the end of April 1945, we were on the road again, marching in the direction of Neustadt-Glewe. En route, sometime between May 3 and May 5, we were liberated jointly by Americans and Russians in a small village called Luebz.

At that time, we were seven Neuendorf girls who made every effort to get accustomed to the situation. We did not know our precise location; only that we were somewhere in Mecklenburg and we were afraid of the Russians. Firstly, they were Tartars and looked very fear-inducing; secondly, we spoke only German which did not actually contribute to our safety. However, soon we encountered former inmates of other countries and it was not so noticeable that we hardly opened our mouths. It was much easier to communicate with the Americans, thanks to our school-English.

Either in Luebz or in Parchim, we went into an empty house to lie down for the first time in a real bed. The Germans had fled and had left everything lying around, even food. We bolted the doors and windows as well as we could, but the Russians tried to enter. With great difficulties we explained to them that we had just been liberated. Then we went to the Russian commandant and, luckily, there was a Jewish officer on duty. It took some time until he believed us since we spoke only German and not Yiddish, but we did know Hebrew prayers. From then on, our house was "off limits" and we also received food. Well, we all had problems with eating. All of us had diarrhea until we were sensible enough to start eating gradually.

After about two weeks, the Americans started to withdraw westward over the Elbe river. The area was going to be solely occupied by the Russians. We did not want to stay behind and joined the march in the direction of the West; particularly since many in our group wanted to go to Palestine. It was not easy to cross the border which was guarded in the East by the Russians and in the West by the Americans with no men's land in between. But, a group of American soldiers that had taken care of us all this time promised to help us. They belonged to the 101st paratroop division and were as good as their word. We arrived safely in Lueneburg.

Lueneburg was full of D. P.'s (displaced persons). There was even a D. P. camp in an old military barrack. We stayed there only a short time and soon obtained an apartment. Then we heard that a Zionist group had been organized in Bergen-Belsen and Kruemel (Esther Loewy) and Miriam Edel went there. Soon, Hannah David disappeared. So, only four of us remained: Anni West (Rosenhain), Irmgard Mueller, Nomi Bachar (Klezewski) and I.

In the fall of 1945, I went to Essen to see whether any of my family had returned. I was unsuccessful and after a month I returned to Lueneburg. During the winter of 1945-1946, I moved to Frankfurt (Main) where I worked as secretary for the Jewish Agency. I had been promised that after a year of work I would be able to emigrate legally to Palestine.

In April 1947, I arrived in Haifa. I knew that the survivors of our group were on hachshara in Afikin and I joined them. Together with other former concentration camp inmates and partisans of the Gordoniah[6] movement in Poland, we founded Kibbutz Netzer Sereni. In 1948, I married a man of the Neuendorf group. We have three children. Our youngest son is, unfortunately, retarded and lives in an institution.

In 1951, we left the Kibbutz and went to a moshav (cooperative village) where we remained for thirty years. For health reasons, and because none of our children wanted to take over the farm, we gave it up and moved to Jerusalem in 1981. Since almost our entire families were exterminated, our friends of the Neuendorf group living in Israel and America are our most immediate and closest family. I know that I can rely on each one of them not one hundred but two hundred percent.

NOTES

Shoshana Heymann

1   In 1935, Hitler promulgated the now infamous Nuremberg Laws which introduced discriminatory measures against all German Jews.

2   A Jewish sports organization for youth.

3   On April 20, 1943, there arrived with a RSHA transport from Neudorf, Niederschlesien (correctly Neuendorf in der Mark, ed.) approximately 1000 Jewish men, women and children. After the selection, 299 men, receiving the numbers 116754-117502, and 158 women, receiving the numbers 41870-42027, were admitted into the camp. The remainder, about 543 deportees, were killed in the gas chambers (Czech, 1989, p. 472).

4   Obergruppenfuehrer Oswald Pohl was chief of the VWHA (Economic-Administrative Main Office). He masterminded the "economic" aspect of the program to exterminate the Jews, as part of Himmler's emphasis on the efficacy and financial independence of the SS. Pohl ensured that all the personal possessions of the gassed Jews—hair, clothing, gold tooth fillings, wedding rings, jewelry, and so on—were sent back to Germany and turned into cash.

Pohl went into hiding at the end of the war. Arrested in 1946, he admitted that the existence of death camps had been no secret in Germany. "Everyone down to the lowest clerk knew what went on in the concentration camps." He was sentenced to death and hanged in 1951. (Wistrich, 1982, pp. 235-236; Gutman, 1990, pp. 1142-1143.

5   On February 29, 1944, SS-Obersturmbannfuehreer Adolf Eichmann, the chief of the Jewish section IV B 4 of the RSHA visited Auschwitz (Czech, 1989, p. 731).

6   A Polish Jewish Zionist youth movement.

CHAPTER 2

The Political Section

(*Politische Abteilung* — Section II)

The Political Section functioned as the representative of the RSHA (Reichssicherheitshauptamt in Berlin, the Central Security Office) in camp. It could independently decide the fate of inmates and was only required to inform the commandant accordingly.

Section II had branches in all of the satellite camps of Auschwitz and was subdivided into six departments: document section, civil registry, interrogation section, legal section, admission and photographic section.

The functions of Section II were the following: maintaining the card file and personal dossiers of all prisoners, corresponding with the RSHA and the various Gestapo offices, responsible for sending prisoners to Auschwitz, receiving prisoner transports, maintaining camp security, combatting any resistance movements among prisoners, interrogating prisoners, keeping the civil registry and administering the crematoria.

The first director of the Political Section was SS-Untersturmfuehrer Maximilian Grabner. On December 1, 1943, he was replaced by SS-Untersturmfuehrer Hans Schurz.

An account of thirty-two former inmates who worked for the Political Section in Auschwitz was published in 1986, entitled *Secretaries of Death*, Shengold Publishers. At that time, the whereabouts of Helena Rotstein had been unknown.

Helena Rotstein (alias Ilonka Gutman)
Melbourne (Australia)

I was born and educated in Lodz (Poland). After finishing high school and obtaining my matric, I took a short course in bookkeeping and typewriting and, soon after got married. Two weeks before the war, my husband went on a business trip to Hungary, and after staying in Yugoslavia and Bulgaria landed in Istanbul, where he lived until the middle of 1943. Then he went to Israel (Palestine at the time).

I came to Birkenau-Auschwitz on March 3, 1943, from Cracow, where I was imprisoned.[1] I had false Hungarian papers (Jewish) which were good at the time. When the Germans liquidated the ghetto, they took the prisoners as well. We were loaded into trucks by SS-men with big dogs, pushing us with rifles and screaming, "Los! Schnell! Schnell!"

The trucks were covered with canvas. We couldn't move. We had to stand all the way to Auschwitz. We were about one hundred people in the truck, packed like sardines and hardly able to breathe. One young man cut the canvas with a razor blade and jumped out. Then three or four people followed him. The SS-men stopped the truck and chased them, shooting all of them on the spot.

The journey from Cracow to Auschwitz took a few hours and when we arrived in Auschwitz the men were taken to one side and the women to the other side, and the selection began. Families were broken up, crying children were taken away from their mothers and the mothers chosen for work. But the mothers didn't abandon their children and went with them to the gas chambers.

Then we came to Birkenau, where I was registered under my false Hungarian name and had the number 38312 tattooed on my left arm. We went for the Entlausung, our hair was shaved off and we were given white and dark blue striped prison dresses. Shoes were thrown at us which didn't fit. We were crying and we did not recognize each other.

They put us into a block which was called the "Quarantine Block." We were about 500 women, under shocking conditions. We slept on stone bunks, eight to ten girls in a bunk and we were freezing. The block was infested with lice, fleas and rats. Two wheelbarrows were put outside the block and these were used as toilets, and we had to relieve ourselves in front of the SS-men and SS-women in the camp.

Every day, someone died or was taken away to be gassed. Every morning we had to stand three to four hours for roll-call—in line. I cannot recall how many of us stood in line. It was still dark and bitterly cold and we only wore our light prison dresses. We were not allowed to talk or move. Lots of girls fainted from exhaustion but we were not allowed to help them. After the roll call they were taken to the gas chambers. We stayed six weeks in this Quarantine Block. Our Blockaelteste was a girl named Edith and she gave me the job of being a "Torwache." I was standing at the door and nobody was allowed to come in or go out and when I saw an Aufseherin approaching our block, I had to warn Edith. As I was standing there, I used to hum songs, mostly very sad and nostalgic songs. Out of my misery and sorrow the humming sounded very beautiful. Edith used to call me in and ask me to sing and they all cried.

One day, several SS-men came into our block looking for girls capable of doing office work. Out of 500 girls, they chose 13, and I was one of them. I must say that Edith helped me, because I had to undergo a small exam and I wasn't so fast on the typewriter. But Edith put in a good word for me, saying that my fingers were frozen and she knew that I was a good typist. And this is how I came to the Politische Abteilung and because of my false papers I was known in the Politische as Ilonka.

There was not enough place in the Stabsgebaeude, so we were put up in "Haus 40," and there already were girls from the Erd und Steinwerke Kommando and a few Jehovah's Witness prisoners.

The name of the Aufseherin was Zimmer. She was a middle-aged woman who was always screaming at us, calling us Saujuden, Stinkjuden, eating our bread.

In the Politische Abteilung, I worked in the Registratur. Unterscharfuehrer Otto Schmidt was watching us in the room, and some time later, Rottenfuehrer Joseph Pach. I worked as a clerk in the section of the Dead Prisoners Division with Willie Pajak and Gisi Herbst. Willie was in charge of this section and we had to write the death notices of the prisoners, the time and cause of death. This was not the case for the dead Jewish prisoners. Only a list came for the dead Jewish prisoners and very often I saw the names of close friends and relatives on this list. I didn't dare make a sound. The Jews who went straight to the crematoria were not registered at all.

For a short time I filed the documents which came from Gestapo or Kripo offices with the personal dossiers of the prisoners, but after a month or so a few new Jewish prisoners came to work in the Politische and I was put in the Karteisection of the Registratur, where Renee Vessely and Janka Berger were working.

The cards were filed in alphabetical order and divided into two sections—that of the living and that of the dead prisoners. And this again was divided into men's and women's cards. Because of my knowledge of the Polish language it was easier for me to find the file of a Polish prisoner. Very often the SS officer would come in pronouncing the Polish surname of a prisoner in a German way and it was very difficult to find the card, but because I knew all the possibilities of the Polish spelling, I always found the card. You had to be fast and efficient. They screamed at you and called you "stupid goat" and other abuses if you were slow. One cannot comprehend the humiliation, the anguish, the tension and the anxiety, besides the fear of being selected for the gas chambers. It was with us every minute of the day.

Very often Herma Hirschler called me in to be an interpreter for Oberscharfuehrer Anton Brose, whose secretary she was. Brose was quite pleasant.

Very often he left food for us and I never saw him beating or torturing prisoners. Quite often I advised the accused on what to say when I was interpreting, or I changed his story myself. I helped many prisoners in this way, but it was only possible to do this with Brose.

Before the war, my husband had been conducting business in many European countries, and I remembered names and addresses of some of his clients. We at the Politische were allowed to write short notes a few times through the Red Cross. So I wrote to some of his clients, telling them who I was (because Ilonka Gutman was not my real name) and that I was in a working camp, Birkenau, and I was "very well." They forwarded the notes to my husband, who was in Istanbul at that time. He didn't know what kind of camp Birkenau was and tried everything to help me get out of there.

One day one of the secretaries in the Politische (I think it was Dunia Ourisson, who worked for Unterscharfuehrer Draser) told me that a letter had come to her SS-man attempting to exchange me for a German prisoner, I don't remember in which country he was. She typed the reply telling them that this was impossible, because I was a "secret-bearer." I was lucky they didn't send me to the crematorium. Several times I received small parcels with sardines from Turkey, where my husband lived, and I shared these with my friends.

I also remember that in the summer of 1944, several high ranking SS-officers came from Germany to Auschwitz. They were in the room with Oberscharfuehrer Brose, where Herma and I were working. When Brose left the room for a few minutes, one of the men asked me whether it was true, that prisoners were gassed here and what happened to the people sent here from a camp in France. I think the name of the camp he mentioned was Vittel[2] (but I can't remember the name for sure). When I told him that they all went to the crematorium, I knew, because I had the list of names in my hand, he couldn't believe it. He told me to be strong, it would not be long any more, something was going to happen soon. I told him about the exchange my husband tried for me, he made a note of my number. After this I was excited for several months, and this kept me going. I think that these SS-men must have belonged to the group that tried to kill Hitler, of which von Staufenberg was the leader.

The Erd und Steinwerke offices were outside the camp, where seven girls from "Haus 40" worked. A few Poles who were not prisoners also worked there. I was particularly friendly with Lotte Frankl, who, incidentally, I see about twice a year. She came from New Zealand and now lives in Sydney. The Poles were active in the Polish underground and very often asked Lotte if she could bring them, through me, information about certain prisoners. I looked up the dossiers of the prisoners concerned and gave them all the information they wanted.

We walked every day from "Haus 40" to work, with an SS-guard and a dog. One day, one of us, a middle-aged woman called Frau Walter, married to a Gentile (eine Deutsche Mischehe), suffered a massive heart attack. We carried her to work but she died in the office after we arrived.

In 1944, the whole "Haus 40" was moved to a brand-new block. The inmates of the Stabsgebaeude also moved in. It was very clean and it had a separate eating room.

In April or May 1944, thousands of Jews arrived from Hungary. The gas chambers worked non-stop day and night. The sky was red from the flames and a horrible smell hung in the air from the burned bodies. Out of every one thousand people, only 80 were registered. The rest went into the gas ovens. Renee's parents were in one of these transports and went straight to be gassed.

At the end of summer a few air-raids took place and we were all overjoyed and happy about this, but unfortunately one of the girls from our kommando, Hedy Winter, was hit by a bomb and died.[3]

On January 18, 1945, we were evacuated and began the tragic death march. The winter was very cold, there was snow everywhere and we had no food. I had a loaf of bread, still from Auschwitz, which I threw away because it was too much for me to carry and walk. My feet were swollen. On the road were many corpses of people who could not keep up the walking or were trying to escape. One had to keep in line while marching, otherwise you were shot. For several days I had nothing to eat and I licked the snow.

Finally, we arrived in Ravensbrueck and then Malchow. I was weak and emaciated and could hardly walk. We sat on the floor and didn't work. Then, I don't remember exactly when it was, I escaped during an air-raid.

After several weeks in Germany, where I stayed for some time with a group of Polish people who had been sent to Germany for forced labor, the Russians came. They put me up with a German family, where I recuperated. I went back to Poland to find out whether anybody of my family had survived.

My whole family had been wiped-out, but for one sister, who now lives here in Melbourne. After a few weeks I went to Hungary, where my sister lived. She survived on false "Aryan" papers there. Then I went to Italy and from there, on April 14, 1946, I went to Palestine, where I was reunited with my husband. I was the only stowaway passenger on the ship "Transylvania" and without a permit to enter Palestine. When we arrived in Haifa, the English authorities came aboard and checked everybody's papers, but also a Jewish delegation came to greet us. They helped me get off the ship, by me pretending to be a member of the greeting delegation. My husband had looked for me and had passed me several times, but had not been able to find me. Of course, he did not recognize me.

After 18 months in Israel we moved to London, then again to Rome and New York, and finally to Australia. Since November 1949, I live with my husband and family in Melbourne. We have two sons, happily married, and five grandchildren. Both sons are medical doctors, one a dermatologist and the other a radiologist. My husband, a former company director, is now retired and we are comfortably off. We used to travel a lot, now we are very happy to stay home. A direct flight from Melbourne to San Francisco takes 13 hours. To Europe much longer, with many stop-overs. We are not conveniently located.

In June 1987, we celebrated our golden wedding anniversary.

After almost 45 years, I cannot forget Auschwitz. For years I used to have nightmares, screamed and cried at night and my husband would wake me and say, "Calm down, you are at home, not in Auschwitz."

It is impossible to describe what Auschwitz was really like. One has to have enormous talent to convey the pictures. Not one of the films made about Auschwitz can portray the real thing. I never thought that I would live to tell this terrible story. I believed that at the end they would kill us all because of us knowing too much and working in this death factory. But the Allies were approaching with such speed that the SS-men didn't have time to do anything and wanted to save their own lives.

One should never lose faith.

NOTES

Helena Rotstein

1   Helena Rotstein probably arrived in Auschwitz on March 13, 1943, not March 3, 1943, because her number 38312 belonged to a group of people who arrived on 3.13.43. Pola Plotnicki, who had number 38309, was among these women (see Shelley, 1991, pp. 256-272). Danuta Czech reports: "About 2,000 Jewish men, women and children arrive from ghetto B in Cracow on March 13, 1943. After selection, 484 men who receive the numbers 107990 to 108498 and the numbers 108467 to 108530 as well as 24 women who receive the numbers 38307 to 38330 are admitted into camp. The remaining 1,492 persons are killed in the gas chambers of crematorium II" (Czech, 1989, p. 440).

2   Vittel was a detention camp near Nancy in France. The camp, established in 1940, was used to intern nationals of enemy and neutral countries whom the Germans wanted to exchange for their own nationals. Unlike other Nazi camps, Vittel consisted of luxurious hotels, located inside a park. The internees were British subjects, American citizens and Polish, Belgian and Dutch Jews. The latter were in possession of Latin American passports. A few succeeded in emigrating to Palestine in July 1944 but the rest were sent to their deaths to Auschwitz. The Vittel camp was liberated in September 1944 (Gutman, 1990, pp. 1578-1579).

3   The air raid during which Hedy Winter was killed occurred on September 13, 1944 (Czech, 1989, p. 876).

CHAPTER 3

Work Allocation Office

(*Arbeitseinsatz* — Section IIIa)

Due to the introduction of files for all prisoners in 1941, those working in the employment bureau were divided into two sections. They were the Arbeitsdienst, whose main task was the organization of prisoner work details and the Arbeitseinsatz, whose task was to maintain files, prepare statistical reports and lists of transports.

On April 15, 1942, Rudolf Hoess, the commandant of Auschwitz, reorganized the Arbeitseinsatzbuero, which until then had belonged to camp Section III and transformed it into an independent department, i.e., Section IIIa. As chief he appointed the second Schutzhaftlagerfuehrer, SS-Obersturmfuehrer Heinrich Schwarz. The non-commissioned officers remained in their positions: Hauptscharfuehrer Franz Hoessler, Unterscharfuehrers Wilhelm Emmerich, Goebbert and Heinrich Schoppe.

During the spring of 1942, four prisoners worked in the Arbeitseinsatz. Several more were added at a later time. During the spring of 1943, the assistant director of the employment bureau—SS-Obersturmfuehrer Sell—released all prisoners working in the Arbeitseinsatz with the exception of two, and brought several new ones as well as several women from Birkenau as a replacement. After the creation of the camp for men in Birkenau in April 1942, an employment bureau was set up there also. The Arbeitseinsatz section was maintaining two files: one according to the inmates' work squads and another according to the professions of the prisoners. All men prisoners from the Birkenau camp except for those from the Gypsy camp were included in the files.

When, in March or April 1942, a camp for women was created in Auschwitz, an employment bureau for women was set up—Arbeitseinsatz Frauen Konzentrationslager. The existing personnel of the bureau in the main camp was charged with the responsibility of supervising the employment of women prisoners. In August 1942 when women were moved to Birkenau, the bureau was reorganized and several women were assigned to work there. They worked in the Arbeitseinsatz section where files were maintained according to names, numbers and professions; a book listing all deceased was also included. Along with the Arbeitseinsatz, an Arbeitsdienst section was established which was responsible for organizing and sending women prisoners to work and for preparing daily reports regarding the state of employment of women for the employment bureau in the main camp.

Some of the women prisoners of the Stabsgebaeude who worked in the main office of the Arbeitseinsatz were: Maria Dummel, Vera Franze, Ibolya Gross, Gisi Holzer, Judith Kahane, Lili Kahane, Marta Weiss and Herta Wilhelm.

Vera Plaskura (née Francee)
Warsaw (Poland)

I was born on November 4, 1924, in Letus-Celje, Slovenia, Yugoslavia. During the war, I lived in Slovengradce/Slovenia. On June 2, 1942, I was arrested and incarcerated in the jails of Celje and Maribor. On March 6, 1943, I arrived in Birkenau (Auschwitz II) where I received the number 37943. After two weeks, I was transferred to Auschwitz I.

The living quarters of the women inmates were in the cellar of the Stabsgebaeude. There were about 500 women prisoners and most of them worked in offices such as: Arbeitseinsatz, Politische Abteilung, Bauleitung and many others. About 40 women worked two shifts (day and night) in the Buegelstube and approximately 100 women worked two shifts in the Waschkueche and Naehstube. There were also 4 hairdressers who did cosmetic work for the SS-women and who also cut the hair of the women prisoners. In addition, there were some Stubendienste (cleaning women).

In the basement of the Stabsgebaeude, we had three-tier bunk beds for sleeping. The sick women were transferred to the Birkenau women's camp. Here, the prisoners were not segregated by nationalities. The "Aryan" women slept close to the entrance and the rest of the space was occupied by Jewish women. This block was a "Musterlager." The SS-women on duty were Clausen, Brunner and Hasse— I do not remember the names of the others.

The first and second floor of the Stabsgebaeude were occupied by SS-women of the Auschwitz and Birkenau concentration camp. The SS-beauty parlor and the SS-tailor studio were also located on the first floor while the workshops for washing, mending and ironing the laundry and clothing of the SS-men were situated in the basement.

I worked in the central Arbeitseinsatz office of the Auschwitz concentration camp. My co-workers were:

"Ibi" Ibolja Pozimska nee Gross, from Czechoslovakia, who now lives in Tarnowskie Gory; Gisi Schloss nee Holzer from Czechoslovakia. She now lives in Ramat Gan, Israel; Herta Wilhelm. She now lives in Germany; Judith Duermayer nee Kachan, now in Vienna, Austria; Lili Kachan, Judith's sister, who now lives in Czechoslovakia; "Pummerl," from Germany, present address unknown; Lilly, Pummerl's sister, an excellent steno-typist, whose current address is also unknown.

The male prisoners who worked in the Arbeitseinsatz were Rudi Kunst from Vienna and Pawel Ludwik, a Pole. The head of the Arbeitseinsatz was SS Obersturmfuehrer Sell. Before the war, he had been a "Schneidermeister" (tailor). He considered himself to be very handsome and elegant—but in reality he was the opposite. Before Sell, we had had Hauptsturmfuehrer Schwarz who later became Lagerfuehrer and then Lagerkommandant in Auschwitz III, Monowitz-Buna. In the end, this function was performed by Lagerfuehrer Hoessler and Untersturmfuehrer Josten. The non-commissioned officer who checked the guards in charge of the workers was Unterscharfuehrer Kapper, while SS-man Emmerich was the head of the work detail Arbeitsdienst.

Our kommando started work at 4 o'clock in the morning and toiled until evening. In the afternoon we had a lunch break, afterward we continued to work until 8 o'clock at night.

At first, we worked in the "Blockfuehrerstube." Subsequently, they built a barrack opposite the Blockfuehrerstube. It served as office for the Lagerfuehrer and the Arbeitseinsatz.

The Arbeitseinsatz had to compute the labor statistics and keep index cards of the entire inmate population. It was our task to assign work to all kommandos and to allot inmates to them. Our filing cabinet contained the following documentation:

Personal Kartei. It consisted of square, plain file cards, imprinted on both sides. On the front right upper corner was the number of the camp. Each card had lines for: name, date of birth, place of origin and date of admission (to the camp) for all inmates. On the reverse of the card we noted the prisoner's place of work, changes of work and dates of work.

The Berufskartei. Its cards were square and vertical and were filed according to occupation. Each occupation in turn was filed according to prison numbers. I do not know what criteria were used to record these items on the Berufskartei. For the Personalkartei we used to copy the occupations from the "Zugangslisten" which we received from the Schreibstube.

The Totenkartei contained all the Personalkarten and Berufskarten of the deceased prisoners. After receiving the cards of the dead from the Haeftlingsschreibstube or a Sonderbehandlungs—list from the Politische Abteilung, we used to transfer the pertinent cards to the Totenkartei.

For instance, before the liquidation of the gypsies, we were told to prepare

cards for living prisoners because they claimed that the gypsies were merely transferred. We issued the cards and placed them separately—but before the evacuation
they were all destroyed.

The writing and sorting out of the Personalkartei was done by women. The
Berufskartei was kept by Lili Kachan and Gisi Holzer. Herta worked with the
Nummernbuch where she registered all those prisoners who died. She was very
musical and was good at composing songs.

In addition to the index card files, we had to take care of the daily correspondence and file the Sonderbehandlung-lists.

When a transport was sent from one camp to another, we had to sort out the
cards of the assigned prisoners and send a list, as well as the cards of the inmates,
with the transport. In the case of the gypsies about whom I wrote before, they
never made a list and their cards were not dispatched. So, we knew that no transport had ever left and that they had all been gassed.

We used to get news and sometimes extra food and clothes through the male
prisoners Pozimski and Werner from the Arbeitsdienst in the men's camp.

Early in the morning, when we arrived at work, we received from the
Haeftlingsschreibstube not only the work assignments but also, illegally, all kinds
of news which made us feel better.

The work was not hard physically but very nerve-wrecking. Everyone had a
special task for which she was responsible. The work had to be accurate and very
precise. We worked in the office together with the SS-men. So we had to be clean,
neatly dressed and well-groomed.

In our office, we were well informed about every transport that left, about
important happenings and work occurrences.

The layout of our barrack was the following: A long hallway ran in the middle with double glass doors at the end. The front door led out onto the square in
front of the gate with the inscription "Arbeit Macht Frei." The back door was in
the direction of the Aufnahmegebaeude. Entering the barrack from the direction of
the gate with the memorable words, the first room on the left-hand side was the
Melderaum. Here worked Kapper and typist Lilly. In the second room on the left-
hand side worked Sell; in the third Josten; in the fourth Pawel Ludwik, Rudi and
Judith. The fifth room contained the files. Behind the file room was the restroom
for the SS and the last one on the left was the restroom for the inmates. The first
room on the right was for Lagerfuehrer Hoessler. The following two rooms were
occupied by the Arbeitsdienst. The third was for the Arbeitsdienstfuehrer and the
fourth for the inmates working for the Arbeitsdienst. Room #5 on the right was
called Fuehrerheim and the last room on the right was for the cleaning inmates,
the "Kalfaktoren."

I do not know who put together the lists of the manpower prison population
or how they were made up and how much money was paid to the camp for their
labor. I do know that Pawel Ludwik and Rudi used to put together an Uebersicht
(a report about the work performed) every two weeks. These statistics were sent to

the head of the SS in Berlin-Oranimburg.[1]

The longest period of my incarceration was spent in the Stabsgebaeude. One month before the bombardment, we had an Entlausung and were transferred to the Erweiterung. There were new buildings with warehouses and rooms for the SS. One building in the Western corner of the compound was covered with a screen, and behind it were the watch towers for the SS-men. We were transferred to this building.

I worked in the Arbeitseinsatz until the evacuation. In January 1945, Sell ordered us to destroy all documents. We started by burning the lists of the Sonderbehandlung and the cards of the dead inmates. We tried to burn the documents in the ovens of our office but, after putting a lot of paper inside, the fire went out. So they told us to make a bonfire behind the barrack.

We had to pack the current correspondence and the lists of the living into crates. They were locked and put on trucks which left Auschwitz. At the last minute, they wanted to also put me on this truck. It happened during an air raid. I hid on top of a cart used to transport the dead and covered myself with a blanket. In the meantime, the truck left.

We were evacuated on foot (a march, later referred to as the "death march") via Brzeszcz and Pszczyna. After Pszczyna, I had a chance to hide in the forest together with my friend Zofia Burghart. This way I gained my freedom.

Jerzy Pozimski
Tarnowskie-Gory (Poland)

I was born on May 5, 1913, in Szarlej, near Piekar Slaski. On June 24, 1940, I was sent to Auschwitz as a political prisoner, where I received the number 1099.

At first, I worked in various work squads, i.e., Industriehof-Bauhof and others. Later, I was secretary of Block 5a (presently 3a), and after that Block 4a (present number).

In 1941 I was transferred to the "Arbeitseinsatz" in the slot vacated by Czajor.[2] I held that position until December 1942, i.e., until the time of the escape of Otto

Kuesel.[3] and Mietek Januszewski. I then became an "Arbeitsdienst" from the rank of the prisoners, where I remained until January 18, 1945. I testified on the subject of my work before Investigative Judge Sehn.[4]

I believe that the basis for employing prisoners as "Arbeitseinsatz" existed from the outset of the camp. Back in the summer of 1940, Oberscharfuehrer Hoessler always stood at the exit gate situated between Blocks 3 and 14 (present numbers), checking the sizes of the work details and assigning appropriate work stations.[5] When I started to work in that section, it consisted of three people and its office was situated in the so-called "Blockfuehrerstube" (by the main gate). It was one of the rooms on the right side, where at a later time the postal censor (Postzensurstelle) was located. These offices were subsequently moved to a special barrack which no longer exists. During its existence it stood between buildings occupied by the so-called "Aufnahme" (reception) and the stable barracks, on the left side when leaving the camp. In this barrack, apart from the "Arbeitseinsatz," there were also offices of the "Schutzhaftlagerfuehrer" and the officers' canteen, where Bronek Czech, Jan Krokowski, Drygalski, Fliegel and others were employed. In addition, there was the office of the camp director. The entire "Arbeitseinsatz," d/b/a Abteilung IIIa and "Schutzhaftlagerfuehrung" d/b/a/ Abteilung III were located there with the exception of the "Rapportfuehrer's" office.

If I remember correctly, the following prisoners were employed in Section IIIa. I have listed them in alphabetical order:

Josef Baras (Komski)	lived in Regensburg, N.R.F. (West Germany)
Bernard Bialucha	town of Chorzow
Ernest Bieniek	lived in Tarn. Gory (Swierczewskiego 7)
Josef Cyrankiewicz[6]	
Alfons Czajor	shot in June 1942
Josef Gabis[7]	worked in MHD, Krakow
Mieczyslaw Januszewski	escaped from camp in December 1942
Eryk Kalus	(lived in Rudza)—discharged to the army in 1942
Edwin Kofin	N.R.F. (West Germany)
Wincenty Konieczny	shot in camp in 1942
Ernest Kowalski	worked in the "Wirek" mine—Halemba
Kramer	?
Werner Krumme	?
Janusz Kuczbara	escaped from camp in 1942
Otto Kuesel	escaped from camp in December 1942—caught in Warsaw
Josef Kuk	deceased
Pawel Ludwik	lived in Krakow
Nowakowski	?
Karl Ohlez	?
Willibald Pajak[8]	lives in Podlesie K/Puszczyny
Jerzy Pozimski	Tarn. Gory—Powstancow 10
Josef Rogowski	Tarnowskie Gory
Edward Skorupa	died in 1954
Rychard Skorupa	Bytom, "Szombierki" mines
Henryk Szklorz	Chorzow—Batory

Apart from the above there were other prisoners whose names I do not remember.

The SS-Arbeitsdienstfuehrers I remember best were:

Oberscharfuehrer Hoessler, Scharfuehrer Emmerich, Unterscharfuehrer Schoppe and Scharfuehrer Fries. Schoppe and Fries both left for the SS Panzer division. The director of the entire "Arbeitseinsatz" was SS officer Schwarz—then Sell. His assistants were Kapper and Oberscharfuehrer Bogusch.

One of the first Arbeitsdienstfuehrers was Kirschner, then Muller, Schulz, Stiewitz, Lewenda, Jurkowski, Salaban, Mahl, Hertwig and Oppelt. Apart from these, there were others whose names I do not remember.

The function of the "Arbeitseinsatz" was to find out the prisoners' trades and specializations and to employ them accordingly in the respective work stations. In order to achieve this goal, the "Arbeitseinsatz" was subdivided into the following cells or units:

1. "Arbeitseinsatz"—whose duties were:
    a. Upkeep of card files of prisoners in four ways: according to their prison numbers, alphabetically, by work detail and occupation (Alfabetisch, Nummernweise, Berufweise, Kommandoweise).
    b. Upkeep of daily work assignments of prisoners in the respective work squads. This record was based on a daily report produced by the kommando secretaries before the "outmarch" of the kommandos to the Arbeitseinsatz (Abt. Kartei).
    c. Update of the card files according to the hospital reports of the deceased, received in the office, and a list of incoming prisoners from the Political Section. Also recorded were prisoner transfers and releases from the camp, based on reports from the secretaries' office (Abt. Kartei). The accounting of the incoming prisoners was based on the "Zugangsliste," also in cases pertaining to larger transports, the prisoners of "Abt. Kartei" registered the newly arrived prisoners with the Political Section (Aufnahme).
    d. Preparation of statistical reports for Berlin, namely (Uebersicht) work applications).
    e. Preparation of monthly prisoner work plans (Arbeitsdiagramm).
    f. Preparation of statements for autonomous firms (i.e., I.G. Farben, mines, etc.) employing prisoners.

2. The next cell (unit) was "Arbeitsdienstfuehrer," with an assistant/prisoner "Arbeitsdienst" whose tasks were:
    a. Daily allocation to individual kommandos, firms and approval of "Arbeitseinsatzfuehrer" and "Arbeitsdienstfuehrer."
    b. Preparation of daily reports of number of kommandos and number of working prisoners.

The number of all the working prisoners was one of the groups contained in the daily accounting of the entire camp.

Apart from the group of working prisoners there were various other accounted groups such as: the group in the bunker, the ones on a quarantined release, the newcomers' quarantine, the sick in the hospital, and kommandos employed in the camp, including block "caretakers," secretaries and others. All the groups together had to add up to the overall accounting of the camp population. I can't name all of the camp kommandos. I remember, however, that near the end there were close to 130. These kommandos were divided into several basic groups: Kommandantur, Politische Abteilung, Verwaltung, Bauleitung, Landwirtschaft, Kriegswichtige Zwecke, Privatfirmen, etc. I know that there was a bulletin in 1944 put out in connection with the Allied bombing, in which there were kommandos instructed to return to the camp during the bombing and kommandos who were to remain in their workplace.

Abteilung IIIa, in Auschwitz I, conducted the central distribution of working prisoners to other Auschwitz camps and sub-camps. There were, however, appropriate independent units of employment in these camps and sub-camps.

In connection with this type of centralization, the "Arbeitseinsatz" in Auschwitz I worked out lists of prisoners sent to other concentration camps at the request of the WVHA Amtsgruppe D. These lists were established in agreement with the prisoners' secretariat and approved by the Political Section. The approval was necessary, in my opinion, to prevent sending out from Auschwitz prisoners who were sentenced to death, so-called "Geheimnistraeger," i.e., those who worked in confidential units of the camp such as Sonderkommando, Arbeitseinsatz, Politische Abteilung, hospital, etc.

As I recall, at some point the concentration camp fell into three male camps: Auschwitz I, II and III (Buna). The last one contained the entire Aussenkommandos and Aussenlaeger. I remember the following subcamps:

Trzebinia-Trzebionka; Gleiwitz I, II, III, IV; Lagischa; Fuerstengrube; Guentergrube; Sosnowitz; Jawischowitz; Bobrek; Golleschau; Charlottengrube; Bismarckshuette I, II; Hindenburg; Gute Hoffnungshuette; Kobior; Janinagrube; Bruenn; Laurashuette; Neudachs; Blechhammer; Eintrachthuette; Hubertushuette; Buna; Budy; Rajsko; Plawy; Harmeze.

In order to establish an accurate nomenclature I would like to explain the following terms:

1. Lagerkommando—working groups not outside of the camp terrain but within the wires of the camp.

2. Aussenkommando—working groups within or even outside of the perimeter of the Grosse Postenkette (large sentry chain) but returning to camp for the night.

3. Aussenlager or Nebenlager—working groups, small or large, who worked and lived outside the terrain of the said camp, in special camps located near the place of employment, e.g., mines, foundries, factories administered by

Auschwitz III. These sub-camps were self-administered with their own director, usually under the rank of an officer. Sometimes, the director of the camp was referred to as a Kommandofuehrer in lieu of Lagerfuehrer. Dedicated Blockfuehrers were appointed Kommandofuehrers. For example, I remember that Oberscharfuehrer Moll became Kommandofuehrer in Fuerstengrube.

4. There were also kommandos referred to in camp slang as "kommanderowki" in which the prisoners did not return to camp for the night and they did not have an administration with the exception of a secretary. They did not have a Lagerfuehrer or Kommandofuehrer and were not governed by the administration of Auschwitz III except for the women's camp in Birkenau (Harmeze, Budy, Babica, Plawy).

Of the multitude of forms that were used in camp I remember the following:

1. The form "Posteingang/Postausgang" was the card file at the camp mail-censorship office (Postzensurstelle), where the incoming and outgoing prisoner mail was recorded and checked.

2. The "Beschaeftigtenszusammenstellung" was the report on the employment of prisoners connected with the "Industriehof" Auschwitz I.

3. The "Staerke der Arbeitskommandos" was a report on the working units engaged within the camp territory. The report was prepared by the Lageraeltester (camp elder) and forwarded to Arbeitseinsatz.

4. The "Postenanforderung" was a requisition form for SS (Postow) guards for the following day. The form was prepared by the Arbeitsdienstfuehrer and forwarded to the commandant's office, which delivered the required number of guards (Postows).

5. The "Block:...geb:...Staatsangehoerigkeit" was a form categorizing prisoners into occupation groups prepared by the data group of the Arbeitseinsatz. The top left corner of the form was separated by two small lines colored in with the appropriate color by type of prisoner.
The position of "Ausgefallen wegen" was filled in the instance of inability to fill the occupation listed in the register "Beruf." My wife worked in this section. The forms were filled out by women prisoners working with card files. I remember an occurrence when wanting to engage prisoner Josef Cyrankiewicz in the "Arbeitseinsatz." I requested that his old card with the notation of "Beruf—advocate (jurist) be changed to "Urzednik" (office employee). Presenting the changed notation on the card to the Arbeitsdienstfuehrer, I initiated the employment of the above-mentioned prisoner in that kommando. This card file underwent a second change when the men in the Arbeitseinsatz were replaced by women. On the same principle the occupation of prisoner Cyrankiewicz was listed as "medical student," which enabled him to obtain employment as a "Hilfspfleger" in the camp hospital.

6. "An den Fuehrer des Schutzhaftlagers K.L. Auschwitz" was a form reporting the punishment of prisoners. It was prepared on the basis of SS reports to the

camp director. The report was signed by the accusing SS-man, given to Unterscharfuehrer Janson, subsequently to Grohssow, with the intent of forwarding it to the camp director for further action. The director then called in the prisoner to his office with an immediate decision.

7. The "Totenmeldung" was a form prepared by the camp secretary in the event of a death occurring in the block during the night or a free-from-work day. This form was filled out without regard for the type of death, i.e., natural, suicide, etc.

8. "H. Krankenbau des K.L. Auschwitz, An die Politische Abteilung des K.L. Auschwitz" was a form filled out by the camp hospital informing the service centers (listed on the left corner of the form) of a death for the purpose of removal of the prisoner from existing data. Apart from the six service centers listed on the form, the Arbeitseinsatz also received a copy. It was a procedure of eliminating the prisoner from the roster but not mentioning the cause of death.

9. "K.L. Arbeitseinsatz" was a form filled out by the Arbeitseinsatz for all kommandos working outside of the camp. This form, commonly referred to as "Arbeitszettel" was taken by the Kommandofuehrer and returned by him to the Arbeitseinsatzfuehrer upon return from work. In instances where the Kommandofuehrer did not request the prisoners for work but only escorted them to work, the form was signed by the director of the establishment for whom the work was done. Thus, the prepared document was the basis for billing for the work performed by the prisoners.[9]

10. "Arbeitskommando Jeden 15. des Monats auszufuellen" was a form filled out by the Kommandofuehrer on the 15th of each month for the Arbeitseinsatz. The Arbeitseinsatz card files were updated on the basis of the information provided by this form.

11. "Uebersicht ueber den Haeftlingseinsatz im K.L._____ Monat_____ 194_" was a monthly summary report of daily work reports. These reports were produced for the Director and Commandant of the camp.

12. "Fragebogen Fuer Haeftlinge" was a form filled out by the Political Section (Aufnahmekommando). This form was used in the beginning. It was later replaced by a two-sided form.

From the time Untersturmfuehrer Sell became "Arbeitseinsatzfuehrer," most of the prisoners working on the card files were "laid-off" and replaced by about 19 women prisoners from Birkenau.

Among the women I remember the following names:

1.	Balla, Alicja	from Slovakia	no address
2.	Gross, Ibola (Ibi)	from Slovakia	now Pozimska Barbara (my wife) lives in Poland
3.	Holzer, Gizi	from Slovakia	now Schloss, lives in Ramat Gan, Israel

4.	Kahan, Judyta	from Slovakia	now Duermayer, lives in Vienna, Austria
5.	Kahan, Lilli	from Slovakia	now lives in Prague, Czechoslovakia
6.	Wilhelm, Herta	from Slovakia	now lives in Weinheim, West Germany
7.	Franze, Vera	from Yugoslavia	now Plaskura, lives in Warsaw, Poland

The women were in a shocking condition: Hungry, dirty, without proper shoes (they wore heavy wooden clogs) and inappropriate underwear. Although anyone helping Jewish prisoners risked being punished, I decided to help them as much as I could. With the assistance of my prisoner colleagues, I tried to organize food, margarine, jam and later, also sugar and tea.[10]

I would pass on all those food items to Ibola Gross, who, in turn would turn them over to her comrades. In the same way, I would organize medicine and clothing (underwear, shoes, stockings). I had to be extremely careful because the SS-men were watching all (women) prisoners during their work in the office very closely (Kapper—Bogusch). This continued up until the time of evacuation (January 1945), that is, for about two years.

The first group of women was later increased by a number of new women. All were, of course, included in my "plan." In addition to that, often the women would find in the files names of their relatives and family members. I would then receive the name and number written on a small piece of paper and we would try to provide them with food and medication. In the period of two years, there were hundreds of those whom we helped. After the war, a relative of Ibola Gross, by the name of Dezider Kleinhandler, thanked me for all the help and invited me to visit him in Duesseldorf, West Germany. Only someone who has been in Auschwitz could know how much effort, courage, and often shrewdness it took to conduct such a "plan" without exposing oneself to the consequences, which meant death.

Twenty-eight hundred Greek Jews (men and women) arrived on March 20, 1943, in a large group transport from Salonika, Greece. From that group only 417 men and 192 women survived (arrived at the camp). The rest were sent to the gas chambers.[11] After three weeks of the so-called "quarantine," I was told by the chief of the Arbeitsdienstfuehrer's office (Emerich) to assign men to particular jobs in accordance with their professions.

I asked in German, "Who speaks German?" Two prisoners volunteered, young Jacob Maestro and his father. As I found out, Jacob's father had been an interpreter in a hotel in Salonika. From a conversation with them I also discovered that Jacob knew German (a little), Greek, Italian, Spanish and Jewish. I suggested to Emerich to include Jacob in our work group as a translator/interpreter. Since that time (April 1943) until today, my friendship with Jacob has continued.

Extremely intelligent and clever, Jacob, in a short period of time, was able to surround himself with a group of his countrymen and under my leadership organized assistance for them. Although Jacob was still a child, he had a very strong "say" among the Greeks. Within the next few months a number of other transports from Greece arrived. After the quarantine period, the prisoners were assigned to work. Jacob was always a member of the group helping others and advising all newcomers to volunteer as craftsmen in order to get a good job. This saved many sick and older people from death. After a few months in the camp, these people were able to take care of themselves. In addition, Jacob would bring fruits and vegetables to our office for women prisoners: onions, garlic, cucumbers and tomatoes. This "action" continued until the last days of the camp, i.e., until the evacuation. The help he provided to Jews (not necessarily Greek) can best be described by Jacob himself, who presently lives in Tel-Aviv.

I am enclosing a photo taken in 1975. I was invited to a convention in memory of the 30th anniversary of the liberation of the Oswiecim (Auschwitz) concentration camp. I met again with a large group of former French and Greek prisoners living outside the country. All were very happy to see me again.[12]

NOTES

Vera Plaskura

1   An Arbeitseinsatz report about Jewish manpower, preserved in the Auschwitz archives, contains the following information: in Aug./Sept. 1943, SS Untersturmfuehrer Sell of the Arbeitseinsatz informed the chief of Section D II in the WVHA that 3581 able-bodied Jews were employed in the armament industry. Among them were 446 from Germany, 700 from France, 198 from Slovakia, 162 from Czechia, 37 from Croatia, 127 from Holland, 184 from Belgium, 5 from Norway, and 1722 from Greece (Czech, 1989, p. 587).

Jerzy Pozimski

2   The prisoner Alfons Czajor, No. 1193, was shot at the Black Wall on June 12, 1942, together with about 20 comrades, as reprisal for the activities of underground organizations in Upper Silesia (Czech, 1989, p. 226).

3   Otto Kuesel, Pozimski's predecessor as Arbeitsdienst, escaped on January 29, 1942, as told by Danuta Czech: "In the afternoon hours four prisoners escaped—the German Otto Kuesel (No. 2), and the Poles Jan Baras (No. 564), Mieczyslaw Januszewski (No. 711) and Dr. Boleslaw Kuczbara (No. 4308). This prepared and planned escape occurred in the following way: Otto Kuesel, who had the function of Arbeitsdienst in camp, was known to the SS men and had their confidence, drives a car into the camp in front of Block 24, loads four cupboards into the car and leaves the camp without being checked by the Blockfuehrer at the gate. Without being stopped, he passes through the entire industrial camp complex. In an open field he opens one of the cupboards. Mieczyslaw Januszewski, in the uniform of an SS-man and armed with a rifle, gets out and sits down beside Kuesel, posing as SS guard. At the final control of the large sentry chain, Januszewski shows the SS-Unterscharfuehrer on duty a laissez-passer (previously obtained) for one prisoner, accompanied by a guard. After having left the "Interessengebiet" of Auschwitz, the other prisoners also climb out of the cupboards. The escape had been arranged with the support of the A.K. Polish resistance movement.

On September 25, 1943, Otto Kuesel was arrested once more and returned to Auschwitz, from where he was transferred to Flossenbuerg in February 1944. Jan Baras was re-arrested in January 1943 under a different name and was once more sent to Auschwitz without being identified. Mieczyslaw Januszewski was also re-arrested and probably committed suicide on the transport to Auschwitz (Czech, 1989, pp. 367-368).

4   On March 29, 1945, the Polish government decided to create a commission to investigate the crimes committed by the Germans during the war. The investigations were carried out under the direction of judge Dr. Jan Sehn, who prepared the material for the later Auschwitz trials.

5   Garlinski tells us how gradually, Polish prisoners of the underground movement were accepted into the Labor Allocation Office: "Witold Pilecki, the organizer of the underground group in Auschwitz, brought into his organization some young people who worked together with Kuesel and through them was able to influence Kuesel and get his own men into kommandos important to the Organization. This applied especially to all groups of craftsmen. It is difficult to establish exactly when Pilecki got his men into the Assignment Office. From data in statements supplied by others it appears to have been by the beginning of 1941. The earliest contact was Jerzy Pozimski (known in camp as Jork). (Garlinski, 1975, p. 61.)

6   He later became the prime minister of Poland.

7   Josef Gabis was the prisoner to whom Lilly Toffler's letter was destined and on account of which she was executed (see contributions by Anna Urbanova in this volume and Shelley, 1986, p. 350).

8   Willibald Pajak also worked in the Political Section. His story is recorded in Shelley, 1986, pp. 307-322.

9   A request for payment for work performed by prisoners, prepared by the Arbeitseinsatz, has been preserved. It covers the period Sept. 1—Sept. 30, 1943, and is addressed to the Zentralbauleitung, the largest employer of inmate manpower. The bill covers 33,892 journeymen workdays at RM 4.00, 1433 half workdays at RM 2.00, 214,709 auxiliary workers' workdays at RM 3.00 and 11,461 half workdays at RM 1.50. The invoice total was RM 799,752.50 (Czech, 1989, p. 617).

10   Langbein talks about Pozimski's "organizing talents." The higher the rank of an SS-man, the more influential the function of a prisoner. The more generous was the bribing that occurred. Once, Jerzy Pozimski, the Arbeitsdienst in the Stammlager (Auschwitz I), provided a whole shoe box full of watches for his boss, Unterscharfuehrer Wilhelm Emmerich. He could obtain the large quantities of watches because everybody wanted to be on good terms with the Arbeitsdienst. It is understandable that after such gifts Emmerich had to be accommodating when Pozimski came with special requests. Pozimski, who had to supply the SS-men with food on a daily basis, also recounted another episode. SS-Hauptsturmfuehrer Heinrich Schwarz, the chief of the work squad, was once invited to the wedding of an SS-man under his command. He called Pozimski and asked for the preparation of a gift basket filled with alcoholic beverages. The basket was delivered in time. Schwarz never asked Pozimski how he had obtained its contents. In conclusion, Pozimski stated, "I have organized for all of them" (Langbein, 1972, p. 164).

11   On March 20, 1943, approximately 2,800 Jewish men, women and children arrive with a RSHA transport from the ghetto in Saloniki. After selection, 417 men who received the nubmers 109371 to 109787 and 192 women who received the numbers 38721 to 38912 were admitted into camp. The remainder of about 2,191 persons was killed in the gas chamber (Czech, 1989, p. 445).

12   In April 1989 Yad Vashem conferred the title of Righteous Among the Nation, its highest expression of gratitude, upon Jerzy Pozimski.

CHAPTER 4

Administration

(*Verwaltung* — Section IV)

This section was in charge of camp finances, provision of food and clothing for SS-men and prisoners, upkeep of all housing, including the crematoria, supervision of all warehouses, including the ones which held the belongings of the murdered victims, all repair shops and vehicles. The directors were, consecutively, Hauptsturmfuehrer Rudolf Wagner (until the end of 1941), Sturmbannfuehrer Willi Burger (until June 1943) and Obersturmbannfuehrer Karl Moeckel (from July 1943 on).

On July 1, 1943, Section IV, i.e., the Administration of Auschwitz, was transformed into an independent office by the name of SS-Standortverwaltung, run by the following persons.

1. Director of the SS-Standortverwaltung was Obersturmbannfuehrer Moeckel.

2. Director of the Standortkasse (pay office) was Hauptsturmfuehrer Polenz.

3. Director of the Standortlohnstelle (payroll) was Oberscharfuehrer Jordan.

Anny (Ann) Rosenhain (née Neumann)
Cranbury, New Jersey (USA)

When the National Socialists came to power in Germany, I was a young girl growing up in Leipzig. During my teenage years, I came to realize the seriousness of my situation due to all the strict economic and social measures being taken against the Jews.

I became engaged to Heinz Rosenhain and, in view of the dangers surrounding us, we decided that Palestine was our only hope of escaping persecution. For this reason, we both joined a Hachscharah, which was a facility for agricultural retraining of young Jewish people. This took place on an estate in Upper Silesia, and we liked working there because we were idealistic and we enjoyed each other's camaraderie. While we were there, Heinz and I got married.

After some months, a number of us were transferred to another farm named Gut Winkel,[1.] located near Berlin. There we got to know another group of young Zionists. About a year later, we moved again to a place called Landwerk Neuendorf,[2] which was similar in scope and also near Berlin, except that it was not geared toward Palestine, but to emigration to other countries, of which there were not too many. The retraining was still only in agriculture. At this point, the other Hachscharah facilities, which were strictly Zionist, were disbanded by German order and most of the people remaining were transferred to Neuendorf.

We felt fairly secure at Neuendorf, although we were under German control, but we worked in the fields, harvesting produce for the Germans and we assumed that we were needed due to the war-time manpower shortage. We knew that Jews were being deported to concentration camps from all parts of Germany.

Early in April 1943, we were informed that we would be shipped to labor camps. We tried to prepare for this deportation in every way we could. We practiced packing our gear to enable us to carry as much as possible. We tried putting on as much clothing as we could in the naive hope that we would be able to keep what we were wearing.

Around the middle of April 1943, all of us were sent to a point of assembly at the Grosse Hamburgerstrasse in Berlin. We remained there for about one week, and on April 19, 1943, we were loaded onto a train, which consisted of cattle cars and these were sealed. Conditions were extremely crowded; men, women and children packed in, with one pail in the middle to serve as a toilet. We received no food or water during the whole trip which lasted about 24 hours. The next day, April 20. 1943, we arrived at our destination. The rail line ended near a concentration camp. The doors were opened and I witnessed a scene I would never forget and which seemed to me like arriving in hell itself. There were SS-men all over the place shouting at us to get off quickly, while German shepherd dogs were barking. The SS-men were ordering men to one side and women to the other, and we were told to leave our belongings behind. The elderly and the feeble, who could not or would not walk, as well as children with their mothers and/or fathers were loaded into open trucks and these people, as we learned later, went straight into the gas chambers. This whole procedure was carried out very quickly and efficiently. The younger and able bodied men were separated from the women and I, with the rest of the girls, was marched into Birkenau. We were brought into a building and the first thing we were told was to surrender all monies and valuables that we had on our person or hidden in our clothing. If we did not do so, we were warned, and anything would be found later, we would be shot. This was a very effective way of getting hold of our possessions without much trouble or searching. The SS were very ingenious in making us do anything they wanted with sheer terror.

In quick succession, we had to strip naked and were tattooed on our left forearm with a prisoner number. Then our hair was shaved, and after a cold shower we were issued old Russian prisoner of war uniforms and wooden clogs. The same prisoner number that was tattooed on our arm was written on our uniform blouse or jacket with a yellow and red Jewish star.

After all this, we were ordered into a barracks that had two cement platforms above each other all around, separated into compartments and ten of us slept in a space the size of a full bed, packed like sardines, head to foot. We had to sleep on the concrete slabs with nothing to lie on or cover ourselves with. At this point, my mind was completely numb and I could not comprehend or absorb what was happening to us. Everything took place so fast, and the shocks we were dealt simply overwhelmed our minds and we were no longer capable of thinking like a normal human being. This treatment was very well calculated to put us into a state of no resistance and no independent thinking, and it was quite successful. The same evening, we were given a piece of bread and an old rusty metal bowl with tea or coffee; you could not tell which it was. Miriam and I shared one bowl of coffee/tea and the other bowl of coffee/tea we used for washing ourselves. Now we were ready for our first night on our cement beds.

Early the next morning, we were summoned to the so-called "Appell," which was a line-up and body count of the prisoners. This took place twice a day for the rest of our stay in Birkenau, and was just another method of torture because we were then left standing for hours in all kinds of weather and in inadequate clothing. Many girls collapsed during these "Appells," and were taken to the infirmary, never to be seen again.

A few days later, our group was quarantined, and from there most of the girls I knew were sent to the Stabsgebaeude in Auschwitz to work. I remained in Birkenau with a few other girls from our group because I worked in the Blockfuehrerstube. Once, during roll-call they had asked for girls familiar with office work. Out of about fifty girls, I had been the only one chosen. Pretty soon, however, I was fired from the Blockfuehrerstube, because a clothes-louse had crawled down my face. Shortly thereafter, I was called and tested again for an office job.

After delousing and the sauna procedures, I was taken to the Stabsgebaeude with two other women prisoners and a SS-guard. Our new quarters were a vast improvement over Birkenau both in sanitary and living quarter aspects, besides I rejoined the girls from our group. I also received different clothing. My job consisted of record-keeping concerning food distribution and consumption for this and all the surrounding camps.

My work squad was called "Verwaltung" (administration). The overall function of the office I worked in concerned food supplies for the prisoners' kitchens for Auschwitz, Birkenau and all the other satellite camps, also for the gypsy-camp. Every morning we received written reports from each camp as to the number of prisoners. For each prisoner, a certain amount of dried meat, dried vegetable, etc. was allocated. I kept statistics as to the exact amount of food supposedly to be distributed to each inmate.

About 10-12 other Jewish women prisoners worked in our detail, but I remember only a few of them: Boezsi Reich, a Slovakian, was our kapo, and the others were Hilde Gran, Irmgard Mueller and an elderly woman. My immediate supervisor was SS-man Hans Schmidt, who was eventually taken to the SS-bunker because he stole food supplies from arrivals. Afterward, I was supervised by Hans Hoffman from Bamberg, Bavaria, and my last supervisor was called Kleindienst; he was not too pleasant.

Hilde Gran's boss was Oberscharfuehrer Josef Kalisch, who was quite nice. Hilde's work consisted of typing letters and invoices.

The director of the Verwaltung was Hauptsturmfuehrer Sauer. On the whole we were treated fairly well by the SS-men of our kommando.

Because of this job, I was able to procure some extra food now and then for myself and for my friends. My job was under strict SS supervision, and I had to be very careful about what I was doing.

In the Stabsgebaeude, I was in one room with about thirty girls; we slept in double bunk beds. I used my bed at night and my friend Miriam, who worked the night shift in the sewing-room, used it in the day time. We slept on straw mattresses and inside of these we hid our personal items, such as soap, scraps of food, etc. We had showers, and the reason to enable us to keep clean was the fact that we worked close to the SS in the office. We had a little better food and we ate out of crockery bowls. We were also able to obtain food from illegal sources or by trading with others. It was always very important and very essential to have friends in camp, because that was the best way to survive. You needed others who helped you with food or clothing or just advice or sympathy to surmount all the hardship you encountered during all those many months and years in incarceration.

Never in the history of mankind have such vast numbers of people been treated with such cruelty and ruthlessness, been killed in such numbers, been reduced to such a level of suffering, starvation and sickness with such inhumanity that words simply fail to sufficiently describe it.

I managed to stay in this office until January 18, 1945, when the whole camp was evacuated because of the approaching Russian army. We were marched out of camp in deep snow and bitter cold, and anyone unable to walk was shot on the spot. Along the march route we saw lots of dead bodies of prisoners who could not make it; who were too weak and starved to be able to walk. We did not receive any food or drink during this march, all we had to eat was the snow on the ground, which we also used to wash ourselves with. This was the so called "death march."

We marched the first night through the next day, and after some rest in a barn, we continued marching and eventually we were loaded onto open cattle cars, still without food or water. Many died during this train ride. The train brought us to Ravensbrueck, which was another concentration camp. Conditions there were horrendous; we were sitting and sleeping on the floor in a large barrack. Again, there was neither food nor drink, only snow.

After a few days, they shipped some of us to Malchow, a concentration camp in Mecklenburg. There, they divided us and put us in different barracks, and we sat and slept on straw mattresses, eight girls to two mattresses. Finally, we received meager bread and soup rations. One very small loaf of bread was divided by eight girls.

We stayed there until early May when the Russians were approaching again, and we were marched out of Malchow deeper into Germany. During this march, things started disintegrating. The Allied armies were closing in from both east and west and our SS-guards started disappearing one by one. The next day, during a rest period in a field, eight of us ran away and took refuge in a barn of a farm house close by. We told the farmer that we had escaped from the east.

During the night, we heard the sound of fighting and the next morning we started walking in a westerly direction. Along the road, we saw discarded SS and other German uniforms and documents. Later on, we encountered American soldiers on army trucks. We came to a small town where the Americans and the Russians met. Our main concern at this time was looking for food, and it took us weeks to get our fill, and it also took me a long time to get used to the idea of freedom; I always felt like someone was still guarding and following me.

During this time, I also started looking for my husband and my mother. It took me a long while to find out that Heinz had died at Ebensee, a concentration camp in Austria, a few days before liberation. I found out through one of my sisters in the U.S. that my mother had survived Theresienstadt concentration camp, which was quite amazing.

My goal was to leave Germany as soon as possible, and to join my sisters in the United States with my mother. I arrived in New York in July 1946, as a displaced person and my mother followed me from Berlin about a year later.

I became a citizen of the U.S.A. and have lived here for over 40 years. Every day I am thankful for the freedom we have in this country.

❖

Irmgard Mueller
Ithaca, New York (USA)

Life was pleasant when I was very young. My father was a lawyer in Halle an der Saale, Germany; two of my mother's brothers were doctors, my other maternal uncle and my father's brothers owned or managed various family businesses, and so did the men who married my parents' sisters. My parents' friends also were either professionals or businessmen. Their children were the children I knew.

Until I started school in 1926, I actually was unaware that other people elsewhere lived differently from the way we lived!

But, then I learned that each week there were two one-hour periods during which I had to leave the class room. Those periods were called "religion." I did not understand why I should not learn the interesting stories and familiar-sounding songs that constituted religious instruction in the early elementary grades, and I did not understand why I was not invited into the houses of other children, even though we were friends during the days at school. I was, in fact, the only Jewish child in my class during three-and-a-half years of private elementary school and six years of "Lyceum" (High School).

Of course, when I got instruction in Hebrew and in Jewish History, there were some explanations. But my parents were extremely protective, in every sense, and so it happened that the SA-guard posted in front of our house in April of 1933, was a surprise to me.

Because of his distinguished military service in World War I, my father was the only Jewish lawyer still allowed to practice in Halle for a number of months, but, eventually, his office too was liquidated. Despite this and all the other ominous signs, he did not believe that Hitler would succeed and so made no effort to leave Germany, except for arrangements to have my brother transfer from taking law courses at the University of Wuerzburg to studying mathematics and engineering at the Universities of Pisa and Rome.

Again, because of my father's war service, I was allowed to stay in school until I had finished my "Mittlere Reife" examinations in the spring of 1936. Then, complying with my parents' wishes, I first took a business course at a private school, and after that I was apprenticed for a year to a master seamstress. In 1938, I went to live in Berlin while studying at the fashion design school Feige-Strassburger. The Kristallnacht brought an end to that phase.

Imprisonment in Sachsenhausen, and the death there of his younger brother, finally convinced my father that he had been wrong, and when he had recovered from the aftermath of the extreme physical and emotional mistreatment in the camp, he and my mother started vigorously searching for ways to escape from

Germany. It was decided that I should become a nurse in England. All preparations went forward without delay, my belongings were packed and shipped off, and I was to leave on September 3, 1939; however, World War II started on September 1st ...

When the German armies moved into Poland, I quickly got a job as a nanny, but when my employer left Germany, the probability that I would be requisitioned to do agricultural labor near the German-Polish border frightened my parents into giving in to my wishes and letting me go to the "Lehrgut Gross Breesen."[3]

I arrived in Gross-Breesen in January 1940, at a most unpromising time. The winter was very severe and, consequently, all of the plumbing in the Schloss (castle) was frozen. There was very little heat, the walls of one of the rooms on the ground floor were covered with thick sheets of brown ice from the frozen pipes above; every drop of cooking and washing water had to be pumped by hand, and we had to use the latrines behind the horse stables. To a city girl this, combined with the somewhat unkempt appearance of the house and its inhabitants, was almost intolerable. The main reason I stuck it out then was the fact that I had been begging my parents, since 1936, to let me go to Gross Breesen. For reasons known only to them, my parents refused until there was almost no other way for me to escape a draft into temporary forced labor.

At first, Bernstein, our director, put me in with the "Oberen Maedchen," but after a few months, more new girls arrived, so he revived the "Mittleren Maedchen" and put me in with them as their watchdog. The few people who had known the Breesen that was, tried very hard to hang on to as many as possible of the practices and traditions started by Bondy,[4] the first director, and his support staff. I think they were quite successful, so that I got thoroughly steeped in leftover "Breesen Geist." I am sure this contributed considerably to my survival, as did the right genes and a succession of fortuitous circumstances.

To start with, I was to stay in Breesen when some of us were sent into Arbeitseinsatz in the spring of 1941. But, because Ruth Schwartz, who was scheduled to leave with the first group, wanted to marry a young man who had to stay in Breesen, Ruth and I traded places, with Bernstein's help, and I went to the Forsteinsatzlager Kaisermuehl near Frankfurt/Oder. After a few weeks there, we were all transferred to agricultural camps near Fuerstenwalde/Spree.

This transfer brought about another chance event. Neuendorf, which was a short train ride away, functioned as the administrative center for the small Jewish labor camps in the area; it was also the only place where we could see a dentist or doctor, so we were permitted to travel there occasionally. Anny Neumann, the sister-in-law of one of my brother's fraternity brothers, had been training in Neuendorf for some time when I met her there. This meeting was crucial, because later on, Anny helped tremendously in keeping me alive.

In Hasenfelde, life was bearable. The work group was given a small house to live in, and we were assigned to farmers who had lost workers to the military. The work was hard, food rations were restricted, and there also were restrictions on our movements outside a given perimeter, but the farmers always got the restrictions waived whenever we had to work beyond the boundaries. We were under curfew, of course, but in general the tone was one of guarded suspicion rather than hostility, and once we had become established the farmers sometimes padded our rations a bit with expendable food items. Besides, with us, the villagers also had to cope with French POWs, and with Ukrainian and Polish deportees who spoke little or no German; in retrospect, I must say that they managed better than one might have expected. They needed us, of course, and some of them were genuinely upset when we were deported in April 1943.

In the meantime, my parents struggled on in Halle, but all their efforts were in vain. They were deported to Sobibor in 1942. I was given a three-day pass to help them pack and to put everything in order for the local authorities. My parents did not survive.

Our own deportation, in April 1943, was carried out in several stages. We were first assembled in Neuendorf, then spent two weeks in the "Grosse Hamburgerstrasse," and were brought out of Germany on Hitler's birthday.

The long train ride in bone-chilling cold, was frightening and exhausting, but there was some optimism left among us: we still believed that we were just going to a larger labor camp! Any hope was crushed forever when the train reached its destination. The arrival at the ramp was the most shocking experience of my life. There were guns pointed at us all around, and a pandemonium of warning shots, of shouted orders, barking dogs and the screams of terrorized families being torn apart.

On my second day in Birkenau, I realized that half of the women and all of the children who had been on the train, were not with us; I asked one of my block functionaries to show me the part of the camp where I might find the children and their mothers; the woman grabbed my shoulders, turned me around, and pointed to a building with chimneys letting off a large cloud of smoke and an odor I had never smelled before. "There they are," she said.

In the meantime, those of us who survived the ramp selection, were initiated into a scheme of systematic dehumanization so severe and thorough that I still wonder how I managed to pull out of it.

In Birkenau there was, at first, no organized work for us. So I volunteered for work to earn extra bread rations. I scrubbed empty barracks, dug irrigation ditches and repaired uniforms. Then, the next great change took place: after about two months, many from our group were selected to do office or laundry work for the SS and we were transferred to the Stabsgebaeude, an isolated troop barrack on the way to Auschwitz I.

The laundry and our small sleeping rooms were located in the basement of the building, the upper floors contained housing for women SS. Food was distributed and "Appells" were carried out in the basement hallway. We worked day and night shifts which switched weekly, but there was plenty of soap and water, the building had flush toilets and even a small shower room.

I don't remember exactly how many weeks I washed clothes. There came a day when the SS needed another typist in one of the offices of the Standortverwaltung, and Anny, who was already working there, volunteered me for the job. So I became a bookkeeper-typist in the office which masterminded the prisoner kitchens for all of Auschwitz and its satellite camps.

Because I tried to heed my father's warning to mind my own business under conditions of repressive authority, I never tried to find out what was going on elsewhere in the building that housed the many administrative offices. I worked in a room with several SS-men. The ranking officer was an Oberscharfuehrer, I think his name was Schmidt. My immediate supervisor was Unterscharfuehrer Kopetinksy, a Rumanian, who behaved as humanely as possible under the circumstances.

My duties every day consisted of collecting the forms brought to the office by motorcycle SS-troops from different satellite camps. Numbers were on these forms representing the prisoners present that day, and those who were absent on that same day. I copied the numbers into ledgers and multiplied them with various gram amounts of food items such as ersatz coffee, meat, bread, different starches, vegetables, jam, etc., all depending on the day of the week and the menus for that day. Once each month, I was marched by a guard to the prisoner's kitchen in the mens' camp, to compare my ledger with the one kept by the bookkeeper for Unterscharfuehrer Eggersdoerfer, and we then "justified" any discrepancies.

I, occasionally, also typed letters, but I do not remember what they were about, and once or twice I took dictation from one of the men in the main office. I vaguely remember that these had to do with some details of camp management.

There were some privileges attached to working in an office. As soon as the new camp for women at Auschwitz I was ready, we were all transferred there. At this time, I became separated from the rest of the Breesen girls. In comparison with the Stabsgebaeude, the new housing was very good. Besides large dormitories, there was a mess hall with tables and benches, and there were as yet no lice, fleas or bedbugs. We were allowed to grow some hair, and we also got most of the food we were scheduled to get, so that I was in reasonably good physical shape when we were evacuated from Auschwitz on January 18, 1945.

Again, thanks to Anny Neumann, I was sent to Malchow, via Ravensbrueck and a smaller transit camp (Bergen-Belsen or Neustadt-Glewe were two alternatives). As time went on, conditions at Malchow became more and more grim; the one thing that kept me going was the belief that I could hang on until the war would be over, and I was convinced that Germany was about to lose.

Just at a time when existence seemed barely possible, the SS marched everyone who was still able to walk, out of the camp in a westerly direction. This march started in the afternoon. During the night, some of the guards disappeared from the sides of our column, and so, at an appropriate moment, six Neuendorfers and I dropped out of the ranks and hid, first in a haystack and later in a barn near Luebz.

Within two days, some units of the American army advanced beyond this point, and we thought that we were now safe. Unfortunately, we were caught in the unstable border conditions between occupation forces. The Americans left after 24 hours and the Russians took over. We managed to elude their efforts to stop all westward movement on German highways, and eventually, had a few weeks of rest in Ludwigslust, the Headquarters of the 82nd Airborne Division. But again, the Americans left. This time the British took over first, and then, once more the Russians came. We got out of Ludwigslust just ahead of their arrival, and went via Hamburg to Lueneburg.

After a short stay in a DP camp, we got jobs with the BAOR[5] and moved out to try living on our own. Eventually, some of the girls made contact with soldiers from the Palestine contingents in the British army and started their journey southward, and some girls moved to the American occupation zone to be in a better position for their efforts to reach the United States.

Toward the end of 1945, I had been able to correspond with relatives in Sweden and England, and was trying to convince the British authorities to bend their rules a little and let me leave Germany for Sweden. No luck. Finally, with the help of Norbert Wollheim and a Canadian UNRRA[6] officer, I found a way to get out of Germany and arrived in Sweden in April 1946.

It took American immigration ten months to give me a visa, even though my brother was an American citizen, had served honorably in the American army and had found a good sponsor for my affidavit. Ah well! I arrived in the U.S. in February 1947.

For nine months, I lived in New York, then I moved to Washington, D.C., where I lived for twelve years, and finally, I came to Ithaca. Here, I first got a B.S. in Plant Pathology at Cornell, and then I worked there as a technician for 23 years. I retired in July 1986, and ever since, have been trying to get used to that.

NOTES

Anny Rosenhain

1   Gershom Schocken reminisced: "My uncle had a big Gut (country estate) close to Berlin which he had bought as an investment. He died in a car accident and my father took over the Gut and organized training courses for young people who wanted to go to Palestine. At that time, there were a number of such training centers in Germany. Gut Winkel was one of them" (Koelbl, 1989, p. 217).

2   Neuendorf is a village in the Mark Brandenburg, near Fuerstenwalde (Spree). One of the last larger transport of Jews deported from the Berlin area contained a large contingent of young people who worked in Neuendorf and the surrounding labor camps. Eight of the women in this book arrived in Auschwitz with this transport.

Irmgard Mueller

3   Gross Breesen was a training farm near Breslau to prepare young people for emigration from 1936-1938; a labor camp under Gestapo control until 1942.

4   Psychologist Curt Bondy, born in 1894 in Hamburg, was a director of Gross Breesen, a preparatory farm for young Jews from 1936-1939.

5   British Army of the Rhine

6   United Nations Rehabilitation and Relief Association.

PART TWO

Office Work Squads of the Stabsgebaeude
Various Enterprises

CHAPTER 5

Agricultural Division

(Abteilung Landwirtschaft)

The Agricultural Division had the task of developing agriculture, cattle breeding and research concerning the introduction of new agricultural cultivation. Obersturmbannfuehrer Dr. Joachim Caesar was the head of this division and had great power of authority. The camp commandant's supervisorial function, spelled out in almost every area of the concentration camp structure by the SS-WVHA (Economic Administration Head Office) in Berlin, did not apply in the Agricultural Division.

As of 1941, one of the more important areas of employment of prisoners was agriculture. It was the result of the evacuation of the existing population and the confiscation of their farms and agricultural land in order to create the so-called danger free zone. In the several hectare area, in addition to the houses, numerous livestock and farm equipment which those evacuated could not take along were left behind.

On orders of Himmler, himself an agriculturist, the tilling and cultivation of the land by the camp's prisoners was started at once with the creation of the

Landwirtschaftskommando.

Additional agricultural enterprises were created in satellite camps which specialized in different branches of agronomy. For example, at Harmense there was a poultry farm, fish ponds in Plawy and cultivation of vegetables and flowers in Rajsko. The flowers, tomatoes and cucumbers, stamped "KL Auschwitz," which were sent in early spring to Berlin, filled Himmler with pride, proving his participation in the construction of Hitler's "One Thousand Year Reich." At Rajsko, they also conducted kok-saghyz research in the hope of obtaining rubber.

Some of the women prisoners of the Stabsgebaeude who worked in the office of the Landwirtschaft were: Anna Binderova, Gertrude Juppova, Ilse Koehler, Edita Maliarova, Anna Neumannova, Jolan Starkova and Nora Stiefel.

Dr. Anna Urbanova (née Binder)
Prague (Czechoslovakia)

The well-known Italian writer and former Auschwitz prisoner Primo Levi, who is a favorite of mine, differentiates in his essay "Beyond Judgment" (*The New York Review*, December 17, 1987) between two distinct categories of concentration camp inmates: those who talk about their heinous experiences; they tell readily and in detail what pains they endured, and remember their misery and hunger perhaps when sitting down to an opulent meal among family and friends, or they speak as witnesses. The others are silent. They are silent because the wounds are still open, because they "do not feel at peace with themselves" or they are those "who feel more deeply that sense of malaise which I, for simplicity's sake, call 'shame'." I belong unmistakably to the last category. I do not find a more fitting expression for the malaise, this innermost reluctance to speak spontaneously, or when amicably requested, about Auschwitz to people without our background than Levi's term of "shame." However, I am not ashamed of my camp life, of my survival—in which I, as a Non-Jewess, could believe incomparably more hopefully than the Jewish girls. But, in view of these indescribably horrible events I am left with nothing but shame, silence and inability to speak. Nevertheless, I believe it to be right and necessary that the witnesses of these crimes report them, write about them, tell the truth to mankind and appear in public in order to do everything so that such barbarities will never be permitted to occur again.

Many authentic and scientific studies as well as works of fiction have appeared about Auschwitz and the Nazi extermination camps so that I shall limit myself to the purely personal, trying very hard to overcome my malaise in order to contribute to our commemorative book.

I descend from a German-Bohemian Catholic family. My mother, Franziska, came from a German-speaking peasant family in Southern Bohemia close to the Austrian border. My father, Franz Binder, was also the scion of a German family that had resided for a long time in Prague and had owned for many generations a townhouse opposite the city wall of Altstaetten where you can still find the wine cellar-restaurant U. Bindru. My father told me, that in the olden time, i.e., before World War I, it was a very established undertaking frequented by high government officials, writers et al. which was open only in the morning and afternoon and where smoking was prohibited in order not to spoil the flavor of the wine. Among some of the eminent family members were, among others: a prebendary (canon) of the St. Vitus Cathedral in the Hradcany (a castle, towering over the city of Prague), a certain Heinrich Binder who was conductor of the St. Petersburg opera and a grand uncle, Emil Binder, belonging to the Czech side of the family who owned a house with an apothecary's shop in the Karlsgasse and whom I remember well.

After their marriage, my parents moved to Budejovice (Budweis) in Southern Bohemia where they lived contentedly as middle-class trades people until 1946. Here, I was born on June 22, 1912, two years ahead of my sister Josefine. Even as pre-school children, our father, who had previously traveled extensively, began to teach us the rudiments of English and French and instilled in us the love of books. I spent the first three grades in a convent school, but when I proclaimed my vocation to become a nun, my sensible parents transferred me to a German public school. Here a few Jewish classmates assisted the timid child, and thus began a lifelong friendship. Perhaps, it is thanks to them that later in life I felt drawn to Jews that in the midst of a narrow-minded environment of friends and relatives of my parents who—at least in the beginning—were in favor of the Nazis I did not stray one moment from the right path.

However, during the twenties and the first half of the thirties there still existed harmony and an active social communal life among the Czechs, Germans and Jews of Budweis. My Jewish comrades had Czech boyfriends and my first love was a Jewish boy. My classmates of the German "Staatsoberrealgymnasium" attended the dances at the Czech "Beseda;" Czech high school students came to the balls in the "Deutschen Haus" where—next to the "Liedertafelball" Hanukkah was indisputably one of the most beautiful events.

I liked to study, especially languages. Besides Latin and Czech (one hour each daily for eight years in the Gymnasium), I learned French and took private lessons in English, Italian and Dutch. The latter, I studied just before my first big summer vacation trip to Holland and England which I took by myself on my bicycle. I had inherited from my father this love for the whole world— and after further bicycle tours to France, Switzerland, Austria and Italy—I am still faithful to it today.

After the Abitur (high school certificate), I could not study because my parents had financial difficulties. I stayed in Budweis, took as external student the diploma at the teacher training institute and passed university exams in the above mentioned languages as well as in Spanish. I taught languages privately, worked as a tutor, did a lot of reading, got inspired by Schopenhauer's ethics and aesthetics, played and sang Lieder at home by Schubert, Mahler and Wolf and spoiled my piano playing with excerpts from Wagner's operas. By coincidence, I learned about a clerical vacancy in the Czechoslovakian Foreign Ministry. I applied, passed the entrance examination and went to Prague in 1936. The art of typewriting which I had to master stood me in good stead only later in Auschwitz.

In 1938, after the Munich Pact, I was dismissed because of leftist views and again took up language teaching. Instead of high school students who had flunked Latin, or similar customers, I now taught Jewish emigrants from Hitler-Germany who wanted to learn English before emigrating overseas. In addition to private lessons, I taught attorneys and other intellectuals in a German social-democratic circle and communist Jewish laborers in another; these at a time when there was no more money to rent space to be used as a classroom not far from the tiny studio which I shared with my sister. She had been working for some time as an efficient secretary for a foreign car manufacturer's agency and we had a good relationship with each other.

In spite of repeated requests, I had not returned my diplomatic passport to the Foreign Ministry. I was, thus, fortunate to be able to assist friends, acquaintances and later also strangers who wanted to emigrate in dispatching their luggage, silver and other valuables abroad. We also accepted our friends' valuables for safekeeping and returned everything after the war to their rightful owners; except for one small suitcase containing towels. For example, I helped Edith R. my old school friend to obtain a French visa. In addition, I had no difficulties to pass the German border control and financial police and traveled to Leipzig and to Switzerland to settle the affairs of Jewish acquaintances. Soon this risky, still purely private activity, assumed the characteristics of political illegality. Together with my future husband I joined a Czech resistance group, not so much for ideological reasons but out of the overpowering feeling to do something against the Nazi regime which had suffocated the young, free and democratic T. G. Masaryk republic—not without the collaboration of the Western powers—and which had already brought so much suffering to the Jews. Out of my old love for these fellow human beings, there now had developed a sort of co-suffering as well.[1] In spite of the current disdain and even contempt of this emotion, I consider compassion to be the highest of human virtues and the first step to love.

In the summer of 1939, I met Dr. Harry Epstein, my future husband. In 1946, after the birth of our first daughter, we changed the name to Urban. He had been expelled from his medical practice in Brno (Bruenn) by a German "colleague" and, divorced after a short unhappy marriage, had come to Prague in search of work and possibilities to emigrate. We had decided to stay together and to continue our illegal activities.

For conspiratorial purposes, I had applied for and received an "Ahnenpass" (genealogical document attesting to my "Aryan" background) and together with my diplomatic passport and our apartment keys put them at the disposal of the resistance movement in spite of Josefine's scruples. But in our everyday life we attempted to disregard the constant threats and the numerous prohibitions. Dr. E. wore the yellow star very seldom. We frequently went for walks in the park, visited wine-restaurants (cellars) and played music together; he was an excellent cellist.

During one of his visits—the Italian grammar lay on the table as an alibi—we were surprised by the Fipo (financial police). Two giant policemen sent my "pupil" away, phoned my sister at her office and requested from us the handing over of valuables whose owner had already confessed. He was the old uncle of a friend of mine. The papers were well hidden in our apartment; similar to other items. We denied everything, trembling inside because of the search since we had rings and other jewels belonging to our friends concealed in the sugar bowl, the salt shaker and other locations. The huge fellows rummaged through the book shelves and the wardrobe, did not find anything and took us along. For three weeks we were imprisoned in the hall of justice in isolation cells with Czech guards and denied everything steadfastly until the old gentleman begged us during a confrontation to admit the whole bit. The three of us were released and smilingly we greeted Dr. E. who had been waiting for us. Well, that had still been a merry imprisonment. I had been able to complain about food and sneeringly refused to do any type of work in my cell.

The uncle went to Theresienstadt from where he did not return. My doctor found a job, at first as a mason's apprentice (doing evening studies at a construction school) then as assistant laborer in a convent nursery. But all emigration plans failed: he did not receive the visa for Uruguay nor did he go with me as missionary physician to China. The future was hanging over us like a heavy black curtain. But we were still happy together—it was summer and we took bicycle excursions into the countryside. Once, and now when I am writing these lines it is exactly 47 years ago, we listened to Hitler's de facto declaration of war to the Soviet Union on the loudspeaker of a country inn. The doctor said, "That is the beginning of the end. We are going to survive. Wait for me." On November 2, 1941, on All Souls' Day, the Gestapo picked us up—each of us separately. We saw each other once more from afar at the Prague Gestapo headquarters, the former Petschek bankhouse. He was sent to the Little Fortress in Theresienstadt destined for political prisoners. After an interrogation during which I pretended to be mentally disturbed, giving the most absurd answers, I was transferred to the Pankrac prison in Prague.

There was solidarity, confidence and a strong conviction of an early or later end of the Nazi reign of terror among the 10 Czech girls and young women in our cell, intellectuals and workers, all of them resistance fighters, some of whom had returned battered and bloody from their interrogations. I was infected by their courage and overcame the tremors that shook my entire body for fear of my fiance's fate. We became friends fast, and soon I laughed with them about my clumsy endeavors to learn how to use a scrubbing cloth. We were allowed to receive small packages with food and laundry. My sister had written a few words on a tooth brush and I learned that Dr. E. had been deported to Poland. In the beginning of January, I was sent with a women's transport to the concentration camp of Ravensbrueck near Fuerstenberg in Mecklenburg. The train ride, we were still in normal compartments, went via Leipzig where we were retained a few weeks in a work-house (camp). We had to mend soldiers' uniforms and I received my first vigorous box on my ear when I used the scissors in the sewing room to cut off my long blond hair. In the beginning of February during an icy cold, we arrived in Ravensbrueck. At that time, i.e., the beginning of 1942, everything went according to Prussian military style in this first large women's concentration camp. Order, cleanliness and discipline were decreed and kept. In the block of the new arrivals, they were calling for food-carriers: two inmates, each of whom had to carry huge buckets suspended from carrying rods and filled with—during that epoch—still edible soup. Whoever had not received gloves, had her fingers frozen—if they were not burned by spilled soup. We all wore camp clothing: uniformed dresses with blue stripes, similar jackets, white kerchiefs for our heads and shoes. Each had her clean blue-checkered bed linen in three-tier bunk-beds.

My drive for self-preservation sent me the nicest dreams at night about bright spring meadows full of flowers and sunny landscapes. So much worse, however, was the early awakening call and the loud order "to build the beds"—the beds were not made, they were "built." The edge of the blanket had to be ultra-sharp, the head bolster had to cut the correct angle. The SS-woman stood with her horse-whip next to the newcomer and let her try again and again. After this test of nerves followed the long roll-call under the wide free sky which gradually reddened from the rising sun. The fresh morning wind seemed to come from the Baltic Sea. In my first letter after many weeks I wrote my sister in March 1942: "You would be surprised how hardened I am. The air is marvelous here. We have beautiful sunrises and sunsets and flocks of storks and wild geese are flying above us. It is still snowing but soon there will be spring. How I am with you in my thoughts" etc. "Protective custody prisoner Binder, Anna, Nr. 9521, Block 16, Fr. K. L. Ravensbrueck." Every second Sunday of the month we were allowed to write home and we all endeavored to keep the news as harmless as possible in order not to upset our relatives. Besides, censorship was very strict, for example they cancelled a remark in my first letter from Auschwitz of May 1942, stating that now I even liked sitting at my typewriter.

Since I had managed to avoid being assigned to the sewing-room work detail, I was shipped with the first women's transport to Auschwitz, heretofore completely unknown to us. The transport consisted of one thousand German female prisoners who were meant to operate as Kapos, supervisors and block elders for the future Jewish transports.[2] With this goal in mind, our transport was put together; the vast majority were asocial, prostitutes and women unwilling to work—with black triangles; criminals with green triangles—thieves and murderesses who after having served their sentences had been sent to a concentration camp. According to their conversations, they had been promised "a good life" in the new camp.

The few political prisoners with red triangles or red and yellow triangles for "Rassenschande"—altogether perhaps one to two dozen—were all German or Austrian resistance fighters, most of whom had already been imprisoned for many years, such as Gerda Schneider, later camp elder in Birkenau; Orli Reichert, later in charge of the Revier in Birkenau; or Maria Maul, later block-elder of the Stabsgebaeude, et al. From Czechoslovakia, there was Anna Neumann-Petraskova from Usti who now lives in Prague. We are still friends today.

We traveled in cattle cars (however, we could move and breathe), the bucket for our toilet needs was swinging from the ceiling, and reached our destination on March 24, 1942, after a long trip with many stops. From the small, trellised windows of the cattle cars, I saw a gray desolate landscape with a few gray pitiful figures. Everything else was registered by me as a bad dream even if we were not threatened to the same extent as the following transports of Jewish prisoners by the armed SS-men with their guard-dogs who were waiting for us. They took our personal data, I received prison number 725 and Anny Neumann 912, Both of us were assigned to work in the office detail. Together with other political prisoners of our transport, we began to register the young girls from Eastern Slovakia, the first Jewish women's transport that arrived in Auschwitz on or about March 26, 1942. We had to fill out data sheets, listing name, birth date, birth place, occupation, etc. The unsuspecting, totally disturbed girls in their best dresses who had come from well-protected families "for three months of work experience" thought they had landed in a mental institution after having endured the dreadful procedure of confiscation of all belongings including clothing, disinfection and shearing of hair. Some of them heaved a sigh of relief when we talked to them in Czech and told them that we were also prisoners. I thought of the fairy tale of the "Altweibermuehle" (old wives' mill) which has the power to rejuvenate now working in reverse. Here, blossoming young girls were transformed in a short period of time into pallid, trembling creatures with wide terror-stricken eyes of irrecognizable age and gender. The infernal machinery of German and Slovakian Nazis worked perfectly. From this day on, I saw my task and my own chance of mental survival in strengthening the courage of these incomparably harder hit Jewish co-prisoners, in attempting not to extinguish their hopes and in endeavoring to assist them as much as possible.

I also registered the second transport which had come from Western Slovakia. I do not remember how many others did arrive. I was dumfounded by everything I saw and experienced. After long morning roll-calls, the work squads marched out to do outside work led by their kapos and supervisors the "Blacks" and the "Greens." They had quickly understood what was expected of them and exploited their power over life and death of the work slaves. With long bars they hit the marching women, pushed stragglers with sore feet into the water ditches, screamed and raged and assumed an air of importance in front of the SS-men and women. The latter fastened long hooks around the legs of the most pitiful inmates and pulled them out of the rows to be gassed. The political prisoners and a certain number of Jewish girls got a break: they were needed in the offices. Soon, I was transferred to the secretariat of the SS agricultural enterprises of the Auschwitz concentration camp as secretary of the director, Obersturmbannfuehrer Dr. Joachim Caesar. Here I worked for 22 months interrupted only by a three week's stay in the "Bunker."

These agricultural enterprises consisted of approximately five Polish villages (Budy, Brzezinki-Birkenau, Harmense, Rajsko, Plawy among others) which the Nazis had simply confiscated. The inhabitants had been expelled or imprisoned and the work was carried out now by prisoners. The Strafkommando (penal work squad) was stationed in Budy; I know it only from hearsay. Not less feared was the "kommando Teichwirtschaft" (pond detail) in Harmense, commanded by Unterscharfuehrer Martin. I, myself, heard him boast in our office in front of the other SS-men how many Jews had drowned mowing reed or had sunk in the water. He meant the girls who "only in panties"—Martin was grinning profusely when describing the scene—stood barefoot, knee-deep in muddy contaminated water, sore all over the body, exposed to the burning sun and the stinging mosquitos and were driven by him to speed up the mowing of the reed.

On the other hand, Rajsko was almost paradise. In addition to the nursery, there was the plant cultivation station for the rubber plant Kok-Sagyz, equipped with a botanical and a chemical laboratory. It was Caesar's major task, for which he was directly responsible to Himmler, to produce German natural rubber out of the cultivation of this Siberian dandelion plant, because there was a shortage of rubber in Nazi Germany and "Raeder muessen rollen fuer den Sieg" ("wheels had to roll for victory") according to the Nazi slogan. During their initial victorious advances in the Soviet Union, the Germans had stolen a Kok-Sagyz plantation together with the Russian agronomists and had transported it to Auschwitz.

Several SS-men worked in the office of the agricultural enterprises as sort of administrators. Kleinschmidt, Manger, Schulz et al. The head of the office was at first Berger, then Titze. The deputy of the director was Ziemssen, a serious, severe young man who soon went to the front and fell. Except for Titze, everybody behaved correctly, even friendly.

Our work detail "Buero Landwirtschaft" consisted of six girls: Anny Neumann (mentioned previously), I who reluctantly became "Kapo Landwirtschaft," the Czech half-Jewess Dinka Juppova (she died a few years ago in her hometown of Louny), and the Jewish Slovakians Edita Maliarova (who lives in Prague and is my friend), Jolan Stark (who supposedly lives in Bratislava), and Bora or Deborah whom we called Nora from Belgium (present whereabouts or survival not known).

One of the SS-men of the office, a quiet North-German, escorted us in the morning with his police dog from the Stabsgebaeude, back and forth for the soup at lunch, and again at night from the office to our lodgings. I cannot describe what we encountered on the way: the carts full of corpses, pulled or drawn by male prisoners, from which naked arms and legs covered with blood and feces were dangling; long rows of small children, marching in pairs as if in kindergarten, in their best clothes with toys and sandwiches in their hands—Nothing can erase the sadness in their big dark eyes—Compared to this, our life in the office was not so bad.

The director was SS-Obersturmbannfuehrer Joachim Caesar who held a doctorate in agricultural science. Here, only a few words about the human being Caesar, since as such he was born like all of us.

He was a stately man in his forties, a genuine "Herrenmensch" (Master Race) type in shining uniform with riding boots and horse whip (which I never saw him misuse), mostly in a good mood (about my hair ribbon on May 1st, he commented laughingly whether it really had to be red). Ironic to cynical; on hearing the news of the murder of a high SS colleague by partisans in the so-called "Generalgouvernement," he just grinned and asked, "Who is going to be the next one?" Only on the day after his wife had died of typhus did he come with red eyes, but punctually, to the office. Soon he found a replacement and a new mother for his three flaxen-haired children in the young, pretty biology student whom he had requested for the Pflanzenzucht from his former professor in Heidelberg. The latter had delivered the girl in person but had escaped in shock from Auschwitz to Caesar's amusement. The student, Ruth, had her doctoral dissertation written by the prisoner scientists in Rajsko, married her boss and, as far as I know, did no evil. Caesar, himself, never conducted himself like a brute toward us inmates during the almost two years I worked with him in the office on a daily basis. When, during a search of my desk, some cigarettes were found, he insisted on my re-instatement against the wish of the SS woman-in-chief, although I had to spend three weeks in the bunker. Only later, when political poems were found in my desk was I transferred to an outside work squad. During Caesar's post-war trial, some of my French friends were present as witnesses. He is supposed to live, or have lived, as owner of a cleaning establishment near the Swiss border.

My work consisted in taking down in shorthand (I had studied the "Gabelsberger"[3] system while still at the Gymnasium) the letters Caesar dictated and to subsequently type them. He corresponded with different SS leaders and "Gauleiters" (district administrators) in the "Generalgouvernement" (part of Poland): with the RSHA (Gestapo headquarters) in Berlin, mostly directly to the boss, Dr. Kaltenbrunner;[4] with Himmler[5] concerning the cultivation of Kok-Sagyz and with other high officials. Or, he requested from the "Arbeitseinsatz" (work allocation) new prisoners for his agricultural work details. He ordered me to search among the new arrivals for biologists, botanists and chemists and to bring him their prison numbers so that he could request them from the Arbeitseinsatz. The names and numbers of the first three biologists, all of them Catholic Polish women, he dictated to me. This was a very welcome task for me because it allowed me to name, and on Caesar's orders commandeer, those among the newly arrived transport of French Jewesses who at least half-way complied with the criteria and who, because of their physical conditions, most urgently needed a workplace with chances for survival. Knowledge of natural sciences was not a prerequisite in my selection. The entire Kok-Sagyz cultivation was nothing but humbug anyway. Life-long friendships were forged in camp. For example, this was the beginning of my continuing friendship with Claudette Bloch-Kennedy (Oxford) and Marie-Elisa Nordman-Cohen (Paris) and others.

Ella Schliesser, our little "Rosa Luxemburg," was probably physically the weakest of them all but mentally the one with the strongest personality. As the child of a Polish rabbinic family, she had come to Berlin. Early in life, she had left her parents' house and lived among the working youths. At first, she was member and later organizer of a political stage. She studied natural sciences in Paris, was arrested and sent to Auschwitz. We were intimate friends, and even today I have not overcome the tragedy that Ella, run down physically and mentally after liberation, abandoned by friends, in a state of deep depression found no other solution but to commit suicide in a hospital in Dresden by setting herself afire. Shortly beforehand, she had complained in a letter to a third person that she, who lived so close by in Dresden, had lost my address in Prague.

Eva Tichauer, the medical doctor, was also from Germany. She was a pretty, blond woman with a beautiful soul, well versed in German and French poetry. We understood each other well, and after the inmates of the "Pflanzenzucht" (plant cultivation) had been transferred to Rajsko, we wrote to each other long philosophizing letters. After her short post-war visit to Prague I, unfortunately, lost contact with her.

I would also like to remember Eva Gabanyi from Bratislava, the draftswoman of the Pflanzenzucht. She died many years ago in Hamburg. I still cherish a color sketch she once gave me for Christmas.

A little later, Riva, a pharmacist's apprentice, later the wife of Dr. Kriegel, a well-known Czech reform politician, joined the "kommando Pflanzenzucht."

Before this entire group moved to Rajsko, we all lived in the Stabsgebaeude together with secretaries of the Civil Registry; the Political Section and other office details; the two Slovakian beauticians for the SS-women; the Slovakian seamstresses—today, I am still good friends with Marta Fuchs-Minarik (Vysnie Hagy, High Tatra) of the sewing room squad;—the Catholic Polish women prisoners of the SS-laundry detail and ironing room and with other "Vorzugshaeftlingen" (privileged inmates). Our life could not at all be compared with that in Birkenau. Everybody had her own bed in a clean dormitory with three-tier bunks. There was a washroom, and we did not have to fight for the small piece of bread or the thin soup. Sometimes, a few potatoes or an onion were smuggled from the nursery. Here I would like to recall the "organizing" skills of enterprising Dinka J. and the loving care of Anny Neumann. The three of us "kept house" together but I was no good at "organizing." We "Aryans" received parcels twice per month from home which we shared, of course. We could even receive money, but there was nothing to buy at the canteen.

It is well known that people prefer to remember the good things. Thus I see myself sitting or lying on the bunk bed in the evening absorbed in long, low decibel conversations; the longest I usually had with Raya Kagan of the "Standesamt" (civil registry). In whispers, we reported to each other the events of the day, told stories from the past and spoke about our precarious wishes for the future. I loved her very much, and our sincere friendship survived the camp. She visited my husband and me in Prague in 1946, before she went to Israel. We saw each other at Claudette Kennedy's in England. I saw her again in Israel in 1968, and a few years later we made a marvelous trip to Spain. Unfortunately, already at that time, the first signs of her mental lability were apparent, a concentration camp syndrome, which necessitated her institutionalization in Israel since 1983. Camp comrades send me regular reports about her. Her memoirs, published in 1947 in Hebrew are a valuable keepsake, some of them were translated orally for me.

Or, I see myself in the circle of my "apostles," as they were jokingly called, my very young Slovakian friends who were thirsting for knowledge and whom I told about a good book, a concert or a bicycle tour abroad. At other times I attempted, as far as this was possible, to answer their questions as to the origin and meaning of life. Soscha, Magda and Vera, Ruzenka, Irene and especially you, Lisa, with the millennial eyes, you have a permanent place in my heart, you gave me more than I could give you. You reinforced my conviction that I belonged there, in bad times at the only fitting place where I could be of help. Thank God, you survived and wrote to me afterward. Some of you I have seen again in your new home in Israel—wherever you are, I salute you in old friendship.

Many of us did write poems; and not only occasional poems for birthdays and holidays which always provided a reason to celebrate. I recall with melancholy joy my 31st birthday in June of 1943 in the Stabsgebaeude, our merry, nocturnal gathering; the touching self-embroidered, or self-fabricated presents and the many beautiful rhymed wishes for happiness and freedom. My French girl friends wrote an entire notebook with old chansons and revolutionary songs including the Marseillaise. We sang on many an evening and learned Czech, Polish, French and also German folk songs from each other. The French women acted entire scenes from Moliere's comedies by heart and Ella Schliesser recited long passages from Goethe's "Faust" or I read from the first book I came across. It was a German biography of the physicist Roentgen which I had found in front of the block and which I had taken along secretly. The next book—possibly placed in my way by a well-meaning male prisoner—was Margaret Mitchell's novel "Gone with the Wind" in Dutch which I translated into German spontaneously in sequels. All these activities, as well as language lessons, improvised discussions on scientific or philosophical topics and classes in music or liberal arts were tolerated by our block elder, Maria Maul, and took place, of course, in a closed circle of friends.

From the office of the "Landwirtschaft," I also brought political news to my friends. As long as Unterscharfuehrer Berger, a good-hearted Sudetendeutscher, was in charge of the secretariat, I was allowed to read the "Voelkischer Beobachter"[6] or even a book after I had finished my work—he just pretended not to notice. The most important part of the newspaper were Wehrmacht reports and the military reportages. I could also follow the changes at the Eastern front on a wall map in the office. Thus, I transmitted, almost every evening, the latest news which turned more and more hopeful to my friends. The girls no longer believed that the end of Nazi rule would come in two, three, or six months as originally thought. They knew it would take quite a while but, thanks to our conversations, they were deeply convinced of the ultimate defeat of Nazi Germany and this certainly gave them inner strength.

From the beginning, I was incomparably better off than my Jewish co-prisoners. As a Non-Jew, I did not have to fear selection or gas chambers. In addition, I knew why I was in camp: as an outspoken opponent of the Nazi-regime and as resistance fighter, I was guilty in their eyes and deserved to be punished. But all the men, women and children? Of what crimes were they guilty? What had been the meaning of politico-ideological questions to these young girls before their deportation? To the majority of them, nothing. Some, who came from a pious family, found strength in their faith, others lost their faith in God in this inferno. When I was asked as to my relationship with the world's religions, I liked to tell them about the great German humanist Gotthold Ephraim Lessing and about the parable in his play "Nathan der Weise:" "The real ring was probably lost." However, besides all lecturing and recitation, the most important ingredient was sympathy: a compassionate gesture, a kind inquiry, a confident smile or a friendly word. This could bring back the other to the community of humans and restore hope and belief in the future.

After the members of the Kommando Pflanzenzucht had been transferred to Rajsko, we kept up an active illegal correspondence through many channels, even through the men's camp with whom they had contact. We told each other news, exchanged philosophical ideas—for example, about Nietzche; and discussed poetry, perhaps Rilke or French writers. Once, the French women sent me flowers with a note which I still have today. It said, "Ces fleurs, ayant gout de la liberté, que nous retrouverons avant le 1er mai prochain. Les Françaises de la Pflanzenzucht."

We "Vorzugshaeftlinge" (privileged inmates) lived and worked incomparably better than the girls in Birkenau. Poetry sustained us. In the Stabsgebaeude, the rhyming continued. Once Herta wrote ten pages full of Sramek[7] poems. After my liberation, I found one of my letters at home from Auschwitz which contained nothing but a love sonnet by Verlaine destined for "Stefan" one of the pseudonyms of my fiance whose address I did not know. My letters to my sister Josefine must have been so optimistic that she wrote to me at Auschwitz on October 20, 1943, "...I am always very happy when I read your letters. It seems that your often admired sunshine nature [of which she liked to make fun, I may add now] keeps you in shape even when the going is rough..."

The rough times started for me when Unterscharfuehrer Berger was replaced by SS-man Tietze, a sly, squinting man. Right from the beginning, he could not stand me. Once he searched my drawer during my absence and found one of my small poems, unfortunately, an anti-fascistic one. It was reported to Caesar and to

Maria Mandel, the SS-woman in chief. She had had a dislike for me from the very first day when I had worked in the registration office. Naturally, I had put this event into rhymes:

Spinnefeind ist mir die O.[8]	The chief is my bitter enemy
Denn nimmer kann sie mir vergessen,	Since she cannot forget
dass ich die Frechheit hab besessen,	that I had the Chutzpah
zu gehn mit ihr aufs gleiche Klo.	to use the same toilet as she.

In spite of Caesar's intercession, I was sentenced to three weeks in the bunker. We were four women in the dark cell with a tiny roof window. I remember a quite vulgar prostitute from Hamburg's harbor district and a young Ukrainian girl who had been unsuccessful in her escape attempt from her forced labor camp inside the German Reich and who sang beautiful native songs. Bunker-Jacob, a giant of a man who was in charge as block-elder did not harass us needlessly. Of course, we were starving, but we could stand it. After my release, I returned to my work place on orders from Caesar and against the wish of SS-woman Mandel, however, my intercession on account of Lilli Toffler, who had been sentenced to death because of a harmless letter, left Caesar indifferent.[9]

My colleagues reported that during my absence Tietze had announced, "The Binder is going through the chimney anyway." In January 1944, during a renewed search of my office desk, Tietze found a few "organized" cigarettes, rather cigarette-ends. Now Mrs. Mandel insisted on my transfer to a work detail doing outside work in Birkenau as punishment.

In the barrack in Birkenau where I was assigned a bunk bed below, not any more on the top tier as in the Stabsgebaeude, the "Blacks" and the "Greens" made life very difficult for me. During the day, I carried piles of bricks on long bars to and fro. What I saw and experienced around me has been described by others who suffered more than I did. After a short while, I was sitting in the evenings in the "Krankenbau" (hospital) with my new friends, Jewish Czech physicians to relax a little. One of the students, at that time a corpse-bearer, has remained a good friend.

SS-woman Mandel did not leave me alone. One day she called me and reproached me because of my contact with "Jews." She wanted me to work again in an office under the condition that I would cease any contact, there were enough Germans in camp with whom I could be friendly. When I told her openly that those were better people than the German prostitutes and thieves, she furiously chased me away. I did not act intelligently, and did not help anybody except myself because of this urge for self-assertion, for preservation of human dignity gave me further strength. An SS-woman once exclaimed in response to my dare-devil behavior, "Binder is insolent even if she is silent."

I contracted a serious infection on my left leg which developed into phlegmone. I could hardly walk and stayed several weeks in the Revier. Easter 1944, I was discharged and became secretary in one of the barracks of the

Krankenbau. One day we received survivors from Treblinka; their condition was frightful. I befriended two Russian women doctors who were prisoners of war and with whom I was in contact till after liberation.

My most horrible camp experience falls into this period. A comrade of my friend Raya Kagan was in the deathblock, destined to be gassed. Raya asked for my help and I got in touch with the camp elder, a German political prisoner. She was of the opinion that I should simply go to the block and try to get her out by myself. I entered; hundreds of naked, emaciated, skeleton-like arms stretched out from the bunks toward me, wanting to hold me. I called her name, hundreds of voices called "here-no-here." I did not find her and escaped in shock.

The closer the front approached in the summer of 1944, the more nervous the SS became and the more we were looking forward to our speedy salvation. In August, I was sent with a women's transport to Ravensbrueck in cattle cars; according to rumors, Edith Gruenwald, the Kapo of the Political Section, who did not like me had added my name to the transport list. On the trip, we stood for hours on the rails during air raids.

The concentration camp of Ravensbrueck was unrecognizable. All order had disappeared, the barracks were crammed full and the soup was inedible. For many weeks, there was no mail to or from home; but the others had been without news from their loved ones for many years. Former camp-comrades welcomed me and brought me civilian clothes; prison uniforms were non existent. In this chaos, I volunteered for a transport to Graslitz (Kraslice) in the Bohemian Erzgebirge in order to be closer to home.

Graslitz was a satellite camp of Flossenbuerg. Here, I worked from September 1944 until April 1945, again as a secretary in the workshop of a factory manufacturing spare parts for airplanes which had been transferred from Berlin to this area. In the work halls, where in peace time velvet and silk ribbons had been produced, there now stood lathes, fraise-machines and drill machines operated by about a dozen workers, also transferred by force from Berlin. During our short, professional talks, they comforted me with the remark that they, separated from their families and under strict supervision, did not have much better conditions than we prisoners. These inmates consisted, for a large part, of German criminal and asocial women augmented by a few political Poles and Czechs and some gypsy women. One of them, young Rosa, sat with me in the office, probably less because of her qualifications—she could hardly write her name—but thanks to her pretty legs. Where can she be today? There were no Jewish inmates at Graslitz, and during all those months I did not become friendly with anybody.

We were allowed to write home and could receive letters and parcels. Leaves and visits were, of course, forbidden. Nevertheless, my good sister risked it once on a Sunday and was allowed to leave her food package at the gate of the factory where we lived in the attic. I learned about her visit and rushed to the window from where I could see and beckon to Josefine, who was still walking back and forth in front of the house. A violent blow on the head from our chief supervisor threw me to the floor. But this could not spoil my joy of having seen my sister.

Only during air raids did we get outside and I greeted the bombs while squatting on the bare ground and freezing. All hell was loose in the sky, especially during that night in February when the city of Dresden, not too far from us, was destroyed.

Spring came and so did the end. In the middle of April we were evacuated, guarded by SS-men and Volkssturm members (unit of German soldiers consisting of seniors and adolescents). Most of us were dressed in civilian clothes with large white crosses painted on our backs, equipped with one tin spoon each and a carton of detergent which probably had just arrived in accordance with the German proverb "Ordnung muss sein" ("order has to rule supreme"). We had nothing to eat. However, a horse-drawn cart accompanied us, laden with flour and at night, after several hours of marching through the green, sunny hills, we were ordered to rest and everybody received a scoop of raw flour in the hollow of her hand. It was prohibited to make a fire. Night rest!

I decided to disappear and persuaded Anca, a Czech factory worker, to come with me. Since our bivouac was at the foot of a mountainous hill, we succeeded in quickly reaching the cover of high trees without being noticed. We rushed higher up and, in order not to lose our sense of direction in the dark, we lay down and enjoyed our first deep sleep in freedom. When it dawned, we continued to march through the forest in the direction of Karlsbad. Soon we encountered a second group of escapees; two Czechs from Moravia, one Polish physician and a young Ukrainian girl who had even organized some potatoes which she fried for us on an open fire for breakfast. We stumbled for hours on mountain paths, always keeping an eye on the road to Karlsbad below and wearing our civilian clothes inside out because of the white crosses painted on the back. Then we encountered the first deserted Wehrmacht soldiers who rushed by without helmets, without weapons and without looking at us.

In the evening, hunger and exhaustion drove us into a village on the highway. We were lucky. The German peasant woman who took us in and to whom I presented our group as Czechs who had worked in the Reich and were now returning home murmured, "Perhaps God will reward me and protect me from the Russians," and she did not ask any questions. She placed a bowl of boiled potatoes on the table and permitted us to sleep in the haystack. Next day, most of the girls had difficulty in walking. They had callous marks and blisters on their feet and needed a longer rest. We left the woods, crossed the road and a meadow and reached a brook. There we took off our shoes and stockings, washed our sore feet and rested. After a while, a military truck stopped on the highway. Several soldiers stepped out and came to the brook to wash their socks. Since some of us absolutely could not walk any more, we decided to ask them to give us a lift in their truck. The soldiers referred us to the chief of the convoy. To my horror, he turned out to be an SS-man. I related the fairy tale of the "Protektoratsangehoerige" who had been bombed out and who wanted to return home. I presented the Czech woman, who did not know a word of German, as having lost her speech during the bomb attack. He agreed to have them all sit in the back of the open truck next to the soldiers and a huge aircraft part covered with tent cloth; I was to sit in front between him and the driver. The journey went to Vienna, luckily via Prague. We advanced slowly; in the valley of Giesshuebel the truck was pursued by low flying airplanes, but nothing happened.

In the evening, in Duppau, the chief of the convoy invited us to have dinner at the inn. There, everything looked like peace time. The vicar and the forest ranger and other well-to-do citizens and dignitaries sat at their usual table. We girls were sitting alone at a set table and had difficulties eating the potatoes and spinach with fork and knife; for years we only had had a tin spoon. Then the SS-man sent the girls and the soldiers (who, by the way, behaved in a proper way) to sleep in the truck and attempted to pull me into his hotel room. I invoked religion and his "good upbringing and education" and he dismissed me to join the others. Early in the morning, we continued the trip and reached the Prague suburb of Brevno before noon. We descended from the truck, washed ourselves at the water pump and went by streetcar directly to my sister's studio in the center of town. We did not have to pay; the conductor smiled and understood the situation immediately.

I called my sister at her office, she came at once and I do not have to describe our meeting. One after the other she put into the bathtub, fed us and clothed us. Only after having been given a "kapelusz," a little hat, did the Pole feel like a free woman. All received money to be able to continue their journey and said good-by the same or the following day. I never heard from them again, only Anca, with whom I had escaped, sent me one or two nice cards.

Thus, three days after my escape I was home and re-united with my sister who did not let me go into the street because the war was not yet over and Prague was still occupied by the Germans. On May 5, 1945, the Prague uprising occurred and on May 9 the city was liberated by the Red Army. Finally, I wanted to see my parents again and went by bike since civilians were not allowed to use the rail-road. Equipped with an official laissez-passer, I rode a while and then hitchhiked in a Soviet military vehicle. The major was very correct and friendly. He gave me food and sent his men to a farm to get eggs which were immediately fried and consumed. When we entered Budweis, he dispatched some soldiers to the brewery to get a barrel of beer. Then he invited himself and his crew to spend the night at my parents' house. These unexpected visitors saved my disconcerted parents and me many joyful tears. We were all served Russian canned meat, bread and beer. There was an animated conversation going on in Czech, German and Polish and, after having been asked by the major, I played a Viennese waltz on the piano. At 11 p.m. sharp everybody went to bed on the major's orders; the soldiers slept on the floor. Everything seemed to run properly and peacefully. When I woke up late in the morning, my mother told me with embarrassment that our guests had left early and had taken with them all the watches that were in the house. They proba-bly had lots of fun with them.

One year later, my parents were forcefully deported as Czechoslovakian citizens of German nationality and taken to West Germany in spite of my repeated interventions on their behalf. My sister Josefine followed them voluntarily, found work in Munich, supported them, got married and lived in a childless marriage in that beautiful city where I have visited her often. My father died shortly after having been re-settled. The last time I saw him, he was behind the barbed wire fence of the camp in Budweis where I secretly gave him a package of cigarettes and pondered about our world and its strange variations. In 1954, I was allowed to visit my mother for the first time, more frequently later. She also came to Prague twice and enjoyed her grandchildren. Both of my parents are buried in Bad Kissingen, their last residence.

When I returned to Prague in the middle of May 1945 from my second visit to Budweis, happiness was waiting for me; my fiance had come back sane and sound, although very thin. He had been liberated in Buchenwald concentration camp after having been hidden for three days and nights under a pile of wood because he had been called to the gate of the Kommandantur. Now he told about his successful escape from the Theresienstadt transport to Poland; about the hard winter hidden in a bunker deep in the Carpathian Mountains together with refugees from a Jewish village; about his temporary job as railroad signal man in a deserted Polish railway guard-house from where he managed to jump on a moving Hungarian military ambulance train and came to Budapest; about his medical practice in Barcz at the Hungarian-Yugoslavian border which he had obtained through a Catholic priest; of his plans to join the partisans in Yugoslavia; of his arrest by the Gestapo when Hungary was occupied; of the fairy tales he told during his many interrogations in different camps to the Gestapo about his identity until he landed in Buchenwald.

We got married in June 1945, moved to a double garconniere (studio) and started to work. At first, my husband was medical specialist for the repatriation of former concentration camp inmates and D.P.'s (displaced persons); later, until his early death, he was chief physician of the laryngological section of the municipal hospital. Like others in camp, I had had tremendous plans for the future: marriage, giving birth to and bringing up several children, study at the university and perfect my piano playing at the conservatory. My guardian angel protected me and I managed to fulfill all wishes except the piano study. We had three children; two daughters, Jarmila and Daniela and one son, Andrej (Andy), all of them well-bred and already parents of four boys and two girls. From September 1945 on, I studied at the department of philosophy of the Prague Karl's University English, German and philosophy. In 1951, I received my teaching credentials, in 1954, the Ph.D. and in 1964, the so-called "Candidate of Science" (professorship).

Immediately in June 1945, I found congenial work as secretary of the president of IUS, an international students' union. Planned during the final years of war by Czech and English students, it was realized in Prague and comprised, at that time, all national students associations in the East and the West. Chinese, Soviet

Russian, American and other student representatives worked in the Secretariat and everybody was filled with the vision of a better future, a world of fraternity and hope for peace. Many beautiful convictions have since been lost.

After seven years of working for IUS (of course, with interruptions for the births of my daughters in 1946 and 1948) and participation in several international Congresses, even via Siberia to China, I left the Student Union shortly before our son's birth in 1952. One year later, I started to work as assistant for German and English in the Department of Philosophy. Here I remained until my retirement in 1970-71.

During all those years, in addition to my main occupation as language teacher, I also had some extra-curricular jobs such as: interpreting, translating, discussing books on foreign fiction for a publishing house, editing the German edition of an, unfortunately, short-lived journal on Czech and Slovakian literature, etc. For some time, I also worked on the Auschwitz Committee of the Czech union of political prisoners. Today, I am sorry for any hour of our leisure time which I did not spend with my husband; that would have been far more important. We had a very happy marriage living in Prague, a city we knew and loved which owes its unique magic to the merging of three cultures: the Czech, the German-Bohemian and the Jewish. We shared joys and sorrows for our children, had a nice, large apartment with garden and a country home in the Lausitz Mountains and went on marvelous trips abroad. Only the thought that he had not suffered and that, every day of our being together after the war had, after all, been a present from fate could comfort me when he left us so suddenly. He died in 1969, of apoplexy during a lecture tour in his field of rhinology in West Germany. I brought him home and he is buried in the Jewish cemetery of Prague, which will also be my last resting place.

Shortly before his death, in July 1968, we had experienced together the most moving event of my life: the invitation from Yad Vashem to come to Jerusalem and to be honored as a righteous Gentile. My Auschwitz friends, especially Raya Kagan, had worked for my nomination. I insisted that my husband should accompany me. Fortunately, Harry's Israeli relatives donated his ticket since it could not be paid in Czechoslovakian currency. A lot happened in Czechoslovakia in 1968, and many formalities had been simplified. We flew to Athens and continued by Israeli boat. Harry, who had never been among so many Jews, was very impressed with the elegantly dressed crew. He never had had much to do with Judaism, considered himself an atheist and discovered only slowly his "roots" in Israel. He admired the young, beautiful Israelis.

In Haifa, we were most cordially welcomed by Harry's cousins. We had the feeling that we had known each other for a long time. I could not believe my eyes when I encountered the blossoming young women who had once been those pitiful creatures in Auschwitz. Tiny, little Shosha—previously as young as she had been thirsty for knowledge—was now the mother of three splendid sons who courageously defended their country.

In Jerusalem, we stayed with Raya. Before the celebration, she was almost more excited than I. During my speech, I had to fight back tears. The ceremony was marvelous. I was allowed to plant a carob sapling in the Alley of the Righteous. Now, after 20 years, it has become a big tree with large branches according to photos. I received a certificate from Yad Vashem. Under my name it says, "qui, au peril de sa vie, a sauvé des Juifs pendant l'époque d'extermination." In addition, I was presented with a medal on which the Yad Vashem building is engraved with the inscription, "Quiconque sauve une vie sauve l'univers tout entier." I had not deserved so much honor.

After my husband's death and certain public events, I retired from public life; yet continued, after some time, with language lessons, private and in adult classes, at present, almost exclusively in German, which is quite in demand here after having been neglected during the post-war era. Because of eye problems, I have to gradually discontinue the German translations of chiefly art and music literature. But my old hobby of traveling (because of our circumstances, mostly restricted to Europe), I have not yet given up. From my school days, from camp and also from work, I have many good friends dispersed all over the world who come to see me in Prague, or they send their children, grandchildren or friends to me and my younger daughter Daniela (and her husband and my two grandchildren) with whom I share a spacious apartment. Then I visit them, and my friends laugh about the old lady who cannot give up her Wandervogel behavior and arrives with her rucksack and stays overnight cheaply in youth hostels as a senior citizen. I prefer to travel alone, in this manner I toured from Norway to Greece and even went as far as Japan. In our socialist state, I am a lucky exception, thanks to the official letters of invitation from my sister.

If I could stand once more in front of the Western Wall in Jerusalem and place my list of wishes into the cracks, I would have one single, maybe illusory request only: imploring the powerful as well as the powerless, the believers of all creeds as well as the non-believers to heed the lessons of the past, to finally listen to reason and to respect human dignity in everybody.

❖

Edita Maliarova
Prague (Czechoslovakia)

I was born on March 8, 1914, in Bratislava. From October 1932, till June 1937, I studied Romance and Germanic philology at the Komnsky University of my home town. After graduation, I was entitled to use the title of professor. Subsequently, I taught at several secondary schools in Slovakia. On June 2, 1939, I was dismissed as a Slovakian civil servant because of racial laws in conformity with the announcements of the minister of the interior, Dr. Tuka, M.P.[10], and the minister of justice, Dr. Fritz, M.P., of May 16, 1939, c. 8973/39-7.M.V. and E c. 10.552/39-2 M.P. concerning the exclusion of Jews from public service (the schools in Slovakia were state schools). This was the first discrimination I encountered.

I lived then with my parents in Bratislava. In 1940, we were forced to vacate our apartment in one of the main streets of Bratislava, and in the spring of 1941, we had to leave Bratislava, the capital of Slovakia; both times for racial reasons. Already, since 1940, Jews were not allowed to be in the streets after 9 p.m. at night.

In the beginning of June 1939, shortly after my dismissal from the school service, I contracted pneumonia and pleurisy, which lasted till the end of July. In August, my parents sent me to the Tatra mountains following the advice of my physician. In April, I had suffered a serious bout of jaundice and, apparently, my body had been quite weakened. Thus, emigration was out of the question for me in August of 1939, and on September 1, World War II began. I believed I would be able to help my parents at home, especially since my sister and her husband were endangered in Hitler-occupied Prague. I thought if I would be sent to a labor camp in Germany, that would exempt my parents from a similar fate. In the spring of 1941, we moved to Topolcany. My father, who had been employed as an engineer in a cable factory, was already retired by that time.

On March 24, 1942, I was arrested in Topolcany and transported with other young Jewish women in cattle cars to Bratislava, where we were housed in the Patronka, a former cartridge factory. Here, we had to sign our "testament" promising never to file any claims regarding the restitution of our property. Josef Tiso,[11] our president, had sold us, i.e., every single Jew, for 5,000 crowns to the Nazis. Dr. Tiso was a clergyman. On March 31 or April 1, 1942, I was transported, together with approximately one thousand other women, to the Auschwitz concentration camp. Before our departure, we were not told our destination. We were only informed that we would go to Germany to work. We arrived in Auschwitz on April 2, 1942.

After our arrival, at that time there were not yet any selections at the camp, we were chased into the women's camp, located during that period in ten separated blocks of the Stammlager (men's camp), The transport to Auschwitz had been escorted at first by Hlinka guards[12] and later by SS. On the way to the women's camp we passed the gate with the inscription "Arbeit macht frei."

The reception procedure took place in block 1 or 2 close to the gate. It was here that our hair was shorn and that all our belongings were taken away. I told a group of young girls around me, "Keep quiet and don't lose your sense of humor!" I received number 3535. Ours was the fourth transport of women arriving in Auschwitz and the third one from Czechoslovakia. The first transport of non-Jewish women from Ravensbrueck, having received prison numbers between 1 and 999 with red (political), black (a-social), green (criminal) triangles had arrived shortly before us. We were lodged in Block 10, sleeping on straw in a big room. During the following days, we had great difficulties with personal hygiene because there was not always water in the washroom. Often, I got up in the middle of the night in order to wash myself.

At first, I worked in the gardening detail. Our kapo was a German prisoner with a green triangle and the forewoman had a black triangle. Our work squad consisted of approximately fifteen prisoners and we performed the spring work in the gardens of the SS who had requisitioned the houses of the former Polish owners. One day, our kapo ordered us to sit down in a meadow, to our great surprise. She started talking to another female prisoner. I could listen to their conversation and it was then that I heard the word "gas" for the first time. We were near the railroad ramp where a transport with human cargo was standing, probably from Slovakia.

I worked in the gardening detail until the end of May or the beginning of June 1942, when I fell ill and could not march out. I was admitted to the sick bay, either in Block 1 or Block 2, with very high fever. After my release, about a week later, my "place" in the gardening detail was occupied. I then worked in outside work details of the agricultural enterprises doing different types of very hard and exhausting field work. One day, in June 1942, when we returned from work dead-tired, we had to remain in front of the gate and stand barefoot on the graveled square next to commandant Hoess's house. We were wondering what might be the reason for this punishment roll-call. A Czech inmate, who worked in the vicinity, told me that the reason was probably Heydrich's[13] death. He had died as a result of an attempt on his life by Czech patriots, parachutists from England. It was confirmed by the fact that only female prisoners from Slovakia had to be at this punishment roll-call which lasted about two hours, until dusk. This was, of course, "peanuts" compared to what happened to the so-called "Protektorat" of Bohemia and Moravia. Horrible acts of vengeance were perpetrated by the Nazis: two small Czech villages were completely obliterated, Lidice on June 10, 1942, and Lezaky on June 24, 1942, and a multitude of arrests and executions took place.

When one of the comrades from Topolcany noticed that I was in a deplorable condition consisting of nothing but skin and bones and that things got worse daily, she asked the German prisoner Berta, who had been imprisoned since 1933 as a communist and who worked in the Arbeitseinsatz (work allocation office), to help me in obtaining an office job. I had to report to Lagerfuehrer Aumeier. Berta had given me good advice to not mention my university education and to talk only about my knowledge of the German language, paying heed to the Nazi motto: "Whenever I see an intellectual, I reach for my gun."[14]

I was accepted into the kommando (work detail) Truppenwirtschaftslager [TWL] (troop supply). The large TWL building was across the road from the Stabsgebaeude. It was under Wehrmacht (German Army) administration, and the staff consisted mostly of members of the Schutzpolizei (security police). Six female Slovakian prisoners were already working there: Aranka Heitlingerova, the kapo of the kommando and author of the Auschwitz song; Jolan Deutschova (later Grossova); Margita Weissova; Margita Grossmanova (later Bachnerova); Suse and a woman prisoner called "butterfly" by the Schupos. I was the seventh inmate from Slovakia, and later a young Belgian woman called Nora was added to the kommando. The TWL building contained not only offices, but mostly store-room space for food items such as flour, legumes and oatmeal, which were delivered to the SS-troops and the Wehrmacht. My work consisted of registering the pick-up of goods on file cards. A French male inmate, who worked in the TWL warehouse gave me news about the battle-front, if possible.

I worked in the TWL from the end of June or the beginning of July until the end of October 1942. At that time, I weighed approximately 52 kilograms. During the first weeks of August 1942, all inmates of the women's camp were transferred to Birkenau. Those that had contact at their work places with SS-personnel were lodged in the green wooden barracks next to the Revier, and after a week they were moved to the Stabsgebaeude. All the other women were housed on the other side of the Lagerstrasse (camp road) in mud huts. That was the sad beginning of the dreadful conditions in the women's camp of Birkenau.

In August 1942, the inmates of the TWL kommando were tattooed at the side entrance in front of the Stabsgebaeude. At the end of August or beginning of September, I secretly weathered malaria. I had high fever. Once, during the roll-call, before marching out, I fainted and only with the help of the comrades of my kommando did I succeed in reaching the TWL building which was close by.

The SS-Aufseherinnen (female guards) lived in the Stabsgebaeude, including Maria Mandel, the SS-guard in chief, as well as her predecessor, Johanna Langefeld. The inmates were housed in the basement. Our block-elder was Maria Maul, who behaved decently and was helpful to the prisoners. We had showers at our disposal, and I had the feeling that the availability of water and the possibility of keeping oneself clean were the main reasons for our physical survival; although, at that time I had contracted scabies (an unpleasant, infectious disease). Luckily, a small room next to the Stabsgebaeude dormitory had been outfitted as Revier, so that we were not returned immediately to Birkenau. The nurse told me that my recovery was due to my strong will power which prompted me to cover myself incessantly with the tar ointments I received.

In October 1942, a conflict arose between the Wehrmacht and the SS. The SS requested payment for the work performed by the prisoners of the TWL from the Wehrmacht. As a consequence, the TWL administration reduced the number of inmates they employed, which affected those prisoners who had arrived last, i.e., Nora and myself. If they had sent us to Birkenau, we would have been in immediate danger of death. The Schutzpolizei member who was the boss of my department came from Marchegg, a little place near the Czechoslovakian-Austrian border, not far from Bratislava. He asked SS-Aufseherin Wenig to keep us for one day in the sewing room, while he would attempt to find us a job in a different kommando. In addition, prisoner Anka Binderova, now Dr. Urbanova, helped decisively. The very same morning, she told SS-Sturmbannfuehrer Caesar, the director of the Landwirtschaft (agricultural) office, that there were two healthy and clean (i.e., deloused) prisoners with secretarial skills at the Stabsgebaeude at his disposal, and it would take quite some time before he would get the inmates he had requested from Birkenau. So, the next morning we already marched out with the Landwirtschaft kommando. It saved Nora's and my life.

The Landwirtschaft office was located in a brick building between the Kommandantur and the SS-Revier, across the road from the green barrack of the Standesamt. Apart from the two of us, the following inmates were working there: Anka Binderova from Prague, our kapo; Anna Neumannova from Prague; Gertrude Juppova from Louny and Jolan Starkova from Bratislava. Anka typed the letters which Caesar dictated. I registered the incoming and outgoing mail in a book and sorted the arriving mail in a file to present it as fast as possible. Since I had access to Kommandantur orders, I was able to warn prisoners in the men's camp, through comrades in the Stabsgebaeude about various happenings and dangers. We had the possibility of reading the newspapers of the SS and to transmit the news about the battle-front to the comrades in the Stabsgebaeude. For a short period, we even had a map of Europe in the room where Anka and I worked.

For some time, an SS-man without rank sat in the same room together with Anka and me. He was half Pole and half German—referred to as "Wasserpolacken"—and it was his task to put the letters into the envelopes and take them to the post-office, or, perhaps, deliver them personally to different SS departments. After his transfer, a civilian employee came in his place who had no work experience and was not very intelligent, so that I succeeded in smuggling a letter to an acquaintance of Anna Neumannova's father in Prague into the official outgoing mail. The letter was addressed to the firm Labora, Laboratory Instruments, in Prague and succeeded in achieving Anna's release in the summer of 1944.

Anna Binderova was sent to the bunker in the spring of 1944, and later to the penal kommando in Birkenau. She was replaced by Ilse Koehler, a German prisoner who had been arrested in 1939, as a communist in Leipzig.

SS-Sturmbannfuehrer Dr. Joachim Caesar, former functionary of the SS Rasse-and Siedlungshauptamt (Office for Race and Settlement) in Berlin, member of the NSDAP since before 1933, came to Auschwitz in the spring of 1942, as special envoy of Himmler in order to direct a cultivation station of the caoutchouc plants Kok-Sagys and Tau-Sagys. These plants had been taken from the Soviet Union. At the same time, he was in charge of the SS agricultural enterprises of the entire Auschwitz concentration camp complex including all satellite camps which had been formed through the confiscation of Polish manors (such as Bahice, Birkenau, Rajsko, Budy) and large farms whose owners had been arrested or resettled. Robbery was common Nazi practice. In all European countries occupied by them, they confiscated everything they needed for the war effort and for themselves. As director of the SS-Landwirtschaft, Caesar was under the jurisdiction of the SS-Wirtschafts-Verwaltungshauptamt, Amt V5, headed by SS-Sturmbannfuehrer Vogel in Berlin.

Caesar, himself, did not have to dirty his hands with beatings, tortures and killings of prisoners. This work was done for him by his employees. Marianne Klein, the director of the poultry farm at Harmense,[15] who wore an SS-uniform, tormented the prisoners who worked for her. His chief colleagues were SS-men. SS-Obersturmfuehrer Thomsen, his deputy, who supervised the prisoners of the outside kommandos, was feared all over camp because of his cruelty and his killing of inmates. SS-men Rosenthal, Rosenow, Mokrus, Moll and Glaue caused the death of thousands of women prisoners. Rosenthal, for example, used to ride his horse directly into the columns of inmates of the "Wirtschaftsbetriebe" (agricultural enterprises) when they marched out or returned from work, so that usually 10-12 dead or seriously injured women were left lying around. These SS-men habitually were accompanied by huge dogs that they ordered to attack. Many women died from being mauled. Some of the worst conditions prevailed in the swamp and pond kommando under SS-Unterscharfuehrer Martin. Half-naked women cut reeds immersed in water and hundreds of them drowned on a daily basis, after they sank completely exhausted or they drowned themselves out of desperation. Fifty percent of the prisoners of this kommando died from malaria. For the entire day, they had nothing but a small piece of bread. The evening soup was obtained only by those who were able to fight for it. In our office, Martin routinely boasted in front of Caesar about how many women had gone into the water again. All the work was performed at Caesar's orders. The pond kommando was part of the penal kommando. It happened quite frequently, since 1942, that exhausted prisoners who fell down and were unable to continue working, were shot "while escaping"—as it was termed. Quite a number of inmates were liquidated in this fashion.

The last bit of strength was squeezed out of the prisoners since the ones that drowned were easily replaced with new ones. For those few who worked in offices, conditions were a little better but, even here, the perpetual threat of being transferred to the death camp for the tiniest infraction existed. Because of a cigarette and a few written notes, Anka Binderova, prison number 725, who had worked for 22 months as a secretary, was handed over to the Oberaufseherin (chief SS guard of the women). For three weeks, she was incarcerated in the bunker, and then she was sent to the penal kommando in Birkenau, where she had to do very hard field work and where living and health conditions enabled only a few to survive; three out of one thousand. After Anka's departure, the following dictum was heard in Caesar's secretariat, "One word is enough and nothing but a small cloud remains."

The millions in profit from the mills and other enterprises went into the pockets of the SS. The work with the Kok-Sagys plants had been classified as essential for the war industry. In Auschwitz, plant caoutchouc was to be produced for the war effort. Himmler was personally interested in this work, requested detailed annual reports about it, and during his visit in Auschwitz, personally inspected the cultivation station.

Caesar did not undertake anything in favor of the prisoners. He, himself, was responsible for the above-mentioned occurrences since he was well-informed about anything that was going on. The SS-men did everything on his orders. He never once intervened in behalf of the prisoners. For example, twelve Poles of the kommando Messtruppe (land surveyors) of the Landwirtschaft were shot under suspicion of having made preparations to escape. He did not intervene in behalf of a German prisoner who received twenty-five whiplashes on his backside because of insufficient work performance. As a result, he was ill for a long time with erysipelas.

There were attempts to camouflage the plant cultivation station in Rajsko as a private institution. A comedy à la Potemkin was enacted in front of visitors from France. They wanted to create the impression that Rajsko had no connection with the Auschwitz concentration camp. The visitors were accompanied every second of their stay, and the female prisoners of the station had to don fresh, snow-white lab-coats with only tiny numbers above the pockets.

Caesar was a fervent Nazi and a deeply convinced disciple of Hitler. He believed in the victory of Nazi Germany, and his entire work was dedicated to this victory. In Auschwitz, his career advanced greatly, and he was promoted to Obersturmbannfuehrer because of his achievements. There was animosity between him and camp commandant Hoess, a kind of personal rivalry; but Caesar never undertook anything indicating that he disagreed with the extermination of human beings or the atrocities that were committed in camp, which the Germans themselves referred to as "Vernichtungslager" (annihilation camp). Caesar was eminently aware of everything that was going on in Auschwitz. The German physician, Prof. Carl Clauberg, who personally conducted sterilization experiments on Jewish inmate women in Block 10, often visited Caesar in his office. After being used, these female guinea pigs were sent to Birkenau to their deaths. Caesar not only exploited male and female prisoners as laborers who had to work like slaves until completely exhausted, but he knew and concurred that after their last bit of strength had been sapped, or after they were not needed any more, or during the winter months when less manpower was required for agricultural work, they were liquidated in any way customary in Auschwitz: through gas, injections, transfer to Birkenau with its frightful conditions of hunger, cold and rampant infectious diseases.

At the end of May or beginning of June 1944, the female prisoners of the Stabsgebaeude were transferred to Block 6, which was outside the camp but still within the sentry chain. Next door, at a distance of approximately two meters, stood the brick house of the SS-Unterkunft, constructed in similar fashion. In September 1944, this part of Auschwitz was bombed. Block 6 was damaged and one of the prisoners, Hedy Winter of the Political Section, was killed.

In the beginning of October 1944, the office of the kommando Landwirtschaft was transferred to a wooden barrack in Rajsko. Here, we were lodged together with the inmates of the Kok-Sagys cultivation station. We stayed in Rajsko until the evacuation of Auschwitz on January 18, 1945. After the march on the snow-laden roads from Rajsko to the train in Loeslau (we had spent one night in a house where, to our horror, we were together with SS-Obersturmfuehrer Thomsen), Ilse Koehler was waiting for me and helped me into the only covered cattle car. Unterscharfuehrer Tietz had received orders from Caesar to keep our kommandos, i.e., the office of the Landwirtschaft and the Kok-Sagys cultivation station, together. It is almost unbelievable that on January 20, 1945, Caesar still believed that he would be able to continue his work. The train took us to Ravensbrueck. During the march, Ela, a Polish prisoner who also was a high school teacher, had approached me and proposed to escape together with her and her comrades; all from the Stabsgebaeude. I could not make up my mind and thus escaped death once more. The attempted escape of Ela and her friends ended tragically. When they climbed a hill, dawn came upon them and they were discovered and shot.

There might have existed order and discipline in Ravensbrueck before January 1945, but through the influx of a large amount of women prisoners from Auschwitz, the camp was woefully overcrowded. There was no room in the wooden barracks and we were placed in a large tent where several prisoners had to share one bed. In addition, we were threatened with transfer to the so-called Jugendlager (youth camp), the last station before being gassed. The old women were housed in a barrack in front of the Jugendlager and the rest of the inmates were not allowed to enter. On the Lagerstrasse, an acquaintance from Bratislava told me that a friend's mother was in this barrack and that she wanted to see me. I entered the barrack although I knew that I was unable to help. One of the worst Aufseherinnen of Ravensbrueck caught me. It was a calamitous situation. The German woman prisoner who had accompanied the Aufseherin during that inspection told me at night that I had saved my life through stoicism. I had stood erect while being viciously hit and had not blinked an eye when several of my clothing pieces were taken away, but had looked straight into the eyes of the Aufseherin. In the evening, the Czech comrades sent me a sweater which Riva handed over with the latest news.

After some time, I was transported, with a group of Jewish prisoners, to Malchow. We did not have to work in Malchow, but we were starving; all we got was a watery soup all day. A short while later, we were transported to Leipzig. On the way, the train stopped on the open tracks near Magdeburg. There was a terrible air raid. The town was saturated with incendiary and explosive bombs. The camp in Leipzig housed German, French and Polish non-Jewish female prisoners who worked in the Henkel aircraft factory. Conditions in regard to food and lodgings were, luckily, much better. When we arrived, there wasn't any more work. Only once did I march out in order to fill a huge bomb crater. A French woman came every evening to our barrack to report the latest news.

I believe it was in the night of April 14 to April 15, 1945, that we were marched out of the camp at midnight. The death march between the American and the Russian front in Saxony began close to the River Elbe. After a week, during the night of April 21 to April 22, we succeeded in escaping. We crossed the River Elbe in a ferry and marched on without the columns and the SS. We were a group of five women prisoners: Helenka Brody and Klari Weissova from the Standesamt, Inge Kochmann from Germany from the Kok-Sagys kommando and Jolan Stark and I from the Landwirtschaft kommando. Helenka went with a ferry before us and we lost her, but she arrived safely at home. The four of us marched on for another week, still encountering some dangerous situations until we reached the Americans: at first the military government in Colditz, then in Bad Lausitz and at last in Grimma. In Grimma, there was a large American internment camp for prisoners of war and former camp inmates, and from here we were repatriated.

After my return, I stayed in Prague. I did not go on to Bratislava where I had enjoyed a happy youth together with my parents and my sister. Only in Bad Lausitz, did Klari Weiss tell me that my parents had been murdered by the Nazis in September 1942, in Auschwitz; my mother had been taken immediately from the ramp to the gas chamber, she had only been 49 years old; my father, who was almost 63 years old, did not last long in camp.

Since July 1, 1945, I have worked in various cultural institutions in Prague. On March 1, 1973, I retired. Since then, as already beforehand, I have been doing translations into French and German.

I believe it was mostly the strong desire to live to see the end of the war, and to experience the victory over the Nazi domination of Europe, which enabled us to endure spiritually and emotionally the three years of concentration camp. We wanted to be sure that Nazism, with all its horrors, had been vanquished once and for all. Of course, equally important were selfless friendship, willingness to help and the mutual understanding among all comrades who had come from different countries of Europe and different backgrounds. I would like to emphasize the importance of altruistic friendship which was based entirely on mutual sympathy and mutual respect and not on egotism.

The following poems contain a few of my thoughts jotted down in camp.

Mai 1942

Die Kolonnen ruecken aus,
denn Arbeit macht angeblich frei,
bei jedem Schritt -
klingt die Erinnerung an die Heimat mit,
zwischen Gesang und Kommandoruf -
tauchen vergangene Bilder auf,
und die Hoffnung belebt so manchen ver-
    zagten Schritt.

May 1942

Columns are marching out
Since work supposedly liberates
With every step
Memories of home resound
Past images resurface
Between song and kommandoruf
And hope appears in many a hesitant step.

Été 1944

Les jours d'angoisse et d'incertitude
nous font voir
la joie de vivre
en des couleurs rayonnantes.

Summer 1944

The days of anguish and uncertainty
Let us perceive
The joy of living
In radiant colors.

Les rythmes lointains
évoquent le reflet
des jours passés en liberté,
dont les images menues
glissent devant notre oeil intérieur.

Far away rhythms
Evoke the reflection
Of days past in freedom
Whose fragile images
Glide before our inner eye.

Et les yeux et les coeurs
pleins d'amertume
crient sans émettre une voix:
quel sera notre futur invraisemblable?

And our eyes and our hearts
Full of bitterness
Scream without a sound:
What will be our improbable future?

Y aura-t-il encore
un retour dans la vie,
des jours ensoleillés, joyeux, heureux,
avec de la musique et la caresse,
sans l'ombre des nuages
menaçant tout mouvement libre?

Will there still be
A return to life,
To sunny, joyous and happy days
With music and tenderness
Sans cloud cover
Threatening each free move?

Herbst 1944

Grau in Grau verhaengt,
wie dieser Tag,
ist heute deine Seele,
endloser Kummer der Kameraden
steigt wie Nebel am Horizonte auf,
vereinigt sich mit deinem.
Vielleicht gibt dir eines Tages
dieser hasserfuellte Schmerz
Kraft zum Handeln und zum Bestehen.

Fall 1944

Gray in gray concealed
Like this day
Your soul appears today
Endless sorrow of comrades
Rises like mist at the horizon
Unites with yours.
Perhaps one day,
This hate-drenched pain
Will enable you to act and to persist.

Grimma, Mai 1945

Traumhafte Vorstellungen, unwahrscheinliche
    Hoffnungen
tief-innerster Seele haben sich erfuellt.
Wir sind frei! Wir sind endlich wieder frei!
Und dunkler Flieder blueht auf den Wegen,
berauscht uns mit Ahnungen glueckvoller
    Zukunft.

May 1945

Dreamlike imaginations, improbable hopes
Of the innermost soul were fulfilled.
We are free! We are finally free again!
And dark lilac blossoms on the roads
Intoxicates us with presentiments of a happy
    future.

NOTES

Dr. Anna Urbanova

1   A word play on "Mitmenschen" and "Mitleid" which cannot be translated.

2   The first transport of female prisoners from Ravensbrueck arrived on March 26, 1942, in Auschwitz. They were the first prisoners in the women's camp, which initially remained under the command of Ravensbrueck. There were 999 German female prisoners, categorized as asoziale (prostitutes), criminal and a few political inmates. They received the numbers 1-999 and were housed in blocks 1 to 10 of the Stammlager, separated from the men's camp by a wall and, as "founders" were intended to assume functions as block-elders and Kapos (Czech, 1989, p. 189).

3   Franz Xavier Gabelsberger (1789-1849) was the founder of German shorthand; his system carries his name.

4   Ernst Kaltenbrunner (1903-1946) was chief of the Austrian SS and SD, and later head of the RSHA. As one of the worst war criminals, he was sentenced to death by hanging. The sentence was carried out on October 16, 1946.

5   Heinrich Himmler (1900-1945), Reich Leader (Reichsfuehrer) of the SS, head of the Gestapo and Minister of the Interior, was, next to Hitler the most powerful man in Nazi Germany, one of the persons chiefly responsible for the extermination of European Jewry. He took poison after his capture by the British.

6   This was the official newspaper of the Nazi party.

7   Frana Sramek (1877-1952) was a noted Czech poet and playwright.

8   O was the abbreviation for Oberaufseherin = SS woman-in-chief.

9   Naumann describes Caesar's testimony as witness at the Auschwitz trial in Frankfurt/M. The court was mainly interested in obtaining material about the defendants. While Caesar had almost total recall when recounting deeds favorable to him, he hardly seemed to remember anything of importance in the case of Lili Toffler. One of the judges asked him, "What about Lili Toffler? Wasn't this massive interference with your authority? I am surprised that you do not recall anything. They took somebody away from your laboratory whom you required for your work which was extremely important for the war effort?"

Caesar: "She was not one of the highly qualified prisoners."

Judge: "But your rank was similar to that of the camp commandant, while the officer of the Political Section was far below you. How could you tolerate such a tremendous breach of your sphere of responsibility?"

Caesar: "At that time, a dictum prevailed: Be careful 1) with Hoess, and 2) with favoritism towards prisoners. One could not overstep certain limits. If you want to, call it cowardice."

The witness, Joachim Caesar, doctor of natural sciences, former SS-Oberfuehrer (brigadier general) and now proprietor of a laundry, was dismissed by the court. He had been unable to shed light on any accusations of the proceedings. Many among the audience believed he had attempted to justify his own behavior—although he had not even been accused (Naumann, 1965, pp. 121-125).

Edita Maliarova

10   Dr. Vojtech (Bela) Tuka, a professor and frustrated intellectual, served as prime minister in Josef Tiso's one party totalitarian regime which was formed when Slovakia became a separate state (i.e., when Bohemia and Moravia were made a protectorate of the Reich) on March 14, 1939. As chief negotiator of the 1942 deportations, he adamantly rejected intervention against the expulsion of Slovak Jews. After the war, Tuka was condemned to death by the

National Tribunal at Bratislava, but he died while in prison in 1946 (Gutman, 1990, pp. 1365-1366, 1519).

11   Dr. Josef Tiso (1887-1947) a priest, was prime minister and president of Slovakia from 1939-1945. He fled to Austria and surrendered to the Americans, who returned him to stand trial in Bratislava. He was condemned to death as the Slovak "Quisling" and executed.

12   These were the Slovak SS, named after Msgr. Andrej Hlinka (1864-1938), leader of the Catholic conservative Slovak People's Party.

13   Reinhard Heydrich (1904-1942) was head of the Gestapo and in charge of the "Final Solution," Reichsprotektor of Bohemia and Moravia. He was assassinated by Czech patriots.

14   Hanns Johst (1890-1978) was a Nazi writer and president of the Reichschrifttumskammer (authority for literary affairs). In his 1933 play "Schlageter," he wrote: "The people have to scream for priests who shed blood, who slaughter. Don't tell me about education—when I hear about culture I release the trigger of my revolver.

15   Conditions in Harmense are described by the former Polish prisoner Tadeusz Borowski. ("Ein Tag in Harmence" in *Bei Uns In Auschwitz*, 1987, pp. 68-104.)

CHAPTER 6

The German Mineral and Stone Works

(Deutsche Erd- und Steinwerke) or (DEST)

SS-Obergruppenfuehrer Oswald Pohl, the chief of the Economic Administration Head Office (WVHA) had one major objective—gradually to make the SS financially independent of the state and the Party by means of its own business undertakings and thus to guarantee Himmler the necessary freedom of action in his planning. Pohl was the guiding spirit behind almost all of the business undertakings of the SS, such as the German Armament Works (DAW), the porcelain factory (Allach) and the quarries, slagworks, brickyards and cement factories forming the German Mineral and Stone Works (DEST).

As a result of an understanding between Albert Speer, Hitler's advisor in relation to architecture and town planning, Himmler and Pohl, the director of the SS administration, the decision was made to establish on April 29, 1938, the Deutsche Erd- und Steinwerke GmbH—DEST, which would be able to employ the concentration camps' prisoners in large numbers in its quarries, clinkers, gravel pits and brickyards. The location of future concentration camps was not unimportant at the time. Mauthausen (1938), Flossenbuerg (1938), Gross-Rosen (1941) and Natzweiler (1941) camps were established in the area of DEST quarries.

The DEST establishment in Auschwitz would sell its gravel and sand with the help of its own sales offices for DM4.59 for one cubic meter of sand and DM3.42-4.13 for one cubic meter of gravel.

There was pressure from the private sector, which was unable to compete with the cheap articles flooding the market by the various SS establishments. As a result, in the beginning of 1943 and also in the second half of the same year, the rates for the work performed by the prisoners increased notably. For that reason, DEST gradually liquidated some of its shops and leased its production facilities and underground adits in the quarries to certain private firms.

Some of the prisoners of the Stabsgebauede who worked in the office of DEST, located outside of the camp in the town of Auschwitz, were: Berta Benau, Eta Berger, Lotte Frankl, Ruzenka Klein, Julie Schlem and Ili Stern.

Helen Kuban (Klein) (née Stern)
Hollywood, Florida (USA)

Born Twice

My name was Helen Stern when I was born and raised in a small community in Czechoslovakia called Pezinok located at the outskirts of Bratislava, the capital of Slovakia.

I was one of nine children of a moderately well-to-do family. That is, until Hitler invaded Austria causing fear that he would come to Czechoslovakia as well. As a result, most of our Gentile neighbors and friends disassociated themselves from my family and me, and the synagogues of our community were all vandalized.

At that time one of my sisters, Sarah, was already living in Palestine. She went to a Maccabiah[1] in 1935 and loved it so much that she never returned. She wrote to the family from Palestine, "Dear parents, Look around you and see what is happening to Jews after Hitler's invasions. Please sell your belongings, store and house while you still can and come here. You have us here and we will help you with everything possible." However, my parents replied, "We live in a democratic country and Hitler could never possibly come here."

In the middle of August 1939, shortly before the outbreak of war, the borders to other countries were still open. Earlier that year, Zeev, a friend of my sister Margaret, arrived from Palestine, which at that time was under British mandate, thereby making Zeev a British subject. By August, he wished to marry Margaret. The British consulate in Czechoslovakia informed Zeev that, in order to ensure his return to Palestine, he had to leave Czechoslovakia on August 30, the same day that the wedding was planned. The wedding was scheduled for 2:00 in the afternoon. The guests and rabbi were waiting while the groom, the bride and I scurried to obtain the passports and to assure a successful escape following the wedding. The consulate in Bratislava was already packed and only under duress were they willing to include the new bride on Zeev's passport. At the hour of the wedding, I was still trying to arrange for my sister and her husband's departure by train. I was told that no civilians were permitted on the train as it was reserved exclusively for the German army which was moving toward the Polish border. With that information, I bribed a cab driver to drive me to Pezinok, nearly 20 kilometers away. I arrived with the grave information, and Margaret and Zeev decided to continue with the taxi cab and crossed the border just as the war began. At that point, everyone wanted to leave the country and save herself, but there was no place to go.

In March of 1941, they confiscated our store as well as other stores owned by Jews. Our windows were broken; we boarded them up and began to live in constant fear.

In March of 1942, our family received a bulletin indicating that all unmarried children of Jewish families had to report to the railroad station at 8:00 in the morning and that we were all to go to a labor camp.

By that time, most of my sisters and brothers were married, two in Hungary, two in Czechoslovakia, and two in Palestine, including Margaret. Only my younger brother, Isador, and I were left at home. Another older brother had died several years before. Upon our parents' request, we bribed a couple who would lead us to the Hungarian border where, at least temporarily, we would be safe from the Nazis. We intended to live with our married sisters. We both had only three sets of clothes as we were told not to carry anything that would suggest we were trying to escape. With a very heavy heart, we said goodbye to our parents and left.

As we approached the border, we heard from others that in those families whose children did not report on Monday morning for deportation to the labor camp, the parents would be sent instead. Without hesitation, Isador and I turned around and came back to our parents' house. It was late Friday evening. As we entered, we saw the table festively set and lit with the Sabbath candles. My parents had suspected that, when we heard about the new order, we would come back. The greeting between us was as if we had not seen each other for years. My parents constantly repeated that they had their biggest present, their children back...even though it was only for the three-day weekend. The togetherness we felt that weekend was indescribable. Every minute counted. We spent every minute together.

On Monday, March 22, my parents accompanied Isador and me to the railroad station with all our personal belongings in huge suitcases. As we kissed goodbye, I deeply sensed that I would never see my parents again. My heart was breaking. I looked at them and said to myself, "They raised nine children and now, in their fifties, they will be left all alone and helpless."

The train took us to Patronka, an abandoned military camp in Bratislava. Every hour they brought new people in. They took all our belongings; I never again saw our suitcases and bags which our parents packed so lovingly.

We were in Patronka for a few days, sleeping on the floor without food, until there were 1,000 of us. They put us on a cattle train, 80 of us in each car. Each transport, as they called the trainload, consisted of 1,000 people.

We still did not know where we were going. We just hoped and prayed that it would be a labor camp. There was no room on the train to lie down. We sat on the ground or stood, body pressed against body, with the door opened about four inches for ventilation.

The train trip seemed endless. There was no water, no food, no lavatories. Girls were fainting and gasping for air because the air was putrid. Finally, the train stopped. When they opened the door, fifteen of the eighty girls had already died. This was my introduction to Auschwitz, a small town in Poland.

It was March 28, 1942. They led us to a common bathroom, stripped us of all our clothing, made us stand naked, and put us into large tubs five at a time. The water became dirtier and dirtier as each group of girls entered. They shaved all our hair (everywhere). They gave us uncleaned Russian uniforms which they had stripped from dead Russian bodies. My uniform became my only clothing for the next 10 months. As I looked around, I could not believe what the loss of hair could do to one's looks, even to the prettiest of us. They then registered us, and from that moment on until after the war I became nothing but number 2282.

Incidentally, you could tell how long anyone had been in a particular camp by their number. Since the early women's transports came in by numbers of 1,000 at a time, we were the third transport to arrive.

Four of us girls befriended each other from the beginning. We tried to stay together because no matter how bad it was, it made the pain more tolerable to suffer with friends. In addition, we were all separated from our families and we all had a need to belong to someone.

We were assigned to barracks which were divided into coops; five of us had to share the space in each coop. Wooden planks were our mattresses and there was one thin blanket to cover the five of us. When we tried to sleep, we would each pull to have part of this blanket. March in Poland was still quite cold.

We worked, slept and ate in the same uniform. We became drenched in it and dried in it. We found that the uniforms which, as I mentioned, were captured from the Russian army, were infested with lice which we learned to call "clothes lice." I never would have believed that they could grow so big. I personally suffered greatly from them especially at night when I felt them crawling over me, keeping me awake through the night.

Every day we went to work with an armed SS-man or woman and a trained German-Shepherd dog. Each morning before we went to work, and each evening when we returned from work, we underwent a head count, for which we had to stand outside, whether it was raining or snowing. We were lined up five in a row and marched by music out of the camp. We were outfitted with old, poorly-fitting shoes, but were not permitted to wear them to work because they felt we would ruin them too quickly that way. We walked barefoot in the middle of the road as Jews were not allowed to walk on the sidewalk.

We marched about five kilometers to work, and only after we arrived at our destination could we put our shoes back on. I suffered terribly going barefoot as every pebble seemed to hurt. I always prayed it would rain or snow so that I wouldn't feel the stones so much. Until this day, I had never walked with bare feet; even when I used to go to the swimming pool I had worn shoes to the edge of the pool. As we marched, we had to sing all the way, even though we really did not feel like singing. In fact, there were many times when many of us would be singing with tears rolling down our cheeks.

Our job was to demolish buildings so that the Germans could re-use the bricks. We formed a chain and tossed the bricks one-to-another. Most of us were very young and inexperienced. It was very cold; the temperature was in the low 20s, and we had no coats or scarves for our freshly-shaven heads. We wore no gloves on our hands, which made catching the bricks particularly difficult. If one of us accidentally dropped a brick when it was tossed to us, the SS-man or woman immediately ordered the dog after us. The dog would jump and bite; the more one cried, the more they would urge the dog on us. I had been raised with dogs and loved them, but I began to hate and fear them.

By evening, we were generally numb, tired and hungry. We would march back to the camp and had to stand outside until the head count was completed (which they called Zaehlappell), after which they gave us our supper. Supper was one slice of bread and a dark liquid which they called "tea." We fought for this food as if we were afraid that they may not have enough for everyone. The menu for the next three years consisted of the same portion: in the morning, plain dark liquid; at noon, squash soup (which we called karpele); and for dinner, a slice of bread and more dark liquid. To this very day, more than 45 years later, I will not have a slice of bread and tea together.

I learned to divide the slice of bread: two bites in the evening, two bites in the morning and one bite in the late afternoon. However, I had to hide the bread inside my uniform because there were some girls who would steal it at night from the cot. When I lay at night in my coop, there were many times that I could not fall asleep because of my hunger. At those times, I might take a bite, then another and another. I would then suffer terribly the next day because I would have no food to get me through.

One morning, when we marched to work, I saw an orange peel far away on the road. I started to shake as I came closer and closer thinking that I would have such a treat. When I got nearer, however, all of a sudden somebody kicked the peel and rind off the road. I could not step out of line to pick it up since they would shoot, claiming that I was attempting to escape. At that moment, I started to cry as if my whole life would have depended on that orange rind. At that time, it really appeared to me that my life did depend on it. I never before would have comprehended how hunger could hurt physically.

Another day, across the field from where I was working, there was a field filled with clover. I could not resist. Jeopardizing my life, I ran across and started to eat the clover, just to have some moisture in my mouth, until I heard shots over my head.

Each day two or more transports arrived, now with elderly women. The gas chambers were not yet ready so everybody was admitted to the camp. In the morning when the head counts were performed some of the elderly people were slower in moving. This prompted the "block-elder," the manager of a particular block or building, to scream, "Faster!" whipping a leather strap or a bat against the slower people. They seemed to be particularly aggressive toward the elderly who were slow to line up.

My block-elder was a 16 year-old girl from my own home town whom I used to know. Reluctantly, one day I approached her and asked her, "How can you do it? You have a mother, too!" She replied, "Shut up or you will get it, too." This girl's name was Etta Hammer. She survived the war and, after liberation found her whole family, parents and brother, intact. I lost my whole family except for the two sisters in Palestine, and I asked myself and wondered, "Where is justice?"

The Germans knew whom to pick as block-elders. They would choose the young and promised them food, clothing and power.

After about three months, as I looked at my friends and myself, I noted how physically deteriorated we had become. One day, an SS-woman heard me talking. Since I spoke perfect German (my public school education had been in the German language) she told me that the next morning I should come to the office and that I would work there (which really meant the difference between life and death). The implication was that I would be protected from rain, snow and wind. I was ecstatic. That evening I told my good fortune to my friends. I realized that my girlfriend, Julia Schlem, looked so bad that she wouldn't survive another few days; I also knew that she spoke German. I told her that the job was for her and that I could probably not handle it (I thought to myself that I could perhaps last another few months). The next morning she reported in my place and I did not hear from her for seven months.

No matter how sick a person became, there was absolutely no medication that was given nor could we stay away from work. According to the Nazis, if you did not report for work, you were of no use so you were taken to the gas chamber. They would say, "Why should we feed the sick when we can bring enough new people with new strength?"

Since arriving at Auschwitz, all the girls stopped menstruating which was partially a blessing because the conditions were already so unsanitary. I believe they put something into our tea, affecting the minds of some girls, while others grew beards and mustaches. Many of the girls I knew died; some threw themselves against the electric fences.

By now, new transports were constantly arriving with young bodies who were capable of working. As a result, the elderly, children, women with children and the disabled were all led straight from the railroad station to the gas chamber. People descending from the train were told to go to the communal shower where they undressed. Instead of receiving water, however, gas came out. There were three gas chambers that worked 24 hours a day, each consuming 1,000 people at a time. Even so, the facilities could not accommodate all the people that arrived each day. There were lines of people waiting to go to the gas chamber.

Every day, when new people arrived, I searched for someone who might know something about my parents. Each morning before we lined up for head count, I would run to the block where I might see a familiar face. One day a girl from my town, who had just arrived, told me that my parents were in that very block which was the waiting room for the gas chamber (she obviously did not know that meant they were all destined to be gassed). I went crazy. All I wanted to do was to see them, be with them in their last moments and die with them. Knowing that I would not survive anyway, I went to the SS-man and cried and pleaded with him—not for the life of my parents, whom I knew he wouldn't spare—but for him to let me go with my parents, thinking at least I would be a little comfort to them. I bent my lips to his shoe. He kicked me, knocked two of my teeth out, and said, "Today, you watch them die, and tomorrow if you want to, you can go." I dragged myself to work. I don't know how I survived that day. I cannot explain it. I walked and talked like a robot and just made my mind go blank.

The next day I no longer wanted to sacrifice myself. By then the hatred in me grew so large that I wanted to live in the hope of surviving so that I could avenge myself. That gave me strength to go on.

Ultimately, our camp became over-crowded. We began to build a new camp about five miles away called Birkenau. The water line was not put into Birkenau yet, but we moved there anyway. It took us about six months to finish the camp. Those six months were hell on earth. It was bad enough to be without food, but lack of water was just unbearable. It was located near the crematorium. The smell of burning bones was horrible.

Transports were still arriving daily, by now from Poland, Holland, Belgium, France and other countries. There were many "Aryan" non-Jews, as well. Anyone the Germans considered to be against them was brought in. In general, they were also not sent to the gas chambers.

The proudest arrivals were the girls from Holland. When they entered the gates of our camp, they appeared to have a strong spirit and sang their national anthem. As punishment for doing so, they had to stand in a ditch partly filled with water which surrounded the camp. As they stood there, the ditch was further filled with water until it reached above their necks. This was done to the girls after three days of having been on the train under horrible conditions. More than half were found drowned in the morning and many others died over the next few days. This act broke them completely, physically and spiritually.

It was still summer. The smell of the burning bodies made the air foul. Girls were dying and were left to lie until they were piled up on heaps of other bodies and then thrown on a buggy and taken away. Girls were dying without being able to be identified. One day, we came back from work (which, incidentally, we did seven days a week) and after the head count, we were not permitted to go to the barracks. We were told we had to be physically tattooed because the girls were dying in such masses that they did not know who they were. Two Slovak boys were tattooing us manually, stitch by stitch. One of the boys, Laly Sokolov, who now lives in Australia, was tattooing my left arm with an SS-man close by. I whispered that Laly should do it slowly as I wanted to obtain more information about my relatives and brother from the men's camp which was about three miles from our women's camp. That is why the number on my left arm is a bit longer and bigger than most other people's tattoos. Later, they tattooed the people by so-called "professionals."

The men were in a separate camp. We did not have any contact with them except for certain "kommandos" of people assigned to do some work in our camp. News started to infiltrate through these inmates. I found out that my younger brother, Isador, had been clubbed to death. I took this news very hard since we were very close in age and had been exceptionally attached to each other. I also found out that a neighbor of ours, Pollak, was working at the place where they herded people into the gas chamber, the "Sonderkommando." One day he had to put his own mother into the gas chamber. His sister now lives in London, England and his brother lives in Melbourne, Australia.

Occasionally, I would see girls wear new shoes or head scarves or even a brassiere. Whenever I would ask from whom they received these, they would all say, "From Matyi." This Matyi worked as the driver of a horse and buggy, transporting materials taken from the Jews. He would drive these materials to a German warehouse and, whenever he could, he endangered his life and smuggled some of the goods to the girls. I pleaded with my friends to ask Matyi for a pair of new shoes. Little did I know that one day Matyi would be my husband.

My feet were particularly sensitive. After the girls from Holland arrived, my regular shoes were taken away and wooden clogs of the Dutch girls were substituted. I developed large blisters and suffered greatly on account of these wooden shoes.

One day, after the new arrival of a transport, I met a girl from my town and asked her about my married sister, Joly. She told me that Joly had been with her on the same train. The girl with whom I was speaking had been in one line, the line that lived, and Joly had been put into the line headed for the gas chamber. I was shocked because Joly had been married to an engineer who was exceptionally gifted in his field. The Germans had exempted him and his family from deportation until that time. I found out that Joly had told the friend with whom I spoke that her husband had been given the choice either to save his mother or his wife, that he could not save both. He had decided to send his wife, my sister, and save his mother. I was very bitter. After liberation, he sought me out but I always avoided talking to him. Now as the years pass, I, as a mother, know what kind of hard decision that must have been. A human being should never be put in the position where he has to choose between a mother and a wife.

Once, after we came back from work and the head count was over, we were not permitted back to the barracks. To our astonishment, we saw three stockades in the middle of the court. Three girls were tied down to them with their panties down and they received 25 lashes on their bare backs. To this day I don't know why; we were just told that they would do it to all of us unless we behaved.

One day the Germans gave us a post card and allowed us to write home. I wrote to my sisters in Hungary. (They were brought to the camp one year later.) I wrote to them that rather than visit their younger sister (meaning me), they would be better off taking their own lives. I also gave them the day our parents died. In case I should not survive, I wanted them to be able to observe the date of our parents' deaths (Yahrzeit). I found out that the reason for this gesture was the circumstance that the Red Cross had visited Auschwitz and wanted to take the mail with them.

The work became harder and harder for me. I became thinner and thinner and, consequently, weaker and weaker. No matter how hopeless life appeared, the willpower always seemed to eke back. At one point, I heard a rumor (which I later found had been started by the Germans) that they were looking for good workers for easier jobs. At that point I was on a team that built roads with primitive, heavy equipment. My job was to use a sledgehammer to crush the stones on the road. As I weighed 70 pounds, it seemed to me that the sledgehammer was heavier than I was. So I volunteered. I noticed that the Germans were very selective, (choosing only the youngest and prettiest girls down the line). Then I saw a German doctor approaching the girls who volunteered and I knew something was not right; I panicked. I began to hide and I ran and crawled from bush to bush until I could mingle with the rest of the girls. I was very lucky. Later, we found out that not one of those girls survived. They were all used as guinea-pigs and had surgery without anesthesia.

The days became cooler and Rosh Hashanah, our new year, came and went. On the day of Yom Kippur, which is the highest holiday in the Jewish religion, we were working in the field in a severe downpour. It was late September and cold. Our uniforms were drenched, and each time I lifted the shovel, the water ran down my sleeves onto my body. We were all crying and asking our overseers to please let us take shelter, at least for a while. They refused for several hours, but then finally let us go into a hut.

They pushed all 50 of us girls into a room. We were like sardines, wet body on body, shivering. We were told not to talk at all or they would send us out again. We heard the men workers' voices from the next room. Suddenly we heard a clear voice singing "The Kol Nidre," which is the holiest song for that day, and all the girls burst out crying. As punishment we had to leave the building and work again in the rain. To this very day, whenever I hear the song, I have to cry.

October came and we received orders not to go to work. We knew this meant trouble, since the moment you didn't go to work, they put you into the gas chamber. It was cold and we stood outside in one place for hours. Finally, we found out that the Germans had decided that as long as we could not do much productive work during the winter, they would institute more stringent selection procedures. Each day when we passed by the Nazis, five of us in a row, they would point to at least two or three girls in each row, grab them, put them on the waiting trucks and drive them straight to the gas chamber.

In the row in front of me were neighbors of mine from home and good friends of my family. They took the mother and the two daughters. All the rest had to march on as if nothing happened. Their name was Weisse and two of their brothers live today, one in England and the other in Israel. I cannot describe the feeling we had as we marched through the gate every moment thinking, "Will it be me?" The same happened when we returned from work. By now we were exhausted, cold and hungry. They just pointed and that was it. It did not matter if you were sick, well or anything. It all depended on their individual whims.

The weather continued to get colder and there were no additional blankets or clothing. Girls began to develop severe colds, and typhus fever broke out among us. This became an epidemic with absolutely no medication available. At this point, we welcomed sleeping five in one bunk so that we could snuggle together and get some body heat from each other since everyone was pulling on the single blanket from each side.

At this time, our block-elders were three sisters, the Zimmerspitz girls from Slovakia. They had certain privileges like food, clothes and being able to keep themselves clean. Fortunately, there were only very few of us who would stoop so low, even if it meant self-preservation. These girls were very mean to us. When they were to wake us, they came with huge wooden clubs and swung them at us in our bunks. They had the power to assign us to the gas chamber if they happened not to like anything about us, whether it was our walk, our talk, our looks or for no obvious reason. We hated them with a passion and feared them even more. Since I do not want to mention them again, I would like to note at this point what ultimately happened to them. When the end of the war drew to a close and the block-elders had obviously outlived their usefulness, they were executed by the Nazis in a horrible way. The Nazis tortured them cruelly and then sent them to the gas chamber. Even though this was a terrible death, none of us girls felt very sorry for them.

The weather became colder yet and we were still without any water and only very little food or clothing. The situation appeared to be getting worse by the minute. The clothes lice multiplied in our uniforms. There was no way to change or wash clothes; so, when returning to the barracks at nighttime, we tended to undress and try to kill the lice living in our clothes. To our sorrow, it became dark very quickly and we could not continue not having electricity, candles or flashlights. To this day, I have a phobia about darkness in a room. I feel the same way about the space around me. I have a phobia of small rooms; I feel that the walls are closing in around me.

Girls began to die from typhus, and I became very ill as well. I developed a high fever. Without food, water or medications, this became absolutely insufferable. In order to just get some moisture, some girls would drink their own urine. I noticed what this did to these girls. They would get terrible diarrhea which dehydrated them further and then they would just die. I tried to get some moisture by lying down on the ground and sucking the earth after rain or snow.

Conditions for us became worse and worse. Our performance did not meet expectations. As a result, on a very dark day in all our lives, i.e., December 5,

1942, a date that we shall never forget, we all lined up for head count as usual in the morning. We were told that nobody would go to work and we all knew the consequences of not working.[2] It was snowing; we had on our striped uniforms without coats or sweaters and still our heads were shaven. We stood outside, many of us with high fever, from early morning not knowing our fate, until a rumor reached us that only a very few of us would be permitted to survive that day. They lined us up in a long goose line. At the beginning of the line, there were two SS-men on each side and two SS-women with cattle trucks nearby. Each of us was ordered to step out, one by one, as they looked us over. If they pointed to the right, that meant death; they grabbed the girl and threw her on the truck. As each truck filled, it was driven straight to the gas chamber. We all knew what was happening but were unable to do anything about it.

As I mentioned before, I was at the height of my illness and I felt I could not go on any more. My feet wouldn't hold me because of the high fever and the absence of any medication. I sat in the snow with the girls surrounding me so that the SS-men would not see me sitting. By now it was already 3:00 in the afternoon. The line became smaller and smaller and I could see healthy, young girls being sent to the gas chamber. I knew that I did not have a chance to survive. The girl next to me was 16 years old, healthy and strong, with blue eyes and blonde hair and I thought she would certainly live. I asked her to please look up my sisters should she come out of the concentration camp alive and let them know the date that I died.

By now I had to stand up as I watched the line become smaller and smaller. The only thing on my mind was ten more minutes, eight more minutes, four more minutes that I would be alive. With each passing moment, I had a stronger and stronger willpower to live. It was only with this feeling that I could manage to stand. As I watched the line in front of me get shorter, I told my girlfriend, "Trudy, God be with you," and at that moment they shoved her into the truck. I stood paralyzed and shocked before SS Sturmbahnnfuehrer Schwartz, more dead than alive. At that instant, another SS-man asked him a question. As he turned his head, he pointed to the side of the living line without even looking at me. Had he not done so, I would not be here to tell this story. Right after me, it seemed that at least the next 80 girls went to the gas chamber. We were sent back to the camp and many of the girls who saw me felt great resentment. I could sense this in their voices. They would ask, "Helen, you?" I was hurt by this. Later they explained to me that they felt I would not be able to survive and they thought that I had occupied the place that a healthier girl could have had.

I, myself, didn't know how I could survive with my high fever, without water or medication. Yet, I kept going. Everyday I walked to work in the snow without shoes, getting weaker and weaker. I couldn't sleep at night because of the lice. They were multiplying rapidly. My whole body became infected and itched constantly. I also developed diarrhea like most of the other inmates, and this weakened me even more. At that point I weighed about 67 pounds, but kept going on sheer willpower.

Two days before my birthday, which is on December 30, when I was going to work, I told the other girls that this was my last day because, by now, I could hardly lift my feet even to walk. They all insisted that I go on and said, "Helen you have to," because we all knew that the moment you didn't go to work you lost your usefulness to the Germans. With their insistence, I went another day. Finally, my birthday arrived. As we were coming home from work, I could not walk any more, so two girls carried me even though they were weak themselves. At that point, they told me I would be better off staying home the next day (which, of course, would have meant death for me). I was fully aware what this meant. While the others stood outside in the snow for our daily head count, I could only sit because my feet would not hold me any more. It was December 30, my birthday, and bitter cold.

I heard an SS-woman calling out my number "2282!!!" Usually, when they called somebody's number, it meant the person did not work hard enough and had outlived her usefulness. It meant extermination. My first reaction was not to answer, but after they repeated my number, I said to myself with resignation, "I would not have gone to work tomorrow anyway so I might as well get it over with now." Fully aware of my death sentence, I stood up and said, "It's me." The SS-woman approached me and said, "Tomorrow, you won't go to work. You are to report to the office."

There is a saying that, with great shock, one can become speechless. I know this to be true because, for the next ten minutes, I could not talk. I was completely speechless, and my first words were, "My birthday!!" The shock of going from an expectation of death to life was so great that I was sobbing uncontrollably. Since that time, I have always said that I was born twice. To work in an office meant that you had to be clean, thus the chance for survival was much greater. The German and Polish civilians who worked in the office wanted to be sure that they would not get any of the diseases rampant in camp, so we were given showering facilities and medications. We also had shelter and did not have to be in the rain, snow or wind without protection.

The next day, when they prepared to send me to the office, they looked at me and noticed the poor shape I was in. They realized they could not let anyone from the outside see me this way. They put me in a little hospital in which no Jews were allowed, only German political prisoners. There, they cleaned me up for five days until most of the sores on my body had healed. This was the first time in almost a year that I took a shower and put on a dress, the uniform for all office help.

While lying in that hospital, I constantly pondered, "Why me?" until they took me to the office and I saw... Julia. I knew. Julia was the girl whom I had sent to work in the office in my place soon after arriving at the camp. All these months I did not know what had happened to her since nobody had seen her or heard anything from her. She worked in this office and when they needed an additional office person, Julia had asked her supervisor, a very influential German officer, to ask for my number.

I believe in fate. Had they asked for my number one day later, I would not have been alive any more. It also taught me that if you do some good to somebody, sooner or later you will be paid back for it.

In January 1943, a new life began for me. They moved me back to Auschwitz from Birkenau, which, in comparison, was heaven. We moved to a building called "Stabsgebaeude," the dwelling for all girls who worked in offices.

We did not get more food, but we had shower facilities which meant we could keep ourselves clean. That alone helped us survive. There were about 300 girls, but only six of us worked for DEST (Deutsche Erd-und Steinwerke), including Julia and me.

All six of us came from Slovakia and all six were about the same age with the same background. Working and sleeping together, we became so attached to each other that even now, more than 45 years later, we continue to be in touch with each other. Two live in Czechoslovakia, one in Australia, two in Israel, and myself in the United States of America.

For the first time since I left home, I started to feel like a human being. I became a person who didn't just have to be self-centered, fighting for survival. I started to become interested in things outside myself. I began to receive news from civilians, most of them Polish. The news we heard would give all us girls hope for a time when all of this would be over, a nightmare of the past.

It was 1943, and we were able to hear bombs being dropped around us. There was a huge German ammunition factory called Weichsel Union Werke in the vicinity which used inmates as workers. As a result, the British started to bomb our camp. Instead of being frightened by the bombs, we prayed that they would come more often since most of us did not believe we would survive anyway. One day in 1944, our building took a direct hit. The wall beside my bunk bed disappeared but none of us was injured, which was a miracle. A few years later, after having married my husband, Matyi, now known as Martin, he told me that his crew had been working in the fields at this particular time. When they saw the bombs falling, they ran to a nearby ditch set up as a shelter against bombs. After Martin and his co-workers were in the shelter for a few minutes, the SS-men came, ordered them out, and took their places in the bunker. A few minutes later, the bunker was hit directly by a bomb, killing all the SS-men.

For the next few months, I continued to live in the Auschwitz women's camp and worked at the DEST office where the Polish employees treated us humanely. We tried to send word to the other inmates in other barracks that news from the outside world was hopeful for liberation.

We were still very hungry, but now we had hopes that it might all come to an end. That is, until we looked across our offices to the railroad station and saw four or five transports continuing to arrive daily. We would still see the doors open with dead children and people falling out.

Near the end of 1944, we heard rumors that the Germans were in trouble and that they were losing on the front. With us, however, nothing seemed to change until suddenly, the transports stopped. Then, two of the three gas chambers were destroyed by an uprising of the prisoners of the Sonderkommando.

One day, we came back from work and they would not let us into the barracks because we had to witness the hanging execution of the four young girls who had furnished the dynamite for the blast. Only later did I find out that Matyi, my future husband, had personally delivered the dynamite. The girls never revealed his name.

It was rumored that the Russians were coming closer and on January 18, 1945, Auschwitz was evacuated.

We six girls who worked for DEST were very fortunate. Our boss assumed responsibility for us and told the authorities that he would deliver us to the closest concentration camp. He and all of us were convinced that had he handed us over, none of us would have survived.

We spent the entire day helping the Germans pack their pick-up trucks in the middle of a snow blizzard, and then we were evacuated.[3]

The Germans rode inside the cars and trucks while the six of us were outside in the pick-up truck. We were half frozen, but still grateful. We cuddled each other to stay warm. As we rode in the truck, we could see the inmates all in long rows of five walking in the road, chased by the SS-men. If anyone stopped, they were instantly shot. As we rode, we saw multitudes of dead and half-dead bodies strewn along the sides of the road. Many times, I can still hear them screaming in my nightmares.

We were on the road for about two days before we arrived at Gross Rosen, a concentration camp in Germany designated strictly for men.

After a few days, several SS-men put us to work on the roads. One of the SS-men spoke Hungarian and, as we spoke the language, we tried to find out about the situation in the outside world. He was somewhat friendlier than the others. One day, on the way to work, we crossed a railroad with empty coal wagons. We foolishly thought that we could escape by jumping into the empty wagons. We hid, cowered in the corners of the wagon floor, praying no one would notice us. Suddenly, the Hungarian SS-man stood on top of the train car with his gun drawn, shouting for us to come out. We tried to climb out of the wagon, but the walls were so high that we couldn't reach the top; he was yelling at us that he would shoot. As I was the tallest of all the girls, I let them use me as a stepping stone to prop themselves to the top. When it was my turn, I simply could not make it. At that point he began to shoot. To this day, I don't know how I was able to jump to reach the top edge, but I did, and made it out. The Hungarian SS-man did not tell his supervisor or we would have all been executed at once.

At this point, the Russian army was beginning to close in on the camp in which we were staying, so we were transported to Theresienstadt camp in Czechoslovakia near Prague. There, we were kept with very little food, but we were full of hope knowing that the Nazis would be defeated, even if it meant that we would be executed. The rumor we heard throughout the camp was that before the Germans would be captured, they would kill us all so that there would be no witnesses to their deeds. In order to accomplish this, they began to build crematoria with the intent of achieving their goal. Within hours of the order to work, however, we heard loud noises, cars and trucks. As we ran out, we saw the unbelievable: Russian tanks, Russian troops, the Russian army. We were laughing, dancing, hugging each other because we knew that the incredible had happened. We were alive and free. The date was May 9, 1945.

A Czechoslovakian family invited my girlfriend and me for dinner. We did not realize how we looked (for example, I was 5' 3" tall and weighed 68 pounds). When they put the soup on the table, my girlfriend, Ladik, and I pulled over the soup bowl, filled our plates to the brim, and within two minutes had finished it all leaving nothing for the other six members of the family with whom we were dining. We became so engrossed in our eating that we did not notice when we had finished that all the people around us were just looking at us and crying.

The only thing I could think of was to go home. Maybe, maybe I would find some members of my family. Since passenger trains did not run yet, I hopped on a coal wagon heading toward Slovakia and my home town, still dressed in my prison uniform. I arrived in Pezinok and did not find any of my family. All of a sudden the realization hit me. Why did I fight so hard to survive and not find any of my family alive? Here I was, a girl with nobody who cared whether I would eat or had a place to live. I remember tears running down my cheeks. One of my old neighbors came out, looking very prosperous. He asked me, "Aren't you happy to be alive?" I said, "What for, I don't even know where I can put my head down." In that instant, he took out a set of keys and said, "This apartment is yours." He told me that he was in charge of housing and that he fought in the underground during the war in the woods. Immediately, I went to an organization (the American Joint Distribution Committee)[4] where I knew I would find my ex-coworkers. I told three of the girls who were in the same situation as I that we had a roof over our heads and that they could come to live with me. It turned out to be a one-bedroom apartment with two beds, but more than enough for the four of us.

The A.J.D.C. organization gave each of us 200 crowns, sufficient for about one day of food. When I walked out of the building, I was introduced to an ex-inmate, Matyi Klein.

During the first few days, everybody searched for family members. One girl I knew crossed the street to accidentally find her mother. Each of them had thought the other was dead. To witness this reunion was indescribable.

After a few days, however, I realized that even though I had a roof over my head, I also had to eat. So I went to look for a job. One organization sent many of the undernourished to the mountains for recuperation. I said to myself that if I start to accept donations, I would never become independent.

I returned to Pezinok. As I approached my parents' old house, my heart broke seeing our family's drapes in the window. My parents had been highly regarded by the townspeople. They, their parents, their grandparents and all my sisters and brothers were born there. I learned that after my brother and I had been sent to the concentration camp, the mayor had advised my parents to hide before the Germans would come into town. One day, however, when the Germans came to look for them, one of our neighbors thought he could obtain my parents' property and divulged their hiding place, the cemetery, to the Nazis. My parents were picked up, not permitted to go to their home to obtain additional clothing, and were then sent with a transport straight to Auschwitz.

I weighed 68 pounds, I had half-inch long hair, and I had no job. I went to city hall to see the mayor who had advertised for clerical work. I sat in the waiting room for hours until it was closing time. He came out to say that I should return the next day. In desperation, I walked up to him and said, "I am not going to wait another day, I am hungry." He asked if I could type, and I said, "Yes." I was hired. Later I was told that he thought if he had not said yes, I would have passed away right then and there. Thus, I became the only breadwinner for the four of us girls.

I began to date Martin, or Matyi Klein, and we were married in December, 1945. After our marriage, we moved to Bratislava and decided to open a clothing store, the same business that my father had conducted previously in Pezinok. To open such a shop, we were required to obtain a town permit. On three occasions we applied for the permit using the name Martin Klein, and on three occasions the permit was denied. We suspected that anti-semitism that had blazed for so many years had not been smothered so quickly. At that point in time, my job was to register deaths for the city of Bratislava's records. After our permit application was refused for the third time, I registered the death of Martin Klein in place of a person named Kuban and we adopted the name Kuban. The permit was granted. We made a comfortable living, and in August 1947, our son, Karl, was born. Then we saw the nightmare begin to reshape. In March 1948, the Russians occupied Czechoslovakia. Businesses were nationalized one by one. One day Martin and I were asked to subscribe to the communist party.

We had lost our freedom once and we did not want to lose it again. So, one Monday in October 1948, a friend who worked with the Czechoslovakian secret police told us that they received an order from high authorities that we were to be arrested if we did not subscribe to the party by the next day. We had a passport and were able to purchase a visa to France. Thus, with only our child in hand, we left Czechoslovakia. We left our belongings in our apartment as well as our money in the banks in order to avoid raising suspicion. A friend of ours took a few of our suitcases to the border where we met him.

We arrived in Paris, and at once applied for emigration. The following week, we met a friend who had just come from Czechoslovakia, too. He said that two days after our departure, the secret police had issued an arrest for my husband. We lived in Paris, but we could not speak French. The little money we had dwindled. We were able to contact relatives in London, England, of the Gestetner family who had offices around the world. They ordered the president of the Paris office to train us and get us a job. Through that connection, Martin received a job at the United Nations in Paris and finally, in January 1952, we were given permission to emigrate to the United States of America.

My second son, Alan Lincoln Kuban, was born on February 12, 1953, the birthday of the great American emancipator, Abraham Lincoln.

To say life was easy would be a lie, but we were free and we were willing to work hard to make life easier for us as well as our family. We moved to Jersey City, New Jersey, where our cousin had a factory. The very next day, Martin began to work as a cutter's helper. He made $35.00 a week. This was not enough to make it, so I went to work and worked for the next 30 years, until 1981, just to be sure that my children would have it easier than we did.

Lotte (Charlotte) Weiss (née Frankl)
Sydney (Australia)

My name is Lotte (Charlotte) Weiss, née Frankl. I was born on November 28, 1923, in Bratislava (Pressburg), Czechoslovakia, the third daughter in my family. I had 3 sisters and 2 brothers. My father was an accountant and my mother looked after the family. We spent our evenings in discussions, laughing and sometimes going out for walks. I spent the first five years of my schooling in a Jewish Day School and later continued at a State College until 1938. Subsequently, I took classes at a commercial school and after finishing my training, was employed as a clerk/typist in a menswear store.

On March 14, 1939, our part of Czechoslovakia became an autonomous state under the presidency of a Roman Catholic priest, Dr. Josef Tiso. The new state fashioned itself totally after the Nuremberg laws. Daily anti-semitic incidents occurred in our city and Jews were being beaten up on the streets and in their homes. Shops were taken over by "Aryans," and Jewish employees were dismissed without notice. I lost my job in March 1941, and could not find another one because I was Jewish.

Starting in September 1941, all Jews had to wear a yellow Star of David on their left breast and all Jews who lived in the non-Jewish part of the city had to move to the Jewish quarter. We were thrown out of our apartment in October 1941, and were moved to the Jewish section of the city. Although there were eight members in our family, we lived in one room and kitchen. Toward the beginning of 1942, there were rumors that all Jews would be re-settled in Poland or Germany. On March 22, 1942, there was a knock on our door and three Hlinka

Guards (the equivalent of the SS) came to our house and brought a summons for the three oldest girls. We were ordered to assemble the next morning at 7 a.m. at an old magazine factory, called Patronka. My dear parents were terribly upset that we would be leaving the next day and stayed up all night to prepare our rucksacks with all things possible. It was a very sad morning when we said good-bye to our heartbroken parents. I never saw them, my sister or my two brothers again.

We arrived at the Patronka. Many of our friends were already there, and we had to leave all our belongings in the yard. They were never given back to us. We were taken to rooms which had 60 girls in each and the doors were locked. We were totally confused and did not know what was going to happen. We were given food twice a day and allowed to use washing facilities only once a day. We had a bucket for our toilet needs. We had no idea what our future held. We stayed there until March 27, 1942, when we were told to assemble in the yard and then were marched to the railway station. We were put into cattle wagons—60 girls to each—and had buckets for our toilet needs. We hardly had room to move and were squeezed throughout our journey, which lasted 24 hours, until we arrived in Auschwitz.

When we arrived there, we were shouted at and kicked by the SS-men to move faster. When all of us were out, we started to march toward the camp. On the way to the camp, we noticed the infamous gate with the sign "Arbeit macht frei" on it, and we also saw the writing, "Gefahr" (Danger), on the fence of the camp as it was a high voltage wire fence. We realized that we had arrived at a concentration camp and were completely bewildered, not knowing what was going to happen to us. We were marched to the camp and were taken to a large hall where we were registered and given our numbers. I received number 2065. Then we were taken to another hall, where we had to undress and we were shaved by male prisoners. Our hair was suddenly gone, and then we had to go into a shower and afterwards we were given Russian uniforms which consisted of trousers and a jacket. We were bitterly cold, tired and hungry. My two sisters and I were taken, with about 200 girls, to Block 10, and the other girls were taken to other blocks. There were 1000 girls in our transport. The first night, we had to lie on the bare ground without blankets or food, and we were crying the whole night.

The next morning, Sunday, March 29, 1942, we had our first roll-call on the camp street and afterward had to assemble for work formation. My two sisters and I were ordered into a "Kommando" (work group) which was called "Gartenbau." Our work consisted of digging grounds, cutting trees and preparing the ground for gardens. We worked in places which housed the SS-officers and their families. It was very hard and exhausting work, which we had not done before, and all forty girls in this kommando suffered from hunger, thirst and the climate. We were woken up every morning at about 3 a.m. and had to hurry out on the camp street for roll-call which lasted 2-3 hours. We had only our trousers and jackets, and had no underwear or socks. We also suffered from the freezing cold. Going to and from work, we had to carry our wooden clogs and walk barefoot. Whilst marching to work, we had to sing German marching songs. We were accompanied by SS-men with machine guns and Alsatian dogs, which were set upon us at the whim of the SS-men without any reason. On the way to work one morning, one girl collapsed, and my sisters went to help her. The SS-men set the dog on them, and it bit one of my sisters in the thigh. She was ordered back in line in spite of the fact that she was bleeding profusely.

When at work, each girl was allocated a piece of ground to dig, and one day when I finished my digging, I wanted to help my sisters, but the SS-man noticed it. He came over and asked me what I was doing, and when I told him I had finished my task and wanted to help my sisters, he screamed at me, kicked me and told me that we were not in a sanatorium but in a concentration camp. He said he would report my misbehavior to the camp authorities. He did hand in a report and one evening a few weeks later, after roll-call, my number was called out by the block senior, and I was told not to go to work the next morning, but to stay in the camp at the gate. When I asked why my number was called out, she did not want to tell me, but I insisted that I needed to know. Then she told me that I was being sent to the penal colony for my misbehavior. My sisters and I could not sleep all night because we already knew that no one ever came back from there. In the morning, we cried bitterly when we kissed good-bye, and then they had to go to work. I stayed at the gate, and eventually more girls joined me until there were about 20 of us. A couple of hours later, my number was called by an SS-man and he made me march to the men's camp to have my photo taken. After that, we returned to the camp and soon after the gate opened and a black van arrived with two SS-men. They called us to come closer and ordered us into the van. As one SS-man stood by the van, the other was counting. He counted to twenty. I was the 21st. Thereupon, he shouted at me to go to my barrack because he did not have enough room for me. I just could not believe what I had heard and was hesitant, so he told me again to go away. I ran quickly to my barrack and hid under the bunk because I was so frightened that he would come after me. The happiness of my sisters and myself in the evening when we saw each other was tremendous and unbelievable.

During the afternoon of that day, I heard some unusual noises on the camp street and went to investigate. I saw a lot of newcomers, and among them I noticed my cousin from Bratislava. As I approached her, she did not recognize me because I had a shaven head and a Russian uniform and was much thinner than before. When I told her who I was, she started to cry and asked, "In what hell have we landed?" She told me that my parents, my younger sister and my two brothers were in the same transport as she. At their arrival in Auschwitz, they sorted the newcomers into two groups. She went to the right side as did my father and one brother, but my mother and the two youngest in our family went to the left. She had no idea what it meant, but I knew already that the left side was selected to go to the gas chambers. (After about two years in camp, I finally found out their fate. My father was beaten to death after four days, one of my brothers lived for six weeks and then died of typhus, my mother, my youngest sister and brother went straight away to the gas chambers.)

I continued to work in the same kommando. Our kapo was a German prisoner with a black triangle and had been imprisoned because she was a prostitute.
She hated Jews, although she had never had anything to do with them, but was
taught by her father to hate them. Eventually, she became used to us and did not
use her whip and her hands on us as often as in the beginning. She was at times sadistic and always beat us and wanted us to work faster, which became harder and
harder as time went on because we were already completely exhausted.

Our work became almost unbearable, and the food was so little that we collapsed like flies. Day by day, some girls of our group could not march out to work
any more because they were so weak and ill. We noticed that many of our girls
disappeared from work and from our sleeping quarters, and we knew they would
never come back. There were rumors going around at this time (end of May 1942)
that the girls who could not work because of weakness or illness would be gassed.
It was incomprehensible to us, but the rumors became a reality very soon and it
was no secret that the gassing took place. There was a Revier (hospital) in camp
where they took one in only when you had a temperature of 40 degrees centigrade
and we were frightened to go near it because it became obvious that only the ones
who kept healthy would have a chance to carry on for the next hour or day.

One day, at the end of July 1942, when we were at work digging soil and cutting trees, I got a terrible headache. On our way to camp after work, I could not
stand the pain any longer and told my sisters that I would go to the hospital after
roll-call. However, I collapsed at roll-call, and my two sisters and two other girls
carried me in a blanket to the hospital because I was unconscious. I was admitted
and stayed unconscious for three days. I was put on the truck, which came every
day to the hospital to collect the very sick patients and then they were taken to the
gas chambers to be gassed. I was told afterward, when I regained consciousness,
by one nurse (whose mother was a friend of my mother) that she knelt down in
front of the SS-doctor and begged him to let me live because I was young, strong,
a hard worker and had never missed a day of work. And a miracle happened, he
ordered someone to take me off the truck and then sent a German nurse from the
SS-hospital to see what was wrong with me. She diagnosed meningitis and gave
me a lumbar puncture. The pain of this injection brought me back to life, and I
started to scream with pain. She shouted at me, "If you scream, you will die. If
you want to live, you must shut up." I had no idea where I was, but I was told to
go to my bunk. A Jewish nurse in this room helped me go to my bunk. I immediately asked her about my two sisters, and she told me that they came to the
window every evening after work, and that she would take me to the window
when they returned from work so that I could see them. When I saw them, I collapsed again, and had to be taken to my bunk. My recovery was almost non-existent. I was weak and worn-out.

A few days later, an SS-woman came to the hospital and asked which of the
patients could run. Although I could not even walk by myself yet, I told her that I
could run. I already knew that one must not say one is ill because that resulted in

one being sent to the gas chambers. It was the beginning of August 1942, and all women prisoners who were staying in the 10 blocks of the Auschwitz camp were moved to a different camp, located a few kilometers from Auschwitz. It was called Birkenau-Brzezinka. Only thirty girls who were in the hospital, and who had informed the SS-woman that they could run, were taken to the other camp in Birkenau. The rest of the hospital patients went to the gas chambers.

It took me three days to find my sisters in this camp. There was chaos everywhere; there was no water, the camp streets were muddy, the huts were dirty and contained bunks which housed eight girls to one level. There were no toilets in this camp, only latrines. Many girls were so weak that they fell in and drowned in them. The only water we drank was from the puddles in the camp streets after rain.

I eventually found my sisters; they were in Block 27 and I moved in with them and went to work with them. I still felt ill and very weak, but we were happy to be together again.

Around the middle of September 1942, both sisters fell ill with typhus. My two sisters, unfortunately, were too ill to stay in the barracks and they were admitted to the hospital. When I went to see them the next day, I was not allowed in by the block senior who chased me away. I begged her to permit me to visit them, but she just kicked me and would not let me enter. I was desperate and tried the next day to see them again, but the same thing happened and I was not allowed in to see them. Suddenly, I heard my name being called by two girls in the camp street and, when I approached them, I recognized them as friends from my hometown. They were carrying a stretcher with clothing. As I talked to them, I looked at the uniforms on the stretcher and saw the number of my sister on a uniform. When I asked them where the clothes came from, they replied, "From Block 25." This was the collection or death block from which all prisoners went to the gas chambers, or they were brought there because they were already dead. I searched the stretcher for the uniform of my second sister and found it there, too, and so I found out that they were no longer alive.

After learning of my sisters' deaths, I wanted to go in desperation to the electric fence and finish off my miserable life. There was no point in going on since I was alone in this world, desperate, hungry, ill and totally without hope. Suddenly, I heard my name being called, and when I looked around I saw my former kapo, Ulla. She had recently become a very important person because she had been made the secretary of the Camp Commandant. She already knew that my sisters had died and said she wanted to help me. She was horrified when I told her I had lost all hope and did not want to live any more. She took me to her barracks and gave me a drink of water and a piece of bread, and promised to help me find an indoor job where I would be kept away from the horrible climate and would have a better chance to recover. She managed to get me into the kommando "Canada," where clothing was sorted from people who came to Auschwitz and then sent to Germany for distribution to the German people.

In early December 1942 I managed to get out of a frightful situation at the last minute. We were lined up after work on the Lagerstrasse in Birkenau for our evening roll call. When the roll call was finished, two SS-women took out 30 girls at random from the assembled rows. I was amongst the 30. We were taken to the medical block on the opposite side of the Lagerstrasse. We were told to sit down in the ante-room and the first girl was called into the medical rooms. It took at least 20 minutes before the next girl was called in and then another 20 minutes before the third girl was called. Neither of the girls came out to where we were waiting. After a while I became suspicious and wanted to opt out. I asked the SS-woman who looked after us to allow "2065 zum Austreten." ("2065 to relieve herself.") She refused to let me go. I persevered, however, and told her I had diarrhea and persisted that I could not wait any longer. I asked her again, "Entschuldigen Sie bitte, Frau Aufseherin, 2065 meldet sich zum austreten. Ich habe Durchfall und muss dringendst gehen." ("Please excuse me, Mrs. SS-woman, number 2065 requests to be allowed to relieve herself. I have diarrhea and have to go most urgently.") She replied, "Komm bloss zurueck, denn sonst werden wir Dich zurueckholen." ("Come back immediately, otherwise we'll drag you back.") I disappeared and ran to the latrine and stayed there for a considerable time, being afraid to return to my block. I returned much later. At that time, I had no idea what happened to the girls at the medical block.

I do not know who performed the sterilization but I know there were two men in white coats in the ante-room of the medical block when we entered. I do not remember whether the 29 girls came back into our block again. I learned from several girls during the following days that all of them were sterilized. One described the way it was done: "A warm steel plate was inserted into the womb and kept there for about 15 minutes." (How accurate this description was I cannot tell.)

The only girl I knew personally was Judith Kahan. I did not know her intimately but as she came from Czechoslovakia, we saw each other often. I cannot remember seeing her after that. It is quite possible that she worked in the Arbeitseinsatz. I know she had a sister in Birkenau. I knew her sister, too.

I learned after the war that Judith was married to a Viennese who was a political prisoner in Auschwitz. I also heard that he became an important man in Vienna (either in the Austrian police or Buergermeister). I believe his name was Heinz Duermayer.

I worked in Canada until the beginning of 1943, and then Ulla again helped me to get a job in an office. It was called "Deutsche Erd- und Steinwerke" and it was responsible to the Wirtschafts-Verwaltungshauptamt in Berlin. There were about 18 people working at the office. It was "ein kriegswichtiges Unternehmen." Men prisoners worked in the quarries in Rajsko and Babice to produce as much sand, gravel and cement as possible, and this was transported to Germany wherever it was needed for building purposes.

Our boss was Ing. Erich Rupprecht, an Untersturmfuehrer, who never wore his uniform but only his civilian clothing. There were a few Volksdeutsche in the office and also a few Polish civilians. We were treated quite fairly by the men in the office and I did not encounter anything drastic. There were seven girl-prisoners working in our office in different departments. I worked in Accountancy. The accountant, Anton Mecner, was a very decent Pole and tried to bring us a little extra food. As he was Polish, his food rations were much smaller than the German rations, but he was kind and treated us as human beings. (To this day, 43 years later, I am in constant touch with him, and I will never forget his kindness toward me and the other girl-prisoners.) Our office was outside the camp compound, and we were escorted to and from work, either by an SS-man or by an employee of the office.

Our office was the headquarters for DEST (an acronym of the company), hence all correspondence with Berlin and other branches throughout the "Generalgouvernement," as well as all the major bookkeeping was done there. I was keeping the ledger and did all the work connected with accounts. Julie Schlemova was personal secretary of engineer Rupprecht, and did shorthand-typing. Eta Bergerova worked alongside Julie; she looked after in-coming mail and did the filing. Berta Hutzler was in the sales department and checked the order books. Ruzenka Gross worked with Berta in sales. Ili Kuban worked in personnel. Herta Wilhelm worked alongside me for only a few months. She admitted to Oberaufseherin Emma Zimmer in Haus 40 that she smoked. Consequently, she was reported and sent to Birkenau for punishment. However, she returned later to the Stabsgebaeude and was accepted as secretary in the Arbeitsdienst. In 1946, she visited me in Bratislava.

When we were accepted for the office job, we were moved from Birkenau to the Stabsgebaeude, and we were very lucky to have been chosen for the job. There was a vast difference between Birkenau and the Stabsgebaeude and for us, who had been in camp almost a year, quite unbelievable. It was the difference between life and death. We each had our own bunk, a blanket and a sheet on our bed and, although we still had very little food and roll-calls, conditions in the Stabsgebaeude were so much better that we started to regain a little hope for our survival. And through our working with civilians, we were given an opportunity to learn about the world outside the camp. The Polish men followed every move of the German army and kept us informed about political developments. After work and the roll-call, we were allowed to lie down and go to sleep, which meant that we did not feel the hunger as much as before. We also could shower every day, and this was a luxury which was unheard of in Birkenau. We lived in the same block as the girls from the "Politische Abteilung," "Standesamt," "Naehstube" and others. We got on very well with the other girls.

After having spent about two months in the office, I developed very bad boils. I was running a high temperature, and the SS-Woman Commandant of the Stabsgebaeude sent me to the Revier. There was a Polish woman doctor by the name of Janina Koszcziuszkowa, whom I noticed was not very friendly toward Jewish prisoners. However, I had already learned a little Polish, and talked to her about herself. She told me her husband was a judge in Cracow and she had an 8-year old son. I asked her if she wanted to send a message to her husband because our accountant often went to Cracow and could take greetings. She did not trust me at first, but she gave me her address nevertheless, which I memorized. When I was discharged from the hospital and went back to work, I gave Anton Mecner the address and he went there to deliver the message. She was extremely happy when Anton brought a little note from her son, and she cried from happiness. Eventually, she became more trusting and as time went on, she became a very good friend of mine. Anton continued to bring her little notes from her husband and son, which I smuggled into the camp. Later in 1943, she was moved from the Stabsgebaeude into another camp and, although I did not see her any more, I received cards and letters from her after the war because Anton and her family became very close friends. I should mention that she was quite antisemitic in the beginning, but she changed considerably after Anton's courier messages.

I remember one afternoon at the office of DEST when three Gestapo men in civilian clothing arrested four Polish civilian employees: Konstantyn Kempa, Ladislaus Saternus, Anatol Bratek and Anton Mecner, for their underground activities. They were handcuffed and driven away in a car. Anatol Bratek and Anton Mecner were eventually released. We were told by Ing. Erich Rupprecht that it was through his intervention that they were freed. Konstantyn Kempa and Ladislaus Saternus were hanged on August 16, 1944 (I remember the date because Ruzenka had her birthday on August 14).

After Bratek and Mecner returned to work, they told us about some of their experiences. Bratek was savagely beaten at the interrogations but apparently did not disclose anything (Bratek died in 1986 in Poland).

Mecner, who spelled his name "Metzner," was also interrogated and told to disclose the underground activities. He was also told that he was a "Volksdeutscher" and should become a member of the Nazi Party. He strongly denied being of German ancestry and insisted on staying Polish. He was released but subsequently arrested again and then freed. He remained a Pole throughout the war, although many Poles became "Volksdeutsche" during the war.

Although conditions in the Stabsgebaeude were so much better than in Birkenau, I suffered much from boils and also from throat infections. I was fortunate that Dr. Koszcziuszkowa always gave me some tablets which were normally unobtainable, but I felt that my health had deteriorated considerably. The sore throats were repetitive and I also had bad pains in my joints. For two weeks, I could not use my right hand because I could not bend my fingers due to stiffness and pain. The doctor gave me some black ointment (Ichtiol). I put it on every night and morning and, eventually, it became better.

After a few months in the Stabsgebaeude, the Deutsche Erd- und Steinwerke girls were moved to Haus 40, together with about twenty girls from the Politische Abteilung. I do not know the reason for this move, but it was much closer to our office which was located opposite the Auschwitz railway station. The conditions in Haus 40 were not as good as in the Stabsgebaeude. We had no heating there and kept warm by two girls sleeping together in one bunk.

Our supervisor was an old and mean SS-woman called Emma Zimmer. She was vicious and dangerous and frightened us constantly with threats, proclaiming in a sadistic voice, "I will report you and then you will go away, you know where? Just one way—up the chimney." We hated her and were scared of her. She punished us at every opportunity. She undid our bunks and we had to do them over and over again until we were picked up and taken to work. We had to clean the floors and doors, and she was never happy with the results. However, after about a year at Haus 40, we were moved again to the new camp, Frauenlager Auschwitz. We stayed there until the evacuation of the camp on January 18, 1945.

On this day, the whole camp was evacuated to different camps in Germany. Our girls from the Deutsche Erd- und Steinwerke were taken by our boss, Ing. Erich Rupprecht, together with his wife, two SS-men and one civilian by truck to Gross-Rosen, where we remained for approximately three weeks. Then we were taken to New Rohlau in Sudetenland for a few days, after which we were transported to Flossenbuerg. We worked in a temporary office during our stay in Gross-Rosen doing DEST work. We were not inside but outside the camp grounds in Gross-Rosen as well as in Flossenbuerg. Since Flossenbuerg did not have a women's camp, we were put in the Bunker on March 28, 1945. This was the last time I saw engineer Rupprecht.

Shortly after the war, I got a letter through the Red Cross from Mrs. Rupprecht. She wrote that her husband was in prison and needed an affidavit from the six Jewish girls who had worked for him in Auschwitz attesting that he behaved well toward us. We all went to a notary public and signed a declaration to that effect and he was freed. However, we never heard from him after that.

We stayed in the Bunker for 10 days and were then moved to Hainichen. We were marching almost all the way, but toward the end of our march we were put into cattle wagons to Hainichen. There we stayed for one week, from April 6 to April 13, 1945, when the airplane factory at Hainichen (or Heinicken) was heavily bombarded and we were moved again. We partly marched, and were sometimes taken in cattle wagons, on our way to Theresienstadt, where we arrived on April 21, 1945. We stayed in the Dresdner Barrack for three weeks, and were liberated by the Russians on May 9, 1945. On May 12, 1945, we made our way to Prague where we remained for a few days. Then we started our journey back to our hometowns.

After traveling for three days, I arrived in Bratislava on Saturday, May 19, 1945. It was a very strange feeling to arrive "Home," and I simply could not believe that this was true. After 38 months of pain, misery, loss of freedom and family and suffering humiliation, to arrive "Home" was just not real. It was 8:30 p.m. when I arrived at the railway station. Notices on the wall pointed to signs which stated that there was a curfew and that no one was allowed on the street after 9 p.m. I did not know where to go and what to do. I remembered some non-Jewish friends of my parents and made my way toward their home. I was very lucky to find them at home, and they accepted me with friendliness and warmth. They invited me to stay with them, and I happily accepted. They told me that there was an

Office of the Joint Distribution Committee across the road, and I decided to go there the next morning. I went and found out that my uncle and aunt had escaped deportation by living in Budapest on forged Aryan papers, and they offered to take me in at their place and give me board.

After a few days of freedom, to which I had to get used very gradually, I suffered a breakdown and was confined to bed for some time. When I eventually recovered, I found a job in a law office as a clerk. It was a very hard beginning because I was emotionally totally finished. I missed my dear parents, my sisters and brothers and began slowly to realize that no one would have missed me if I would not have come back. Were all the sufferings and deprivations worthwhile? It is true that the first few days of freedom were unbelievably joyous and the relief indescribable; I could look over my shoulders and not see an SS-officer ready to beat me or send me to join my parents and sisters and brothers in the gas chambers. But, gradually came the shocking realization that difficulties were being placed in my way with regard to finding a way back to life. No one wanted to know, or was prepared to come to terms with, what had happened. Why, I thought, had I struggled to remain alive through the hell of Auschwitz? Being the only one in my family to remain alive, I felt guilty that I had been spared. My family and the six million others had committed no crime except to be born Jewish and they had been condemned to death. But, I "had been condemned to life."

In the beginning of 1946, I started to go out with a man who was 20 years older than myself. I felt that I needed a very mature person to replace my mother, father, sisters, brothers and friends and I started to be happier when I was in his company. We were married in 1947, and life slowly began to give me a little happiness from then on. We prepared ourselves to emigrate to New Zealand because my husband had one surviving brother who lived there. We arrived in Wellington in August 1949. I was much happier being so far away from Europe, and slowly began to lead a normal life. My husband worked as a storeman-packer in the beginning and in 1956, he and his brother opened a manufacturing business for covered buttons. I was very fortunate to have two sons, born in 1951 and 1953. My husband had also been in concentration camps and never recovered from his experiences. He was a sick man, and suffered ill health throughout our married life. He died in 1982, at the age of 78. My sons, John and Gary, moved to Sydney, Australia, and I decided to join them in 1986 so that I would be close to my dear children and grandchildren.

As a result of my experiences, my nerves have suffered greatly and I have arthritis in my joints. Here in Sydney I found a part-time job as a bookkeeper, and I am happy that I do not have much time to think. I love to spend time with my dear family and with friends. The beginning in Sydney was very hard and traumatic because I missed my friends in New Zealand. Sydney is a very large city and it took a long time to get adjusted. But, now I am happy that I live here and that I am surrounded with love and understanding. I am very fortunate to have four grandsons and one granddaughter who give me a lot of joy.

I still have nightmares about Auschwitz, but I try to cope. I taught my children to be aware and to watch for any signs of antisemitism and to always be involved in Jewish affairs. I am very grateful to the Almighty that they are decent human beings who are active in the Jewish community and that my grandchildren attend Jewish dayschools. May we all have a happy life and may there be peace in Israel and the World.

NOTES

Helen Kuban

1   An international Jewish sports festival, generally held every four years.

2   The date was easy to remember since December 5, 1942, was Shabat Chanukah as well as St. Nicolaus' Day (Czech, 1989, p. 351 and Skodova, 1962, p. 79).

3   On January 20, 1945, the chief of Section W I of DEST in Oranienburg wrote to the chief of section W of the WVHA that Auschwitz had been evacuated because of the approaching front and that with the permission of the commandant the six Jewish women prisoners working in their office had been transferred to the KL-Gross Rosen (Czech, 1989, p. 980).

4   The American Joint Distribution Committee (A.J.D.C.), also known as "Joint," was an organization for relief to Jews in need in other countries.

CHAPTER 7

The German Armaments Works

(Deutsche Ausruestungswerke) or (DAW)

The DAW was established on May 3, 1939, with headquarters in Berlin. Standartenfuehrer Walter Salpeter was appointed as its head. DAW assumed control of the production plants that the SS had established in order to exploit the labor of inmates of the Dachau, Sachsenhausen, Buchenwald and later Auschwitz concentration camps.

As time went on, more such factories were set up in the Lublin, Stutthof, Ravensbrueck, Neuengamme and other camps. The number of prisoners employed in these plants rose from 1,220 on December 31, 1940, to 15,000 in 1943. Most of the prisoners who worked in the DAW factories perished, either through the policy of Vernichtung durch Arbeit (extermination through work) or by mass-slaughter Aktionen.

The decision to establish the woodworking shops of DAW in Auschwitz had already been made in 1940. The actual construction started in the beginning of 1941 and production began probably in the second half of that year. They manufactured mainly furniture, ammunition cases, timber construction items and coffins for the Wehrmacht.

As of 1942, in accordance with the general employment strategy aiming at the maximal use of all available manpower in the arms industry, the DAW shops in the concentration camp areas were supposed to be turned into shops producing material and equipment for the army. However, in spite of Himmler's urging for the SS to establish its own arms industry, the DAW shops only partially produced war supplies.

Due to the lack of security guards, a special passage of wires was built in the main camp of Auschwitz to be used by prisoners to walk from the camp to the DAW shops. The passage was called the Loewengang (lion's walk).

In 1944, approximately 2000 prisoners worked for the DAW in Auschwitz. The DAW also directed the Luftwaffen Zerlegebetriebe (aircraft disassembly works) and here approximately 1300 prisoners worked.

Esther K. Atlas (née Kassvan)
New York, New York (USA)

My name is Esther K. Atlas, born on May 20, 1908, in Radautz, Bucovina, formerly Austria, presently Rumania, and I am now residing in New York City. I was married to Arnold Atlas, an engineer, in 1941, who died in May 1972, in New York. Due to the Holocaust, we decided not to have any children. My parents, Moses and Mathilde Kassvan, had eight children; I was one of the youngest. My father was the son of a rabbi, Avner Kassvan, who is written up in the Jewish Encyclopedia and who was a renowned author of Jewish books. Both the rabbi and the father of my mother, Moshe Mattes of Jassy, Rumania, met at the first Zionist Congress at Basel, Switzerland, with Theodor Herzl. After their marriage, my parents settled in the Bucovina, Rumania, and had a factory for manufacturing cigarette paper. We had a nice house with servants, and I remember a beautiful garden with an orchard in which I played with my sisters and brothers. Joseph Kassvan, my father's brother, was the mayor of the town of Radautz which had a large Jewish population. My father, being an ardent Zionist, enrolled me in the first Hebrew kindergarten at the age of about three, and I still remember a few lines from the Hebrew song about the boy and the bird.

When the first world war broke out, my family had to flee the invading Russians and after a very hard and long journey, having taken only the bare minimum with us, we arrived in Berlin, Germany, where I was enrolled in the school of the Berlin Jewish Congregation at Kaiserstrasse, which had an excellent curriculum, both in secular and Jewish studies. I liked the school very much and usually finished at the head of the class. I also joined the Zionist Sport Club, Bar Kochba, and was a member of the club until it was dissolved around 1940; I was voted President of the women's division. I made a lot of friends and, thinking back, I feel that these were the happiest times in my life.

Although my teachers encouraged me to go to college for further studies, I felt that it would be a financial hardship for my parents and decided to take an office job. Besides, it was understood at that time that only the boys in the family, of which there were four, should get a formal education.

Around 1930, the Nazis made their presence felt in Germany, although most Jews did not believe that it was serious. However, in 1933, when Hitler came to power, the impact was severe. Jews and Socialists were arrested and sometimes no longer seen. There was talk of torture and killings. Jewish Government officials and workers were summarily dismissed, Jewish lawyers could no longer practice, and many Jewish businesses were "arisiert," that is, taken over by a Nazi supervisor. Many Jews tried to flee over the border to Holland or France, but many were captured and imprisoned. My brother, Avner, and his wife, Golda, and their two children escaped to France; after a short while, my sister, Judith, got a visa to France and left for Paris. My brother, Fritz, was in Radautz, Rumania at that time, where he had married and had settled down as a printer. My brother, Elieser, and my sister, Shoshanna, the youngest of the family, who were active enemies of the Nazis, had managed to get out to London and Shanghai, respectively. My oldest sister, Rebecca, with her husband and their two children got a visa for Palestine and left.

My father had died in 1936, and when the war broke out in 1939, only mother, my brother, Simon, and I were left in Berlin. I had obtained an immigration visa to Australia, which became void with the outbreak of the war. I could not bring myself to leave my mother, nor for that matter my brother, Simon, who was rather apathetic, having never fully recovered from the effects of the first war in which he served as an officer in the Austrian army, taken there from medical college. All my efforts to obtain a visa for them failed. I was still employed by the Patent Attorney, George Weinhausen, who had taken over the practice from the Jewish Patent Attorney, Albert Elliot, for whom I had worked for over 15 years. The Jewish community had organized classes in English as a refresher course. There, I met my future husband, Arnold Atlas. Since his parents fell under the Russian quota and had influential friends in the U.S.A. who gave the necessary affidavits of support, their application for a visa to the U.S.A. was being processed. I fell under the Rumanian quota with a waiting period of about ten years. By now, almost all Jewish employees had been dismissed, and my boss was under pressure to dismiss me too, which he very reluctantly did. He was a democrat, and his father had been instrumental in writing the Weimarer Verfassung.[1] I applied for, and was admitted to, Hachscharah in Gut Winkel bei Berlin, but after less than a year, the Hachscharah Center was closed by the Gestapo. In the meantime, Arnold and his parents obtained the U.S. visas and one day before he left, on March 25, 1941, we were married. We hoped that I could get a U.S. visa under a preference quota, but the U.S. Consulate closed in June 1941, and no more visa applications were being processed. The U.S. Consul was married to a White-Russian woman who was known for her Anti-semitic feelings, and Berlin was the worst place to obtain a visa to the U.S.A. We heard later that the Consuls in the southern part of Germany were much more compassionate, or at least fair.

From the Hachscharah Gut, I went back to Berlin and to my mother, and was inscribed for slave work in the factory of Tewes in Berlin-Wittenau, manufacturing small armaments. We were in a division of about 50 Jewish women, segregated in a cage where we polished and examined piston rings for planes and trucks. The German foreman was a Socialist who secretly tried to make our lives easier, and never failed to be polite to us. We worked in three shifts; travel time was about four hours on foot and by railroads. We wore the yellow star and were allowed only two hours in the afternoon for shopping; our ration cards had a big J and, in addition to the very meager ration of bread, butter and meat, very few vegetable, but not tomatoes or the like, could be bought. Anyway, by the time we were allowed to shop, the stores were empty of goods. In addition to Jewish workers, there were many Belgian and French workers in the plant, also a few Germans, mostly in supervisory capacity. I must say, in all fairness, that the Germans were not hostile to us, after all, we were all co-workers, although the Germans got their regular pay, whereas most of ours was deducted by the Government as Jew tax.

In August 1942, we heard that Jewish elderly people were deported to Theresienstadt, which was supposed to be a model camp for the privileged ones, and one day the Gestapo came for my aged mother. She had been a wonderful mother, a good Jewish woman who did not have it in her heart to do anything wrong or hurt anybody. It was the worst experience of my life to see her being taken away. I blamed myself for having failed so miserably to save her. She wrote me a few cards, the last one from Theresienstadt to Auschwitz, which miraculously reached me, and which I still treasure among my possessions. She was later transferred from her camp to Auschwitz and was killed there.

Now only my brother, Simon, and I were left. One day, in February 1943, he did not come home from his night shift working in the railroad yards. I had to leave for the afternoon shift, and when I arrived at the railroad station Wittenau, one of the French workers pleaded with his eyes to follow him out of the station. When we were in the fields, feeling unobserved, he told me that the Gestapo had been in the plant with trucks and had taken all the Jewish workers with them without giving them time to take warm clothes or any of their belongings. He warned me not to go to work, and even offered to try to hide me, which I could not accept. I knew that he had an affair with a Jewish woman who recently had not shown up for work and evidently had gone underground. I learned after the war that she had been saved and that the two had gotten married.

I went back to the house, staying there for several days and not answering the knocks at the door, having heard the heavy footsteps of the soldiers on the stairway. By this time, Berlin was supposed to be "judenrein," and no ration coupons could be obtained. However, the "Aryan" neighbors in the building, who saw me coming and going (I had removed the yellow star from my clothes), smiled at me and did not give me away. I had a Jewish neighbor who was married to an "Aryan" and had two children. Her name was Elfriede Kuesell. Her mother and my mother were together in Theresienstadt. She helped me a lot, and whenever I felt alone and miserable, I went up to her apartment and received a hearty welcome from her and her little children, and always a warm meal. They all somehow survived, and we are still good friends in New York. Berlin had been under steady bombardment by the Allied air forces for years. We took refuge in the air raid shelter in the basement of our building. But toward the end, I became fatalistic and no longer went down. In the mornings after the air raid, we found that many houses near us were erased. However, Berlin without its big Jewish community and my numerous friends became a strange town to me, and after about a week of holding out alone in the apartment, I lost my nerve and finally opened the door when the SS knocked again, and was taken to the center for deportees, which was in a school of the Jewish congregation, Grosse Hamburgerstrasse. There, we were registered by the staff of the Jewish congregation, many of whom knew me from my Zionist activities, and who could not hide their anguish at seeing me captured. They embraced me wordlessly.

On March 5, 1943, the center was cleared and the group of about 600 men, women and children were herded into railroad cattle cars fitted out with straw and a big bucket. I detected my former teacher, Mrs. Fischer, in the same car. I made my way over to her to tell her how much I had always loved and admired her and how she had taught me that a woman can be married and also have a career, retaining her femininity. I never saw her again.

After days of travel, we arrived at the railroad yards of Auschwitz-Birkenau. Waiting for us were many SS-men with their ferocious-looking dogs, chasing us out of the cars, telling us to leave all our belongings behind for the time being, immediately separating the men from the women, telling us to line up in rows of five, and there I experienced my first "Sortierung," of which there were many thereafter. The SS went through the rows, looked everyone over with steely eyes and *sorted* us out. I was told to go to the shorter line which was destined for a work camp. They assured us that the others, being too old or too young or too feeble were to go to another camp where the conditions were better. We desperately wanted to believe them, especially the ones that were separated from their young children. (They were all taken to the gas chambers.)

Our group of about 60 women (only three of whom survived), mostly young and good looking, hardly anyone over 30, were marched into the camp of Birkenau, entering through the gate bearing the inscription, "Arbeit Macht Frei" (work makes you free). In the reception barracks, older inmates tattooed our serial number on our left forearm (mine was 38003 with a triangle), identifying us as Jews. We wore the same triangle in yellow on our prison clothes, political German prisoners wore the triangle in red, former convicts in green, homosexuals in pink, prostitutes in black. We then were registered with German thoroughness, and later taken to the so-called Sauna, where we stripped, had our hair shorn off and took a shower, were given men's pants and jackets of light weight, some of which had holes in them. We now received our first meal, potatoes in their jackets which we learned to skin with our bare hands.

We were then marched into the camp proper, shoved into a cell block containing rows of 3-tier bunks; we had to scramble for a vacant bunk and were lucky to find a horse blanket on the straw mattress. We were exhausted and tried to sleep, but the moaning and crying of the others and the putrid smell pervading the barracks, coming mostly from the buckets which served as the indoor toilet during the night, kept us awake. At the crack of dawn, we were all chased out to stand "Appell" (head count); the inmates of each cell block had to line up in single rows of ten and the count began. The SS-women conducting the count, the lowest of the low, were obviously not very good in arithmetic, and we had to stand for hours shivering in the cold March mornings in our light attire. There, I caught sight of human heaps, women who had given up, unable to walk anymore, or who could not take it any longer, voluntarily offering themselves to be taken to the infamous Block 25 which was the holding block for the gas chambers. Some women who did not have shoes or blankets took them from these unfortunate women and did not find much resistance, after all; they would not need them anymore.

After the Appell, we were given our first work assignment, ours was to shovel loose soil or sand into heavy wooden troughs and to carry them to the other end of a huge square. We were working in pairs, and when, on the way, we tried to put the trough down for a short respite, we were beaten by the supervising German inmates or the SS-women. The German inmates, who had been incarcerated for quite some time, let out all their anger and frustration over their imprisonment on the other inmates. When they noticed that some of the Jewish women no longer made an attempt to shield themselves from their blows, they kept on beating them until they died. We then had to carry the corpses back to the camp high over our heads. We met columns of men also carrying their corpses at the end of the work day, hardly able to march themselves, so exhausted were they and so were we. I swore to myself that I would never let that happen to me, that I would not march out if I felt that I would not be able to live through the day. One of my partners was a girl whom I knew from the factory. She had been working there for some days and was at the end of her strength. She was of no help and I tried to outwit the supervisors and put the trough down any minute I noticed that their attention was focused on somebody else. At the end of the day, we were marched back to our cell blocks, outside of which we were given our daily bread ration, but my partner was no longer able to stand in line for bread and went without it to her bunk; the next morning she joined the heap.

A few days later, I was assigned to field work. We marched for hours, then worked the fields with our bare hands, and the only way to wash them and our bodies was to use our precious tea ration given for supper. There was no water except in the saunas to which we had no access, no plumbing and the open latrines and raw sewage fouled the air and the grounds, inevitably bringing on typhoid fever and other diseases. Shortly after our arrival, almost all of the girls menstruated. We were given sanitary napkins. It was the last time we had to use them for a long, long time, nature helping us to avoid additional strain and handicap. This, and with my hair shorn, looking like a man in those trousers, I no longer believed myself to be a woman, nor ever again to be one. I had been a healthy young woman, life in a big family, in the sports arenas and on Hachscharah had toughened me, but as the days went by, I felt my energy shrinking and the final solution of the Heap became more and more attractive.

After an exhaustive field trip, one night I fell down on my bunk vowing not to get up before the next morning, when I heard somebody shouting into the cell block that they were looking for good office workers and that applicants should immediately come to the block at the gate. I gathered up all my strength and proceeded to the cell block where I found a long line of applicants. The woman in charge warned us that only the most experienced office workers would be considered and the ones who tried to fake it would be sent to a penalty camp or the gas. The lines thinned considerably, but since I was confident that I knew everything connected with office work, worked myself up to the head of the line, and was given a typing test and had to write a short resume, stating my prison number and name on top.

At roll call the next morning, my number was called out and I was told to stay in the camp. The SS-Obersturmfuehrer in charge of labor was expected to see me. Around noontime, we were called to line up before him. We were about twenty girls, not only office workers but women trained in handicrafts. He interrogated us one by one, selected a few and did *not* take me. He made the rounds again, I tried to change my story a bit, stressing my proficiency in French and English languages, but again he rejected me. I resigned myself to the idea that I had to die. When he turned angrily to a woman and berated her for having picked such an incompetent bunch of women, she became indignant, insisting she had selected the best of the camp, took out one of the slips from the stack of the resume slips and showed it to him. He glanced at it, said "This is good, who is it, 38003?" When I raised my hand, he said, "Also doch." (So, it is you, after all.)

About ten of us were selected and taken to the sauna, showered and given new clothes, the prestigious blue and white striped dress and jacket, worn only by non-Jewish inmates and some privileged Jewish workers to whom we now belonged. We were marched to the Stabsgebaeude (Staff Building), a four story building located between Birkenau and the men's camp of Auschwitz, housing the staff of SS-women on the upper floors, the basement was used for the SS-laundry, the mending room on one side and the dormitory for us inmates on the other side. Compared to Birkenau, this was paradise. There was a shower room and a wash room with hot and cold running water, and water closets. We got, or "organized," sheets and blankets for our bunk beds and got white porcelain bowls for our food, as well as spoons, forks and knives.

We were about 300 women in the Stabsgebaeude, most of them office workers, almost all of them young and beautiful and of above average intelligence. It was seldom by pure chance that they were chosen to be in the Stabsgebaeude. The largest group of girls worked in the Politische Abteilung, where prisoners were interrogated and very often beaten by the SS-men. They had to march out early in the morning and came back late in the evening. It was one of the toughest assignments. The next group was the one working in the Standesamt. They had the records of all the inmates, had to fabricate medical stories when the prisoners were gassed or otherwise killed, and every so often, had to compile lists of those to go on a transport, which they knew meant that they were being transported to the gas chambers. Whenever they had to do this, both the Politische and the Standesamt, who usually marched out and back together, returned after the lights were out in our block. They were given their ration, but could hardly eat and did not talk at all. We knew then what had happened and our hearts sank.

Other girls worked in the offices of the Verwaltung, where all kinds of administration records were maintained: Bauleitung, Pflanzenzucht and other smaller offices. They were mostly from Slovakia. They had been rounded up there already in early 1942, immediately separated from their families and practically built up the cell blocks with their bare hands. They were the ones that had survived, most of the others were killed or died from typhoid or exhaustion. Being the first ones to arrive in the camp, they held the better positions. There was a large contingent of young girls working in the laundry and sewing room, often in several shifts.

From the girls working in the Standesamt, I soon found out that my oldest brother, Simon, had died within two weeks, so had my brother, Avner, his wife, Golda and their two children. We newcomers were held in quarantine for four weeks, since the SS knew full well to what diseases we had been exposed. During that time, I felt weaker and weaker. A check in the infirmary showed that I had high fever which was a sure sign of typhoid fever. I was given a bunk bed in the infirmary, headed by a Polish woman doctor, Pani Kosciuszko, who was heard to remark, "The best Jews are the dead Jews." She gave me pills to swallow, but my fever rose, and I must have become delirious, because they all complained that I screamed and cried during the night and talked a lot. Miraculously, I recovered from typhoid fever, but one morning my head became clearer, I noticed a small hole in my right second finger with some liquid oozing out of it. When I showed it to the doctor, she remarked, "Oh, you can die from this," but she did not take any steps to give me any medication. I finally joined the group of women who showed up after working hours for ambulatory treatment, and she smeared some black ointment on my hand, wrapping it in paper bandage. My hand became very swollen and severe pain set in and I suffered through several days.

One evening, we had inspection by the SS camp doctor. He was in a jovial mood and chatted with the patients, asking the Polish doctor about her cases. Again, she ignored me, so I got up from my bunk and somehow drew his attention to my bandaged hand. He asked her what ailment I had and she said, "It is probably going to be a 'plegmone,'" (an inflammation with an extraordinary quantity of mucus or pus prevalent in the camp and a common occurrence after typhoid fever). He said, it was already one, and a very severe one and I was to be taken to the men's camp in Auschwitz where they had a large medical facility, staffed by Polish doctors or medics for an operation. When he saw me blanch at the idea of having my hand cut open and thereby retaining a scar (vanity of a woman being more dead than alive), he said soothingly, that the doctors would cut it from the inside. Of course, they did not. They took at least a gallon of pus and water out, but the wound did not heal and after a while the palm of my hand began to swell as well, and they performed another operation which was more successful. However, two of my fingers remain stiff. I cannot make a fist and I have a big ugly scar on my right hand.

The SS-doctor paid us another surprise visit one night, and noticing me with my paper bandages on my right arm, asked to see my hand. When I told him that the wound did not heal in the beginning and that I had to undergo another operation since the palm of my hand had been swollen, he said, "I told you that they should make the incision on the palm." He remembered!

The long stay in the infirmary (about two months) had one good result. I more or less regained my health and after my hand had healed enough to be able to hold a pen and later to operate a typewriter, albeit with only two fingers of my right hand to this day, I was finally assigned to office work. I was very lucky. The office was one of the Deutsche Ausruestungswerke making coffins for the Armed Forces and employing about 1,000 male prisoners, mostly in carpentry. At that time, we were only three women working in the office; the men had been imprisoned for two years and were more than glad to see and talk to a woman. I was loved by the inmates, and respected by the SS since I was a very good worker, and I thanked God every day for helping me.

In the meantime, another small camp was built between Birkenau and the men's camp of Auschwitz, and we were transferred to a block in this camp. It was a spacious block, kept clean by inmates assigned to this task, we got sheets and even comforters, apparently brought in by prisoners from Hungary who arrived in great numbers in the summer of 1944. The infirmary was enlarged, we had a big wash room with hot and cold running water and private toilets. We heard that the infamous Block 25 was no longer in operation. It seemed they needed all the workers they could get. Whereas, before only men were assigned to work in the ammunition factories in a separate camp "Buna," they now had built another factory called "Union," in which women were employed. These factory workers were housed in another block in this smaller camp, and I found among them friends from the Hachscharah.

The ground floor of our block, the so-called Elite block also housed the girls from the bordello, and they were proud to identify themselves as such. These were German prostitutes who had been jailed before, but after expiration of their jail sentence, were not released, but shipped out to the concentration camp where they could now ply their chosen profession legitimately. They slept most of the day, marched out to the men's camp in the evening and came back late at night, singing at the top of their lungs. We did not have much contact with them.

The cell block next to ours was occupied by women selected for medical experiments. Some of these experiments consisted of sterilizing them by injections into the womb. Many ran a high fever thereafter, many of them died, but quite a few survived, among them a relative of mine, Friedel Milner; the sterilization experiment apparently worked, since she could not have any children after the war.

I had the opportunity to read German newspapers left behind by our SS-supervisors and was aware of the defeats and retreats of the German army. I knew that the Russians were coming nearer and nearer. Inmates arrived from the evacuated camp in Cracow. Polish inmates were being shipped out to camps in inner Germany and I figured that, pretty soon, we would be evacuated from Auschwitz, too. This happened on January 18, 1945. We had to march for days in the snow-covered Beskiden Mountains; long columns of men and women, many falling to the wayside, either from exhaustion or gun shots, eating the little bread each of us had been given on the day of evacuation, but suffering from thirst and extreme fatigue. After days, we arrived at a railroad yard, were jammed into waiting railroad cattle cars, and finally deposited at the camp of Ravensbrueck near Berlin. This was a camp for mostly Aryan women. There was no gas chamber, but the discipline was tough. When we arrived, I saw women kneeling in punishment for a long time. We only stayed for a few days in this relatively clean camp. We were transported to a camp in Mecklenburg named Malchow which had been empty, although there was hardly any food; the daily soup consisted mainly of water and the bread seemed like straw. There was clean water to drink and wash with and clean outhouses. At that time, I heard through the grapevine that President Roosevelt had died. But food became scarcer every day. It also seemed that the Russian army was advancing and they decided to send a transport, as they called it, to another camp. I was selected to go there. There was a rumor that the camp was in an ammunition factory in the German town of Leipzig in Saxony, which so far had not had an air attack. We were again put into cattle cars, we saw loaves of bread loaded into a separate car, but although the journey lasted for more than two days, no bread was being distributed. At nightfall, we stopped at a bombed-out railroad station. I read that it was in Magdeburg. The SS-men went away, and we were still lying in the open-top cars when we experienced and watched the heaviest bombardment by the Russians we had ever seen, and we had seen many on our marches. The long railroad cars we were in were, of course, perfect targets. The young kids cried in fear and panic, but I remembered how my mother calmed us when we were afraid, and I said loudly over and over, "Don't be afraid, God is with us," and somehow I believed it. To our surprise, and obviously the surprise of the SS-men who had hoped to get rid of us, we were not bombed. The next morning, they distributed the loaves of bread to one person in the car, and the girls unanimously elected me to receive the bread in appreciation for my keeping them calm during the air raid. However, two girls, who had their old mother with them during all the time in Auschwitz, took over the distribution, and I did not mind. I would not have been able to withstand the onslaught of all the hungry women by myself.

The next day, we arrived in Leipzig. The factory was an ultra-modern multi-story glass building. There still were Polish women employed as ammunition workers. There was a huge washroom with—wonder over wonder—scraps of soap left behind on some wash basins. We had not seen soap since the Auschwitz soap bars made from human corpses and I took a long, delicious hot shower. There was even a long dining hall to which we were escorted twice a day, being served on long tables with a thick, hot soup. The dormitory with three-tier bunk beds was light and clean; however, it adjoined the dormitory of the Polish workers who were on night shift. We were lying on our bunks all day. There was no other place for us and, of course, we talked to each other. After a few days, the Poles complained that "the Jews were making so much noise, they could not sleep," and we were taken out of the big building and put into wooden barracks on the grounds. I was delighted. It was spring, the bushes were green. There were even some flowers. We could walk around and we were no longer in the glass building so prone to an air attack. Sure enough, the attack came after a few days. The glass building was damaged considerably, but we Jews were unharmed. However, food became scarce again. There were no more regular meals and after a few days, we were again sent out on the road. On April 20, in honor of Hitler's birthday, we encountered one of the worst air attacks which lasted for hours, but by that time, the pilots must have been aware that the long lines of marchers were prisoners, not Germans, and spared us. Of course, we could never be sure and stretched out on the road shoulders trembling.

A few days later, we came across a big farm (Rittergut). We could hardly walk any more, but we sensed that we were near the end, and when the SS-men told us that we were given shelter in the barns, we asked them to separate us from the Poles and the Russians, because the Polish women stole our belongings at night, and the Russians attacked us openly in gangs even during day time. We fell down in the straw, got some hot potatoes and milk and, since we had not eaten for days, we promptly got diarrhea. The next morning, SS-men who had guarded us on the long march, came into the barns and, although they had promised us that we could take a long rest there, asked us to get ready to march on, but very politely. This gave us the cue to plead with them, saying we were very tired and could not walk any more. We were given thirty minutes to think it over, but after a while, a Polish girl from the other barn came in and told us that they would not march out and had told them so. This gave me courage, and I told the other women that we would do the same, unless he threatened us with a gun. Since I spoke German best, the other Jewish women were mostly from Poland, there were also French women who chose to stay with us, I told the guard that we had decided to stay. I noticed that he already wore civilian clothes under his SS-overcoat. He warned us that he would alert the local police and I said that we would take that chance. So, the SS left.

We watched through the slits in the barn wall how the German population loaded some of their belongings onto carts with horses and one after the other left the village. After a day or two, we felt more secure and physically strong enough to force the doors open and ventured out, realizing that nobody would stop us now. We were still given daily rations of potatoes and milk, but the neighboring farmers grudgingly supplied us with additional food. At that time, the village elders decided to take us out of the barns and assigned us to individual farmers, of which there were still quite a few left. Since I spoke French, the French women asked me to join them to be their interpreter, and the eleven of us were sent to a farmer, on whose grounds the prison of the Russian POW's was located, guarded by a German sergeant. Before we arrived, the Soviet army was already there, had freed the Russian prisoners and arrested the German guard. We now made ourselves comfortable on the bunk beds, although there was no change of linen. The German farmer supplied us with hot meals, and the French civilian workers of the village showed up; they brought us additional food and wine, and the women started to cook on the small stove in the barracks and produced delicious meals, à la française.

One morning, probably May 5, I detected a white flag on top of the farm house and shortly thereafter, a big detachment of Russian soldiers arrived. They were happy like children, riding around on bicycles which they had confiscated, sporting watches on their arms, sometimes as many as eight or ten. However, they also raped the women and often could or would not distinguish us from the German women and we had trouble persuading them that we were friends, not foes. After one of them had paid me a polite visit on the ground floor of the barracks, where I had taken over the bed of the arrested German soldier (the French women occupying the bunk beds of the freed Russian prisoners were on the upper floor), he came back at night, knocked at my locked door at night and pleaded with me to let him in. It took a long time, with me screaming and shouting and threatening to report him to the "Commandant," for him to give up but, of course, I did not close my eyes that night and the next day we all decided that it was time to leave. The Frenchmen hired a driver with a horse-drawn cart, and started loading their little carriages, bicycles and other belongings on it (the women did not possess anything), and filled it up, not leaving any room for passengers. So we once again walked, but it was much harder for the men who were soon exhausted, and were ashamed to admit it, but after all, we women had more practice in walking.

At the end of the day, we arrived at a makeshift displaced person's camp in a village near the river Elbe, and we discharged the driver. We were deloused, given shelter and food and were thinking of ways to continue our journey. We were still in the Russian-held part of Germany and eager to get to the part occupied by the Americans. Strolling around the camp, I came across a hut with an open door. Several Polish men were sitting at a small table and they invited me in. We were trying to make conversation in halting German or Polish, which by now I could also understand somehow, when I noticed a snow-white loaf of bread on the table. I had not seen white bread in Germany since the outbreak of the war, and when I asked them from where they had gotten the white bread, they answered that the American Red Cross had given it to them. It turned out that the American Red

Cross was located in a small building down the road of the village. I jubilantly told my French friends about it, and two men and another woman joined me in going to find out about our possible repatriation. On our arrival, we were told that the truck had left for the big Displaced Persons Camp in Halle and was expected back around noontime. We all gathered our belongings and were there at noon, when the truck with tired U.S. soldiers returned, not very happy to see us, because they had thought that they were through for the day. They wanted to take the women only, but we did not want to leave without the men. We had all become very good friends. The other condition was to leave all the bicycles, carts and other heavy objects behind, to which the men agreed, and the Americans speeded with us along the Autobahn to Halle.

We enjoyed our stay in Halle. U.S. soldiers were in charge and took good care of us. In addition to a lot of other French former inmates waiting for repatriation, there were also quite a few of East European nationality. Preparing for the repatriation, several Frenchmen in charge told the non-French that they would have to return to the eastern part of Germany. Realizing that they detected an accent in my otherwise pretty fluent French, I told them that I was married to an American and was to be repatriated to America via France. They became very respectful. I was "l'Américaine," and they allowed me to go with the French nationals to France.

The repatriation began in open small trucks. Only half of us had seats, and we took turns sitting down. The American drivers did not find their way around, road signs probably had been taken off deliberately and we rode around until late into the night. It had started to rain, drenching us thoroughly, but we took it in stride, happy in the knowledge that we were leaving Germany. We finally did arrive at a railroad station and entered cattle cars again, but did not mind. We passed Holland and Belgium, and the Dutch and Belgian prisoners got off in their countries. We were greeted by the citizens of these countries at the railroad stations enthusiastically. They passed along food and drink and wished us luck on our further journey to France. We had one more stop before we reached Paris, our final destination. There, we were invited to a dinner in a long hall. We were asked how much money we had since the French authorities allowed us to bring into the country only a limited amount of foreign money. Those of us who did not have any money were given the maximum amount of French Francs. I arrived in Paris by the end of May 1945, greeted by a staff of French volunteers who screened us and put us up in the Hotel Lutece which served as reception headquarters for the repatriates. We rejoiced in meeting friends, congratulating each other that we had survived.

I located relatives, cousins with whom I had grown up in Berlin, and whom I had visited before the war. They took me to their houses, clothed and fed me. These families had left Paris for the south of France when the Germans advanced, changed their identities and all but their old parents survived. Their parents' names were Rudolf and Rosa Schwarz; they were killed in Auschwitz.

I now tried to get in touch with my husband in America. At the American Red Cross, I was told that there were two Jewish organizations who were supposed to take care of people like me. It was the HIAS and the Joint Distribution Committee.

I remembered that a close friend of my father-in-law, Dr. Rosen, was the President of the Joint. When I asked about him at my visit to the Joint, I was told that he was still the President and through him, my husband was located. He sent me a cable full of joy and gratefulness for my survival. But, there was still a war on in the Pacific, and it took a year before I could join him in New York.

He lived with his parents in a small walk-up apartment on the west side of New York, commuted every day by railroad to Bethpage, Long Island, his place of work, in one of the largest aviation corporations in the country. Grumman's. We were happy to be together. After a few weeks of rest, I got myself an office job, and together, we made a good living, had a circle of friends, many of them survivors, and lived happily until his untimely death at the age of 63. I am lonely now. Many of our friends have died or moved away and I have more time to reflect upon the strange fate that has befallen me and so many others. The more removed I am in time from the Holocaust, the less I can understand how this could have happened.

I hope it will never happen again.

NOTES

Esther K. Atlas

1   The Constitution of the Weimar Republic.

CHAPTER 8

Supply Storage Facility for the Troops

Truppenwirtschaftslager (TWL)

It was the task of the TWL to purchase and furnish food supplies to the SS-kitchen in camp as well as to the German troops at the Eastern front. The TWL building was located within the camp area directly opposite the Stabsgebaeude, but did not belong to the concentration camp administration. It operated under the supervision of SS-Standartenfuehrer Oswald Pohl, the head of WVHA (Wirtschafts-verwaltungshauptamt, the SS Economic and Administrative Department) in Berlin.

In Auschwitz, the following persons were consecutively the director of the TWL: Hauptsturmfuehrer Kreuzmann, Obersturmfuehrer Meyer, Sturm-bannfuehrer Winkler, Untersturmfuehrer Desch, and from the beginning of 1944 on, once again Obersturmfuehrer Meyer.

Some of the women prisoners of the Stabsgebaeude who worked at the TWL were: Jolan Deutsch, Margit Bachner, Margaret Weiss, Margarete Reich, Aranka Heitlinger, Julia Foeldy, Alice Balla and Elisabeth Reich.

Margit Bachner (née Grossberg)
Rishon L'Zion (Israel)

I was born on April 19, 1916 in Kezmarok, Czechoslovakia as the daughter of Adolf Grossberg and his wife, Hermine, nee Drechsler-Gabel. My father was a lumber merchant and I had six siblings: Paula, Therese, Max, Heinrich, Josef and Zoltan.

After graduating from a commercial school, I worked as a bookkeeper and secretary. Even after the introduction of the yellow star for all Jews in the fall of 1941, I continued to be employed as the only Jew in a cabinet-making factory which had fifty employees and was considered an economically essential enterprise.

On March 27, 1942 an armed Slovakian policeman called Jacob Stetz—a former classmate and playmate of mine—came to arrest me, in spite of my employer's protest of being willing to pay a large sum of money as guarantee that I would not escape. Notwithstanding his bail offer, I was arrested together with my sister, Therese, and delivered to the district office from where we were taken to the gathering camp in Poprad. Here, we were put into cattle cars and at the border station of Zvardon we were handed over to the SS.

We arrived in Auschwitz on April 3, 1942. They chased us out of the cattle cars by screaming, "Faster, faster you dirty pigs, whores, faster." Lagerfuehrer Aumeier kicked the accompanying physician, who reported to him, a few times in the stomach until he did not get up any more. Then we had to form rows of five and were led to the woman's camp in Auschwitz. We were put into the attic of Block 6 together with our luggage. Looking out of the window, we perceived bald-shaved creatures in uniforms in the opposite-lying Block 7 who were wildly gesticulating and trying to establish contact with us. We thought they were mentally deranged men—but they turned out to be girls who had arrived with a transport the previous day and wanted to let us know to hide or keep our combs, soap, handkerchiefs, etc.

By the way, I immediately had an inkling that we were in a concentration camp. When I saw the huge gate with the inscription "Arbeit Macht Frei" (work liberates), the guard towers and the barbed wire fences, I remembered a line of the Dachau moor soldiers' song "Dreifach ist umzaeunt die Burg" (thrice the fortress is fenced in).

We spent a horrible night on the bare floor. The next morning, we were led to the so-called "delousing," all our belongings were taken away, we were shorn, received Russian uniforms for clothing and looked exactly like the figures we had seen the day before through the window. I looked for my sister, called her, and when she stood in front of me, still did not recognize her. It was so horrible and comical that I burst into hysterical laughter.

My first work assignment was the cleaning of the Sola river. We stood up to our knees in water and had to fish out everything, starting with leaves up to entire tree trunks that went downstream. It was meaningless work. Soon my hand was full of festering pustules.

This continued for several weeks. In the meantime, we were transferred to Block 10. We slept on the floor, one closely pressed against the other. If somebody moved, perhaps to turn over, she would not have any more place to lie down. One day, when we were standing for the roll-call, I saw two neatly dressed girls in striped dresses and white headkerchiefs accompanied by an SS-man. I did not rest until I found out where the two worked. They were Else Gruen from Bratislava and Alice Reiner from Presov, two of the first secretaries of the Political Section.

I pondered for a long time how I could obtain such a job, and one day I gathered all my courage and addressed the SS Blockfuehrerin. Luckily, she asked me what I wanted. I told her that I was an excellent office worker and perhaps I would be of greater value in such a capacity. She ordered me to register my number with the block-elder. About two weeks passed, when suddenly, my number was called during roll-call. When I stepped forward to report to the Blockfuehrerin who was in the company of Arbeitsdienstfuehrer Stiebitz, I expected the worst. I was relieved when Unterscharfuehrer Stiebitz asked me for other girls who were also experienced secretaries. I named two from my home town: Margarete Reich and Serene Klein, who lived in the same block with me. He ordered me to let them know to report to the gate the following day.

The next morning, there were about one hundred girls at the gate, and the chance to be selected was very slim. SS Hauptsturmfuehrer Schwarz came on horseback and questioned each of us as to her skills. When it was my turn, I enumerated my capabilities and also mentioned that I was familiar with Gothic script. He told me, "Woe to you if it is not true. All of you step aside, you are going to be tested." He selected 20 girls, among them my acquaintance, Margarete Reich. During the exam, we had to write our curriculum vitae, half in Latin script and half in Gothic letters. My penmanship was very good. Behind me stood Untersturmfuehrer Conrad from the HWL (Hauptwirtschaftslager der Waffen SS) and he said—without examining me—"I take this one." I was blissful. Apart from me, seven other women were chosen for the HWL, among them Margarete Reich. The remaining twelve girls were assigned to the Political Section and the Standesamt (civil registry). It was April 20, 1942.

In the beginning, I worked for Untersturmfuehrer Conrad who was in charge of cash disbursements. I prepared the payroll lists, executed transportation I.D.'s and took down letters in shorthand. Six months later, Conrad was transferred to a front unit and SS-Hauptsturmfuehrer Kreuzmann, the boss of the HWL was also replaced. In his place came Obersturmfuehrer Valentin Meyer who, in addition to his other duties, took over cash disbursements as well. From then on, I became sort of the boss's secretary and typed official instructions and many other documents. In 1943, the HWL became the TWL (Truppenwirtschaftslager) but our tasks remained the same. In 1944, the Oberaufseherin (SS-woman in chief) appointed me to be the head of our work detail. My only duties in this capacity were to report the number of prisoners of the squad when marching out to and returning from work. It sounded like this: "Protective custody prisoner #3755 obediently reports five prisoners for work."

The heads of the TWL were Hauptsturmfuehrer Kreuzmann, Obersturmfuehrer Meyer, Sturmbannfuehrer Winkler and Untersturmfuehrer Desch.

Some of the other personnel were: Untersturmfuehrer Conrad and Oberscharfuehrer Tusche in cash disbursements, Unterscharfuehrer Graebner in shipping, Unterscharfuehrer Hampel in empty containers, Unterscharfuehrer Dietz in purchasing and bookkeeping, SS-man Saecker for general use, Unterscharfuehrer Schiller in sutlery, Oberwachtmeister of the Schupo (Schutzpolizei, protective police) Walter and Oberwachtmeister of the Schupo Sucker administrators of goods, Unterscharfuehrer Sepp Holzknecht administrator of storage facility #2.

The girls of the Stabsgebaeude who worked together with me in the TWL were: Jolan Deutsch (now Gross). She worked in bookkeeping and had to order railroad cars for delivery to the Eastern front. She now lives in Zurich, Switzerland. Margaret (called Muli) Weiss, who now lives in Kent, England and Margaret Reich, who is deceased, both worked in bookkeeping and sutlery. Aranka Heitlinger, who is deceased, worked as shorthand typist and in purchasing. Julia Foeldy, who committed suicide after the war, worked in bookkeeping and took care of the index file. Alice Balla, who now lives in Kezmarok, and Elisabeth Reich, whose address is unknown, worked in bookkeeping and kept the lists of the sutlery.

In 1943, when the HWL (Hauptwirtschaftslager, the main supply warehouses) was transferred to Breslau and transformed into the TWL, there was less work in Auschwitz because a major part of the goods was shipped directly from Breslau. They started to save manpower. The cleaning work squad, which had consisted of female prisoners, was put at the disposal of the camp administrators and we, the secretaries, had to clean the offices from that period onward. A large part of the male prisoners was dismissed and the same happened to three of our comrades. Alice Balla, Elisabeth Reich and Aranka Heitlinger lost their jobs. However, they were lucky and were accepted as office workers by the SS administration work squad. Julia Foeldy had previously been transferred to the Standesamt office.

About forty male prisoners worked for the TWL loading and unloading goods, pushing and shunting railroad cars, carrying heavy sacks, etc. Five of them worked in Camp II and did not have such a bad time because Unterscharfuehrer Holzknecht was very decent toward them and even helped them to "organize." Willi Rzepka, Roman Ivoras and a third inmate were released as political Polish Volksdeutsche (ethnic Germans) and sent as members of the Wehrmacht to the front.

We worked from 6 a.m. until 8 p.m., so we were seldom present for the rollcall. We received our food regularly and, already in 1943, Obersturmfuehrer

Meyer had arranged for us to obtain additional bread rations so that we could help others. Later, we even got premiums, i.e. coupons for items at the prisoner canteen in the men's camp where we could go only in the company of an SS-man (the women's canteen had nothing but shoe polish). That's why we gave away the coupons to the male prisoners who purchased Machorka tobacco.

The SS-men behaved correctly toward us in an impersonal way since it was strictly prohibited to have private contact with inmates. However, frequently we managed to obtain little tidbits. For example, my boss, Obersturmfuehrer Meyer, told me to go to the basement to empty the wastepaper basket. I did so and always found something edible among the papers, once even an apple. Of course, we shared everything. The same happened to the other girls, each boss secretly gave a little something to his secretary.

Here and there, when it was not dangerous and when the SS-guard left us alone in the building and locked us in in order to fetch the male prisoners, we succeeded in stealing the key to the food storage area for a few minutes to "organize" ready-made soup mixes, sugar and semolino. We always took only small quantities, for example, in letter-envelopes, and smuggled them into the Stabsgebaeude. The major portion of the sugar and the semolino we gave to the Revier (camp hospital) to help the sick. Sometimes, cabbage heads or similar vegetables fell from the railroad cars; we ate them raw to get some vitamins. Every day I searched the SS offices for cigarette ends and took them to my sister. She shared them with friends in the restroom—i.e. everybody got a puff.

I did not have a direct Kochani, but, sometimes, I could organize some items from the kapos of the male prisoners. For example, my shoe size was #41 and I had great difficulties in obtaining a pair that would fit from the women inmates' clothing warehouse. The kapo of the clothing facility for male prisoners (Haeftlingsbekleidungskammer) frequently came to the TWL and I had an opportunity to exchange a few words with him. He supplied, without any reciprocity on my part, a pair of large sandals for me and, toward the end in the Winter of 1944, even a pair of boots. One was half a size larger than the other, but they served me well during the evacuation of Auschwitz and especially for smuggling letters. The requested shoes always reached me through the office of our block-elder, Maria Maul. How the kapo managed to pull it off, I still don't know. Maria Maul, a political German prisoner, was one of my friends in the Stabsgebaeude.

As supervisor of the TWL women's work squad, I was allowed to move freely within the sentry chain with an I.D. from the camp administration. In my boots, I often hid notes with news about imprisoned men for their wives, or vice versa. Without fully realizing it, I transported information for the underground movement, risking my life each time.

The male prisoners had more possibilities for sabotage and resistance. There was a clothing warehouse as well as an arms depot in the TWL building. In 1942, shortly after we started to work for this work detail, two men escaped.[1] On a Saturday afternoon when the TWL had been closed, they had broken into the clothing magazine and had stolen SS uniforms. With a TWL truck parked in the garage and forged papers which they had received from the Polish underground organization, they drove away and were not recaptured. Only at the end of 1944, one of the escapees was caught, returned to camp and revealed the secret of his escape under torture at the Political Section. He was hanged. One of the women who at that time typed the interrogation protocols for Oberscharfuehrer Boger of the camp Gestapo (I believe it was Maryla Obstfeld), told me the story.

Sometimes, I was sent by the TWL with different reports and invoices to the SS administration. In addition, every day I went to the agricultural section in order to pick up milk for the SS. Every morning, when I cleaned the boss's room, I had the opportunity to study the map on which the front lines were marked with colored pins. Once in a while, between 6 and 7 a.m., I could listen to the BBC broadcast in various languages because our guard locked us in and went to pick up the male prisoners. Of course, two girls always stood guard at the window and watched for somebody approaching. I had to be very careful to put the knob back onto the identical position in which I had found it. The BBC often gave reports and even names of concentration camps and SS personnel, so the British and all the Allies knew what was going on in Auschwitz.

I took an active part in the everyday life at the Stabsgebaeude. Every Saturday afternoon, when the others were resting, I wrote the prisoner lists according to work details for SS-woman Volkenrath, nee Muehlan, in her official office. Consequently, with time, a more informal relationship developed and one day she asked me if I had any relative in camp. I literally kneeled in front of her and asked her in tears to save my sister, a very good seamstress in Birkenau, and have her transferred to the Stabsgebaeude. The SS-woman jotted down my sister's number and her block and a few days before Christmas 1942, my sister, Therese, stood in front of me in such horrible condition that I did not recognize her. We had a very emotional reunion.

The behavior of the SS-women on duty in the Stabsgebaeude in regards to the inmates varied widely. The SS-women Drexler and Hasse were real beasts, but SS-woman Volkenrath behaved correctly toward the prisoners. SS-woman Lotte Klaus was good to everybody. She closed both eyes when the girls were "organizing" and even admitted male prisoners under the pretext of "making essential repairs," so the women could meet their "kochanis."

About the SS-men of the TWL, I can report only in a positive sense. Once, in 1944, Obersturmfuehrer Meyer told me point blank, "Believe me, Margarete, I don't agree with that which is going on in Birkenau." He was the only one who addressed us as "Sie," all the others called us "Du" (thou) but by our first names.

By the way, in August 1942, we were transferred for a week to Birkenau. Once, when we returned from work, we witnessed a gruesome event. Birkenau was not only surrounded by electrically charged wire, but also by the "Koenigsgraben,"[2] a wide and deep ditch filled with water. When we marched back to camp, we saw many corpses in the water. There were a few survivors who desperately tried to crawl out of the ditch with their last strength. They let them climb up a little way and then pushed them back into the water with long iron bars. This game was repeated over and over. More and more drowned bodies were in the water, and the next morning when we marched out to work, the corpses were still in the ditch. It was awful. The recollection of this experience still pursues me today.[3]

Although I was sometimes desperate, I am usually an optimist, and this optimism I conveyed skillfully and strenuously to my co-prisoners. I often told them that the Germans suffered heavy losses at the front, and I fervently believed that we would be liberated one day. However, my sister was a big pessimist and it took a lot of energy to strengthen her will to survive. Especially when the bombardments became more frequent, I was firmly convinced that we would be free one day.

I had a lot of friends in camp and was well liked. Many girls waited impatiently for me to return from work because I told them what I had seen and heard. Sometimes I invented some favorable rumors just to shake the girls out of their despair. Aranka Heitlinger and I were co-authors of the Auschwitz song which surreptitiously was spread to all satellite camps of Auschwitz and clandestinely was sung by many prisoners as an act of defiance. (See Appendix C, pp. 271-273.) Of course, I was especially close to the women of the TWL. We lived together, ate together and shared everything with each other, and I still correspond with the two survivors: Jolan Gross and Muli Weiss.

We also practiced solidarity. One night, when it was dark and almost everybody was asleep, we administered a sound beating ("Kameradschaftskeile") to Boezsi Reich. We threw a blanket over her so that she would not see anything and gave her a good thrashing because she had betrayed Alice Balla who had smoked and had been punished with bunker arrest. The case was investigated but nothing was found out because everybody pretended not to have seen or heard anything.

In January 1945, we were evacuated by TWL personnel with the permission of the commandant of Auschwitz to Breslau. However, they could not keep us there because everybody was fleeing from the Russians. We spent a horrible night at the Gestapo in Breslau, then we were taken to Gross Rosen. From there, we went by foot and by train to Mauthausen. After two days, they evacuated us again. We were supposed to go to Buchenwald. However, Weimar and Buchenwald were heavily bombarded and we landed in Bergen-Belsen, one of the worst camps.

It was a nightmare. The camp was overcrowded, the corpses were lying around, there was a dreadful stench, we did not receive any bread only very watery soup made of yellow turnips and, in the end, nothing at all. At first, Joli Deutsch fell ill with typhus, then I developed pleurisy as was attested by a physician after the war. Muli nursed me devotedly. The SS escaped and left behind only Hungarian Volksdeutsche volunteers to man the guard towers.

On April 15, 1945, we were liberated by the British Army. Luckily, the entire TWL work squad survived.

Czechoslovakian liaison officers came to Bergen-Belsen, at first Captain

Gutrig, and later Captain Nekola. They were looking for assistants to register all Czechoslovakian nationals. We volunteered and were scrupulously interrogated before being accepted. They gave us a navy-blue uniform as well as underwear, and we worked until the beginning of August 1945, when we returned home.

I went back to my former job as bookkeeper and secretary. In January 1949, I emigrated to Israel. There was an unscheduled delay in the port of Naples and I walked along our boat on the pier. Suddenly, I heard somebody call out my name. Next to us there was a ship of the Haganah[4] at anchor which was transporting weapons, Red Cross ambulances and other equipment from Czechoslovakia to Israel and one of the soldiers on duty on the deck had called me. He was Bernard Bachner from Maehrisch Ostrau, a former friend of my sister Therese, who had recognized me from afar. We talked for a while and he gave me his address in Israel.

I arrived in Israel on February 3, 1949. Bernard did not wait until I visited him but inquired in the port of Haifa as to which reception camp I had been sent. One day before my departure to Ramat Gan, he came to see me and three months later we were happily married. We have one daughter and four grandchildren. My husband passed away in 1977.

My health is not the best. I suffer from neurovegetative disturbances and problems with my spine; both of these ailments were contracted in camp. I often dream dreadful things about Auschwitz and wake up screaming. Once, when I saw red-burning flames shooting from the chimney of a steel plant in Acco, I imagined it to be the crematorium of Auschwitz. I even smelled the odor of burning flesh and I became so sick that I had to vomit.

I think it is tragic that almost all over the world people make believe—as if Auschwitz had never existed. Not only that, all those events were considered to be nothing but a chimera (vide "The Auschwitz Lie" and other publications). In Germany, and even in the United States of America, Neo-nazism surfaces. Mankind wants to forget but we will never forget nor forgive.

NOTES

Margit Bachner

1   Czech reports that not two, but four prisoners escaped: "On June 20, 1942, four Polish prisoners of the TWL fled from Auschwitz: Kazimierz Piechowski (No. 918), Jozef Lempart (No. 3419), Stanislaw Jaster (No. 6438) and Eugeniusz Bendera (No. 8502). They left the camp in a Steyer 220 automobile dressed in SS uniforms. Eighty kilometers from Auschwitz they abandoned the car in a forest. After their successful escape they sent a letter to the camp commandant apologizing ironically for the theft of the automobile" (Czech, 1989, p. 232).

2   A water ditch outside the Birkenau camp.

3   Orli Reichert-Wald described this incident in her story, *Die Engelmacherin* (Steger & Thiele, 1989, pp. 100-101).

4   The Haganah was the defense group of the Palestine settlers. Later it was incorporated into the Israeli army.

CHAPTER 9

The Central Construction Division

(Zentralbauleitung der Waffen SS und Polizei in Auschwitz)

The Zentralbauleitung der Waffen SS und Polizei in Auschwitz, which was not part of the camp's administration but rather part of the WVHA (Wirtschafts-Verwaltungshauptamt der SS in Berlin), was responsible for the enlargement of the camp. Originally, the organization's name was SS-Neubauleitung Auschwitz and was led by SS-Untersturmfuehrer Schlachter. The Zentralbauleitung der Waffen SS und Polizei in Auschwitz was formed in November 1941 as a result of a merger of the Sonderbauleitung fuer die Errichtung eines Kriegsgefang-enenlagers der Waffen SS Auschwitz and the SS-Neubauleitung Auschwitz and was entrusted with the responsibility for overseeing the construction of the concentration camp in Auschwitz as well as the already, at the time, under construction prisoner-of-war camp in Birkenau. SS-Sturmbannfuehrer Bischoff was appointed to be the head of the Zentralbauleitung der Waffen SS und Polizei in Auschwitz. SS-Obersturmfuehrer Jotham became the new head of the organization in November 1943, after Bischoff was appointed chief of the newly created Inspectorate in Slask. The Zentralbauleitung oversaw the various constructions, as well as the stores—Bauhof and Holzhof, the car-park and the building shops. At first, the Zentralbauleitung was under the Inspectorate-East with headquarters in Poznan and then, after December 1943, under the Inspectorate Slask, which, in turn, was under the Hauptamt Haushalt und Bauten.

The Zentralbauleitung's functions were threefold: investing, architectural planning and general execution. Most of the work associated with the construction of the camp was to be performed by the prisoners themselves under the supervision of the Zentralbauleitung. However, due to lack of a sufficient number of specialists among the prisoners, the Zentralbauleitung hired outside firms to do the more sophisticated work. The firms used their own workers as well as the prisoners.

One of the first prisoner work details set up as a result of the construction of the camp was the Baubuero-Bauleitung. It was established in June 1940 and was part of the Zentralbauleitung. In the beginning, the group was composed of four prisoners. Four more were added later. During the heaviest periods of the construction of the camp (1942-1943), over one hundred women and men prisoners worked in the Baubuero-Bauleitung, which was divided into four sections: architectural, installation, drafting and measuring. Prisoners of this group who were under the supervision of the SS-men participated in designing the plans for the camp, technical plans of new objects and buildings, marked out the area for future buildings, roads, etc. The first task of the prisoners working for the Zentralbauleitung consisted of topographical measurements of the camp site and the area around it, and then, preparation of precise maps and plans of objects in the area. These tasks were performed by a group of land surveyors who, later, set up their own group called Baubuero-Vermessungskommando. Qualified geodesists were part of the group. One of the first plans prepared by the group was the plan of an ammunition bunker, which was later turned into a camp crematorium.

One of the major undertakings of the Zentralbauleitung was the construction of the Auschwitz crematoria. On July 1, 1942, they asked the firms Huta, Hoch- und Tiefbau, A.G. and Schlesischer Industriebau Lenz & Co., A.G. in Kattowitz to submit bids for the construction of new crematoria. The installations for the gas chambers would be supplied by J.A. Topf & Sons in Erfurt.

The firm Lenz declined the crematorium construction for lack of manpower. Consequently, on July 15, 1942, the Zentralbauleitung accepted the bid of RM 133,765.65, submitted by the firm Huta on July 13, 1942, and ordered the company to start immediately on the project. Engineer-in-chief Pruefer of Topf & Sons in Erfurt arrived in Auschwitz on January 29, 1943, to discuss with the Zentralbauleitung the completion date of the four crematoria. He also inspected the sites.

The four new crematoria and gas chambers were completed in 1943: Crematorium IV on March 22, 1943, Crematorium II on March 31, 1943, Crematorium V on April 4, 1943, and Crematorium III on June 25, 1943. Thus on June 28, 1943, SS Sturmbannfuehrer Karl Bischoff, the director of the Zentralbauleitung, informed Heinz Kammler, the chief of Section C of the WVHA, that the construction of the requested crematoria had been completed. From now on they could count on a cremation capacity per 24 hours as follows:

1.	old crematorium	(Auschwitz)	340 corpses
2.	new crematorium II	(Birkenau)	1440 corpses

3.	new crematorium III	(Birkenau)	1440 corpses
4.	new crematorium IV	(Birkenau)	768 corpses
5.	new crematorium V	(Birkenau)	768 corpses
		Total	4756 corpses

SS-man Pery Broad recounts that the Zentralbauleitung was so proud of their achievements that they placed a series of pictures of the crematoria in the hall of their main building for everybody to see. They had overlooked the fact that the civilians coming and going there would be less taken with the technological achievements of the Bauleitung on seeing the enlarged photos of fifteen ovens, neatly arranged side by side, they would, instead, be rather apt to ponder on the very strange contrivances of the Third Reich. Untersturmfuehrer Grabner of the Political Section soon took care to squash that queer publicity (Broad, 1965, p. 70).

Some of the women prisoners of the Stabsgebaeude who worked in the office of the Zentralbauleitung were: Hedda Birnbaum, Margot Leiter, Herta Mehl, Margita Milch, Henny Lipschitz, Lotte Lipschitz, Helene Pfeffer and Baba Weinberger.

Herta Soswinski (née Mehl)
Vienna (Austria)

Why We Have to Tell about It

The Stabsgebaeude in Auschwitz was the prison block for a variety of work squads: office workers, laundry workers, seamstresses, beauticians, etc.

The block was not exclusively Jewish. We were together with "Aryan" women of many nationalities: Germans, Poles, French women, Czechs, etc., and also, for some time with German women from Siebenbuergen.[1] There was only a dormitory, no living room. The food was distributed in the hallway. During the summer months, we ate in the meadow in front of the building and in the winter wherever there was space.

In regards to the prisoners from Transylvania: the husbands were German soldiers and their families had been persuaded to resettle "heim im Reich" (in the homeland) through the "Fuehrer's" promises. Instead of on farms and manor houses, they had simply been placed into a gathering camp. Since the women complained constantly and demanded to speak to the camp commandant, not only in regards to the unkept promises but also because of insufficient food and lodgings, they were picked up one morning by truck, supposedly for a meeting with the camp commandant but, instead, they were sent straight to the Stabsgebaeude in Auschwitz (I believe for three months) in order to wean them from complaining. Before I relate how I came to the block, I'll perhaps give some information about myself.

I was born on April 16, 1917, in Znaim (Znojmo) (Southern Moravia) which belonged at that time to the Austro-Hungarian monarchy and later to Czechoslovakia. My mother tongue was German and, until I was 6 years old, I did not know a word of Czech.

On my mother's side, I descend from a pure Sephardic family which can be traced back to Don Abarbanel,[2] a great Jewish scholar and secretary of the treasury of Ferdinand, the Catholic, who escaped with his entire family from the inquisition in Spain via Holland. One branch of his descendants settled in Southern Moravia, the other in the Burgenland (the most easterly portion of Austria, near the Hungarian border). I learned all of this during a chance encounter and conversation with a woman belonging to the Burgenlandic branch of the family (what is the favorite topic of conversation among Jews? of course, the Mishpoche and you find it in the most unexpected places.) Later, the fact of my Sephardic descendance was confirmed by my only surviving maternal relative, a cousin who had emigrated with the Youth Aliyah[3] to Israel in 1939.

Two months after my sixth birthday, my mother, who had been ill for many years, died and I soon got a very evil stepmother. No fairy tale could describe a worse one. I have not been able to repress these events for all these many years; although the poor woman, as well as my beloved stepsister, both became victims of Hitler's barbarity.

As a result of my father's second marriage, we moved from Znaim to a small place in the vicinity of Prague. I learned Czech, and a month after our arrival I already attended a Czech elementary school consisting of five grades. During these five years, I almost forgot the German language, but when I returned to my grandmother in Znaim, everything came back at once as if it had only slumbered subconsciously. By the way, during all those years, I recited the evening prayer, "Muede bin ich, geh zur Ruh" in German as a legacy to my mother. However, once I relearned German, I noticed the inappropriateness of the words I had recited.

There was a large and active Jewish community in Znaim. I have pleasant memories of the Makkabi or the temple choir, where I was allowed to sing under the direction of chief cantor Handgiff during the entire four years I lived in Znaim. Simultaneously, I received a profoundly nationalistic Czech education in my Czech school; as a matter of fact, the patriotic movement among the Jews in Bohemia was very strong; but the two did not interfere with each other. There was no antisemitism in my environment.

After a two-year sojourn in Northern Bohemia, I came to Prague at the age of 17 and started to work. My generation grew up in an era in which political interest and political activities were omnipresent. Soon I joined Techeleth Lavan[4] in Prague, a Zionist organization of the second International, with which I strongly identified. The association was not only of a politico-cultural nature. I felt this powerful bond when my father died in November 1936, after having been unemployed for three years, and suddenly, I remained all by myself. My chaverim and chaverot took very good care of me, picked me up from the office at noon and at night and did not leave me in the lurch until I had, at least halfway, recovered from this blow. Our group had a rich cultural program: theater, concerts, films and, during the first years, in addition to my job, I also studied at a private commercial academy and at an English Institute (since I never used the language, I forgot it completely).

Thus, the events of 1938 came to pass, much noticed and emotionally felt by all of us: at first the occupation of Austria, then the separation of the Sudetenland, i.e., the Pact of Munich. Who could remain passive in such a time? I could not. I worked with refugees, with the youth division of the Red Cross, and belonged to a leftist youth organization with whom I went underground after the occupation of the remainder of Czechoslovakia. I would like to mention that the communists did belong to the most active and courageous fighters, when living underground in freedom, as well as later in the illegal organizations of the different concentration camps.

The occupation of Bohemia and Moravia (Slovakia had established an independent state one day before the occupation) did not come as a surprise to us. The Munich Pact[5] and the loss of the Sudetenland, where all defense establishments of Czechoslovakia had been located, had been a dreadful shock; not to talk about the separation of many Sudeten-Germans who had been ready to risk their lives for Czechoslovakia and to fight side-by-side together with the inhabitants of Bohemia and Moravia. The betrayal of our allies, England and France, had been a heavy blow for all of us. After Hitler's victory, our minister President Beran declared, during a proclamation at the Altstaedter Ring: the only nation faithful to us had been the Soviet Union. If we would have accepted their assistance, we would have been regarded as the representatives of Bolshevist Russia in Europe. We all cried. How could we have known. . .?

In 1940, my boss and his entire family committed suicide. The firm was taken over by his "Aryan" brother-in-law. He had nothing better to do than to fire all the Jewish employees immediately. I was the first victim. After I had given him a piece of my mind and told him how shabby he, as a Czech, had acted, I received three months' severance pay. This money kept me going for the following weeks until my arrest; there was even a little left over. It almost sounds like a joke, but after Hitler's occupation I received a juicy increase in my salary as foreign language secretary according to the new labor laws which went into force for the brand-new "Protectorate" of Bohemia and Moravia; only to be fired at once because of these new laws.

On August 27, 1940, I was arrested because of my underground activity. Two weeks beforehand, I had taken a rather difficult entrance test at the Jewish Community Federation which I had passed with flying colors, and I had been scheduled to start my new job on September 1. Well, it had not been meant to occur;

instead of to the Jewish Federation, I marched to the Petschek Palais, the seat of the Gestapo in Prague.

I did not actually march, but was taken out of bed in the early morning hours by two giant Gestapo men and delivered to headquarters. The very first day, I experienced several times, on my very own body, how criminals of my kind were treated and in the evening I was transferred to Pankrac jail. And the interrogations? We could hear the beatings in the "waiting room" where those who were waiting for their first interrogation were sitting; and I believe I was used as a deterrent; but mine was a special case, not related to any of the others who had been arrested, except for the fact that, like the majority, I had been betrayed by somebody who, after the first box on his ear, had "spilled all the beans." The one who nailed me did not even know my name and only knew approximately where I lived, i.e., after a meeting, he must have followed me secretly.

These interrogations were repeated daily during the first period. Then they only started again in December 1941, but on a very intensive basis so that I lost one tooth and a large part of my hearing (which is rather tragic, particularly now in old age when I can hardly go to my beloved theater or mingle with people; no hearing aid can help here). But, although they had to carry me out on a stretcher several times during the first as well as during the last series of interrogations, they were not successful with me. I still derive satisfaction from this fact. It went so far that I was given over to another interrogator. "Whom do you have there?— you don't say, I have been looking for her all over Prague. We don't know whom we have under our own roof. No, I don't want this dirty sow—I'll only take a deposition from her." He did not even attempt to achieve his goal through beatings, he just, more or less, finalized the case. The first one was called Zander and the second one Friedrich. And their conversation which interrupted the interrogation did me a lot of good—not the interruption, but the knowledge that nobody wanted to have anything more to do with me...

I was first jailed in Pankrac, as already mentioned, and later, i.e., in the summer of 1941, in the prison on the Karlsplatz, also located in Prague. On January 14, 1942, I was sent with a transport to Ravensbrueck concentration camp.

We traveled in a roomy car of a passenger train, Jewesses as well as non-Jewesses, could talk freely and were not in a bad mood. We did not know what fate awaited us, but we had left the Gestapo beasts behind! We changed trains in Berlin, and at our arrival in Ravensbrueck, i.e., in Fuerstenfeld, the howling, the barking of dogs, the beatings until we had climbed into the trucks to be taken to camp, were such a shock that my menstrual period, which was due the following day, did not come. They did not have to put any medication into our food, I doubt that they would have wasted them on us, the desired effect was achieved without it. And I was not the only one.

The next day, we were assigned to our blocks. For me, it was the Jewish Block Number 9; at that time, there were two Jewish blocks in Ravensbrueck, #11 and #9. I had to do outside work: filling straw mattresses, carrying heavy cement sacks, digging a ditch with a pick ax in the middle of winter when the soil was completely frozen, etc. Our block also provided the woman-power for cleaning the sewers. They gave us summer clothes for this hard work when the temperature reached -20°. In addition, since we were only allowed to relieve ourselves if the SS-woman permitted us to do so, we often had wet panties, which we washed at night, but which were still frozen stiff the next morning when we had to get up. Bladder infections were the consequence. During that time, they checked strictly that we were lying in bed by ourselves. We had three thin "horse blankets" and one summer nightgown and icicles were hanging at the ceiling. With two together in bed, we would have had six blankets and could have warmed each other a little. The prohibition was supposedly for the protection of our morals. Later, when we were five women in two beds, nobody was concerned with morals any more. In Auschwitz, we were three or two women in one bed. My bed partner at that time was Gitti Milch from Slovakia.

During that period, there did not yet exist an underground movement in Ravensbrueck; that only started toward the end of my stay, at least for the Czechoslovakian group. Nationalities kept more or less together, although there also existed some cross-national friendships. I was the first, and of course, after Ravensbrueck had become "judenrein" (free from Jews), the last member of the leadership circle for the Jewish block. Ilse Kreibich was in charge. But solidarity was practiced right from the start, and I experienced it myself. In the beginning, my friend, who worked together with Milena Jesenska[6] in the Revier (hospital), told me, "Look around and try to find out how things are working here. Then I'll help you." A short while later, she realized that I was helpless in the face of camp conditions and incapable of "organizing" and taking proper care of myself. So I received a morsel of bread here and there, a pullover from the warehouse and a plate of soup on those days when we did not get any as punishment.

One day, two SS-women were in charge of the penal squad. During roll-call, a work detail was formed from our block to shovel snow. Unfortunately, I was among those that were selected, although I was still quite weak from the interrogations and unable to eat much. I just fainted, right in front of the Kommandantur. One SS-woman commanded her dog to attack me, the other restrained the animal. The commandant looked out the window, and I received a "Meldung" (was cited) and the entire work squad was punished by having to stand at the gate without food. (All of this was later told to me because I had lost consciousness and had been completely out of it.) It weighed very heavy on me that the entire "kommando" had been punished because of me. But in regards to the "Meldung," I was to experience the solidarity of inmates. With the help of women from Block 11, for example, Kaethe Leichter,[7] from Vienna and a prominent prisoner from Prague, whose name I have forgotten, a relative of my Prague friends who had represented Czechoslovakia at an international forum, the "Meldung" just "disappeared." It would have meant bunker, and this I would not have survived, given my weakened physical condition, not to mention the notorious SS-woman in charge of the bunker at that time, Oberaufseherin Maria Mandel, who was to accompany us to Auschwitz later. After this event, my friend, Esther Klima, wanted to renounce her work place in the sewing room in my favor, but against my wish, so that I would be able to sit during work. However, the exchange did not go through, and I was happy that it did not.

Suddenly, in March 1942, a transport of 1,000 women prisoners went to Auschwitz to work as inmate functionaries, as we learned later. Then a Gypsy transport was sent, and also a transport of prisoners from the two Jewish blocks who had arrived in Ravensbrueck before the middle of December 1941. We did not know their destination, but it was strange that their prison uniforms, they had received new clothing before leaving, was returned to camp a few days later. We had arranged with Ruth, our table-elder, to send us some news, if possible, under the star of her jacket. She did so, and the girls from the clothing detail, informed by us, gave us the note. She wrote that she did not know where she was, but that they had been received by a group of physicians which even comprised a dentist. She could not write us any more because it was her turn to get undressed. Thus, we knew just as much as before. Today, however, we know that the women were sent to Bernburg[8] and were all gassed. The dentist was present in order to ascertain how much dental gold could be expected from the transport. Even now, writing down this information, I still get goose pimples; it is so horrible. Thinking of all the dead, the later ones, including the members of my family, I can only repeat Friedrich Torberg's words, "Wherever I go, the dark gowns of the deceased flutter about me."[9]

From summer 1942, I worked in the furrier's cutting workshop. From furs stolen all over Europe, jackets, gloves and shoes for the soldiers at the front were cut. We also received brand new fur trousers directly from the factory. In the pocket of one pair of pants, I found a letter from a factory girl to an unknown soldier at the front. We had to open the seams and cut them in order to produce the above-mentioned items. One day, we received a shipment of beautifully embroidered children's furs from Rumania or the Ukraine. We all choked and many a tear fell on those furs.

There was a group of peasant girls from Germany among us who were imprisoned because of "Rassenschande" with prisoners of war, Frenchmen or Poles, who had been assigned to their farms. Some of them had children at home who were the results of their relationships. When they were caught (most of them had been betrayed), they were shorn, tarred and feathered and driven through the village like that before they were sent to Ravensbrueck. We could imagine what had happened to their male partners.

But, even in these cases, there was reason to smirk: among these women, there were a mother and her 15-year old daughter, who had been arrested because of the same man. Even in camp, they still quarreled a number of times because of him.

We also received minks and silver foxes, and it was soon discovered that, frequently, jewelry and foreign currency were sewn into the heads. These pieces then came to a separate table to which several SS-women were also assigned. There, the furs were opened and searched. The items they found constituted a fortune. They obviously came from Jewish transports. The people had thought that they would be "resettled" and had tried to at least save a small part of their belongings for their future life. Eventually, everything landed with the SS.

Another aspect of camp life also has to be noted, which I know best from the point of view of the Czechoslovakian group, to which women of German nationality belonged, namely: the cultural side. We knew many poems by heart, each one of us learned from the other at night on the Lagerstrasse (camp street). It is almost unbelievable to what an extent memory can be trained. I, myself, knew, in addition to my own poems which were created in prison, in Ravensbrueck and later in Auschwitz, more than 300 Czech and German poems and ballads by heart. One cannot imagine how much strength a poem or a song recalled can provide in sleepless nights. My own poems, and also those of my comrades, were written down and made the rounds within our group.[10] One day, Bozenka, from the laundry detail, came to me and brought me a little notebook, exclaiming warningly, "You have to be careful. I found this in the blouse of an SS-woman." What had happened? The girl who had the poems last had lost them. She did not tell me anything, believing if they would be found she would confess to be the author. An SS-woman found them, put them into her blouse, forgot about them and then gave the blouse to the laundry. I was lucky that Bozenka was the one to wash the blouse. Later on in Auschwitz, a prisoner from Brno, who was released, took the poems home and gave them to me in 1945.

After the March transports, only half a Jewish block remained and we were transferred to Block 7. Gradually, more and more Jewesses arrived so that finally five persons were sleeping in two beds. In the beginning of October 1942, we heard that we would leave with a transport to Auschwitz. The name did not mean anything to us, all of us had been imprisoned for a long time and no news had penetrated. Even when the construction of a crematorium had been considered in Ravensbrueck, we had asked "why?" Until then, the undertaker of Fuerstenfeld had picked up the dead. Manya, a physician in our group, explained that the term crematorium was used for everything that was being burnt, including garbage. Well, I know such naivete is unimaginable. The last day at work in Ravensbrueck, a Russian partisan, a medical student from Kiev, who worked together with me at the same table, cried so hard that I asked her whether somebody had hurt her. Nina answered, "I am so sorry for you. You are so young." But why she pitied me, she did not tell me, although she obviously knew something.

On the eve of the transport, which was scheduled for October 5, 1942, our friends from the Revier bandaged our wounds. (By the way, I had been very ill in Ravensbrueck, and with the assistance of a friend, had received a bed card for one week with 39.4° Centigrade fever. The card was then illegally renewed for an additional week. Later, I found out that I had had tuberculosis). Early in the morning during the roll-call, the SS-women had intended to march the prisoners of the Jewish block out of camp quietly. But, then something happened which the guards had not expected, and even we did not imagine: they were not in charge of the camp any more. All the women ran to us, and we were literally embraced by each one of the prisoners. This is something which one cannot forget; this comradeship and love which was shown to us by the other inmates, disregarding their own safety. I learned in 1945, that for every one of us, the death notice had been sent to the Gestapo at home (and from there, if still existing, to the family). I often thought whether some of these women knew or surmised the fate of the March transports. However that may be, it was a unique event! I don't remember how we came from the square in front of the kitchen to the train. I only know that we traveled in prisoner compartments, that there was a thunderstorm at night, that it was raining, and that there was an SS-woman who had some human emotions and provided us with some drinking water when we were standing at a station. I don't recall how we got from the train to Birkenau.

In Birkenau, we had to stand on the left side of the gate. We perspired in our winter prison uniforms which were too little for the winter, but too much for the heat. Here we stood until afternoon. In the meantime, Regine, our former block-elder, who had arrived with the transport of the German non-Jewish prisoners, visited us once in a white apron with red dots, then in a blue one with white dots, and once again in a red one with white dots. She obviously wanted to show us that she was a prominent prisoner.

There was a ditch between us and the camp.[11] In the afternoon, they placed a plank over it and we were individually called and tattooed. This was done by a Czech political prisoner, according to his triangle, and since he thought that we came from "outside" he made my number, 21709, extremely large so that he could ask me for news in whispers. Moreover, he probably thought, big or small, it's all the same; the chimneys are waiting anyway. After the tattooing, we were sent to tables on the Lagerstrasse where we were registered. All of us had been arrested by the Gestapo, thus this formality had to be taken care of. I asked a girl that worked next to the Lagerstrasse about life here. Her reply is still ringing in my ear: One would be able to live if they would let us live. What did this mean? The girl who registered me looked at me, noticed my bandage and said very softly, "Take all bandages off." Since she was very insisting, I followed her advice and told the others whom I could reach unobtrusively. Why this was important, we understood later.

We then came into a sort of barn and received civilian clothes, i.e., they were just thrown at us. For example, I got a long black dress and an older woman from my block whom I had called "Mutti" (mother), she had been a member of the sect "Herz Jesu" (Heart of Jesus)[12] a checkered young girl's dress. Laughingly, we exchanged; and suddenly we were shaved and deeply shocked. A tea kettle was brought and was taken away without being distributed, and we were so thirsty! Then an SS-man appeared and sat down. Individually, we had to step in front of him and he motioned with his thumb: left or right. All elderly women went to the left, but also all of those who had a bandage, for example a young, buxom blond and blue-eyed girl, Erika from Berlin. There was a rumor that all of those would receive lighter work. It seemed plausible to us, especially since afterward, we were all together led to a barrack. We did not manage to sleep in the "kojen" (stone berths); we were so pestered by fleas that two hours later, when we were chased outside for roll-call, we had stockings formed by fleas.

An SS-woman called, "Whoever was standing to the left yesterday, step forward." Probably, we were counted beforehand and afterward, I, therefore, remember that we used to be 530 and later, only 210. I do not recall that during the selection (because that was what we had experienced at night) a list had been made. We were so unsuspecting that, indeed, everybody stepped forward; not even the mother of one of the girls attempted to stay with her daughter. The SS-woman looked for women inmates to accompany the transport among the block personnel. We heard loud weeping and thought at first that if friends have to separate they cry; we would do the same. Then the SS-woman screamed, "Whoever cries, goes along." Momentarily, this was incomprehensible for us, but did strike us as ominous. Was it a punishment to accompany the transport? In the course of the morning, we learned what had happened. We had learned, but not understood; today, I am still pondering the question of how one could send people like vermin into the gas. The case of Katja is unforgettable; she came into the camp pregnant, worked with us in the Bauleitung, delivered in Birkenau, still sent us a desperate letter: hunger; and then went with a transport of mothers with children into the gas...

After the roll-call, an SS-man came and looked for office workers skilled in typing. I am short and stood with my friend in the last row. Nobody saw my raised hand. Esther pushed me and commanded, "Say something." I uttered, "Zehn-fingersysten" (typing with ten fingers). My number was listed and in the afternoon they called us for a test. We were six—I believe only two from our transport—Li, a Berliner who came from Holland and I. I could not elbow myself ahead, that's why I was the last to be examined. And the SS-man said, "I do not need more than six." The one who tested us replied, "But number six did write very fast." "O.K.," the SS-man said. And so I came to the Stabsgebaeude; a giant step closer to survival. This group of six girls was the beginning of the kommando, "Zentral-Bauleitung."

I have to mention one installation in the basement of the Stabsgebaeude which did us a lot of good, although it was not intended to be for our benefit: there were two showers in a tiled room which we could use on a daily basis, even if only for a few minutes, and perhaps 8-10 of us simultaneously, but we could wash ourselves thoroughly. Since we had contact with the SS, we had the possibility of keeping ourselves clean. In the Auschwitz women's camp, to which we were later transferred, there was a real washroom, without a door and three steps from the entrance of the block, which was always open. I was not the only one who washed herself daily from head to foot with the ice cold water. This also was a path to survival.

Auschwitz; one could write volumes about it. Soon I found friends, two women from Prague and their colleagues from the kommando Landwirtschaft (agricultural office work squad). They loved to listen to poems and songs. When they heard that my friend, Lilly Riegelhaupt, who had arrived together with me, was still in Birkenau, Anni immediately tried to requisition her for the kommando Landwirtschaft. But by the time everything was taken care of, Lilly did not exist any more. She could not stand Birkenau, and at night, when the others were asleep, she had run into the electrically charged fence. Neither did we succeed in having Esther transferred from Birkenau to Auschwitz. Thus, although no SS-woman chased me with her dog, and I could work in my own field, all of this greatly depressed me. Physically, I was also not in the best of health; later I weathered intestinal typhus, dysentery, intestinal flu and mumps (a human being can stand a lot when survival is at stake); but at that particular period, I just could not bear it any more.

One day, a certain prisoner from Prague called Stahl, who worked as engineer in the drafting section of the Zentral-Bauleitung, and with whom, up to then, I had not exchanged many words, approached me and asked whether I would be willing to join the illegal camp underground organization. I would have loved to have screamed, "Hurrah!" I had neither scruples nor fear. It is impossible to work illegally if one is afraid and I had already proven myself beforehand. My dark moods disappeared, and I concentrated on my task: to organize a women's resistance movement from whom I could gather information, and to which I could supply information; to draw in girls who knew what was going on, what was planned, etc. In some girls, I confided what it was all about, some suspected it and some had no inkling whatsoever; I just involved them in conversations. The more my news about the outside situation turned out to be correct (I received the news from the leaders of the men's underground), the more their confidence in me increased and the more information I collected. The tiny nucleus of our organization immediately requested poison so that we would be able to kill ourselves in case we should be sent to the gas chamber (after all, we were "bearers of secrets" and had no lease on survival, but nobody in Auschwitz had). I told the girls if I would ask for something, I would rather choose a weapon to take somebody else along in case I had to go. I transmitted the request which, of course, was not granted.[13]

Ernstl Burger, a Viennese, was the leader of the Auschwitz underground. Unfortunately, I did not know him personally. Engineer Stahl was our liaison. But he must have been a fantastic person, judging from everything I heard about him.

I also organized news myself. There was an illegal radio in the workshop detail, and each afternoon an inmate came to our section of the Bauleitung to deliver letters that had to be signed. When I saw him, I went into the hallway. He walked behind me and seemingly, in a monologue, related everything he had heard during the British broadcast. One day, however, he remained silent, until, desperately, he burst out that the previous day the Blockfuehrer had come to the block drunk and had arbitrarily made a selection, my informant was also among those destined for the gas. The same evening, when I returned to our block, I looked for the girl who most probably would have to type the list, somebody from the Political Section. We discussed the fact that, since the SS-man had been drunk, he certainly would only remember that he had filled two sheets with names, but most probably he would not recall an accurate figure. The girl agreed to type the list double-spaced and to leave out my informant as well as a few other unknown prisoners, and to save them from the gas chamber.

The Zentralbauleitung (ZB) was subdivided into several sections, each one under the direction of an Obersturmfuehrer, e.g., Obersturmfuehrer Pollok was the head of the raw material division, Obersturmfuehrer Jotham became chief of the ZB when part of it was transferred to Kattowitz (his secretary was Baba Weinberger), Obersturmfuehrer Jahn was the fiance of SS-woman-in-chief Maria Mandel (both of these two resembled each other—I believe more information is superfluous). But I remember mostly the two divisions for which I worked, namely the material section supervised by Obersturmfuehrer Pollok and the planning division. These larger units were in turn subdivided. Thus, Unterscharfuehrer Wilk was the head of a subsection and worked together with Unterscharfuehrer Pruchnik and SS-man Kunert. The director of the workshops was sitting in the next room. His name started with B. He had a hardware store in Upper Silesia and delivered large quantities of merchandise to Auschwitz. Leo, a Polish prisoner, worked for him. In 1944 he escaped together with his friend.

Shortly afterwards, Unterscharfuehrer Pruchnik told our kapo, Hedi (Leo's kochanka) and me that he had seen Leo in the street in Kattowitz. I asked immediately whether he had pursued this matter and he replied that he was not obligated to see everything. He might also have looked the other way. This answer was quite in line with his behavior. I breathed a sigh of relief and Hedi also calmed down.

The planning division also comprised the drafting section, the planning archives and the blueprint room. Here I worked for Wilk and also for Dejacco, who was the director. Two of his employees were SS-man Gierisch and a civilian worker called Gottlieb. The latter came from Vienna and had connections with the Perlmoser cement factory. In 1945 he contacted me in Vienna (how he tracked me down is still a mystery to me) and requested a certificate that he had not belonged to the SS. My answer was, "I can only give you an affidavit that you were wearing civilian clothing in Auschwitz, but, considering your views, I don't know whether or not you were a member of the SS." (After the departure of Dejacco and Gierisch when he replaced both of them, we had some arguments which he settled by declaring that the Fuehrer knew full well what he was doing.) Well, he was not interested in such a certificate and I never saw him again.

Jotham and Jahn were feared by the prisoners. Although nothing drastic happened in the offices of the ZB, the reputation of many SS-men originated because of their behavior on the construction sites. This was the case, for example, of Unterscharfuehrer Swoboda and his colleague, who was from Saxony. Swoboda himself was Viennese. He had an oven company in Vienna and also diligently delivered merchandise to Auschwitz. After 1945, I found out that there were two oven manufacturers called Swoboda in Vienna. I don't know which one belonged to the former SS-man. We also received ovens from the firm of Topf and Sons, Erfurt.

We had two SS-men who volunteered for front service. I knew because both told me about it. One had been working as a land surveyor at the ZB. He was the one who gave us some bread when we started to work in the office. Shortly afterwards, he disappeared, only to resurface one day in the hallway. He informed me that he still had to settle a few things and that he had volunteered for front duty because he did not want to participate in what happened in Auschwitz.[14] The second one came to us after his wounds, received at the front, had healed. Whenever he met me in the hallway he asked, "Spitzmaeuschen, how are you?" I did not stop and did not answer. However, one day he blocked my way and said, "Spitzmaeuschen ["little shrew-mouse"—he probably used this term because of my dejected countenance], at home I was brought up in the following way—my father whipped me when I played with Jewish children from the neighborhood. But that, what is happening here we did not want." And a few days later he was gone, back to the front. I don't remember his name nor the name of the first SS-man.

Later, Czech civilian employees worked in the drafting room. They were rather despondent in this environment. One day, I had to write a letter for one of the SS-men, architect Gierisch, to a Nazi office in Prague. I "forgot" to add "Protectorate of Bohemia and Moravia" on the address. Gierisch asked whether I did not know and I answered, "No. I have been imprisoned for such a long time that I only remember facts, and that, for me, is not a fact." Naturally, I knew that I did not run any risks with Gierisch. He just turned around in order to hide his smile. The young Czech draftsmen raised their heads and stared at me. I then started to write permissions for leave on the official letterheads of the Bauleitung, I had no access to the official forms, stamped them with a normal rubberstamp of the Bauleitung and scrawled some kind of illegible signature. The trick succeeded, from now on, they went more often on home leave and, eventually, sometime in 1944, they all joined the partisans in the Bohemian/Moravian mountains. Only one of them returned shortly to Auschwitz to let me know that everything had gone well and to inform me where the boys were.

On a steady basis, we smuggled plans of the SS and information about happenings in camp to confidants outside.[15] A German prisoner worked in the draft room, who often went into the field together with an SS to survey the area. Afterward, he always came to me at the secretariat to have the legend put on the plans. I was very curious and inquired about everything in such an innocent way that he told me all. That's why I was well informed about several actions of the SS and transmitted this news to the movement. In an emergency, some Polish prisoners acted as couriers. They knew how to get the warning outside. Once, I learned from the German prisoner that the SS wanted to raid an underground communication center in a nearby village. Quickly, I told the Poles. When the SS came to the village, nobody was there.

My liaison engineer, Mirek Stahl, was transferred to Buchenwald in 1944, from then on the connection to me worked only sporadically. In August 1944, I already worked full time in the planning division and my boss was the already mentioned architect Gierisch from Munich. Although he was an SS-man, the Polish prisoners and I addressed him only as "Herr Architekt" when we were alone, and he called me "Fraulein Mehl." But Gierisch's behavior was exceptional.

Of course, all SS-men, as well as civilian workers, knew what happened in Auschwitz, even if they dispute this today. Only a few years ago, they caught the former director of the planning section of the Bauleitung, Dejacco, an Austrian. After the war, he lived as master builder in the Tyrol. During his trial here in Vienna, he claimed that he knew nothing and was acquitted. But on every plan, also those of the crematoria, there had been his signature.[16]

What upset me during the trial was not only his denial, but his statement that he had not known what was going on in Auschwitz, in conformity with all SS criminals. He would have been acquitted even if he would have admitted his activities in Auschwitz and his knowledge of occurrences in camp because many former prisoners testified on his behalf.

Architect and former SS-man Gierisch behaved in an entirely different manner. Immediately after the war he reported his membership in the SS and his duties in camp, and was extradited to Poland although they had not even requested him. For three years he was imprisoned until his trial took place. The examining magistrate stated that he had received such a multitude of depositions in his favor that he would surely be acquitted—and that's what happened. Later Gierisch told me that those years had not been a picnic but understandable in light of everything that had happened.

One day, Gierisch said, "Fraulein Mehl, there is a new transport in the basement, see if we can use anybody of them." I went to the basement and looked around. I noticed a prisoner with a red triangle without a letter for the nationality, signifying a German political prisoner.

"From where are you, and how long have you been in prison?"

"Seven years, and I am from Vienna."

This was enough information for me; as a seasoned inmate one develops a sixth sense for people. I talked to other prisoners and learned from a newly arrived Czech prisoner that the person who had betrayed me to the Gestapo had perished in a concentration camp; looked further, asked for occupations (professions, skills, etc.). Then I returned to the Viennese and we talked about the situation, the reasons for incarceration, resistance in general and in relation to the concentration camp. Well, the prisoner had been instructed by the underground to get in touch with me; that's why he had been sent to the Bauleitungskommando, but they had advised him that I would have to receive notice first. In the evening, when he told Ernstl Burger he had already spoken with me, the latter did not believe him, "Herta does not talk to anybody who has not been announced in advance." But it was true. This was the first and only time that I did not stick to my principle. This called for revenge. For 43 years, I have been married to this man.

His arrival and our collaboration brought about a tremendous change in my life. I already mentioned that I was incapable of organizing anything for myself, although, especially in Auschwitz, commandant Aumeier's dictum was valid: "He, who lives longer than three months here, does not live by camp food alone." I depended on occasional donations, and for some time Gitti and I washed dishes after lunch, actually the task of the block personnel, and received a piece of bread in return. I received a parcel from my step-aunt three times. Just looking at the way it was packed caused me to cry.

I forgot to relate that, although my relatives at home had received my death notice, after having been in Auschwitz three months, we received permission to write. At first, I wrote to an aunt and later a cousin by marriage took over the correspondence until he himself disappeared in Theresienstadt. I can imagine that my aunt must have been dumfounded when she heard from me for the first time. That, at least, was the reaction of an acquaintance of mine when he met me in Prague in 1945.

SS Unterscharfuehrer Wilk, for whom I worked a long time at the Bauleitung, once put a piece of bread in the office. But I was too proud to take it and left it there. Two or three days later, he asked me why I had not taken it. My answer, "You should have told me that it was for me. I do not steal."

Healthwise, I went downhill. The Polish male prisoners in our kommando organized forty-six liver extract injections, thirty-six of these were administered, illegally of course, by our Polish woman prisoner physician, ten were drinking vials. My liver was swollen and my face was covered with yellow spots. My future husband was appalled at my appearance. He asked me why I had not demanded anything from the underground movement, and I told him that they were not an institute of supplies for me. He replied, "However, we cannot afford to lose our functionaries in this manner." From that moment on, he took care of me.

Before I was transferred to the planning division, a part of the Bauleitung was moved to Kattowitz without the prisoners. On this occasion, a case with different documents was discovered. When my former boss asked me about the contents, I had to confess that these were open files yet to be processed. He raised his hand to hit me; it was a precarious situation. After reflecting a moment, he lowered his hand, turned around and left the room. This had been my personal sabotage.

Before the arrival of the Hungarian transports in 1944, additional barracks for gassing were constructed, camouflaged—according to the plans—with straw mats. Architect Gierisch called them "the Hungarian barracks." I don't know whether this was the official work designation or whether he only referred to them privately in this fashion. Moreover, ditches were dug for the burning of corpses.

In the fall of 1944, architect Gierisch asked for a transfer to Gross-Rosen. When I remonstrated and told him that we had counted on him, he answered, "My child, they (meaning the Russians) will be here so fast that the others will not even turn around. Nothing can happen to you any more." Well, he was not right; but, probably, he would not have been able to help us.

Sometime in 1944, we were moved from the Stabsgebaeude to the newly constructed women's camp in Auschwitz. Next to us was an empty block, separated from us by barbed wire. One day, the telephone headquarters of the SS division Dirlewanger[17] moved into that block. Like all plans and reports, this news was transmitted outside. Not long afterward, we had an air raid.[18] The pilots accurately hit that particular block and many SS-men were killed. Usually, when I heard airplanes, I did not go to the basement. This time, I stood together with about ten other girls next to the rear wall of our block. Suddenly, I had such a strange feeling and persuaded the others to go down with me. Only Hedi remained, and that was the only one of our block who was killed by the tumbling wall. When the wall collapsed we all tried to run outside. Edith Gruenwald, the kapo of the Politische Abteilung, attempted to block our way. We had to push her aside before we reached the outdoors. The clothing warehouse was located in one of the front blocks. Here, a German inmate, who had been imprisoned since 1933, was killed. He had been a nice fellow and was mourned by many.

In the fall of 1944, we suddenly had to return from work in the middle of the day without knowing why. I strolled with a group of girls along the fence; perhaps I would learn something. Two Yugoslavian political women were also in our group. On the other side, two SS-men were walking, and I heard that they were conversing in a Slavic language. I told one of the women to verify whether I had heard correctly. Yes, there was an uprising of the Krematorium-Kommando in Birkenau, the two SS-men answered. Finally! I had known about the endeavors of the camp underground to convince these prisoners to resist because their particular work detail was being gassed regularly every few months. This was as predictable as the Amen after the prayer. Finally, they succeeded. Of this particular squad, two—I repeat, two—prisoners have survived as compared with the previous zero survival rate. Again, we had the confirmation: resistance is always worthwhile, while passivity means death. I am certain this would have happened in my case if I would not have contributed a little to the organization of the resistance movement. It gave me strength and the conviction: whether with or without me, the others are going to croak. To be completely honest, I really did not believe that I would survive, but I was not downhearted because of it; that always signified death, as I have learned in three or four cases in my kommando. While most of the girls said, "We are not going to survive except if we are lucky," I was of the opinion, "We are going to survive except if we have bad luck." The end result of these two assertions was the same, but mine sounded different and helped to keep one's head erect.

For a long time, we did not have a kapo for our work detail. Maria Maul, our blockelder, who had come with us from Ravensbrueck and who knew me from there, told me that I should report at the office the number of prisoners of the squad when we marched out and returned from work. I complied—and that was it.

Then, an "Aryan," a German political prisoner who was to be released soon, appeared in our kommando. At once she told me at night when we came back from work that I did not have to report any more "since I am here now." That was O.K. with me. Since she immediately got the kapo arm band, she was our first kapo. On the day of her release, she transferred this honor to Hedi.

There was a woman from Berlin in the Stabsgebaeude who worked in the laundry detail. She probably had been a prostitute beforehand. She had sent a petition to the authorities requesting to be released, and claimed that she had not only learned how to work, but had also realized the benefit and necessity of work. When a bordello was opened in Auschwitz, this woman was one of the first members of the crew. This kommando resided in our block in a special room and marched out to work every evening with bolsters and make-up kits. It was, perhaps, understandable that we did not exactly go out of our way to have contact with them. They complained about this. One day, during roll-call, commandant Hoessler stood in front of our block and roared at us, "... and we should take notice that everybody was working for the Reich. One in this fashion, and the other in another ..." I was standing in the first row, and was not allowed to move a muscle in my face, but I had to bite on my lower lip very hard in order not to roar with laughter. Once, when we had returned from work, there were a multitude of SS-women waiting for us and all reflector lights were turned on. We were to be checked. My heart sank, because I had newspapers underneath my dress. We were not allowed to have any, not even official, newspapers; it was a clear-cut crime, and I would be bombarded with questions such as: "Why? From whom? For whom?" etc. At first, the SS-women searched our apron pockets and I was delighted, since I had a very severe head cold and my pockets were full of wet handkerchiefs. Then it was the turn of our kapo, Hedi. They found lingerie and a pair of shoes on her. She received a box on the ear and a Meldung (report for punishment); I believe it was a week in the bunker. "Exit." And when they ordered her to exit, I just followed her; none of the SS-women noticed. Only a few of our girls were trembling. As long as I was within the radius of the reflectors, I walked very slowly, but in the dark I started to run and fell on my bed; only now did I begin to shake. It was my sixth sense that caused me to disappear; it has saved me in quite a number of dangerous situations.

In October 1944, five of our comrades, among them Ernstl Burger, attempted to escape and were betrayed by the "helpful" SS-man. The SS could not make up their minds whether or not to execute them. Three times, the gallows were erected in the men's camp, and the third time they were hanged.[19] A week later, the four girls of the kommando "Union," who had smuggled explosives for the uprising of the Sonderkommando, were hanged.[20]

In December 1944, I erroneously addressed SS-Obersturmfuehrer Pollok, whom we had feared all those years, as "Unterscharfuehrer." To my surprise, he retorted, "It seems you would like to degrade me." Well, if you talk to me, you'll get an appropriate answer, that had been my motto throughout all of those years:

"Herr Obersturmfuehrer, if already, then all the way." "But I am going to fight dearly for my life ..."

"You? If I would say so ..."

He turned red, turned around and was quiet. That is an illustration of the mood among the SS.

At the beginning of January 1945, there suddenly appeared a new SS-man in the planning archives, where I had been in charge since the Polish prisoner who had worked there had been sent to Gross-Rosen. And the SS-man barked at me, "Where are the plans for the crematorium?" I went to the drawer and opened it; the plans were gone. "Well, you probably knew what to do with them." I became furious, "Do you believe we would have waited until you came along?" Indeed, all the plans had been smuggled out of camp; not in vain did we have the blue print room and the connection to Polish civilian employees. The SS-man then dictated a list of the crematorium plans and even took the carbon away from me. Of course, we knew that Auschwitz was going to be evacuated; we learned it the instant the plan arrived at the Political Section. The camp underground decided to attempt to prevent the evacuation. They wanted to accomplish this with the help of the SS-Standortarzt (camp physician-in-chief) Wirths. My future husband was given the task to get in touch with Wirths because he had experience in this field; he had been evacuated from Lublin to Auschwitz. Thus, he wrote a letter to Wirths, without his prison number and asked for an appointment, just signing "Dr. Soswinski." Our comrade, Karl Lill, who worked for Wirths, gave him the letter. One day later, when I came to the Bauleitung, my husband told me that he had received a summons to appear before Kirschner at the Political Section. It is superfluous to describe how we both felt. Then he was gone for two hours; it seemed an eternity to me. Kirschner had the letter he had written to Dr. Wirths, and my husband already saw himself dangling from the gallows. But the more questions Kirschner posed, the calmer he became. Finally, this notorious murderer told him, "If you want something in the future, address yourself directly to me." Even this happened in Auschwitz in 1945—notabene only 40 kilometers away from the front.

When we heard about the planned evacuation, I immediately said I would try to escape, come what may. I simply had the feeling I would not be able to survive a third concentration camp. I believe my husband was not convinced of my succeeding in such an undertaking, otherwise he would not have asked so desperately for news about me in May 1945, when he was already back in Vienna, from many returnees of different camps. Nobody could tell him about me. I, on the other hand, learned that he was alive and already in Vienna from a friend, a former prisoner who had also been evacuated from Auschwitz to Mauthausen. Then I met a Viennese who was returning from Dachau and on his way to Vienna via Prague. I gave him a note; the first news. And by the middle of June 1945, I was already in Vienna.

To write about my escape, respectively the escape of almost the entire Bauleitungskommando, would prolong this essay considerably. Let me only mention that we were helped by a little SS-man, a Volksdeutscher from Rumania, who had had more than enough and also wanted to get away. His only weapon was a "Panzerfaust" (kind of rocket used against tanks) of which he was more afraid than of the devil. Moreover, three Polish peasant families helped us, risking their lives. In Upper Silesia, the front had formed a basin and German gendarmes and Gestapo who had already escaped returned for some time. We, therefore, divided our group into pairs. I went with Trude, since both of us wanted to go to Prague. In Strumienie (Schwarzwasser), the front passed us during the second week of February 1945. When spring commenced, we entered the former territory of Czechoslovakia, the Carpatho-Ukraine, which now belongs to the Soviet Union. We were free!

However, today I still cannot forget, and it is probably the same for all of us who have survived the inferno. Physically and mentally, I am a marked person. But we all have to write about it, we have to tell about it so that it will never, never occur again!!!

Looking at our world at present, I wonder whether humanity did learn anything from this enormous catastrophe?!

NOTES

Herta Soswinski

1   Siebenbuergen is German for Transylvania.

2   Don Isaac Abarbanel (1437-1508) was a religious philosopher and influential minister at the court of Ferdinand and Isabella in Spain.

3   Youth Aliyah (or Aliya), a Zionist organization for the transfer of children and young persons to Israel, founded in 1933 by Recha Freyer.

4   Techelet Lavan is a Hebrew name (Blau-Weiss in German) for a Zionist youth movement.

5   The Munich Pact was an agreement between Hitler, Chamberlain, Mussolini and Daladier in September 1938 for the partition of Czechoslovakia.

6   The story of the writer, Milena Jesenska, who died in Ravensbrueck, is told by her friend and co-prisoner Margarete Buber-Neumann (Buber-Neumann, 1988).

7   Kaethe Leichter was a militant Austrian Social Democrat arrested in Vienna during the Nazi occupation. Rosa Jochmann paid tribute to her in her reminiscences *Mit Offenen Augen* and told how she received the last communication from Kaethe, after she had been transferred from Ravensbrueck with the first transport of Jewish women:

   ... Kaethe told me "if it will be possible, I'll send you a note." When the dresses of the women were returned I told the prisoners of the disinfection detail: be careful, in case you have number so-and-so please look under the sewn number for some kind of news. There was a torn-off yellow slip: "We are driving through Dessau. Good reception everywhere," and then, as if somebody had pushed her. Now I know what it was. In Dessau they were led directly into the gas chamber (Berger, Holzinger, Podgornik, Trallori, 1987, pp. 182-184).

8   According to Fernando Morais, who chronicled the life of Olga Benario-Prestes, the Ravensbrueck prisoners knew that the transferred Jewish women had been sent to Bernburg,

but they did not know what it stood for. He writes:

A plan was devised to learn where the prisoners were being taken. Several of the transferees were given pencil and paper and asked to record the name of every place they could identify along the way and stuff the small scraps of paper into the hems of their skirts when they arrived at their final destination. Once the clothes were returned to the camp it would be possible to pinpoint exactly where they had been taken. The first truck to return after the scheme was put into action did not completely clarify the women's fate. The notes found in their skirt hems repeated the same name: Bernburg. But what did that mean? (Morais, 1990, p. 231).

9   Friedrich Torberg, a deceased Viennese writer born in 1908, lived from 1938-51 as an emigrant in Switzerland and the USA.

10   "In 1941 the first Ravensbrueck 'book' appeared. Conceived by Anicka Kvapilova, it was dedicated to Milena. It was an anthology of remembered Czech poems, written in pencil on stolen paper and carefully bound in stolen toweling, colored with light blue tailor's chalk" (Buber-Neumann, 1988, p. 160).

11   On October 6, 1942, 622 women prisoners, transferred from KL Ravensbrueck, receive the numbers 21428 to 22049. There are 522 Jewish prisoners among them. During the reception procedure these prisoners watch the truck carrying the murdered women from the penal Kommando in Budy pass by (Czech, 1989, p. 315). One of the prisoners of this transport was Dagmar Ostermann, #21946 (Shelley, 1986, pp. 170-183); another was Charlotte Tetzner, #21962.

12   *Herz Jesu Verehrung* is German for Adoration of the Heart of Jesus, a sect propagated by the nun Marie Alacoque (1647-1690), canonized in 1920.

13   Garlinski reports about Herta's activity in the camp's resistance movement: "When the women took over Section B I b in the summer of 1943, an underground group was set up there too, led by Herta Soswinski. To this group belonged the Russians Irina Ivannikova, Zhenia Sarycheva and Viktoria Nikitina" (Garlinski, 1975, p. 125).

14   It might have been the SS-man described by Vera Foltynova, a prisoner of the Bauleitung work squad, in the following way: "When SS-Hauptsturmfuehrer Schosenow, who came from Latvia and had been transferred recently to the Bauleitung in Birkenau in the summer of 1944, saw the long trains moving in the direction of the crematoria and learned the fate of the human cargo, he said, 'I am not a murderer, I am a soldier.' In a few days he went to the front" (Langbein, 1972, p. 478).

15   Langbein confirms that the inmates Krystyna Horczak, Waleria Walova and Vera Foltynova, who worked in the office of the Zentralbauleitung, secretly made copies of the camp plans and of the construction plans of the crematoria with gas chambers which were sent, together with other information, to Czechoslovakia (Langbein, 1972, p. 291).

16   Dejaco was involved in a search for a practical method to dispose of the bodies in the mass graves of Birkenau, since fisheries in the surrounding areas were complaining about poisoning of the groundwater through cadaver toxin. "On September 16, 1942, Rudolf Hoess, the commandant of Auschwitz, SS-Untersturmfuehrer Hoessler and SS-Untersturmfuehrer Dejaco of the Zentralbauleitung went to Chelmno, where SS-Standartenfuehrer Blobel showed them the installation for the cremation of corpses. The purpose of the inspection was to discover a way to empty the mass graves of Birkenau, to cremate the bodies and to remove the ashes in order to eliminate all traces of the crime" (Czech, 1989, p. 301).

17   SS-Obersturmbannfuehrer Oskar Dirlewanger, the commandant of the special SS unit (Sondereinheit) recruited from among German concentration camp inmates with black or

green triangles.

18   On September 13, 1944, from 11:17 a.m. to 11:30 a.m., the I.G. Farben factory at Dwory, near Auschwitz, was bombed. As in previous air raids, no attempts were made to destroy the extermination facilities. Some bombs also fell on the KL Auschwitz. In the camp extension, four SS residences were damaged as well as half of Block 6, where women prisoners working in SS offices were lodged. Fifteen SS men were killed and 28 severely injured in their living quarters, and one female prisoner was killed in Block 6 (Czech, 1989, p. 876).

19   On December 30, 1944, five members of the camp resistance movement Kampfgruppe Auschwitz whose attempted escape had been betrayed by SS Rottenfuehrer Johannes Roth were hanged: the Austrian prisoners Ernst Burger (#23850), Rudolf Friemel (#25173) and Ludwig Vesely (#38169); and the Polish prisoners Piotr Piaty (#130380) and Bernard Swierczyna (#1393). They refused to have their eyes covered and shouted before the hanging: "Down with Hitler!", "Down with Fascism!", "Today we—tomorrow you!", "Long live Poland!" (Sobanski, 1980, pp. 207-219; Czech, 1989, pp. 917, 944, 953-954).

20   The first memorial plaque for the four girls who had smuggled the gunpowder out of the Union factory was dedicated on May 22, 1985, in Froendenberg, Germany, a little town where the headquarters of the Weichselmetall Union Werke were located. In Jerusalem there is a memorial for the four heroines.

PART THREE
Different Workshops of the Stabsgebaeude

On June 14, 1940, the first transport arrived at the Stabsgebaeude, receiving prison numbers 31-758. This started KZ-Auschwitz, which became the largest extermination camp in Europe.

(Inscription at the Monopol building in Auschwitz)

The Stabsgebaeude (staff building), i.e., the pre- and post-World War II monopoly building in Auschwitz, was the beginning of the most notorious of Nazi concentration camps.

In 1942 it was used as living quarters for the SS-women. In the basement, the SS laundry was washed, ironed and mended. After the transfer of the women's camp from Auschwitz to Birkenau the women prisoners of the laundry, ironing and mending work squads were equally housed in the cellar of the Stabsgebaeude, together with the girls of several office kommandos. For the convenience of the SS Aufseherinnen, a work detail of expert seamstresses and of beauticians was added.

During the summer of 1944 all inmates were transferred to the new camp extension. The workshops of the laundry, ironing, mending and sewing details were moved to the "leather factory." Like all other prisoners, the women of these work squads now marched out to work, enabling them to catch at least a breath of fresh air, while beforehand, they had not been able to leave the building.

CHAPTER 10

Laundry Detail

Eva Brewster (widowed Raphael, née Levy)
Coutts, Alberta (Canada)

I was born on December 28, 1922, near the end of the terrible post-World War I inflation in Germany. My father, Albert Levy, owned one of the largest food import/export firms in Berlin. His first wife had died during the flu epidemic of 1918, leaving him with three young children. At the time he married my mother, Elizabeth Moses, who was only 19 years old herself, my oldest stepsister was already 12, my stepbrother ten and the youngest girl three years old. So, from the day I was born in the house in Berlin, where I was to live for the first 16 years of my life, I was spoiled and pampered, not only by my parents but also by the three older siblings, a nanny, a cook and three maids.

Because my father could pay his hundreds of employees with ample supplies of sugar, flour, cocoa, coffee, etc., when millions of marks wouldn't buy a single egg, we survived the inflation and later, the great depression, relatively well, keeping not only our family but also innumerable German staff, their wives and children afloat. They all adored my father, and since our ancestors had lived in the Berlin area for centuries and my father had fought in the First World War and lost his younger brother on the battlefield, he never saw the handwriting on the wall when Hitler first surfaced in German politics. Nor did he heed the warnings of "brothers" who—one after another, deserted his Freemasons' Lodge to join the

Nazi party.

I remember my paternal grandfather only as an independently wealthy old gentleman, very tall with silver-white hair and a long, white beard. His name was Joseph Levy and he took me for long walks through the Berlin parks, the zoo, and the famous, later infamous, Unter den Linden Boulevard. He introduced me to our family history and well-known ancestors, including one who was physician to King Frederic the Great, another, the composer Meyerbeer, and the "Spanish connection," his wife's ancestors. The latter had fled to Germany via France during the Spanish Inquisition and married into our already well-established family in Berlin.

I never knew this grandmother. She died very young of diabetes before insulin was discovered. But she was a wonderful painter and left behind the most beautiful oils and water colors. All her large oil paintings were lost during World War II, but I still have a very beautiful water color flower painting she did as a young girl in March 1872, signed "Martha Cohen," her maiden name. She was a recognized artist in her lifetime and had been asked to exhibit her paintings in Berlin, Paris and London, but my grandfather wouldn't allow her to do this. It wasn't done in the Victorian age and socially unacceptable in patrician circles for a wife to appear in public as a "bohemian." I realize now that my own early painting and writing ventures were a subconscious attempt to right a wrong done to outstanding women of another generation.

My maternal grandfather, Simon Moses, owned a brewery in Gleiwitz, Upper Silesia. He and my grandmother Else, née Schweitzer, had five children, one boy and four girls, of which my mother was the second youngest. The brewery went bankrupt in the stock market crash of 1929. My lovely grandmother couldn't face the "disgrace" and committed suicide. My grandfather moved to Berlin and lived with us until after my father's death in 1938. He then joined his two elderly sisters and all three swallowed lethal pills during a Gestapo raid and mass arrests of old people who were to be deported to a then unknown destination.

My younger brother, Stefan, born January 15, 1924, and I knew little about political developments and economic disasters before 1933. Our parents protected us from any outside influences they thought might ruin our happy childhood. I went to elementary school in Berlin from 1928 until 1932 and then to high school from 1932 till 1938, when Jewish children were expelled from all public schools.

On January 25, 1938, my father was "invited"—it was a summons—to have dinner with the then Minister of State Backe.[1] When he came home after midnight, my mother wakened me and asked me to stay with him while she phoned our family doctor. My father was very ill, but still tried to stop my worrying. "You don't have to order a wreath yet," he said. "Backe made me eat oysters before telling me that an 'Aryan' would take over my business next Monday. So, darling, don't cry. We'll go on a long, lovely holiday. Just be a good girl and get me a glass of water with ice cubes. I'm very thirsty." By the time I got back with the water and before the doctor arrived, he was dead—heart failure.

My mother was inconsolable and decided to leave home to take up nursing at the Jewish Hospital in Berlin. But first she arranged for my younger brother to be sent to a boarding school in Sweden. She would have liked me to go with him, but I still wasn't ready to leave. After I was expelled from high school, she enrolled me in the Jewish Domestic Science School in August Strasse, which, a few years later, would be the collection center for Jews to be deported.

I was left alone with my grandfather and a succession of Jewish maids in our huge, deserted house. The "Aryan" maids and cook were forced to leave us because of a new racial law that forbade "Aryan" women to stay in a household where there was a man under the age of 70. In spite of everything, I still enjoyed life with the boy I had loved since I was 12 years old. We had a sailing yacht on which we sailed on the many lakes around Berlin, making crazy plans to escape via canals to the North Sea and across the Channel to England. The plan never materialized because all exits were too heavily guarded by then. We applied for visas to the U.S., Canada and just about every country in the free world.

Still, with the optimism of youth, I married the boy I would have married anyway some day. My father already knew that we were engaged although he didn't take this too seriously. He had told me that I would have his blessings in ten years' time if or when we both had finished our studies and if we were still as much in love by then. We got married on the 9th of February, 1939. But by the time we got permission and an exit visa to leave, war had broken out and we were trapped.

Our baby daughter, Reha, was born on July 11, 1940, by which time my parents' house had been requisitioned by the German Broadcasting Company's executives and we had moved in with my husband's parents, who also had a large home.

For the next two years, we lived like most other Jews left in Berlin. Both my husband and I were forced into slave labor factories and had to leave our little girl in a Jewish day-care center. Food rations for Jews were reduced constantly, but my husband was a very good carpenter and managed to sell odd pieces of small furniture or book shelves privately. We then had a little money to buy supplements to our meager rations in the thriving black market.

Our child was just two and a half years old when my mother suddenly appeared one night to warn us of an impending roundup of young mothers and children. A Gestapo officer attached to the Jewish Hospital by then, had told her that all Jewish families with babies would soon be evacuated and deported to the East. I immediately decided to hide our small daughter. My mother-in-law vetoed the plan. She said that we would all be killed if the Gestapo discovered that the child had disappeared from our home. I, therefore, took no chances and with my husband's consent got a quick, uncontested divorce to enable him and his mother—my father-in-law had died of a heart attack before this happened—to swear that they knew nothing of my whereabouts or of what I had done with the child. I then moved with Reha into a room rented from another Jewish family and arranged with a Christian nurse, a friend of my mother, for her to take my little daughter to her brother's farm in East Prussia. She would tell him that Reha's parents had been killed in an early bombing raid. We had never taught Reha her real name; all she knew were her pet names so that she could not give herself away.

As soon as my child had been taken into hiding, I joined the Resistance and, after a short period of training in disguise, memorizing my fictitious past in case I was caught, and given false identity papers, I was sent to Strassbourg for further instructions. Shortly after that, the Resistance dispatched me to Dornbirn, a German border post to Switzerland, with some technical drawings I was to take to agents across the border, crossing illegally, of course. Another Resistance member by the name of Peter was to guide me over the mountains. After three similar missions I was promised that I could stay in Switzerland and that my husband and child would be helped to join me.

However, I was arrested on arrival in Dornbirn before my guide could contact me. The headquarters of the Berlin section of the Resistance had been raided and, probably to save more important members, the Gestapo had been given the names of a few new and inexperienced ones like me who couldn't reveal any secrets or names even under torture. The equally inexperienced young Gestapo officers didn't wait long enough to meet my Resistance guide as well and that saved me from a firing squad. "Peter" turned out to be the regular police officer in charge of the border station. He came to the cellar room I had been locked up in, quietly identified himself and burned the documents I was carrying before the Gestapo could search me. Although the latter didn't find any proof that I was the person they were looking for, they did condemn me to death by firing squad, that decision based on a telegram from Berlin which gave details of my real name and my intended mission. "Peter" took it upon himself to call the Gestapo headquarters in Berlin and told them that I might or might not be the person they were looking for; but, he explained, the officers attached to his police station were not experienced enough to find that out. So, Berlin ordered him to have me sent back for further interrogation. That was on February 4, 1943.

Two months and eleven prisons later—I described that tortuous transit in my book *Vanished in Darkness*—I landed in Berlin again. Given official release papers, the woman in charge of female prisoners told me I could go home and admonished me to "behave" and to keep away from jail in the future. German prison staff seemed completely unaware that there was a campaign to eliminate Jews from the community. They presumed or were told that young people like me had committed some petty crimes and should be returned to their parents.

My husband, too, had been arrested trying to escape to Switzerland and while we were both on the run and returned to the capital, his mother had been deported and her house and property had been confiscated. My freedom was short-lived. While I was still contemplating how to get from Moabit to the Jewish Hospital and to my mother, the Gestapo shadowed and rearrested me in the first side-street I had walked to. They pushed me into a waiting taxi, took me to their dreaded headquarters and there, interrogated me for what seemed hours. They obviously knew all about me and didn't ask a single question concerning the Resistance. All they wanted to know was where I had hidden my child and when they realized that I wasn't going to tell them, they beat and kicked me into unconsciousness. I screamed at one point, "Oh, mother, help!" After that, they stopped beating me and promised to get my mother, to do the same to her and to get her to answer their questions. I was then taken to the deportation center, my former domestic science school, where a transport of mainly very young people was being prepared. They came from different agricultural camps where they had worked in preparation for emigration to Palestine.

A girl, Anne Borinski, took care of me immediately, bandaged my lacerated back and put a cool, damp facecloth on my bruised face. Still barely conscious, I don't know how much later my mother arrived, still in her nurse's uniform and unharmed. She had been arrested at work and was taken to the same two men who had interrogated me. Although we had originally agreed to say my child had been taken to Italy if we were ever asked, we both realized at Gestapo headquarters that Italy was no longer a safe place since Hitler had concluded a pact with Mussolini. So, on the spur of the moment, we both told the Gestapo that my daughter was safe in Switzerland. I don't think the officers believed either of us. There is evidence that the Gestapo officer attached to the Jewish Hospital, my torturers' superior, protected her and probably told his underlings that they were not to touch her. He even came to the train depot the day we were finally deported, brought her back to me from the cattle car filled with old people she had been told to join and said to me, "Tell me where you have hidden your child and I'll take your mother back to the hospital in my own car. I promise you that nothing will happen to your baby. She'll be with you and you will not be separated again. And your mother will remain safely in Berlin under my protection and continue nursing the sick here. I think the world of her and her life is in your hands. If you don't confess, I can't help her either." It was a terrible decision to make, but since we both thought Reha was safe, my mother signaled me not to talk and insisted on going with me into what we thought was going to be a family camp somewhere in the East. On April 20, 1943, in honor of Hitler's birthday, this last and largest transport of young German Jews, joined at the last minute by remnants of two Jewish senior citizens' homes and some young mothers with children, left for an unknown destination.

Much has been written about those terrifying days and nights in overcrowded, airless cattle trains which had been bolted and locked from the outside prior to departure. None of us knew where we were going and what to expect.

On arrival, after two or three days and nights in a cattle train, we arrived in Auschwitz although, at that time, we didn't know where we were. There was no station, just a platform of yellow mud trampled hard by previous arrivals. Brutal SS guards, under the supervision of the infamous Dr. Mengele, immediately separated young men and women. The old people, mothers and children, also stood apart. "They'll go to a better camp for a good, long rest," we were told. Only my mother, probably because she looked much younger than her 41 years and because Mengele still had some respect for her nurse's uniform, was allowed to stay with us girls.

Still dazed from the trauma and degradation of being tattooed (I became number 41959), from having our heads, underarm and pubic hair shaved in front of leering guards and having our good clothes replaced with old rags, we spent a miserable night. Cold and hungry, a Blockova roused us from the bare brick shelves to scramble out of the barracks over dead bodies of inmates who had died overnight.

A 17-year-old SS-woman took that first interminable roll call that morning. Her name was Irma Grese and after the war she was tried and condemned to death by hanging for her sadistic cruelty and the large number of deaths she was personally responsible for. I had to look at the tattoo on my arm before I realized my number had been called. But what struck me most on that cold April morning was the smirk and air of satisfaction on our Blockova's face. A Jewish prisoner like ourselves, who had arrived in Auschwitz with one of the early transports from Czechoslovakia, she seemed proud and happy to report the number of dead found in our barracks during the night.[2]

That day I received my first lesson in survival. After working prisoners had moved out, the camp was deserted. Except for the guards on watchtowers, there wasn't a soul to be seen, no sound of any living creature, not even birds. Even the tall chimneys just outside the electric fence of Birkenau which, we had been told on arrival, were "Germany's most productive factories" and which had been smoking furiously the night before, were dead.

Turning a corner, I saw an old woman sitting in the early morning sun, leaning against the wall of a hut, trying to warm her wrinkled face and claw-like hands. She asked me to sit down and knew already what transport I had arrived with. "We know everything here," she said. "Just looking at a fellow inmate's eyes, I can tell you when they are going to die. But I also know you are going to live. You may be a skeleton soon, but unlike me, you are a fighter. Would you believe that I was 19 years old two days ago?"

That little person's name was Ruth Cohen, the last of the Cohens from Hamburg. Her parents and little sister had never been admitted into the camp and had been killed on arrival. She put a gentle, cold hand on mine: "May I tell you a few facts about Birkenau that might help you to survive? They are horrible, but you'd find out sooner or later. The sooner you know what is going on, the better a chance you'll have to brace yourself while you are still strong enough to have some initiative."

The "factories," she told me, were huge gas chambers where old people, mothers and children, the weak and the sick were sent for that "good, long rest" the SS doctor had mentioned when we arrived. "Don't ever report sick," Ruth warned me, "and if you are ill, don't volunteer for a 'better camp.' Such an offer of 'new opportunities' is a ruse the SS use to bring sick prisoners out of hiding.

And never run from an SS dog. Stand still and he'll not attack or, if he's already got his teeth in you, he'll let go." She told me of a very beautiful woman, the only woman over 40 in her transport allowed into the camp, who had been torn apart by those dogs just a few days prior to my arrival. She had tried to get away when a vicious guard had set the dog on her. That woman, I learned, was Paula Raphael, my lovely mother-in-law. "Don't be ashamed to cry," said Ruth. "Only tears can save your sanity here."

She spent her last energy telling me all this and much more. Much of her advice did indeed help me later to survive in situations where a wrong move or decision would have meant certain death. But at that moment all I could think about was how to help her. When I had to leave and promised to come back later with some bread as soon as we would receive our ration, she smiled and said in a voice so low I had to bend down to hear her, "I'm tired, so tired of this rotten life and, really, I'm not hungry anymore while you need every crust of bread you can get hold of just to survive. Anyway, I won't be here anymore. Good bye and good luck. Look after your mother; you are so lucky to have her." I had not mentioned my mother; but I was to learn much later and from bitter experience the kind of extrasensory perception one can develop when being starved to death or about to die.

Not until the next day did I manage to get back to Ruth with an extra ration we had been given. But her Blockova, a dragon of a woman, told me with great satisfaction that Ruth had "kicked the bucket" during the night. "Good riddance," she added. "That miserable Muselmann refused to work from the start, was always moping and can now rot in her grave for long enough!"

The previous day, when I got back after meeting Ruth, the girls of my transport had already lined up for an unannounced roll call in front of an SS officer who said he was the "Labor Leader." Because he came from Berlin and claimed to have a "soft spot" for the girls from "our great capital," he promised to give us a break, a good working commando and double rations. And then, probably because I drew his attention by turning up late and, when asked what I thought of Birkenau, told him what an evil, cruel place it was, he appointed me Capo of the new crew. We were to collect "vegetables" for the camp kitchen, that is, nettles which grew in abundance in the vicinity of the camp.

My mother was already ill when we started. She couldn't keep down even the black brew we got to drink, had dysentery and was too weak to move out with us. After a few days, when we returned from outside work, she had disappeared. Our Blockova said she had been chosen for the sewing room in the SS staff headquarters near Auschwitz, but I didn't believe her. Unhappy and more defiant than ever, I told a passing Capo what I thought of her cruelty to the poor skeletons she was in charge of, was duly deported and was given two weeks hard labor as punishment.

Hard labor consisted of carrying big, heavy rocks from one place to another; I still don't know what, if anything, they were used for. But if 20 prisoners went out in the morning, no more than ten returned at night. Half our number was beaten to death if they collapsed, or if they didn't, sent by the guards to retrieve their drinking bottles or caps dropped at the perimeter of our place of work and then shot or torn up by the dogs for "trying to escape."

The day my punishment ended on May 19, 1943, I was returned to our Blockova with instructions that I was to have a delousing session, a hot bath in the sauna and double rations again. The next day, I was to rejoin the girls of my transport to be incorporated in the "white caps," a kommando working in the men's camp in Birkenau sorting out and bundling for dispatch to Germany the clothes and possessions of newly arrived transports.

That day, I experienced for the first time the kind of ESP Ruth had demonstrated just before her death, something I have, since then, associated with extreme starvation. The few prisoners who survived and who had that inexplicable knowledge of events to come or taking place elsewhere, lost that "second sight" as soon as they were free and well-fed again.

It is impossible for me to relive again that terrible day in the spring of 1943 when my husband and child arrived in an unexpected transport from Berlin. I have written about it in my book. Suffice it to say that I knew it and nobody believed me. My husband, who was allowed into the Birkenau men's camp, was to tell me later how the Gestapo had discovered our little daughter.

The farmer, who had taken her into his home, was being badgered and threatened by the local Nazi party boss because he could not produce identity papers or birth certificate for the child. Frightened, he asked his sister to take her back to Berlin if she could not get the necessary documents. So, the Christian nurse collected her and left her in a Catholic orphanage. The nuns had loved her and looked after her well, but could not prevent the Gestapo taking photographs of those of their charges whose background and identity were unknown. A plainclothes police woman then took the pictures to various Jewish organizations and institutions, including the Jewish Hospital. She left them on the matron's desk and sat quietly in a corner when a young nurse came in to see the matron about something. She took one look at the photos and said, "What a lovely child! Isn't that Elizabeth's granddaughter? She is her spitting image!"

The police woman soon returned with Reha and, having found out that my husband was still on the isolation ward with scarlet fever, confronted him with our little daughter. She ran to him immediately, of course, climbed on the bed, threw her little arms around him and cried, "My Daddy!" Both of them were then included in the transport that arrived in Auschwitz on May 19, 1943.

Also in that transport was a former teacher of mine, a Mrs. Unger. She had been in hiding with her six-year-old stepson, a child from her husband's previous marriage. On arrival when men, women and children were separated, she persuaded my husband to let her take our daughter to me. As ignorant of what was happening to women (or men) with young children as we had been, she was convinced that a mother could do a better job of looking after the kids than a father, no matter under what circumstances. That teacher I had loved long before I was married, went to the gas chambers with two children—neither of them her own.

I lost my will to live then, but my friends and the incentive to see my husband and to keep him alive made me carry on. Working in the "Canada" kommando in the men's camp gave me the chance to give him clean clothes and would have enabled him to get extra food rations, had he accepted them. But he was so terrified of the man in charge of his barracks, one of the most sadistic German criminals, that he refused to take them.

A few weeks later, a new kommando was formed which was to load shoes onto trains bound for Germany outside the SS staff quarters. Our Blockova persuaded me to join that new group with a dual purpose in mind—I could find out at last whether my mother was alive and working in the sewing room there, and at the same time, ask the Blockova's sister why she had not kept her promise to get a transfer for the Blockova to the staff quarters.

It took days of loading mountains of shoes, the good footwear of probably thousands of now barefooted prisoners and thousands of dead, before I could even get a glimpse of staff-quarter girls through their basement windows. But eventually, when the first full train moved off, we got a chance to talk to the prisoners there and found out that my mother really was alive. For once, the "job offer" had been genuine. Because everybody else had gone into hiding that day, believing it was a selection for the gas chambers, the SS took my mother—the only volunteer—in spite of her poor health.

Whenever our guards looked the other way, I could talk to my mother until, one day, my friends brought me a note from my husband telling me that he would be working in the women's camp putting a roof on latrines. Our Blockova agreed to keep me off work for a few days so that I could meet him after one more day loading shoes, when I could tell my mother why she wouldn't see me for a while. I stayed behind in Birkenau the following day, but it was one day too late. The men had a selection for the gas chambers the night before where 1000 of them were killed—my husband among them. One of his friends told me that there was nothing wrong with him except that he had a sore throat and lost his voice. Asked by the SS for his number, he whispered in reply and trying to talk louder, his voice broke. That was enough to condemn him to death.

Desperate to see my mother, the only loved person left to me now, I jumped across the fenders of the train the following morning while the other prisoners were starting to load shoes. I hadn't noticed that we had different, brutal guards that day. One of them let his dog off the leash and set it on me. It got hold of my leg but, remembering what Ruth had told me, I didn't move and the dog let go of me. Before that happened, my mother had thrown me a loaf of white bread which the guard took and trampled into the mud. On return to the camp that night, he reported me at the gate and, once again, I was condemned to hard labor, this time for an indefinite period.

Again, more than half of our daily contingent died. Their bodies were thrown into an open mass grave close to the trenches we had to dig. I, too, was getting weaker and weaker, unable to eat even the small food ration we got at night. But, plagued by thirst, I accepted a bowl of water from passing gypsies which, I was told by a guard, came from the swamps beside the crematorium. That water was probably the cause of typhoid fever that landed me in the hospital barracks eventually. That sojourn too, the inhuman treatment of patients there, being left without even straw mattresses and blankets which were sent for "delousing," without medical or any other help is described in my book. And so is the death of a very young Greek girl who died with her arms round me in the narrow bunk we had to share. She didn't know a word of German or any language other than Greek and probably never understood how or why she had come to this death camp.

I was in a coma then, thrown on the stone floor in a corner and declared dead, but came to when a rat was crawling on my legs. I managed, somehow, to get back into a bunk bed and was found there by Doctor Mengele during one of his inspection tours. When I asked him to release me and claimed I was fit enough to go back to work, he remembered, and mistook me for, my mother. Once again, he saved the person he thought of as a qualified nurse. I was the last prisoner to get out of those hospital barracks alive. All other patients were taken to the gas chambers the following night.

Even then, I would not have survived without the constant help of my friends. They had to hold me up and practically carry me to work or roll calls, do my quota of sorting clothes back in the men's camp and left me to rest covered with blankets. Inevitably, I failed the next selection tests and fell into the ditch we had to jump over in order to survive. At the very last minute, I was saved from the gas chambers by the SS woman in charge of the staff quarters, SS Brunner. She had promised my mother months ago to get me transferred to the staff quarters and my mother, worried because she hadn't heard from me for so long, had reminded her constantly until, perhaps by coincidence, Brunner decided to go to Birkenau and get me the day that would have been my last.

How I managed to get from Birkenau to the staff quarters, running after the SS-woman's bicycle and prodded along at the point of a guard's bayonet behind me, is still a mystery to me. But once there and united with my mother, life became a lot easier than it had been in Birkenau.

With more and better food, the physical help from all the girls in the SS laundry—they did part of my allotted washing for me until I regained some strength—and my mother's love and care, I recovered fairly quickly. Our food rations were augmented by almost daily gifts from a young Dutch SS-woman—I have forgotten her name. She had come to love my mother and got into the habit of calling her upstairs, presumably to get a massage for pain in her neck or shoulder muscles. In reality, she just wanted to talk and confide her fears of the future, once the war was over, and her regrets of the past. Her father had thrown her out and disowned her when he found out that she had an affair with a German SS officer after the Nazis occupied Holland. She had followed her lover to Auschwitz, not knowing what she was coming to. She never got used to the brutality and death around her but, I suppose, was too weak and scared to leave. But to us, in the staff quarters, and previously in Birkenau, she was consistently kind, always tried to help us and never betrayed us, knowing full well if or when we secretly talked to men or managed to "organize" extra food.

On December 27, 1943, we received our very first Red Cross parcel. I remember the exact date because it happened to be the day before my 21st birthday and I had hoped to divide the sardines and chocolate cookies among all the girls in my dormitory on the 28th. When we went to work, the Red Cross parcels were left on our bunk beds. There were no lockers or any other place to keep them. When we returned, they were gone. The SS raided our bunks for any unauthorized possessions most of us collected from time to time and hid under the mattresses, such as combs, small cracked mirrors or pencil stubs found in the SS-women's waste paper baskets. This time, they took the authorized parcel as well. The Dutch SS-woman replaced all my losses and gave my mother a few additional goodies that night as a birthday present to me.

In 1944, all prisoners housed in the staff quarter basement—laundry, sewing room and the so-called political department personnel—were moved out and transferred to a brand-new camp near Auschwitz consisting of four identical two-story solid houses surrounded by a single-strand barbed wire fence. Only one of those houses was separated from the others by an additional double fence—a camp within the camp. It was to house the "guinea pigs," female prisoners undergoing the most cruel "medical" experiments of modern times, on orders and under supervision of SS doctors. Their crimes have been revealed in trials and in books.

One of the other three new blocks was reserved for prostitutes, prisoners kept to amuse SS guards and passing German soldiers on their way to or back from the Russian front. The latter were billeted in houses identical to ours, built on the other side of the wire fencing. The prisoners' accommodation was unbelievably luxurious by Auschwitz standards—clean, airy dormitories, no bars on the windows, bunk beds with matching eiderdown covers, tables and chairs, and woven mats on the stone floors. There were tiled shower rooms and toilets. We soon learned that this camp had been built with the intention of throwing it open to International Red Cross inspection to show the world how well prisoners had been treated.

Before we had left the SS staff quarters, SS Brunner had asked us for a list of any friends we knew were still alive in Birkenau. She promised us their transfer to the new camp, where much larger premises for the SS laundry and sewing room would require a lot more workers. SS Brunner kept her promise and the girls we had named were already in the camp when we arrived.

The laundry and sewing room were now established in a complex of buildings which, built round a cobblestoned yard, was probably a small factory before the war. It was always referred to as "the factory" for the period we worked there. It was about a mile's march from our new camp. We had to work even harder here than we did in the staff quarters. Now, in addition to the clothes of SS-women and a limited number of guards, we got the uniforms of male SS officers from sur-

rounding camps as well as those of passing soldiers billeted in the barracks close
to ours. But there were compensations. While our food was once again brought
from the Auschwitz camp kitchens, almost as bad as it had been in Birkenau, we
now had the opportunity to meet with privileged, mostly German male prisoners
who worked in another building within the complex. They traded for food and
other items required by the SS in the town of Auschwitz, accompanied by only
one guard, often a guard who could be bribed to keep his mouth shut if the prisoners did a little trading for themselves. Some of these men brought us their washing
and paid with food. Some fell in love with a girl and would look after her, keeping
her supplied with almost anything she needed.

Otto, the man who singled me out, was the men's Capo. He had been in various concentration camps since 1933 for having been involved in a street brawl between Hitler Youth and young Communists shortly after Hitler came to power. He
befriended my mother first and was old-fashioned enough to ask her permission to
meet and talk with me. Unlike many of the other men, he never asked for any fa-
vors in return and if he had any plans for the future which included me, he never
once talked about them. All he wanted to do was to see us through ordeals to
come, to feed and clothe us adequately and to keep us fit and strong enough for
the exodus he foresaw once the Russians advanced into Poland. He schemed end-
lessly in the hope of escaping with us and had enough uncut diamonds stashed
away—I have no idea how he got them—to bribe guards. But his plans never materialized because he knew that a majority of Poles hated Jews as much or more
than the Germans and wouldn't have hesitated to hand us over to the SS.

In the meantime, we had yet to live through the summer, fall and winter of
1944. Otto kept us well-informed of allied victories and advances. He was, and remained, a dedicated, idealistic Communist and was one of the men operating a secret radio transmitter and receiver in the men's camp. Unfortunately, the Nazis
were equally well-informed and every German retreat and defeat was triggering
reprisals on the helpless prisoners in the Birkenau death camp.

That summer, we were also at the receiving end of an allied bombing raid
which accurately destroyed the barracks outside our camp which, at the time, were
filled with German soldiers on their way to the Russian front. Only one stray
bomb hit the block we, that is, the night shift of laundry and sewing room workers, were sleeping in. I have written about this raid and its aftermath in my book
and so have others; the final evacuation of Birkenau and Auschwitz concentration
camps and the death march of January 1945 has also been described by survivors.
No amount of imagination can conjure up the terror of endless columns of starving
prisoners being whipped on through deep snow, shot at and killed if they couldn't
move fast enough through the day and through the night.

All German prisoners, most SS officers, men and women, had already been
transferred to Germany. Privileged German inmates were promised their freedom
in November 1944 if they volunteered to join the SS or army. Otto said that all his
men had chosen that option, but he preferred to remain a prisoner until liberation,

which he expected very soon. However, he knew from experience what happened to prisoners, especially German prisoners, when they were driven from one concentration camp to another.

The day before he and his men were to be evacuated, he came into the drying room of the laundry and told me everything he knew would happen to us. He warned me of every danger, how and where to walk and what position in the ranks to keep away from. He told me how to protect my mother and begged me not to let her out of my sight. Finally and very reluctantly, he advised me to escape with her from the evacuation transport as soon as we arrived in Germany and as soon as an opportunity presented itself after leaving the hostile Polish population behind us. He had organized good winter boots for my mother and me and told me to take warm civilian clothes from the drying room to wear under our striped camp dresses. He said that most of the SS-women were to be evacuated with his transport and their clothes left behind in the laundry would never be missed. He was convinced that my mother could not survive another concentration camp, even if she was left alive to enter one, which he doubted.

I followed his advice and, after all German prisoners and most of the SS officers—men and women—had left, I organized and removed from the drying room civilian clothes for as many remaining women as I could.

In early January of 1945, we heard the first shells and machine gun fire, a sure sign that the Russian front line was advancing toward Auschwitz. As we lined up for the early morning roll call, the SS guards carried full marching kits and machine guns and the SS-women didn't even take time to count us. Within minutes, we saw the first group of prisoners from the fenced-off compound of "guinea pigs" being marched out of the camp. Our block was told to wait and while we waited, at least two messengers turned up with conflicting orders for the guards. The first, we were told, indicated that Auschwitz was surrounded by Russian troops and that we would not be evacuated.

The brutal SS-woman who had already started to strip prisoners in the front row of the warm clothes I had so carefully accumulated, who had beaten and insulted the poor girls and had left them standing almost naked in the deep snow, suddenly changed her tune. She broke her whip into pieces, ground them into the snow, put her arms around the women closest to her and begged us to help her when the Russians arrived and took over. If we said that she had been forced to "only do her duty" and had never been cruel, she would demand help for us and a speedy return to our homes, as well as money and food. She told us to get inside, to put extra coal in the heating ovens and to warm ourselves. Needless to say, the girls she had previously stripped, quickly dressed again in their warm civilian clothes under their striped camp outfits.

However, as soon as the second messenger arrived with an evacuation order, the miserable SS-woman started hitting the prisoners again to get them out of the building. She kicked my mother in the back with her boot and I swore I'd kill that woman if or when I was free again. Soon after we were finally marched out and had passed endless columns of prisoners from Birkenau, we were whipped on past a ditch filled with bodies of women.

Three days later, having marched through forests, snow and ice, having suffered terrible losses of life and with nothing to eat other than snow, we were finally loaded onto open coal cars, a hundred women to each car, more than a third of it being occupied by two guards and their dogs. We had no room to sit, stretch or even move arms and legs and, of course, nothing to eat and nothing except the inadequate clothing to prevent freezing. The guards had furs and warm blankets, ample food rations and lots of booze.

By the time the train had crossed from Poland into Germany and the guards had been given new rations, eaten and fed their dogs and thrown over the side what they didn't want, I was determined to follow Otto's advice. As soon as the opportunity presented itself I was going to get out. It came in the very early hours of January 26. The guards were drunk and snoring under their blankets, which also covered their sleeping dogs. The train was moving very slowly and, having told my mother and my friend Susi what I intended to do, Susi let me climb on her back to swing over the side of the train and jump. She and another girl, Herta, helped my mother to follow me. I had asked Susi to come with us, but she felt that there was no safety in numbers and decided to stay on a trip to yet another concentration camp few would survive.

My mother and I made it across a snow-covered field and into a forest before we heard the train stop, a lot of screaming, dogs barking and shots being fired. I don't know what happened or whether other prisoners had tried to escape from some of the many overcrowded cars. But when we finally heard the train moving on and had shed our prisoners' clothes, my mother and I walked away through forests and villages, all of which were deserted, until we finally caught up with long columns of German refugees trying to get away from their homes and farms before the Russian front moved any closer.

Our escape may sound easy now, but you have to read my book to fully understand the terrible dangers, adventures and threats to our lives and freedom we had yet to go through before the war was to be finally over and before we were truly liberated. My mother, who was 87 on January 1, 1989, and still lives in Kibbutz Sarid, Israel, lives very much in the past. She often remembers our escape and keeps saying, "I couldn't jump off a moving train now!" She forgets that this was the easiest part and that everything that was to follow was even harder to live through—the long walk in a bitterly cold winter until we came to a train station where trains were still leaving for Berlin. Getting through identity controls on arrival there; getting to and finding the house of a German friend who had kept some of our clothes and money before we were arrested. Just to get to her home in a totally bombed-out district in West Berlin was a monumental task in the middle of the night. We were very lucky to find that one house still intact and that friend willing to take us in and to help us get to Mecklemburg to be billeted as "refugees from Silesia" with a Nazi family which, until the day the Americans marched into their village, Gadebusch, believed that Hitler had a secret weapon up his sleeve and would still win the war. To hide the tattoo on our arms under long sleeves when the weather turned hot, to escape the recruitment into the Nazi army when all girls of my age group were still being called up, and to finally work in a jam factory as an interpreter with French prisoners of war was trying, to say the least. A Nazi foreman was forever threatening to have me arrested and sent to a concentration camp if I refused to translate his foul language and his endless harangues on the "glorious" Nazi doctrines. But the hardest test to my will to survive was the realization that I had lost my family, my husband and child I had loved so much, and without them life did not then seem worth living.

Only when the 7th American Army marched into the German village and Axel Springer, son of the well-known German publisher, took over as the first Town Mayor in Gadesbusch, did I rediscover a purpose in life. Axel Springer had left Berlin shortly after Hitler got into power, had become an American citizen, married an American girl and returned to Germany with the victorious U.S. army. He identified my mother and me, appointed me as an interpreter and, reluctantly, allowed me to take part in the hunt for war criminals, straying SS, mostly former concentration camp guards hiding in nearby woods.

There, among many others, I found and identified the woman who had beaten our girls and kicked my mother downstairs before we were evacuated from Auschwitz. I was given the opportunity to kill her as I promised myself I would. A Jewish lieutenant in charge of the Nazi hunters left me alone to interrogate the SS-woman. Having told him about her infamous past, he gave me his service revolver "for my protection" and said, "She is all yours!" But when that creature cringed before me and begged for her life, I could not shoot her in cold blood and despised myself for that weakness. Still, she didn't get away. She never even came to trial. During that brief period of rough justice, the soldiers who had covered us in the woods in Gadesbusch and had subdued her when we found her, I was told later, took her back into the woods and hanged her after presumably giving her a trial hearing. There was no inquiry and I don't even remember her name. Perhaps some others of her surviving victims will still know who I am talking about.

During the summer of 1945, after the end of the war in Europe, the 7th American Army was posted to Japan and I was transferred to Lueneburg to work with and for the British Control Commission in the Department of Property Control, dealing with former Nazi estates. My mother started working there immediately as a nurse in the large and understaffed hospital for refugees and former prisoners. And there, I met Ross Brewster, who had fought in the British army from the beaches of Normandy to Hannover as a frontline soldier and had now been posted to Special Branch Investigation because of his knowledge of German and of German mentality. We got married on April 1, 1947, two days before he was to be demobilized and sent home to Scotland and a few days before my mother was to leave for Palestine, a year before the State of Israel was born.

She was going to work in Haifa throughout the Arab siege and attacks, and was there reunited with my younger brother, then a soldier in the Haganah and my older brother in Kibbutz Hazorea. My younger stepsister also returned to Israel after the war. She had joined the British army as a nurse in North Africa, stationed in Egypt, and had been the first to get compassionate leave to visit us in Lueneburg.

A British subject myself now, I joined my husband a few weeks after his release and debriefing from Special Branch. He returned to the university to take up again his long-interrupted studies and I finished my even longer-interrupted high school education, sat and passed the A-level exams with distinction and then attended college in Glasgow, Scotland, to become a physiotherapist. I graduated a year before my husband became a veterinary surgeon and, during that year, worked as a physiotherapist in a large rehabilitation hospital.

After he graduated, I joined him again and took a Cambridge University course in English, French and German Literature and, at the same time, a Journalism course taught by the Fleet Street (London) School of Journalism. From then on, we lived in Devon, England, where my husband was in practice and from there went to West Africa, where he started as a veterinary officer under the British Colonial Office in Lagos, Nigeria. From there, he was posted to Vom, a veterinary research center in northern Nigeria and finally, after Nigeria got its independence, we were posted to the then British Cameroons, where my husband was appointed Director of Veterinary Services under the United Nations.

I had to teach our two children myself there, since there was no school for Europeans and we finally went back to Britain for their sake and their education. Again, my husband started his own veterinary practice in Devon, England, but had to move to Scotland a few very happy and successful years later to take over his family's farm in Rossshire, Scotland. However, every one of our six men earned more in our farm than we did without having the responsibility of planning, weekend work and costs. When the Canadian government sent a representative to Scotland to offer my husband a post in Canada because of his, by then, well-known experience and achievements as a veterinarian and worldwide knowledge of animal health and diseases, we accepted and moved to Canada in 1969.

Although I had written many stories over the years, most of which were published, I now started working as a professional freelance journalist almost by accident. I began by taking issue with a German youth band in the Calgary Stampede playing a number of old Nazi songs. My objection caused an outcry of considerable magnitude among the large German population in southern Alberta. A newspaper publisher, who was just as fed up with the unreal German arguments asked me to "shut them up," which I did successfully once and for all. Ever since, I have been a contributor to Canadian newspapers and, for years, a commentator for radio and television.

I wrote articles for Alberta Teachers' Magazines and school broadcasts for Alberta Education's Social Studies. In 1973, the then Minister of Agriculture, having read many of my reports from Israel during my almost annual visits there, commissioned me to research into structure, methods and development of cooperative farming in Israel. The resulting two-part report and films were widely distributed to Canadian universities and colleges, and a number of cooperatives were started in different Canadian provinces and on a few native Indian reserves, some of them very successful.

In 1984, after a teacher was discovered to have taught his high school students for 14 years that the Holocaust was a "hoax," my book, *Vanished in Darkness*, was published, reprinted a number of times, and finally a new edition was printed for domestic and international distribution in 1987. For my writing, radio and TV work, the women's magazine *Chatelaine* and the Y.W.C.A. gave me the "Woman of the Year" awards in 1976 and 1977 respectively. In 1985, I received honors for the book on the Holocaust in the annual Alberta Culture Awards for the best non-fiction books published during the year. And in 1986 I received an Honorary Doctor of Laws degree from the University of Lethbridge. Also in 1986, in the municipal elections I was voted into our town council and am now Deputy Mayor of Coutts, Alberta.

My husband, who I had thought would survive me, died of heart and kidney failure in October 1986. We had been married nearly 40 years. The day before he died, he still voted for me in the 1986 municipal elections, confident that I would do everything possible to improve the living standards of all our citizens and to strengthen our democracy. He left me a legacy of love and caring that has kept me going against all odds.

Still busy writing weekly columns for newspapers and magazines, as Deputy Mayor of my municipality, and as a director of a number of boards where I represent the Council, I have little time and inclination to dwell on my past as a rule. I have had little contact with Auschwitz and Birkenau survivors over the past 40 years except when I visited my mother in Israel.

There are many questions I am being asked whenever I give a lecture in schools, colleges and Canadian universities on my ideas on democracy, racial discrimination in Canada and elsewhere, immigration policies and Nazi hunting as well as trials of convicted Nazis. Has "justice been done?" Of course not. And it can never be done. All countries have been dragging their feet far too long except in the very few cases like Eichmann's, which got worldwide publicity. I have no illusions that many more will be brought to trial and concentrate on the neo-Nazis who keep popping up all over the Western world. In short, I try to do everything in my power to make sure that history will not repeat itself, at least not in my corner of the world. I know from the many letters and calls I get from school children and students that I have made an impact and that they will not forget. As far as I am concerned, Germany is no longer on the map as a tourist attraction. For me it remains only as a huge cemetery. But, at the same time, I don't hold a new generation of Germans responsible for their grandparents' crime. Every time I visited Israel over the past 40 years, I have met young German students doing volunteer work on kibbutzim and elsewhere. All of them felt they have to atone for what was done to the Jews under the Hitler regime. Many of those young Germans gave up or interrupted their university or other secondary schooling to try and make up for past sins. While I always encourage them, or take them myself to see Yad Vashem, I also suggest they go home and make sure that neo-Nazism doesn't get a foothold there.

❖

Sophie Sohlberg (née Loewenstein)
Jerusalem (Israel)

I was born on September 15, 1923 in Munich, Germany.

My mother was Erna née Cohen from Koeln. My father, Victor Loewenstein, was from Ichenhausen, a small town in Schwaben with a 200-year old Jewish community which came to an end by Hitler.

My father was a genius. He never studied in any yeshiva, but was a talmud chachem (expert). He didn't finish more than ten years of school and was an expert in mathematics, history, physics and whatnot. He was interested in everything and knew the method of quick-reading two generations before it was invented. He worked as a procurist (head clerk) at the "Bayerische Hypotheken and Wechselbank" in Munich until the end of 1938, when he was asked to retire (with a full pension). He had been the head of the "Rechtsabteilung" (legal section), and when he left, it took four persons to replace him.

My father was very involved, too, in the life of the Jewish community. He was very active in the fight for ritual slaughter in Germany. Everybody came to him for advice in any field you can think of. He had connections with the right people, Jews and non-Jews. Among these were Anna von Hentig who was, together with her sisters, the Misses Beckmann, the owner of "Henkel's Zwillingswerk," and her brother-in-law, Dr. Werner Otto von Hentig, who was a high official in the foreign ministry in Berlin. They helped Jews which ever way they could, in spite of the danger involved. Dr. W. O. von Hentig, his wife and five children—none of whom served in the Hitlerjugend—Hitler Youth—were an outstanding family.

Then there were Mr. Fulham, the English consul in Munich, and Mr. Folley, the consul general in Berlin until the outbreak of the war. Through these and other connections, my father was able to help many people leave Germany long before that was his "job" when he became one of the directors of the "Hilfsverein der Juden in Deutschland"[3] (Aid Association of Jews in Germany), after he had retired from the bank and we had moved to Berlin (in October 1938).

My mother was a real helpmate who assisted him in every way she could.

Our home was always full of guests.

I had a sister, Rose, almost two years younger than myself. She was very intelligent and gifted in every way. At the age of 17½, she married her teacher (14 years older than she), Ernst Kordheimer, four months before they were sent to Auschwitz on February 28, 1943. Two days later, my parents were killed by a bomb. Before being deported from Berlin, both my sister and her husband had to work in some factory.

When I arrived in Auschwitz-Birkenau seven weeks after her, she was not alive anymore. I met friends of hers in camp who had been with her. Her husband died there, too.

I was born, as I mentioned before, in Munich. For eight years I attended the Jewish primary school, and during the ninth school year (1938) I studied at a private Catholic Lyceum (High School). They accepted me there only after very difficult examinations lasting three days. A friend of mine failed and was not accepted.

But that was unrelated to anti-Semitism. I had a very nice time there and the girls as well as the teachers accepted me as one of them. (I was, at that time, the only Jew in the school.) During that period, only children of veterans of the First World War were allowed to study at secondary schools. My father had been a soldier during the war and had even lost an eye.

When we moved to Berlin in October 1938, I studied about six weeks at the Jewish "Realschule" until the ninth of November, when the male teachers were imprisoned. Then I stopped studying altogether and became my mother's "helper." I was seventeen when the Germans decreed in 1941 that every woman aged 16-45 had to work in a factory. My father was able to send me to Neuendorf, a farm belonging to a Jew who had converted it into a training camp to prepare people for emigration to Eretz Yisroel. When I arrived in May 1941, nobody could leave Germany anymore, but there, at least, I was not forced to work on Shabbat as I would have in a factory in Berlin. I even managed not to work on Shabbat when the N.S.D.A.P. took over Neuendorf and it became an "Arbeitslager" (Forced Labor Camp).

Before the outbreak of war, my father had the opportunity to send my sister and me to England. But he did not want to send us alone. (He had had to leave home at the age of twelve because there was no school for him in Ichenhausen. He went through very hard times far from home, and did not want the same fate for his daughters.) He and my mother had permits for England, too, but he thought he had no right to run away from his job of helping others to get out of Germany. Besides, my mother's parents lived with us at that time and we could not leave them by themselves. My grandmother's brother and nephews, who had been living in Eretz Yisroel for 60 or 70 years, were not very keen to help them obtain certificates. My father used his special connections for people in direct danger only, never for his family. My grandmother died in 1939, and my grandfather in 1942. Both died a normal death.

Altogether, the two years in Neuendorf were a very nice time. We lived there like on an island, far away from the war. I belonged to a small group (if I remember correctly, 24 boys and six girls) of the Noar Agudati. We had our own kitchen. We had Gemara[4] (Talmud) lessons for the boys and Chumash[5] (Torah) lessons for the girls in the evenings after work.

A few weeks before we were sent to Auschwitz, we were informed of our imminent deportation. We were told that Auschwitz was a transit camp for other "work camps." We were not worried about it. We did not mind working and thought that the war could not go on much longer, and that, too, would end.

On April 9, 1943, we were sent to a "Sammellager" (holding camp) in Berlin, and on the 20th of April (Hitler's (may his name be cursed) birthday, we were sent to Auschwitz.

It was the day before Pesach. While still in Neuendorf, we had baked matzot and taken them with us, and we held the Seder in the railway car. All our group was together in the same wagon—an animal wagon without windows. On the first day of Pesach, we arrived in Birkenau. I found it very kind and thoughtful that only the young people had to walk and the old people and mothers with children were sent by lorries. Only after some days, did we learn where they had been sent.

I don't remember the walk from the railway station in Birkenau, but I remember the inscription on the gate: "Arbeit Macht Frei." I recall the following events like a bad dream. Somebody took away everything we had with us and threw it all onto a blanket on the floor. (The first thing was a small prayerbook I had gotten as a present a week before the outbreak of the war.) Then the undressing, the shaving of all hair, the "sauna" where we all looked like monkeys, the trousers and shirts we got to wear, and the tattooing of the numbers (41956 for me). After all that, everybody got a piece of bread with an awful taste, very salty and sour. Then we were sent, five girls together, to a "koje" (berth). I don't remember who the three others were, but I remember that Ruth Libman was together with me (Ruth Weill, now in Kibbutz Chafetz Chaim). She was very depressed, and I remember her saying, "You can't stand that for long!" That was the second Seder night.

I fell ill with typhoid, but because we were not sent to work during the first month, I could manage with it. I somehow got through the roll-calls with the support of some girls, and the rest of the day I could stay in the "koje." After about a month, the girls of our transport were sent to the Stabsgebaeude, I was left behind because the SS-man realized that I was hardly able to stand on my feet. At that time, there were no selections in Birkenau, or else I would not be here to write this.

The block nurse sent me to the "Revier" (infirmary) every day. There they took my temperature. I saw to it that it didn't climb to 39° Celsius and they sent me back to the Block. This continued until one day I thought I had no fever anymore, and they took my temperature correctly. It climbed to more than 39°, and they kept me at the "Revier." There I was afraid of catching more illnesses. Zilla Orlean (today Zilla Sorotzkin, 34 Rashi Street, Jerusalem) helped me very much. She was a nurse there. I don't remember how long I stayed at the "Revier"—a week or more. When I came back to the block, the girls could not believe their eyes. Not many came back from the "Revier."

For a short time, I was sent to pick thistles for the kitchen. Sometimes I worked in the "Flickstube" (sewing room), and once or twice I went with the shoe-detail. They worked near the Stabsgebaeude, and we could see the girls who were there. We were very much impressed with how well and clean they looked. (They even had hair again!)

The only time in Birkenau-Auschwitz I volunteered, was for the shoe-detail because I very much wanted to see our girls, even from afar. Generally, I made it a rule to do only what I was told to do and not to volunteer for anything. I thought that that way I need not regret anything. I never really believed in my heart that we would live to see the end of the war and be free. I was quite sure that in the end the Germans would kill the whole camp and nobody would be left to tell our story. I never told my thoughts to anybody. On the contrary, I always tried to seem optimistic and would not let the other girls utter pessimistic thoughts. Although in my heart I was very pessimistic, I hoped for a miracle and had a very strong desire to live on, and wanted to do everything in my power to achieve that goal. I hoped, that as long as we were able to do our work, the Germans would let us live.

I don't remember when it happened. I think about two or three months after our girls were sent to the Stabsgebaeude, I was told by the Blockaelteste, "Tomorrow, you are going to the Stabsgebaeude." I could hardly believe it, but it was true. The next day I got clean Lagerkleidung (clothing) and, together with 16 Slovakian girls, we were marched to the Stabsgebaeude. There I found out why it all had happened. Ruth Libman had been working on the night-shift in the Buegelstube (ironing room) of the SS laundry. One night, the kapo told the girls that they needed more workers. One of the girls said that she had a friend who knew how to iron, but she was in Birkenau. The kapo told her to give her her friend's number; then she could bring her over from Birkenau. When Ruth heard that, she told the kapo that she too had a friend in Birkenau who knew how to iron and gave the kapo my number. She knew it by heart because it was one number after hers. In the morning Ruth informed the other girls, and everyone who knew the number of a girl in Birkenau added it to the list. But only I was called to the Stabsgebaeude.

The Stabsgebaeude was a paradise compared to Birkenau. Instead of standing for roll-call for hours twice a day, the Blockaelteste counted us, I think only at night, on the way to the dormitories. Instead of at most one liter of water a day for drinking and washing ourselves, we bathed every day in the washing buckets when we finished work.

The food was not much better, but there was more of it, and we were not hungry anymore. In Birkenau, in the women's camp, they put something into the food to stop the monthly period. In the Stabsgebaeude, we got the food from the men's camp and the period returned. In all the camps, they put bromate into the food to calm us down. We had lice, bedbugs and fleas in the Stabsgebaeude as well as in Birkenau.

Two girls had a bed together, but we met there only from Saturday afternoon to Monday morning when we did not work. During the week, one of us worked by day and one at night.

In the beginning, I was put into the SS laundry "Truppenwaesche." My task, then, was to wash the underwear, shirts and trousers of the SS-men by hand. Later on, when the SS laundry moved to the "leather factory," we got machines for this kind of laundry, but continued to wash "private laundry" by hand. I had the dubious "honor" of washing the underwear of all the "important people" like Dr. Mengele, the Oberaufseherin Irma Grese and Lagerkommandant Kramer. I don't remember any other names. I also don't remember who was the second girl who was with me at the private laundry. At the machines were, if I remember correctly, Ruth Carliner and Susi Kurzweil. Other girls worked labeling the laundry, in the Buegelstube (ironing room), in the Trockenraum (drying room) and in the Flickstube (sewing room). Every girl had friends in the other parts of the laundry who washed, ironed, dried or mended their things. I washed for several girls, and they dried, ironed or mended for me. We were allowed to wash our things on Shabbat but not during the week. I washed all week for the girls or myself, but not on Shabbat, and was always afraid of being caught. One day I explained to the SS-Aufseherin (woman) that it would be much more useful if we were allowed to wash our things on Monday at the time when we had to wait until the new laundry of the week was being signed out and we could start washing, instead of on Shabbat when we had too much to do to finish all the laundry of the week. (In reality, we never had any difficulty finishing it.) The Aufseherin swallowed my explanation and from then on we were allowed to wash our own things on Monday. One of the Aufseherinnen wanted me to wash the things of her Kochani (boyfriend), one of the SS-men, by hand. The moment she turned her back, I threw them into the machine. She never found out that I did not wash them myself.

When the SS laundry was in the "leather factory," some men worked there, too. I don't remember what their task was. I remember only one of them by name. He was the son of Rabbi Weill of Colmar.

Every day when we finished work, we were occupied with searching for lice in our dresses, underwear and hair. We often had a rash all over our bodies. When we moved from the Stabsgebaeude into the new F.K.L. Auschwitz, we got rid of those troubles. I don't remember when that was.—Sometimes there were books among the threads and other mending articles they received in the Flickstube, and we read them. One day they got a small book with short stories in Hebrew. They gave it to me. I read it and started to teach Hebrew with it. One night one of the SS-men decided to search our little sacks. (Everyone had a little sack for her bread. We got it once a day in the evening and we had to keep it somewhere for the next day.) I don't know what the SS-man was after, but he found the book, threw it on the floor and called, "What, have you got Talmud here, too?" and took the book with him.

Once I got a Chumash (bible)—also from the girls of the Flickstube. I studied it with Irene Kunstler. It was the first time in her life she learned Chumash. At the Seder night, we used it instead of a Haggadah.[6] At the midnight break, we put a white (wet) sheet on the table in the laundry. We, the girls of the night shift and several girls who got up and joined us, sat around the table. I read the chapters which tell of the Exodus from the Chumash and translated them. Sarah Hirschberg (now Schoenthal, Chofetz Chaim) sang the songs of the Haggadah. That was our Seder. We had no matzoh and maror (bitter herbs) we did not need. We had more than enough there. We sat there much longer than the hour of our break, but the Aufseherin did not disturb us.

One night when Irene was reading in the Chumash during the night break, an SS-man came and took it away from her. Many years later, she told me that she had been afraid much more of what I would say when I heard of it in the morning than of the SS-man! I remember her being in tears when she told me about it.

Just before Hanukkah 1943, I received some small parcels from a non-Jewish friend of my parents. I don't remember her name and I never found out how she knew where I was, and was very astonished that I got the parcel at all. There was some food in it and a small packet of candles. So I was able to light one candle every night of that Hanukkah. We lit it on the lowest of three beds (one on top of the other) in a corner of our dormitory. We succeeded in setting nothing on fire and were not caught.

How did we know at all the exact date of the Jewish Holy Days? About ten years before Auschwitz, at the Jewish Primary school in Munich, I had learned the rules of the Jewish calendar. This knowledge helped me to make a calendar for each of the two years I spent in Auschwitz. The first one—which I wrote in a little copybook with a cover embroidered by Anne Borinsky (today Orah), who gave it to me on my twentieth birthday—was stolen together with a small piece of bread I had saved for the next morning. That was in the last camp Neustadt-Glewe. By the way, I did not go without food that morning. Several girls, when they heard that my little sack with my piece of bread was stolen, shared theirs with me. So in the end, I had more than any other day.

The second calendar, which I kept along with a very small siddur (prayer book), is still with me today.

In the late afternoon and evenings when we were in the dormitories of the Stabsgebauede and afterward in Block II of the F.K.L. Auschwitz, we were generally not under the immediate control of the SS. We could not run away. There were iron bars on the windows and the iron doors were locked by key. So, generally, we were left alone by the SS. Sometimes we got a book to read. And we arranged some lessons, too. There was Pesja Schereschewsky, a Beit Yaacov[7] teacher from Poland. She had a tremendous Bible-knowledge in Tenach and other Jewish fields, all by heart. Not long ago, I learned (through a book by Yehuda Nachschoni) that she wrote lessons for the men who worked with us and explained the difficulties which arose in their studying. Everything was solely by writing notes, because to talk to a man was the biggest sin you could commit in camp. To write was forbidden, too, but it was easier to hide. Pesya lived in Tel Aviv for a short time after the war. I went to see her when she came. She died there about 40 years ago. We had some other lessons by Anne Borinsky—she got some book, for example "Faust" by Goethe, and read it with us.

Just in front of the window of our dormitory in the Stabsgebaeude were the railways. One of our Neuendorf boys, Willy Reich, was working there pushing wagons. Several time he brought me little presents, such as food and other small things. I remember that on my birthday he gave me Quaker Oats with sugar. That was something the boys in Neuendorf had liked very much. There, too, we had not had too much to eat. I knitted gloves for him. I got the wool and the knitting needles from the girls of the Flickstube. One day Sarah Hirschberg (today Schoenthal, Chofetz Chaim) fell ill. She seemed to have malaria, and we were very afraid she would be sent to the "Revier." In the morning I told Willy about it, and that we urgently needed Chinin (quinine) for her. The same afternoon he brought it to us, and Sarah got well.

One of the things Willy gave me was a prayerbook. Because it was quite big, I could not take it with me everywhere, and hid it under the mattress of some bed at the back of the dormitory (that was in Block II already). I don't remember, either, why my bed was not safe enough, nor whose bed it was. One day—if I remember right, it was September 14, 1944—we were attacked by airplanes. (British or Russian? I don't know.) I was with the girls of the day-shift at work in the Stabsgebaeude. When the bombs started falling, all of us, together with the SS-men and women, were put into an inner hall. There was no shelter in the Stabsgebaeude. I saw one of the SS-men shiver and start to pray. That day several bombs fell on Auschwitz, one of them near the house of Oberaufseherin Grese, but I don't think that much more was broken there than a pot with jam. The next day I had to wash a curtain full of jam. Just beside Block II there were two barracks of SS-men. One bomb fell on each of them, and a third one on the end of our barrack. It fell through the roof and the floor into the shelter. One girl was killed and several wounded (many of the SS-men were killed). The bomb made a big hole in the floor exactly in front of the bed with my prayerbook, and it was impossible to get there to retrieve it. When I told Willy that my prayerbook was "bombed," he brought me a new one, a very small one which I could hide on my body—and I have it still. I met Willy on the first night of the Todesmarsch (deathmarch). He gave me a loaf of bread and a packet of margarine. That was the last time I saw him. He did not live to see the liberation.

I remember another bomb attack. It was at night in Block II. We were told to go down into the shelter. There was a big commotion among the girls on the stairs, and some of them were getting nervous. Then one of the SS-men shouted at them, "Be quiet! The bombs are not meant for you, only for us!"

There were very good relations among the girls in the Stabsgebaeude, not only among those in the same kommando. There were too many girls to be close friends with all of them, or even to know all of them. But if someone needed help, everybody was ready. For example, Miene Trenk had T.B. (tuberculosis). She was weak and had to have enough to eat. So seven girls gave her in turn, their bread and margarine portions—each day, another one. She never forgot that, and when she died about three years ago in the U.S.A., she remembered those girls in her will. I had many friends in Auschwitz, and I am still in touch with many of them.

I had, thank G-d, almost nothing to do with the SS-men and Aufseherinnen. I hardly remember them. Except one Aufseherin. She was a Dutch girl who had followed an SS-man who had promised to marry her. He brought her to Auschwitz as an Aufseherin and left her there. She hated being there. One day one of the girls ran away. I do not remember who she was. I think I didn't even know her. As far as I know, she was the only one who tried to run away from the Stabsgebaeude, and they caught her and killed her. When that Aufseherin heard of it, she was terribly afraid that she would be punished for it. I do not remember whether she was.

The saddest remembrance is of that Friday night when two girls were hanged. I do not remember what they were accused of. It happened when we were already in F.K.L. Auschwitz. The entire camp had to stand outside as if for roll-call. When they were hanged, all of us were marched around the place. May the Almighty take revenge for their blood. It was Friday night—Shabbat—and when we were allowed to go back to our barracks, we took the two loaves of bread which we had gotten whole, because several of us girls had taken our portion of bread together, like we did every Friday in order to have two whole loaves—and made kiddush over them with very heavy hearts.

At the end of 1944, we knew (I don't know how) that the Russians were driving the Germans back and were coming closer to Auschwitz. In my heart, I never believed that the Germans would let us be liberated by the Russians. Although the gas chambers did not work anymore in Auschwitz, I was quite sure that the Germans would find some other way to kill us all before the Russians would come. Common sense told me that the Germans would not leave anybody alive who was able to tell the world what had happened in the concentration camps, and the thought that the world would never know was very hard for me. As I said already, I never revealed those black thoughts to anybody. On the other hand, I still hoped and prayed for some miracle to happen.

On January 18, 1945, we were told that all the prisoners of Auschwitz, except those in the Revier, would be moved westward. That strengthened my belief that they wanted to kill us all. For the Revier alone they could manage without gas chambers, and I was sure that they would send us to Gross-Rosen where the gas chambers were still working, according to rumors. Only when we had passed the railway station of Gross-Rosen, did I begin to believe that there was reasonable hope of getting out of the hell alive. On Thursday, January 18, we started the death march in the late evening. Before we left, we recited the road prayer together with such fervor as I have never done in my life, not beforehand and not afterward. We marched all Thursday night and all Friday with only some very short breaks at the road side. The earth was frozen. The night was very cold, and very clear with many stars in the sky. It was hard to walk because of the ice. Ruth Libman fell several times, until she put a pair of socks over her shoes. People that lived along the way put out pails with water at the road side for us to drink. Everybody who was not able to walk on was shot. There was Julchen Preuss. She was much older than we and suffered from heart trouble. At the roll-calls in Auschwitz, we had had to support her because it was very hard for her to be standing for a long time. Now on the way, she told us that she could not go on anymore. We could not leave her, and dragged her on two of us, each one taking one of her arms. She lived through it, and returned after the liberation to Munich, where she was a secretary for the Jewish community as she had been before Auschwitz. She died after several years there.

Friday night, they let us sleep in some barracks. I don't remember where it was. I could not take off my shoes. My feet were very swollen and wet, and I was afraid I would not be able to put my shoes on again if I took them off. Many of us had frozen feet or hands, or both. Part of us went on Saturday morning. I was with the group who went only on Sunday morning. From there, we continued our "journey" by railway in open freight cars. It was our luck that they were open. They stuffed us in like sardines. There was no room to sit down. We were standing all the way, three days and nights. We had no food anymore, except for the snow which was covering everything. After a three day "journey," we arrived in Ravensbrueck, Ruth Libman had a hole in her head, because the iron door of the car had fallen on her head.

I don't remember anything of the month in Ravensbrueck. After a month there, we were sent by railway—and this time in really "human" wagons and with enough room to sit down—to Neustadt-Glewe in Mecklenburg in the north of Germany. There was a small camp next to a soldier's camp of the Wehrmacht. We got very little food. But food was very rare then in Germany, and even the soldiers got very little. On Pesach, I exchanged my small piece of bread for a carrot or an uncooked potato or some leaves of cabbage (a girl who worked in the kitchen could organize that for me.) There were girls who were jealous of how much I had gotten to eat...

In Neustadt-Glewe, we worked a little for the soldiers. We had to dig holes big enough for one soldier to stand in along the roads, or to hide roads in the woods by covering them with pieces of wood and leaves. Once while doing this with a group of other girls, I got a kick in my behind from the Lagerkommandant's foot itself. He had come to see what we were doing and I, for a fraction of a second, had turned my head to look at him.

Toward the end, we could hear and see the front coming nearer. At night, we heard the cannons shooting not far away. By day, we saw airplanes fighting each other.

We knew that the Russians as well as the Americans were very near and soon would meet in the middle of Germany. I never believed that that would end the war. I thought that they would go on with it, fighting each other. Luckily, I was mistaken.

On May 1, 1945—Lag B'Omer[8]—there was no roll-call. We got nothing to eat. We heard no shooting, saw no airplanes. It was very quiet outside. We heard from somewhere that the Russians were very close. We were sitting in our barracks very hungry. All of a sudden many girls started running to the kitchen and taking all they could find there. The SS-men on the watch towers started to shoot at them. It was a terrible turmoil. Ruth Carliner got a bullet in her foot. All of a sudden the shooting stopped. Our SS-men, as well as the soldiers of the camp nearby, had run away. We were free!

Somebody spread the rumor that the Germans had mined our camp and we had better leave it, the quicker the better. So we moved to the soldiers' camp. There we found some tins of sardines, pots of coffee and cooked potatoes still warm on the tables. It seemed that the soldiers had run away in the middle of their meal. We finished their meal. But it is not too wise to eat sardines on an empty stomach. We all got sick from it, and I have trouble with my stomach to this day.

It seemed the SS had not had enough time to mine our camp, and nothing happened there. But the soldiers had hidden some gunpowder in one of the stoves in their camp. One of the women was killed when she tried to make a fire in order to cook something.

The Russians arrived the next day. They started to give out some food. Not much. After a few days, they asked us to leave the soldiers' camp because of the dirt in it. So we moved to a small house on the outskirts of Neustadt. It was a district of very small houses, each one with three rooms. One of them and the kitchen were on the ground floor, and two bedrooms were upstairs. The male inhabitants of the houses were in the army, and the women were afraid to stay alone; some of them went to live together, so that many of the houses were empty. Seven us of went together to live in one of them: Ruth Libman (Weill), Ruth Mayersohn (Muller), Irene Kuenstler (Stiefel), Jutta Pels (Bergt), Dietel and Ruth Carliner and myself. The first night in that house, three Russian soldiers came, broke the windows on the ground floor and came up to us in the bedrooms. We tried to explain to them that we had been prisoners, and that we were Jews. They didn't understand German, and we didn't understand Russian. Our tattoo numbers didn't make any impression on them. They were tattooed, too. We succeeded in getting through that night without being harmed, but we were quite afraid. After that night we slept during the day in turn, and all of us stayed up together downstairs in the kitchen by night.

A week after our liberation, on May 8th, two of us went to find out where the Americans were. We had heard that they were not far from us. The girls stayed in a deserted house for the night, where they found a radio which was working. They turned it on and heard that the war had come to an end. The next day, they came back and told us that the war was over and the Americans were fifteen kilometers from us. Ruth Libman, Ruth Mayersohn and I decided to try to get to the Americans, but to wait until after Shavuos.[9] Meanwhile, the Russians put up some collecting stations for the French, Dutch or Belgian people to send them back home. We had made small French flags for ourselves and had been wearing them on our dresses in order to be left alone by the Russian soldiers. They raped only German women. So we decided to "remain" French and to try to go "back home" to France. All three of us had been born in Germany, but had no intention whatsoever to remain there. Besides, we wanted to get away from the Russians, the quicker the better.

On May 21st, we went to the collecting station and the next day we were sent among a group of others to the Americans. I started keeping a kind of diary. On May 23rd, I wrote in it, "Last night for the first time we could sleep quietly." We were on our way eight days, through Holland and Belgium by trains decorated with flowers.

On May 30th, we arrived in Lille. There we told the truth, because our French was not good enough to tell French people we were French. So we were sent to some kind of prison and told we would be sent back to Germany because there was no Hitler anymore—why couldn't we remain there! Men from the Jewish community got us out after three days and sent us to Paris. There I met a cousin of mine at the kosher restaurant. I had not seen her in fifteen years. At that restaurant, we met someone, too, who worked at the Jewish Agency,[10] and he promised to send us at the first opportunity to Eretz Yisroel.

My grandmother (my father's mother) and an aunt of mine lived in Aix les Bain. I went to them on June 28th (17th of Tamuz).[11] There, I sewed for friends of my aunt and worked one month in a children's home. On August 7th, I was called back to Paris because we were supposed to start for Eretz Yisroel. But we stayed three more weeks in Paris. We lived six or eight people in some family's flat (Rabbi Frankforter's), who was not in Paris at that time and left their flat to us, with all the food that was in it. And, it was enough for us for three weeks.

On August 24th, we were sent by train—three special cars full—to Marseille. There was hora dancing and singing in the station before the train left. We arrived in Marseille on Friday morning and were put into a camp for German prisoners of war. First of all, we saw to it to arrange for something to eat for the 160 people who wanted kosher food. Ruth Mayersohn announced that I knew how to cook (I had done it most of the time in Neuendorf as well as after the liberation in Neustadt and in Paris). So with the help of some boy I "Kashered" pots and a stove. The carpenter made a big wooden spoon for me (I had to stand on a chair in order to be able to stir the food in the pot). Some women who could have been my mothers helped me. We stayed in Marseille twelve days. The last two days there were 100 additional eaters from a group from Switzerland. Among the entire group was Jacob Zwi Sohlberg, who 15½ years later was to become my husband. But, that we found out only on Pesach 1961, when he first came to visit me. It seems that his mother had given him enough food on the way so he didn't need "mine." And so we didn't meet then.

On September 8th, we went by cars to Tullon where the ship "Mataroah" waited for us, an English ship on her way to bring soldiers to India. The soldiers occupied the cabins. Only some women with small children were given cabins. All the others were stuffed down in the belly of the ship. Those who didn't find room there, slept on benches and tables on deck. Half of us were illegal. Nobody got his papers into his hands. Nobody counted us, thus everybody got on board. I was one of the last ones, about a quarter of an hour before the ship lifted anchor. I know I had a certificate and was not afraid of being left behind. To this day, I hate being in a pushing crowd.

We arrived in Haifa on September 2nd, in the afternoon. It was Shabbat and the first day of Rosh Hashana. We had to get off the ship because she was continuing on her way. We were told that we couldn't stay in the harbor until after Rosh Hashana because there were rats in the barracks that had been prepared for us and there was danger of cholera there. The truth was that because of Rosh Hashana the English did not control our papers. The Jews wanted them to send us to Athlid so that they could pick out the illegals. It was night when we departed, first by train, and then we walked about half an hour. There, on the sides of the road, waited people of the kibbutzim in the neighborhood and they took the illegals with them. I think the English soldiers had been bribed because all of them looked at the stars and none of them saw anything.

Because of Shabbat, we had left all our belongings on the ship. But we found everything in Athlid. I even found parcels belonging to friends of mine who had come illegally and were spending the second day of Rosh Hashana in some kibbutz. I took their things with me for them.

Now in Athlid, we were again shut up in a prisoners' camp with an iron fence around it. Some friends of mine who lived in Haifa came to visit me, but they were not allowed to come in. We could only talk through iron bars. Except for that, of Athlid I only remember the very big green peppers and plums we got there. I had never before seen such big fruits and vegetables.

In order to get out of Athlid as quickly as possible, I went to Kibbutz Chofetz Chaim together with Ruth Libman. Ruth intended to stay in Chofetz Chaim, and that is what she did. She still lives there. I didn't mind visiting there. I knew most of the people there were friends of mine from the time before the war. But I did not want to live in a kibbutz. I had had enough of living in a crowd and wanted to be on my own and to decide about my future by myself without asking permission from anybody.

We arrived in Chofetz Chaim September 15th (Tishrei[12] 6th, my 22nd birthday). I enjoyed the six days in Chofetz Chaim very much. After Yom Kippur,[13] I went through Tel Aviv (four days with an aunt and cousins who lived there) to Jerusalem. There, too, lived an uncle and aunt with two cousins of mine. I met lots of people who had come here with the help of my father. Everyone received me with open arms and tried to help me. Friends and distant relations sent me parcels from America and England. Here, as well as it had been in Paris, everybody wanted to share with me the little he himself had.

I had no problem whatsoever geting used to normal life. I started studying at the Bais Yaacov teachers' seminary. Thus a very old dream of mine I had given up long ago had become true. As long as I could remember, I had wanted to become a teacher. The almost two years I studied, I lived with my uncle's family. For my living, I sewed for my aunt, my cousin and their friends. When I finished seminary and started teaching, I rented a very small room, and eleven years later when I got some money from Germany, I bought a small flat where I am still living. There was much discussion here of whether to take the money or not. I never liked the term "Wiedergutmachung." The Germans cannot make anything good with money. Money cannot bring to life those they murdered, and it cannot give back the years we were shut up in concentration camps. But it can pay back at least part of the things they stole from us. It cannot make healthy those who came out of all that, but suffer all kinds of illnesses, but it can make life a bit easier for them.

I worked as a teacher for 17 years, until my second son was born. I married in 1961 at the age of 37, when all my friends had given me up long ago. As I mentioned, my husband came with me on the same ship to Eretz Yisroel. He was born in Switzerland. Here he joined Kibbutz Yavneh and lived there for 12 years. He left the kibbutz for Jerusalem in order to find a wife. He started to work as a clerk at the Bituach Leumi and in addition to sell books for some publisher. The publisher's wife was a teacher in Bais Yaacov. She knew me and sent him to me. We have three sons, and so far one daughter-in-law and a little granddaughter.

I have good connections with many of the "girls," although most of them I don't see too often. Everybody is busy and for me, especially, it is difficult to leave home.

From the first day after the liberation, I have been trying to live an absolutely normal life. I never thought that others must care for me, and although everybody tried to help me, I started to work for my living from the beginning.

It took me quite some time until I learned what had been going on in the world during the time I had been shut off from it. But I don't believe that those 25 months in Auschwitz are missing from my life. I am convinced that anything that happens to you has a reason and comes to teach you something. This belief helped me very much. If you are in a situation where you have no power whatsoever to change things—because any kind of resistance would be suicide—then at least try to get something positive out of it, or else you cease to want to live on. Lack of will power to continue to live killed many people in the camps.

I have no idea what has happened to any of our SS-watchmen or women. I can't say that I care about it. I am absolutely sure that in the end everybody will get exactly what he deserves. I don't even mind, whether Hitler (may his name be cursed) is still alive hiding in some hole or if he was killed by the attack on him, or if it is true that he committed suicide. That, however, I never believed. He had not enough courage for that. I was 6 or 7 years old (1929-30) when we lived just opposite him in the Tierschstrasse in Munich. He was already known then as a coward and a sadist. But I think that nobody dreamed of it then that he could set half of the world on fire ten years later.

I think trials like those of Eichmann or Demjanjuk are important in order that the world should never forget what has happened. But I would have preferred that the trials had taken place in Germany and having them hanged there and not in Israel—I think that would have been more useful for history.

NOTES

Eva Brewster

1   Herbert Backe joined the Nazi party early. In October 1933 he was State Secretary in the Ministry of Food and Agriculture. In 1936 he was made Food Commissioner for the Four Year Plan, responsible to Goering for the coordination of agrarian and industrial policy. At the end of 1943 he was promoted to Reich Minister and Reichsbauernfuehrer (Reich Farmers' Leader) and in April 1944 he was appointed Reich Food Minister serving in Hitler's last cabinet. He committed suicide by hanging himself at Nuremberg prison on April 6, 1947 (Wistrich, 1982, p. 10).

2   The blocks of the Jewish Zugaenge, like all other blocks, were ruled by the Jewish women from Slovakia ... They were the real aristocrats of the camp. It seems strange, but in this congregation of misery, baseness and fear, they sparkled with an unusual luster. They were the first prisoners in Auschwitz, and they felt a certain pride in having built the camp. When they were brought here ... there was nothing but swampland, but now there were barracks, blocks, offices and streets.

"While we were building this place," they said, "and were being plagued by malaria, you were sleeping in warm beds." They spoke with such hatred and contempt to the Zugaenge as if the Zugaenge deserved nothing better than ill treatment and death. We existed only so they might have somebody to beat up on, somebody to serve as a background to their reflected glory (Nomberg-Przytyk, 1985, p. 20).

Sophie Sohlberg

3   *Hilfsverein der Deutschen Juden*, the German Jewish Aid Society, was founded in 1901 for social and political assistance to needy Jews.

4   The explanation of the Mishnah by the Amoraim, i.e., the Talmud.

5   *Chumash* is the Hebrew term for Pentateuch.

6   The *Haggadah* is the prescribed service and narrative relating the Exodus from Egypt and recited during the Seder on Passover.

7   Beit Yaacov (or *Beth Yaakov*) is an Orthodox girls' school.

8   Lag B'Omer (or *Lag Ba Omer*) is the 33rd day of Omer, corresponding to Iyyar 18, a semi-holiday.

9   Shavuos (or *Shavuot*) is the second of the Pilgrim Festivals; also called Pentecost because it falls on the 50th day after Passover.

10   The Jewish Agency is the executive of the World Zionist Organization.

11   Tamuz (or *Tammuz*) is the fourth month of the Jewish religious and tenth month of the Jewish civil year.

12   Tishrei (or *Tishri*) is the first month of the Jewish civil and seventh month of the Jewish religious year.

13   The Day of Atonement.

CHAPTER 11

Mending Room

Ora Aloni (née Borinski)
Kibbutz Maayan-Zvi (Israel)

From Berlin to Maayan-Zvi via Auschwitz

I was born in September 1914 in Berlin as the oldest child of an upper middle-class family. My father, Dr. Paul Borinski, a chemist and hygienist, was director of the chemical section of the Department of Health in the city of Berlin. My mother, Alice, was the daughter of a family of professionals who had been living for many generations in Berlin. My brother, Fritz, Shmuel, was born in 1919. He now lives with his family in Israel.

Our education was absolutely non-Jewish and emphasized obedience and responsibility as "German citizens" (Deutsche Staatsbuerger). I attended the Dorotheen-Oberlyzeum (a girls' high school) and received my Abitur (high school diploma) in 1933. My highest grades were in German and mathematics. There were very few Jewish classmates in my grade and my best friends were Christian girls. Even my parents' circle of friends consisted mostly of couples from mixed marriages. In this way, the events of 1933 caught us completely unprepared. It was an earthquake which threw me into another life and which, at first, was felt painfully. My father was very rudely fired from his job in April 1933. Later, my parents were invited to go to Norway, thanks to my father's professional reputation. However, after the German invasion, they were deported to Auschwitz and were exterminated in the Spring of 1943.

It took me a long time to get used to the idea that I was Jewish and to the steadily deteriorating situation of Jews in Germany.

Between 1937 and 1939 I attended the college for "German Elementary School Teachers of the Jewish Faith" and graduated in the Summer of 1939. During the course of these two years I not only learned that I was Jewish, but I also encountered Zionism and decided to choose it as my direction in life.

In the Fall of 1939 I went as a Madricha (youth leader) to the Hechaluz-Hachsharah[1] Kibbutz Ahrensdorf, which belonged to the Macabi-Hatzair (movement). In 1941 Ahrensdorf was liquidated and we, together with other Chalutzim who still lived in Germany, were transferred to the agriculture estate in Neuendorf.

With the assistance of other Madrichim and especially with the assistance of my fellow youthful students, I completed my "Inner education as a Zionist." From that time until today, the relationship between these young chaverim and myself developed into a close friendship. The daily forced labor in and near Neuendorf under S.A. supervision did not prevent us from preparing ourselves further for a life in Eretz Israel. But far more demanding was the preparation, mentally as well as physically, for the imminent deportation from Germany.

It came to pass in the middle of April 1943. After a short stay in a gathering camp in Berlin, we were transported in cattle cars toward the East—it was the Seder night and in each of the four cars which contained members of our Chevrah, one of us conducted the Seder.

I want to emphasize once more that our Chevrah was an extremely closely-knit group. This sense of belonging helped us enormously throughout the horrible days that were to come. During our final days in Neuendorf and throughout our journey in the cattle cars, we fervently wished only that we might be able to stay together!

Shortly after we passed the sign "AUSCHWITZ," the train came to a standstill and we heard the harsh commands, "Get out! Fast! Women, here, men there across the rails," and we felt a sharp pang in our hearts. But obediently, holding hands and upright, we marched through the large gate. There was barbed wire everywhere, with SS-men and women holding back snarling dogs on their leashes.

It was April 20, 1943.

At first, they took us to Birkenau. There we had to undergo the customary procedures: sauna, confiscation of our last personal items, having our heads shaved, being tattooed with an identification number and finally, receiving our prison clothes. All of this has been told numerous times, so I will leave out the details. However, it is important to mention that, to the best of my memory, I and possibly my Chaverot, were hardly affected by the activity going on around us. This new situation seemed unreal to me. The SS-men, whom I did not think of as men even during later periods, stared at our nakedness. I remember that the female prisoner who tattooed the number into my arm asked me in astonishment, "Why are you laughing? Doesn't it hurt?" Then we were led to a block, where my chaveroth again tried very hard to stay together. I saw rows of tiered bunks with paltry straw. Eight of us were assigned one row. One of the eight had to stand in a long line in order to receive a little bowl of pitiable watery soup and one tiny dish of water for the entire group for drinking, washing and rinsing our mouths. I don't remember any more.

The next morning after the roll-call, we were assigned to the herb-kommando. Now that it was daylight, I felt oppressed by the endless rows of blocks, the narrow camp road with its grayish-brown clay soil and its accompanying odor. Our work was not hard. We had to gather stinging nettles and throw them into sacks. The nettles were probably used for the SS kitchen. In the beginning it was painful to our hands, but later we did not feel it. In the background, at a distance, I saw white lilac.

Thus a week passed, perhaps more—I don't remember exactly. Then the inmates of our block were called to undergo the "first selection." At that time we did not know that this was the term for what was happening to us.

Whispered through the rows came advice: "Always say that you are feeling fine! Try not to show wounds, pimples or skin eruptions! If you are given a thermometer, don't put it in all the way, just pretend to." We were sent in long lines from one SS-man to the next. They asked our occupation, special talents, state of health, and all of them looked us over very thoroughly. It was fortunate that we had received the warning—almost no thermometer reading indicated fever, although many of us were probably running a temperature. Then we were divided into different groups. To some they said,:"Orchestra" and two or three of our chaveroth were among those chosen. The second group, which also had some of the chaveroth, consisted of secretaries. I was among the third group, which was the largest and was destined for laundry detail and the sewing room. The fourth group was placed aside—here also were some of our chaveroth. We never saw any of those again.

Our group was led a short distance until we reached the vicinity of the main camp of Auschwitz. In the center there was a large, multi-story stone building which—as we learned later—was called the Stabsgebaeude. This was the residence of the SS-women, but the basement was reserved for female prisoners. It was an impressive contrast to the barrack-blocks we had known in Birkenau. It was not until later that we discovered that the Stabsgebaeude housed only those prisoners whose capacity to work for the SS was being attempted to be kept intact as long as possible. That our chevrah belonged to this "select group" was explained by the fact that we were young and used to physical work. Even before our arrival it had been planned that we would be transferred to the Stabsgebaeude for special work. How lucky we were—if one can speak about luck under the circumstances—I should experience myself very soon.

Our kommando (laundry detail/sewing room) was assigned a rather roomy hall with about 30-40 beds. Two women received one bed, and since we worked day and night shifts, it was easy for one to sleep during the day and the other at night. I was assigned to the laundry detail. The work was, for me and certainly for the others, quite exhausting. Everything was washed by hand and rubbed on a washboard placed in a tub which was too high for me. There were brown SS blouses, brown slacks, brown shirts, underpants and brown socks—the color of brown similar to the clay soil outside.

I stood, or better hung, for a week at my giant wash tub and felt myself becoming weaker every day. Maybe I had a fever? I went with two chaveroth who also did not feel well, to the Revier. The doctor who received us was Polish, Christian and a political prisoner. Later we heard that she had many different moods—at times she could be very mean, at other times very good. She only looked at us and said, "It's clear that you have typhus. You are lucky that you have already been at the Stabsgebaeude a week. So you can go to the hospital. Otherwise, they would have sent you immediately to the gas ovens ..."

How I got to the hospital I never knew. I only remember that I woke up after being unconscious for a number of days and felt miserable. Three of us were lying in two beds. On one side next to me was a professional bicycle thief and on the other side a prostitute. Both were quite nice to me. When I wanted to speak I could hardly utter a word, certainly not coherent phrases. An elderly German Jewish doctor was responsible for the hospital—she wanted to help but was so weak that she could hardly do anything. We did not receive any medication. The little that was available was being sold by the prisoners who worked as nurses in exchange for food or cigarettes. After some time, I discovered the two chaverot not too far from me, in a similar condition. One was very quiet, but the other talked interminably—nonsensical material, fantasies, etc. But we established contact very quickly, at first from our beds. Later, we attempted to walk slowly from one to the other, grasping the bed posts.

Perhaps two weeks passed, during which time we gradually improved and we decided to make every effort to return to our work as fast as possible. We noticed that even from here those patients who did not recover were sent away—probably to Birkenau. Thus, we did walking exercises for several days and I can still see myself stumbling around my bed. I do not know how we recuperated. Perhaps it was tremendous willpower, some still existing strength, certainly our obligation toward the chaverim and our desire to reach Eretz Israel. I personally was helped by a young Dutch nurse. In fact, she probably saved my life. She saw that day after day I pushed away the horrible camp food which she served and told me, "You have to eat something in order to gain strength. If you'll give me your daily camp ration, I'll bring you something in exchange which you'll be able to eat." Of course I agreed, and for several days she brought me small appetite-inducing sandwiches, sometimes with a pickle, at other times with tomato or cheese. I devoured these joyfully and gradually my strength returned.

The three of us declared ourselves "OK" and the following morning we joined a group of inmates who were returned to the Stabsgebaeude. As far as I remember, I was the last among us, supported by my chaverot and stumbling behind the small column. The next day I resumed my work in the laundry detail. I did not work very much that day. I was still quite weak and was more leaning than standing in front of my washboard and the huge tub full of "brown." I do not know how long I would have lasted, but a miracle happened—it was another one of those in the chain of miracles that helped me to stay alive. In the evening, I was sitting with my friend, who also had a bed on the upper tier on the bed corner. I had intended to cut the small piece of bread which we had saved for the evening meal into two pieces. But the knife, which we had found somewhere, instead of cutting the bread sliced between the thumb and index finger of my right hand and created a deep wound. I saw a stream of blood spurting out and hysterically I ran with my friend to the "Revier." The Polish doctor bandaged my hand and asked me where I was working. After she heard that I was in the laundry detail, she looked at both of my hands, lifted them up and walked around in the room with me. She talked to everybody present, nurses as well as patients. "Look at these hands. With these tiny, tender hands, the child has to work in the laundry. No, I will not permit this. I'll talk to the block elder, Maria. First you'll get three days sick leave, to allow the wound to heal and then you'll go to the sewing room." Thus, after three days of leave, which did me a lot of good, I went to the sewing room, which became my permanent kommando.

The sewing room kommando also worked day and night shifts. The chaverot tried as much as possible to be on the same shift. Each shift had about thirty women. There were also a few older women with us—some of whom were from "mixed marriages" and received preferential treatment. Many of them had also arrived with our transport. The Kapos of the sewing room were three sisters from Slovakia who had been in the camp the longest. They did not behave especially badly toward us, and not particularly well, either. After all, we could stand it.

After having been at the Stabsgebaeude for about two months, we managed to establish contact with our chaverim who had been separated from us when we had gotten off the train. We received small notes very cautiously through the male Kapos who were allowed to circulate freely between the men's and the women's camps. Naturally, the delivery as well as the sending and receiving of these notes was done at the risk of one's life—we were very happy to learn something about our chaverim in this way. We could even send and receive small personal letters, always with the hope that nobody would discover them. We also learned details about our chaverim through our chaverot who worked as secretaries for the SS. They had access to lists from which they gained information about their camp numbers, their working place and any changes in their status, which they communicated to us. Although this was very important information, this type of news also caused us a lot of pain. We had assumed that one or the other had perished, but these had only been guesses, which we tried to forget as fast as possible. But now they became facts, "officially certified" news, which could no longer be denied. At first, only a very few chaverim were affected—but for us, every name which was extinguished caused us profound anguish.

All in all, the time we spent in the sewing room passed quietly. During the day shift we endeavored to work properly (even if, sometimes, we cut holes into the brown material on purpose). The interesting part was the night shift. Then, generally, nobody entered our room. The Kapos were relaxed. We performed the necessary work on the side, but mainly we talked. Of course we spoke about home, about future plans, described gourmet meals, beautiful clothes and hairdos. I would like to emphasize that with all this fantasizing, we were quite aware of the reality of the extermination camp. One was never sure what the next day, even the next minute, would bring and whether or not we would live to see it.

The nights, not only in the sewing room, but also in our bedroom, gave us the possibility to pursue different activities in order to maintain the life of our chevrah. The seven original chaverot in our kommando had been gradually joined by several other women, to whom it was important to belong to us. We were now about 10-12 chaverot. From time to time we succeeded in arranging an Oneg Shabbat on Friday night. We chose a time during which it was unlikely that the block-elder or the SS-woman would enter. Then we sat closely together on beds facing each other and recited and very softly hummed Shabbat songs. Also, on Yom Kippur, we held a small secret ceremony with some solemn words. None of us fasted, because we could not afford to.

On Chanukah 1943, the year we arrived in Auschwitz, we had a sort of "Askarah." It was one year after the murder of Alfred Selbiger, the director of the youth movement of Macabi-Hatzair. Since we did not know the exact date of the assassination, we scheduled the Askarah to be on the last day of Chanukah. Behind a blanket we kindled the last Chanukah light on a yarn spool, and afterwards the Jarhzeit-Licht for Alfred. Very softly, we sang his favorite songs, talked about him and revived old memories. We were lucky that nobody ever discovered these nocturnal activities—otherwise it might have been the end of us.

Generally, life during the night shift in the sewing room was less dangerous. Apart from the ordinary conversation, I tried to avail myself of the time in order to pull the chaverot out of our dismal everyday life. I recited poems by heart (my memory was functioning much better at that time) and told stories from Greek and Roman mythology. At the same time I could assist in their general education, which had been interrupted much too early in most cases.

Much more dangerous was another activity which became a habit during our night shift. The SS-woman who guarded us always appeared in our room at a fixed time and stayed for about one hour. Most of the time she slept, putting her head on the table around which we were sitting doing our work. She was quite stupid, primitive and generally good-hearted. At present, I don't remember from where we took the courage, but it is a fact that we accomplished what we wanted to do and were lucky enough that nobody ever caught us. In the basement of the Stabsgebaeude, there was a room reserved for the SS-women on duty. It contained a radio set. It appeared that we were pretty sure that, apart from "our SS-woman," nobody else was around at night. Thus, when she was asleep, two or three of us sneaked to her room. One of us kept guard outside. We put on the radio and searched until we found the B.B.C. and were hoping to hear that the Russians or Americans would liberate us soon. Unfortunately, at this time we had no possibility of delivering some comforting news to our comrades who were waiting in the sewing room.

This was, approximately, the usual course of our day and night shifts. Special events occurred in the winter of 1943. We had the idea to arrange a performance for the morale of the inmates. We chose as contents a fairy tale, "Pechvogel und Glueckskind" (the Ill-fortuned and the Lucky One) by Volkmann-Leander.[2] A Dutch girl who worked with us and who was a dancer took over the choreography. I wrote the text, mostly in rhymes. The performance was a big success with the inmates—unfortunately, the SS-men heard about it and demanded that we give a second performance for Christmas for them and their families. Of course, we did not want to comply under any circumstances and tried to refuse with all kinds of pretexts. But we were told: the SS commands and so we had to perform our fairy tale once more—not with much enthusiasm on our part but with a lot of applause from the SS-families.

I personally had a very upsetting experience around Christmas. When there was not too much work, I had started to make little dolls to give as presents to the chaverot. At first I did it under the table—then a kapo saw it and requested a doll—and from that time on she allowed me to make dolls and other small gifts officially. Naturally, this was more pleasant than darning brown socks, and above all, I could make others happy. But it started a new problem for me. One of our kapos showed a doll to the SS-woman on duty. Immediately, she wanted one, too. I tried to distract her under all kinds of pretexts, but she said, "I order you to make one." So I had to manufacture one for her. A few nights later one SS-woman officer came. Everybody was afraid of her. She usually walked around with a dog on a leash. I don't remember her name, only that she was known as the "Death Angel of Auschwitz." Now she was quite friendly and said she wanted to see the girl who made the dolls. Then she told me that I was to make a doll for her for Christmas—not an ordinary one, but a very beautiful one—a very dainty doll with lace, and especially, with golden curls. I could only reply that I did not have any supplies for this, hoping she would give up her request. But she took me outside and opened a door in the hallway. The room was filled with clothing. I knew instantly that this was one of the rooms where the belongings of those arriving in camp were collected. Here were only selected precious pieces. She said, "Just take whatever you need. I'll pick you up later." I understood that I had no choice but to choose something and was hoping that she would come soon to fetch me. The minutes in this clothing warehouse were horrible. I took a few pieces without really looking and was happy when she let me out. But this was not the worst. Then she said, "And the golden curls," and already she had unlocked another room and I was standing in front of an enormous pile of hair—hair of all kinds, hair of all colors. I needed some time to collect myself until I was capable of talking. "No, I cannot use genuine hair. It's easier to make curls from embroidery yarn." Then she returned me to the sewing room and I had to make the doll for her also.

All of these events occurred during the last winter months of 1943. Nineteen forty-four was a year of restlessness which was especially strongly felt by the SS. There was tremendous tension for us also. Day in, day out, we were waiting for scraps of news which we could gather here and there. The question which preoccupied us was, "how and when will the war be over?" Some time, I don't remember exactly when, there was a violent air raid. The alarm sounded but we had no place to go to be safe. Of course, we were ambivalent. On the one hand, we were happy that Germany' enemies had chosen this goal, but at the same time we feared that something might happen to us. One bomb fell next to our block. Later, we saw the huge crater it created. I believe one or two prisoners from our block were killed. The SS became more fearful and nervous than beforehand.

Toward the end of 1944 the restlessness grew, together with the certainty that the war would soon be over. What would happen to us? Would we be liberated by the Russians? Or would the SS exterminate all of us beforehand? It was a very cold winter. The clay streets were covered with snow. Our bedroom was no longer in the Stabsgebaeude, but we slept in a new block above the kommando of the "officially certified prostitutes." We still worked in the sewing room and walked through the snow to work. Now we were preparing for the evacuation. Secretly, we made for ourselves and the other chaverot, carrying bags in which to keep a piece of bread. We found some warm blouses, which we hid in order to wear them underneath our prison uniforms, and also found some warm SS-socks. The last day we went to work, we saw an older civilian worker. He waved to us from afar and shouted, "Don't be afraid, we will be all right. The Russians are very close!" This encounter gave us a lot of strength.

The night of January 17-18, 1945, the end started. Which end? The end of our imprisonment in the extermination camp of Auschwitz! But for us, also the end of a relatively orderly daily way of life, of relatively orderly eating, sleeping, washing and of the slightly privileged treatment we had been receiving. During this night I awoke because I noticed that the block-elder together with an SS-woman were in our room. I understood that they were looking for women who— for any reason—were not employed at that time, in order to send them on transport.

The next morning we were sent to work as usual, but they soon sent us back. Then came the order: "Get in line to take food for several days." Many inmates were already gathered who immediately started to throw themselves on the portions that were supposed to be distributed. Skirmishes started which developed into regular fights. We were no match for these battles and decided to make do with a small piece of bread that one of us had managed to obtain. In the meantime, the quarrel continued. One woman climbed on top of another, one hit another with a bottle and she lost an eye. We went outside to line up for the march. Beforehand, we had decided to hold each other's hand very tightly to stay together. We knew that was very important for us. We were three rows of five chaverot each. The SS tried to arrange an orderly evacuation, but they also were very nervous and it was not as orderly as usual. We started to march—five and five—and suddenly, I noticed that I had lost my row of five. One SS-woman saw me and boxed my ear viciously. She asked, "Why are you not in your row?" She took my hand and pulled me along, at first in the direction of the march, and then back again, in order to find a hole for me. I only thought, "What is going to become of me? With which strangers will I have to walk? How will my chaverot look for me?" Finally, the SS-woman stopped, pushed me into a row where she had found a place, and disappeared. When I looked up, I was standing next to my friend in my row of five. We were all happy. We marched in a group of twenty rows of five women each. In front of every group was an SS-man with a bicycle and a dog, and at the rear of every group there was also an SS-man with a bicycle and dog.

Thus, we marched through the big gate through which we had entered almost two years ago, only this time, in the opposite direction. I still can hear the words which one SS-man uttered to the next: "The transport is marching." That's the way we left the extermination camp and started the death march. It was January 18, 1945.

If I were to start now to give many details about the "death march" and also to talk about events after the liberation, then this report would be very long. That's why I'll talk only in general terms about the march and will mainly mention events that were of personal importance to me.

Our first station was the Ravensbrueck concentration camp. It took us seven days to get there. Five of those days we walked, and two days we were transported in open coal cars, lying on the snow which was covering the coal. These were seven horrible days. In the beginning, we marched quite well, but every day it became harder and harder and whoever could not keep up was shot by the SS. We supported each other in order to stay in the row. We marched day and night, and only in the early morning hours, between 3-5 A.M. were we allowed to rest a bit. Then we lay down in the snow the way we were, at the roadside, and slept in spite of the cold. When we were awakened, our three rows of five got up fast, threw down our clothes and, naked, washed ourselves in the snow. It did not disturb us that the SS-men were watching—it was important to do something for our health and for our "morale." After the first two or three days we did not have anything to eat, so we ate and drank snow. Luckily there was plenty of snow during the entire march.

During the third day of our exodus, something happened that is still in my mind's eye. I believe I never felt as strongly as in that hour that our end was near. In the morning, we were told that we could rest a little longer and we were led to a big crater located between two rocks. The SS-men stood in a circle with rifles and machine guns. We also stood in a circle, more toward the middle. The command, "Stand still!" was heard, and I was sure that soon we would be shot. The image—

how we were standing in a circle in the crater with the rays of the rising sun, and behind us the SS-men with their rifles I still see today. But nothing happened—after approximately an hour, the command "Stand up in rows of five and continue to march" was given. It might have been that they were waiting for orders which never arrived. Later we heard that during this time, there was already great chaos in Germany so that nobody knew what to do, and they certainly did not know where to go with us.

Thus we were led further to Ravensbrueck. There we stayed for about two weeks, received a little bread and perhaps even a few spoonsful of soup. Then, when there was no more food, we were transferred to the Malchow camp. We arrived in Malchow on February 11 and stayed until April 2, 1945. Then we were transported to Leipzig. On the way, we thought for the second time that our end had come, although in a different way. We were again shipped in open coal cars. Somewhere on a railroad station, our car was put on a secondary track. And then a horrible air raid started which was concentrated directly above us. The SS jumped from their cars in order to hide underneath, but we were not allowed to move—they threatened to shoot us if one would stir. I was lying next to my friend. We were holding hands and waiting. After every bomb from the sky we counted, we knew if we could count to three, we were still alive.

From Leipzig we marched two days and two nights through the snow to the Tauchnitz camp. Again we ate, drank and washed with snow. Never did we experience as many air raids as in those days. Usually, there were small planes of the Allied forces, who flew very low and shot at our columns with machine guns. They probably thought we were German refugees. This fright has stayed with me until today. I get very scared whenever an airplane above me starts to descend rapidly.

We passed masses of German refugees between tanks. They usually had horse-drawn carriages or perhaps hand-drawn carts, laden with household goods. And all around on the horizon, we saw their villages going up in flames, one after the other. Of course, it filled us with a certain satisfaction. Then we arrived in Tauchnitz, which actually was no longer a concentration camp but a work camp. Here also there was no work for us; it seemed that again the SS did not know what to do with us. And there was no food. Luckily, snow was still available. And for drinking purposes we had water—yes, real water. We stayed in Tauchnitz until Friday, April 13. In the morning I had an uncanny feeling that this would be a lucky day for us. It turned out to be true. Again we were on the road to be transported to another camp. After having walked for about two hours, we saw a Russian airplane above our heads which flew very low. It appeared that the pilot had recognized our column, because he started to wave. We pulled off our head scarves and waved back, joyfully. Slowly, the rows of the SS began to get smaller. Many were afraid and tried to disappear. Now, one of our chaverot who worked as secretary for an officer came to our row of five and said, "Just now my officer told me, 'If you want to escape, now is the time.'" We decided to follow this advice. The SS-men in front and behind our group had disappeared. When the transport came to a small fork in the road, the five of us turned off and continued on a narrow path which led into the woods. There we hid for some time. Good that in those hours we did not yet know what we later learned, namely that many prisoners attempted to escape and the Germans were searching the woods for many days, and shot without pity everybody they found. Again, a miracle happened. We waited in our hideaway in the bushes another day and night. And what was the first thing we did in the morning? We took off our clothes and examined everything carefully for lice. After some time had elapsed and we could safely assume that by now the marchers were away from us, we tried to pretend being civilians and invented a story which would portray us as prisoners of war. We felt more and more free and secure. Most probably we had lost all frames of reference. Yes, we were free for the moment, but the road to ultimate freedom was still long and filled with danger.

On April 17 we left the woods and came to a large manor house. We told our story to the owner, but he replied, "I know exactly who you are. A transport of Auschwitz prisoners passed by here and you escaped from there. I am willing to hide you under one condition—when the Russians come to the farm, tell them that I treated you fairly and that they should treat my children and myself fairly." We promised and he took us to an attic which was covered with straw. An old woman brought us some milk soup and a little bread. It tasted marvelous. And they were clever to provide us only with light food in small quantities. Later we heard about ex-prisoners who devoured everything they could get their hands on and they fell seriously ill. Some of them even died.

We stayed about six days, then the farmer called me and said, "I just received a call that in half an hour an SS patrol is going to search my house. They have already been all over the neighborhood. Under no circumstances must they find you here. I have a suggestion for you. A good friend of mine has a large farm, about thirty minutes from here. I'll explain to you how to get there. He will help you further. Now you have to leave quickly."

We were already at the gate of the manor when I suddenly remembered something. I ran back to the owner and asked him to give me a short note for his friend explaining the situation. He complied and I took the note. When we came to the other farmer, we told him that his friend had sent us with the request to hide us. He opened the door and told us to come to a certain room. We complied, but suddenly, I remembered the letter. I went back to him and gave it to him. He read it, looked at me and stated, "You know, you just saved your lives. I was about to phone so that the SS could come and pick you up, because I did not believe you. After having read my friend's letter, I am willing to hide you. Come!" He took us to a small room behind his house, brought us food and allowed us to lock the door ourselves.

After two nights he told us, "They just announced on the radio that all prisoners and prisoners of war should gather in Oschatz, a small town nearby. The Americans occupied it a short while ago. Go there and they'll welcome you with open arms." To each of us he gave a little package with sandwiches which had been prepared in advance. We thanked him, said goodbye and walked in the direction he had indicated. But we were almost certain that this was a trap and that he had sent us directly into the arms of the SS. So, after about fifteen minutes, we turned around and marched in the opposite direction.

While we were stumbling along on the highway, sad and unsure of ourselves, we saw two women on bicycles coming toward us and heard one tell the other, "How wonderful that the Americans are already in Oschatz and how beautiful the little town is with all those white flags." They passed us and all five of us sat down at the roadside and started to cry. Then we ate our bread—now we could do it—and then we got up and marched quickly in the right direction.

Finally, the death march and Auschwitz were behind us. The war was over, at least in our region. Yes, and we were free, but still very far from our goal—Israel. We stayed in Oschatz for about a month under the protection of a group of French prisoners of war. I'll give only one example of their touching consideration. The first thing they did after they had given us shelter was to give us marvelous French soap. Only later did they shower us with good food. After a month they told us that they would soon return to France and that Russian soldiers would come in their place. It would be advisable for us to move as fast as possible to the American sector.

Two evenings later there was a loud noise in front of our house, which had been used beforehand by German officers. Two drunken Russian soldiers crashed into the room. One threatened us with his rifle—he would shoot if we would resist. The other one approached the chaverah whose bed was closest to the door, with unmistakable intentions. We protested and screamed, "Auschwitz! Auschwitz!" showed him our arms with the tattooed numbers—nothing seemed to help. The soldier started to take aim, and suddenly, there stood a Russian officer in the door. He had the two drunkards removed and apologized politely in French. He had entered because he had heard our screams while passing by. From now on he would post a guard in front of our door.

But the next day we went to the Frenchmen to decide what to do next. They suggested attempting to take us with them as their wives to the American sector. They helped us cross the large bridge. On the one side there was a Russian soldier, on the other side an American soldier. We reached Grimma, located in the American zone and begged the Frenchmen to take us with them to Marseilles. Naively we thought it would be easy to get from there directly to Palestine. Of course, it was impossible for them but they took us to the American Commander-in-Chief and there they most cordially took leave of us. The chief officer of the American troops whom I managed to approach was unable to help us. He only told us we should be happy that we had "crossed the bridge" and were now in Western territory. He also promised to look after us. The "care" consisted in sending us, accompanied by an American soldier, to a camp for German homeless women. The camp was under the direction of Germans and was surrounded by a wall and a gate. It was clear to us that we would not stay behind walls any longer. They treated us decently, but the second day, early in the morning when everybody was still asleep, we climbed the wall and left.

Then our "row of five" separated from each other. My friend and I went in the direction of Leipzig, the next large city. It seemed to us quite normal that there, in the middle of the street, we met one of our chaverim. He was the son of a "mixed marriage" and had not been deported. He had lived underground in Berlin and had managed to survive all the horrors of the battle and occupation of Berlin. Now, here in Leipzig, he put his hand into his pocket and gave us something as if it was the most natural thing in the world. "This I kept especially for you!" It was a piece of material on which a bridge, the symbol of the group which I had led in Neuendorf, had been embroidered. During our last moments before our deportation two years ago, I had given him this piece of material for safekeeping—and he had kept it on his person during all the horrors of the last twenty-four months.

Then he told us that we should go to Weimar. Close by was the former camp of Buchenwald, where part of our chaverim and other former prisoners had gathered. Most likely, a Red Cross transport would soon be sent to Switzerland from there. So we went on the road again, partly walking, partly hitchhiking and even using the train a short distance, for which we ex-concentration camp inmates required special permission. In general, our encounters with Germans were not unpleasant. Once it happened that a farmer who had given us a ride on a buggy asked us from where we came and who we were. On hearing our reply, he managed to give each of us a resounding smack before we succeeded in jumping down from the buggy.

In Buchenwald, we rejoiced in meeting and seeing our chaverim again. They were waiting for the delegation from the Red Cross. When it arrived, there was great disappointment on both sides. It turned out that the Red Cross was supposed to take only children up to twelve years old to Switzerland, but there were no children of this age (they had all been exterminated). They negotiated with Switzerland, which finally agreed to admit teenagers between the ages of 17-18. Of course, all of us were interested in going to Switzerland because it meant getting out of Germany, one step closer to our goal. And for me it was especially important to reach Switzerland in order to find out from Natan Schwalb, our emissary of the Hechaluz in Europe, details about the fate of our missing chaverim. I finally obtained an identification card from our chaverim who had worked in the office in Buchenwald which showed me as being fourteen years younger than my actual age. In spite of repeated inspections by Red Cross personnel, I was included in the children's transport. We departed on June 19, 1945, and traveled for five days, sometimes over rails which had been placed across deep chasms because a lot had been destroyed.

After two weeks of quarantine in Switzerland, we were sent to a children's home of the Red Cross, from where I could get in touch with Natan Schwalb. After about three to four months, we were transferred to a house of the Youth Aliyah. There I met Akiba Lewinski, a member of Kibbutz Maayan Zvi. At that time he had come to Geneva as the Israeli representative of the Youth Aliyah in order to re-organize the Youth Aliyah in Europe. Akiba adopted me from the Red Cross as his daughter. In addition, I worked as his secretary in Switzerland for two years. At our first meeting, when I glanced toward the mountains across Lake Geneva, Akiba told me, "It is beautiful here, but at home in Maayan it is far more beautiful!" Then I knew that I would go to Maayan.

I also worked for half a year in the Paris office of Youth Aliyah and then I was allowed, under the auspices of the Aliyah, to go to Israel with a forged tourist passport. Our boat arrived in Haifa on June 28, 1947. Some chaverim of Maayan met me at the port in Haifa and took me to the Kvutzah.

And I knew that I had finally arrived home.

I should mention that my husband was born in Breslau, Germany, and has been in Israel since 1939. We have two married sons and eleven grandchildren.

Rachel Moses (née Inge Petzal)
Kibbutz Kabri (Israel)

I am writing about events which occurred almost 45 years ago. I have not consulted any books for assistance and give almost no dates or names because I do not recall them precisely. Everything is recorded the way I remember it. Certainly, friends and others who have survived the Holocaust as I have will write about different occurrences or recall things in a different light. The way I write it is the way I remember it. This is essential for me. In order to understand how I view the Germans through the years 1939-1945, I have to go back to my childhood.

I was born Ingeborg Petzal in 1922 in Arnswalde, a county seat in the province of Brandenburg, Germany. It was a beautiful town, surrounded by four lakes and much beloved by me. Today, Arnswalde is Polish. The present inhabitants, so I was told, have no feeling for the town (Heimatgefuehl), they yearn for Poland and the former inhabitants of Arnswalde long for their homeland.

My parents, Hilde and Arnold Petzal, were respected citizens. We lived very comfortably. My maternal grandparents, Heimann and Johanna Bieber, owned two large houses. In one of these houses, which had three floors, my parents; my sister, two years my elder; my brother, one year my junior; and I, as well as my grandparents and all employees of the two households lived. The employees had a floor to themselves and were very devoted to us. My great-grandfather lived in the second house. He was killed in 1935 by stones thrown by members of the S.A.

My parents and grandparents were loyal German citizens and we were brought up with the same philosophy. All of our friends and acquaintances were Germans. We mainly celebrated Christian holidays. Until 1934, I had never seen a Hanukkah menorah; in its place in our living room stood a Christmas tree that we enjoyed along with our employees. On all national holidays we put out the German flag. My father, a veteran of World War I who had been seriously wounded during the war, taught us to stand up while listening to the national anthem.

As a result of such an upbringing, I, of course, considered myself German and was proud of it. The teachers in elementary school were all friends of my parents and grandparents. I was popular in class, and on free afternoons many friends from school came to my house to play in the yard. We were my grandfather's first grandchildren and he spoiled us rotten. Nobody was allowed to say anything bad against us, not even my father. Punishment did not exist and every wish was granted.

Toward 1932, I noticed changes in my close environment which at first I did not understand. The adults often sat together and discussed politics. I always heard the phrase, "It won't be so bad, everything will come to an end soon." In 1933, Adolf Hitler was elected chancellor and for all of us a new era began.

My grandfather and father declared that as Germans we would not leave Germany. In school, I did not feel at ease any more. In the meantime, I attended High School and the children of higher echelon Nazis did not want to sit at the same table with me. I only had contact with children whose parents were against the Nazi government. I did not understand my world any more. At home, everybody was very concerned because it was impossible to continue the business. Our employees left us. New laws were enacted daily. Every night our windows were smashed, and we were forced to have them replaced the following morning. I was so afraid of the Nazis that I could not sleep any more at night. My sister was sent to a school in Hamburg where she stayed until 1940. So she did not experience first-hand the loss of our fortune and the total collapse of our life. Everything was taken away from us. My mother comforted us with some words which I'll never forget, "The Pope will not permit the worst." My question, what the worst would be, was not answered. I got the reply in 1943, when I was told that my parents, sister, grandmother and many relatives had been shot by the Germans.

In 1936, I was sent to a Jewish school in Berlin. My brother went with my parents to Stettin and my grandparents moved to Koenigsberg. This signified the end of my childhood. It was not easy to adjust to Berlin. I was homesick for my parents. Finally, the sense of security which Berlin Jews were still feeling got the upper hand.

In 1939, shortly before the outbreak of war, my brother went to the former Palestine with the last youth Aliyah group to leave Germany. The parting was very difficult for my mother who had accompanied my brother to Berlin. My father had not had enough courage to go with them. At the station where the train was departing, there were heart-rending scenes when children said good-bye to their loved ones for the last time.

In the meantime, the Jewish schools were closed and I took a course in infant care. The first heavy blow occurred when my parents were deported, together with all Jews of Stettin, to Piaski near Lublin. The postcards which I received from there were hopeless; a single scream for help. My sister, who had visited them just by chance at that moment, was deported with them. The first two years I could send a weekly parcel of four kilos, but most of the contents were usually stolen. Since I belonged to a Zionist organization, I was admitted to the Beth-Noar in Hamburg. I continued sending packages to my parents.

In 1941, the Beth-Noar was liquidated and I came to Neuendorf, a large manor about 30 km. from Berlin. A group of young Jews was living there preparing for emigration while being trained in the field of agriculture. About 80 youngsters, who were Zionists like myself, lived with them. They were lodged in barracks, a short distance away from the manor house. They came from many different Hachshara locations which had gradually been liquidated and had been concentrated in Neuendorf. The group was under the direction of three responsible youth leaders. After the hard and long work day, they then taught evenings: Hebrew language and songs, history and geography of Palestine. They led their own very active and intense life, apart from the general group, and I joined them. It was difficult to get used to the hard work and the new life-style, but slowly I got accustomed. I was greatly assisted by a friendship which was forged there. Rachel and I became comrades and she tremendously facilitated my admission into the group.

I could not help my parents any longer because it was forbidden to send packages to Poland. From time to time I received news, the tone of the letters sounded more and more desperate. Life in our group, and particularly my friendship with Rachel, helped me a lot. I became a part of the group and felt protected by it.

In the meantime, all over Germany transports of Jews rolled toward the East. Many parents and young relatives were in these transports, the letters we received were sad and hopeless and our group was greatly affected by these events. Our leaders helped and comforted us as much as they could. Our chevrah (circle) became more and more cohesive. We promised to stay together and support each other and remain strong.

The time of our deportation drew closer. The administration of Neuendorf attempted everything to keep us there. If they would have sent us away two months earlier, most probably hardly any of us would have survived. Of all Hachshara groups who had stayed together illegally and been deported in the beginning of 1943, we met only two girls when we arrived in Birkenau, and these two were Mueselmaenner (walking skeletons).

In April 1943, the date of our deportation was fixed. We were prepared for everything—but not for an extermination camp. We had expected hard work, and extremely difficult conditions—but were unprepared to learn that the word "transport" was almost one hundred percent synonymous to annihilation. Shortly before we left Neuendorf, I received the news of the murder of my parents, sister and grandmother. My parents were shot by the Germans in whom they had blindly believed. My grandfather had been able to save himself. I met him in Palestine after the war. He was still hoping that a part of the family had survived. I had to destroy this hope.

Before our departure, we were gathered in the Grosse Hamburger Strasse in Berlin where we were told the date of our deportation. It was the Seder evening of April 19, 1943. Auschwitz was given as our destination. The name instilled fear in us, but we were young and full of hope. Our greatest desire was not to be separated from each other. Once more we swore to help each other.

The large trucks arrived, taking us to the railroad tracks located far away from the city where the cattle cars were ready for us. We sat down on the floor of these cars, very closely one next to the other because there was extremely little space. I was sitting beside Rachel. The doors were banged shut and locked from the outside. I am certain that no one in those cattle cars ever forgot the banging and locking of the doors.

In spite of the crammed car, we prepared for the Seder evening. One of us told stories from the Hagadah and we all sang Pessach songs. The train rushed along as if it could not reach its destination fast enough. We hardly slept this night. The next day, I attempted to reach the only opening, a tiny window without glass but with iron bars. I perceived an unknown landscape. We reached Upper Silesia. Coal mines replaced the green countryside. I saw forced laborers and prisoners of war guarded by Germans during their work. The train was still hurrying, but suddenly it started to slow down. By now, I did not want it to stop. I noticed strange people outside, the kind of which I had never seen before. They were dressed in striped prison clothes or in old, torn rags and were guarded by SS-men carrying whips, accompanied by barking and tugging dogs. There was the same expression of hunger and hopelessness in everybody's eyes. I asked them, "Where are we going?"—"Auschwitz," was the reply and they pointed toward heaven. Others made a cut-throat gesture with their hands.

I went back to Rachel and said, "Believe me, Eliyahu-ha-Navi has to come fast, otherwise it will be too late." Rachel smiled, "How can he come when the door is closed!"

The train stopped, the first doors were opened and we heard screaming and barking dogs; everything around us trembled. Our door was unbolted and we heard the command, "Raus, raus, schnell, schnell—everybody out fast leave all your belongings." Hand in hand, Rachel and I jumped down. Immediately, we were separated from the men. There was no time to say good-bye. A large truck was parked next to the ramp. The SS-men announced that all old people, mother and children, pregnant women, and weak and sick persons should climb into the trucks, they would be driven. Many people ran to the truck, including the lazy bones who were looking for an easy life. As soon as a truck was full, the next one arrived. We never saw any of those children, mothers or anybody else who had climbed onto the truck again.

We were put into rows of five. Our group was close together, holding hands; next to us were the other comrades from Neuendorf. The SS-men checked the rows once more. Whoever appeared too old, they sent to the truck. Then we started to march, accompanied by SS-women and an SS-man of the dog patrol unit. Everywhere we encountered electrically charged barbed wire fences. We passed a gigantic gate with the inscription "Arbeit Macht Frei." The gate was surrounded by SS guards with barking and panting dogs. We entered through this gate upright and without actually realizing that we were now in the concentration and extermination camp of Auschwitz-Birkenau. It was Pessach (Passover), April 20, 1943.

We marched inside the camp on a straight, large road, the "Lagerstrasse." Nobody uttered a word. I was convinced that we were only passing through and would, eventually, be taken to a labor camp; because what we perceived was so unimaginably gruesome that we could not bring this reality into relation with us. We were young, and the creatures lying or standing around the camp were old, desperate human beings, dressed partly in striped prison clothes or in torn rags. They tried to approach us with outstretched hands, calling "Bread, bread." The SS-women chased them away.

We were driven to a large barrack, located approximately in the middle of the camp. Today, I do not remember the exact order of what was done to us. But in the end, we all appeared with shaven heads in huge non-fitting "Bresent" suits which did not provide any warmth. All of us were in a state of shock, some cried and some were entirely mute. After every procedure, we had to stand at attention in rows of five, and our group always fought to stay together. Rachel and I were inseparable. She was just ahead of me when we were tattooed with our camp numbers. I believe this event shook me up the most. Never had I seen, outside in the free world, human beings with tattooed numbers and, somehow, I had the feeling that this number was decisive. Since Rachel and I had consecutive numbers (hers was one digit lower than mine), we could remember each other's number.

Small, measly portions of dark, badly baked bread were distributed. Most of us did not take it. We could not swallow anything. Again, we were taken to another barrack. Here we were registered. At first we had to give our number, then our name, our parents' names, occupation and other demographic data. Finally, we were led into the block destined for us. Even without us it was overcrowded. We were assigned a koje (berth) where we spent our first night. Screams and shouts resounded in the block in a variety of languages, but not in German. The women I saw seemed to be insane. There must have been more than one thousand persons in our block.

The first days in Birkenau were especially difficult. The roll-calls lasted several hours. We hardly received any tea or soup, the masses pushing around the food distribution location were enormous. A dreadful inexplicable stench hung over Birkenau. Gigantic chimneys bordered the camp on one side, spitting smoke and fire against the sky. Corpses were lying all over, even in the latrines. In the morning, they were carted away. The sight of the corpses depressed me immensely, and in order to calm myself, I imagined them to be dummies. I stuck to this belief, and only after having already lived for twelve years in Israel did I admit that these dummies had actually been dead bodies.

After having been in Birkenau a short time, I noticed drastic changes in my physique; I lost weight rapidly. The girls from Neuendorf kept close together, we did not separate even for a minute. The hatred of the other prisoners from many European countries against the German Jews was omnipresent. We could not convince them that we had not caused the war.

During a typhus epidemic, I fell ill. I did not tell anybody because no-one would have been able to help me. From day to day, I felt worse. Only the news that a part of our transport would shortly be transferred to Auschwitz where conditions were much better made me hang on. After a long waiting period, we were actually ordered to report to a certain barrack. At that time, Rachel decided to stay in Birkenau in order to assist those who might still be arriving. The separation was very difficult, but it had to be. In the barrack, we had to individually file past an SS-physician in the nude. The sick were sent to one corner and the healthy to another side. I was among the sick and the doctor came to our group and promised medication, beds and special care. I did not believe his promises, and behind his back, I crawled on all fours toward the side of the healthy. They helped me to get dressed. Then we had to step outside. The sick remained and we never saw one of them again. The physician stood in the open door and observed us. He asked me why I had not remained with the sick. I answered that I was healthy and my comrades pulled me outside, away from the doctor.

We marched in rows of five a few kilometers out of Birkenau until we reached a building standing all by itself, not far from the men's camp in Auschwitz. It was the Stabsgebaeude. The basement housed the SS-sewing room, the SS-ironing room, the SS-laundry and sleeping facilities for prisoners. We had been up since 4 a.m. and arrived exhausted. The reception of the block elder was not very enthusiastic. She assigned us to different work details, I was delegated to the sewing room. Since there were no sleeping quarters available for us, we had to work that night.

During that night, I gave up. I could not continue to work. In the morning I reported to the Polish prisoner physician. She saw immediately that I had typhus, ordered me screamingly to undress and locked me without any clothing in one of the shower stalls to await the arrival of the SS-physician. I passed horrible hours in the stall, calling for help but nobody came. Only the following day, the door was opened and again I was standing in front of the same SS-doctor who had selected me in Birkenau; luckily he was not Mengele. He glanced at me questioningly. In spite of my wretched condition, I had confidence in him, and said, "I want to live, Herr Doktor, please help me." I still did not know in which direction he would send me. But I believe I made it clear to him that he was also a healer and that his work did not consist entirely of pointing to the right or to the left. I heard when he instructed the driver, "Take the little one to the Aryan hospital in Birkenau."

There I lay for many weeks, very ill and without any care. When I regained consciousness and my desire to live, I started to observe my surroundings. I noticed that the same SS-physician passed through the block every day surrounded by nursing staff. The patients were not allowed to speak to the doctor. I knew that I was unable to pull through without help and was looking for a pretext. When the physician passed my bed on his round the next morning, I raised myself a little in spite of the prohibition and said, "It's me, Herr Doktor. The little one from Auschwitz." All the prisoner nurses ran to make me shut up, but the physician came closer stating, "Here you are. How are you?" I asked him to send me back to my work place. He promised to see me the next day. Then he told his staff, "I want to see this patient tomorrow morning," and so he saved my life a third time. The following day he returned and ordered my transfer to another hospital block where the conditions were better. Even there he still came to look after me.—Only here in Israel did I find out that this physician committed suicide in Birkenau before the Russians reached the camp. His name is mentioned on many pages in the court proceedings of the Nuernberg SS doctors' trial. He was among the major SS-physicians who committed medical crimes during the Nazi period. I am convinced that my parents' belief in the German people which had served as leitmotif for my upbringing helped me persuade the physician to spare my life.

After many long weeks, I returned to the Stabsgebaeude and once more joined the girls of my group. They helped me regain my strength. Conditions in the Stabsgebaeude were immensely better than in Birkenau. The behavior of the SS-women toward us was a little more humane. We were able to take showers and keep ourselves clean. But, even here diseases were rampant and our group diminished.

I received the news that Rachel was very ill in Birkenau. In my despair I approached the highest ranking SS-man, an act which was strictly prohibited. He listened to me and wrote down Rachel's number. A few days later he returned and told me that he could not help. Rachel's number had appeared on the death list. It took me a long time to recover from this blow.

A short time after this occurrence, we were transferred. Military barracks had been constructed for the SS. They stood in long rows, visible to everybody. In order to protect them from air raids, we and other prisoners were housed in the middle row of these barracks. Before the underground movement, which had been in existence in Auschwitz for a long time, could inform the Allies not to bomb this particular area an air raid occurred. To be sure they hit their target, they aimed at the middle row and our barrack was heavily damaged.

The end of the year 1944 approached and so did the Russians. We were hoping for a speedy liberation; instead four girls who had worked in the Union factory were hanged in front of our eyes. They had stolen explosives from the factory which had been used to blow up one of the crematoria.

We heard that the Russians were coming closer, but before they appeared in front of the gates we were driven on the road. The death march began in the middle of January 1945, when it was icy cold. A multitude of prisoners was killed on this march. Those that had been shot lined the sides of the highway. They served as road markers for the SS—who often could not recognize the street due to hugh snow drifts. We were without food and water and had very thin clothing. The frost was horrible. We marched without hope, driven by the SS.

On the third day, I had a frightful experience which I will never forget. I marched in my row of five and suddenly one of the shot and wounded men—who probably had been lying by the roadside for hours—crawled toward me. He propped himself up a little, embraced me in an iron grip and begged for water. I could not free myself and did not even attempt to do so. The man was very seriously injured and I was horrified by his appearance. All I could do was to tell him that I did not have any water and to advise him to eat snow. Already, an SS-man with a pointed gun approached. The girls of my row pulled me fast and forcefully away from the wounded man and the march continued. I was in a state of shock. "The man wanted nothing but water," I tried to explain to the girls. "We don't have any water ourselves," they replied. At that moment we did not realize that we were lacking many other items besides water.

We walked until we reached cattle cars which were waiting for us. I don't remember the name of the railroad station. In these open cars we crossed half of Germany. At that time, a good part of Germany had already been destroyed and in the midst of this destruction we were on our way to another concentration camp.

We reached Ravensbrueck and lay in front of the gate exhausted, sleeping. Only the shouts of the SS woke us from time to time. Ravensbrueck was overcrowded and without food—they did not want to accept us. Eventually, the camp administration and our SS-leaders worked out an agreement. We were admitted for a few days. Once we even received some watery soup, but our major nourishment consisted of snow, similar to the deathmarch and cattle car diet. From Ravensbrueck we were sent to a camp in Malchow, a small town not far from Rostock. The next days we spent lying on the barrack floors. We saw food very rarely. They were literally starving us. Many women fell ill.

When the Russians drew closer to Rostock, we were again shipped in open cattle cars, this time to Leipzig. All of Germany seemed to be on the road during that period and everything was chaotic. Whoever could, tried to escape from the Russians. Some prisoners who had already been liberated were streaming back to their homelands. In the midst of this disorder, we were taken to Leipzig.

The cattle cars had transported coal previously and we looked like moors because of the coal dust. En route, we encountered a very severe air raid. The SS-men ran for cover, but we were sitting in the open cars and trembled with fear. However, we were not hit and arrived in Leipzig where we were lodged in an empty factory. We had been starving in Malchow, yet in Leipzig it was even worse. We were so weak that we were lying down most of the time and hardly talked. The SS was invisible. Again, many of us fell ill. Our only hope was the Americans who were already close-by.

During the night in which the Americans conquered Leipzig, we were once more driven by the SS to march on the road. We had to run on-the-double and once more the dead bodies were lining the highway. Our strength was waning. Allied planes shook us up. They must have seen the SS-men and thought we were German refugees. They passed us, returned and shot into our rows. I don't know how many casualties there were. I was close to losing my mind. But we fast followed the example of the SS and threw ourselves flat down in the ditches as soon as we heard the engines of the planes.

Finally, came the most beautiful moment of my captivity. An airplane approached, flying very slowly and low above us. We saw two men in the plane gesticulating and we understood the message: they knew who we were and they asked us to hold out a little longer. The plane returned a few times. We drew new strength and embraced each other joyfully.

And then, at long last, the instant arrived for which we had waited since 1943. We heard the message, "Run, run to freedom." At first, I did not understand the meaning of the words. But then I saw that everything was in disarray and people were disappearing around me and I did comprehend. My first thought was, "Why did so many people have to die before these words were spoken?" And at that time, I did not yet know how many millions had been killed.

We were in the vicinity of a small town called Oschatz. White flags were hanging out to indicate that the town had surrendered. Together with many others, I ran into town. We could not get to the Americans who were sitting in two cars in the center of town. There was a curfew, and the mayor was in the process of signing some documents to hand over the town peacefully.

We had to wait another day and another day, until we finally stood in front of the Americans and asked them for help. They did not know who we were, had never seen a concentration camp, and the name "Auschwitz" did not mean anything to them. They knew that there was a refugee camp in Grimma and sent us there.

Anew, we marched about 30 km. We reached the camp and were welcomed by German women. I immediately asked to be put in touch with the International Red Cross but they did not have any contact. We were told that there was a group of liberated prisoners in the former concentration camp of Buchenwald who could help us. In addition, there were American physicians in Buchenwald.

The distance between Grimma and Buchenwald was approximately 120 km. We took to the road at once. Most of the way we walked, trains had started to run again, but part of the rails had been destroyed. In Weimar, the last stop before Buchenwald, we met a group of men. They introduced themselves as former inmates of Buchenwald, mostly communists and other political prisoners. We were the first women from Auschwitz who arrived in Buchenwald. They immediately provided cars and drove us to the camp. At first, we were taken to the clinic. The American physicians were in uniform; there were also some German doctors. One of the American physicians spoke to me in German. He asked me to get undressed. When he noticed the poor physical condition I was in, he ordered the German doctor to come closer and examine me. However, I did not let him—I had had enough of German doctors!

In the meantime, a room had been prepared for us. We could wash ourselves and started to eat slowly—and at long last, we finally felt secure.

This is my story, the way I remember it. It will accompany me until my last day.

Jutta Bergt (née Pelz)
Weil am Rhein (West Germany)

I was born in Berlin on June 23, 1924. My parents were Ludwig and Regina Pelz, née Kallmann. My father had worked as an independent businessman operating a chain of movie theaters, but he already had to give up his business before Hitler came to power because of some shady deals made by his partners.

After attending several primary schools in Berlin, the last one at the Mariannen Platz in Kreuzberg, I entered Gross-Breesen, an agricultural school near Breslau, in Lower Silesia in May 1939, and transferred to Landwerk Neuendorf located in the Mark Brandenburg, one year later. From here I was deported via the gathering camp "Grosse Hamburger Strasse)" in Berlin and arrived in Auschwitz on April 20, 1943.

It was a big exception that relatively quite a few members of our transport survived Auschwitz. Since we were good workers, our deportation had frequently been postponed and we were the last large Jewish convoy that was shipped officially from Berlin. The Scharfuehrer who accompanied our transport was so touched by these facts that he felt personally responsible for us. In Auschwitz, he delivered the necessary declarations on our behalf. That's why we were treated in a privileged manner right from the first day.

However, thanks to some Slovakian Jewish women, we obtained the best possible work detail in the entire women's camp. They had been afraid of losing an inexhaustible source of "organizing." We had been earmarked for work in the Effektenkammer (warehouse), an excellent work squad of an elite Slovakian group. Here, the belongings of new arrivals were sorted out and possibilities for "organizing" were enormous.

The Slovakians had been destined for the Stabsgebaeude, situated outside of camp. Over there, one was isolated from all dirt and misery, one didn't see or hear anything—but there was nothing to "organize." In addition, the SS-woman in chief had a very bad reputation. The Slovakians knew all of this. They started to pull strings, contacted their friends—who as prisoners with the highest seniority occupied all kinds of key positions in camp—and asked to have the German girls sent to the laundry-detail instead. They preferred to remain in their old work squad because they were scared they would starve in the Stabsgebaeude. Their request was granted and we obtained the ideal "kommando." If the power of the strong would always be used in such a way in favor of the weak, the world would be a better place.

Unfortunately, only approximately one half of our group was chosen for this work detail. The selection process depended on the data we had submitted during registration at our arrival in camp, i.e., whether we had claimed to be farm hands or factory workers. I had registered as an agricultural worker because I believed that there would always be work in the fields, and it might be easier to obtain something edible. All the "farm hands" came into the Stabsgebaeude.

After this division, the protective (privileged) treatment of the group that remained in Birkenau came to a halt. Only much later were they destined to get good jobs in the ammunition factory which, at that time, had not yet been completed. Merely four girls actually obtained this work—all the others had perished in the meantime.

Thus we came to the Stabsgebaeude to inaugurate the night-shift in the SS-laundry. The Stabsgebaeude was located outside the large sentry chain. The SS-women lived upstairs, and in the cellar were the SS-laundry, SS-sewing room and SS-ironing room. There was also a large dormitory in the cellar connected by a hallway with the work-halls.

This work squad was really excellent if compared to conditions in Birkenau. We could keep ourselves clean and did not have to be afraid of selections. If I think back today that as a young girl I had to spend a year and a half locked up in a cellar, I feel sick. I love fresh air and spend every free minute out of doors amidst Mother Nature. Nevertheless, the cellar was our salvation. Contrary to Birkenau, where the inmates had to stand for hours outside during the roll-call in snow, rain and blistering heat, the counting in the Stabsgebaeude was accomplished very fast; the roll-call did not last longer than one half hour. And in the winter when the weather was bad, it took place indoors.

▼

For about twenty months, i.e., until the evacuation of Auschwitz, I worked in the sewing room, mending SS clothing. In the following pages I'll relate a little about our life in the Stabsgebaeude, as well as in the Lagererweiterung (camp extension) by drawing a few vignettes of some co-prisoners.

Irene Kuenstler

Irene's parents worked in Neuendorf. They came with us together to Auschwitz; in addition, there were her grandmother and her eleven year old sister. At our arrival, after we had descended from the cattle cars, the selection process started. To the accompaniment of screams and curses, young men and women were separated and the older people and children were put on trucks. We considered this to be a good sign which showed respect for seniors and children. When we did not find these persons in the barracks where we were processed, we assumed they had been admitted to a camp with more favorable conditions.

The next morning, we learned the truth from our new comrades. Most of them were Slovakian Jewesses who had not welcomed us too well. For them, we were not fellow sufferers in the same predicament but simply Germans, personally responsible for Hitler and his regime. That's why they did not even try to inform us tactfully about the trucks' destination. "You can't imagine where those trucks went? You didn't hear anything about it in Germany? "—No we had not." "Well, to the gas chamber. Didn't you see the high chimney outside the camp which spits flames day and night? That was the final stop of the people on the trucks. Don't think that you are safe. There are daily selections at the camp gate when you return from work. The ones chosen for the gas first go to Block 25. There they can prepare quietly for the last trip."

We were shaken—not so much about the facts which we did not yet believe, but mainly about the tactless and heartless way in which the message was delivered. These girls had already been in Auschwitz one horrifying year and only through brutalization of the innermost feelings had they been able to bear camp life without cracking up.[3]

These revelations were particularly painful for sixteen-year old Irene who could not grasp that her mother, grandmother and little sister were not alive any more.

After we had been in the Stabsgebaeude approximately three months, somebody told Irene that her father was in the hospital in the men's camp. Some of the girls of our youth group worked in SS offices where the inmate files were kept. They always informed up about the location and work place of the men who had arrived with our transport. Our men were in Monowitz, a satellite camp of Auschwitz a few miles away, while the men's main camp (Stammlager) was in our neighborhood and could be reached with some cunning. Once a week, a small group was allowed to visit the dental station. The Polish inmate physician who put the group together through pre-registration had full understanding for special cases if one confided in her. Once one was in the men's camp, there was always an opportunity to arrange a meeting.

We usually went to the dentist on Wednesday. Since there were a few days left, Irene started to eat only one half of her bread ration and saved the entire special portions of sausage and margarine which we only received twice a week in order to bring everything to her father, who could surely use it to regain his strength. For some reason, that Wednesday the visit to the dental station did not take place, it was postponed for the following Monday. The waiting and the saving started all over again because the sausage did not keep that long. Monday arrived and there was another delay. The same situation prevailed for the next two weeks; always great expectations that the meeting would finally take place and then again the big disappointment because the visit to the men's camp was cancelled. Until it was too late, and the father had been selected for the gas chamber. Thus, Irene had watched closely as her family disappeared till she herself was the only one left.

All of us had come to Auschwitz by ourselves. Our parents had been deported before us, and there was a little more distance between the extermination process and our realization of it, although we were certain that our parents had not fared any better.

Later, Irene and I became friends. While I attempted to have an optimistic outlook, she was far more realistic. In our numerous discussions she often said,

"I am not even concerned whether or not I'll survive. That is really not so important. But I wonder how everything will turn out in case we should survive. I am afraid of freedom. We all have no parents, no occupation and no home. We won't be able to return to Germany. For all the others it is easier than for the German Jews. Talk to the Dutch, Belgian, French, Greek and even the Polish, Czechoslovakian and Hungarian Jews. They all have only one desire; to go home. For us, there is only Palestine and I don't know if we'll be able to get there so fast."

In camp, I laughed at her, "You'll see, everything will be all right. Surely, there will be organizations to help us and possibilities to learn."

Now, 45 years after our conversation, I don't know which of us proved to be right. Everything was not as rosy as I had imagined it to be, but also not as hopeless as Irene saw it.

Mrs. Litwak

We met Mrs. Litwak in the Grosse Hamburger Strasse in Berlin where Jews were gathered before deportation. By coincidence, Mrs. Litwak came to our youth group's cattle car and was later transferred along with us to the Stabsgebaeude (only afterward did we learn that merely five cars of our transport had been destined for the camp, the rest had been disconnected and switched for dispatch to the "Beyond").

Mrs. Litwak's husband and twin daughters had been caught in the street, arrested and deported a few weeks earlier. I had known Hanna, one of the twins, from Gross Breesen. She was a good-looking 17 year old girl. Both sisters could sing and dance very well. They often performed at the Jewish cultural club. Under normal conditions, they would probably have become professional artists. In Auschwitz, I learned about Hanna's tragic end. When we were in camp a few days, our room elder started talking to us,

"You are all from Berlin?"

"We were deported from Berlin because we worked in the surrounding areas," one of us answered.

"Six weeks ago we had a transport from Berlin. But none of them is alive any more. The last four girls were shot last week while trying to escape."

"Is it really true that people are being shot while trying to escape?" I asked. "Since November 1938, many wives received notices about their husbands' death in this way. But here escape seems to be hopeless. Do many attempt to flee or is it just a euphemism for murder?"

"In this case it was a genuine attempt at escape," the room elder answered. "But in general, not many are trying. And these girls were better off than most. They were friends, and two of them were twins. The twins were well-liked here in the block. They could dance and sing and we saw to it that they obtained a good work detail. We made it easier for them here in the block because they lit up our hopeless evenings a little with their singing and dancing. And last week, they tried to run away from work. Of course, they did not get far. It was soon discovered that they were missing and the trained dogs were sent after them. Nobody has seen them anymore. I don't know whether they were shot or gassed." The Slovakian stopped.

During the entire conversation, Mrs. Litwak, who stood next to me, became more and more agitated. Like her, I also thought of Hanna and her sister.

"All last week we only talked about the girls' folly. Helga, one of the sisters, often spoke about escape..."

Mrs. Litwak screamed when she heard the name. "And the other was called Hanna, right?"

"Yes" the Slovakian replied surprised.

"They are my daughters," Mrs. Litwak uttered with difficulty. "I knew it immediately when you started your story. Now you have to tell me everything about them."

"That is horrible," Hanka, the room-elder, muttered. "If I had known that the mother was listening, I would not have told the tale.

We retreated and left Hanka and Mrs. Litwak by themselves. If Hanna and Helga would have lived a few more days, they most probably would have come with us to the Stabsgebaeude. Above all, there would have occurred the miracle that a mother found her children in this inferno and survived together with them.

We were transferred to the Stabsgebaeude and Mrs. Litwak sat together with us in the sewing room. Apathetically, she did her work. Since I had been friends with Hanna for a short while, I took special care of Mrs. Litwak. One day, after we had been in the Stabsgebaeude for approximately six months, she told me excitedly, "Imagine. I heard that Hanna and Helga are alive. They are said to be in an outside work detail with good conditions. It seems they were not killed after their attempted escape."

"Who tried to tell you this? It sounds completely unbelievable. We all know from experience that in cases of attempted escape the prisoners are always executed."

"I heard it from two girls, Ilona and Katja. You don't know them. They work in the administration and by coincidence saw the files of Hanna and Helga who are in a satellite camp. They told me to write a short note which they promised to deliver."

"I don't know. Don't you think we should have their story checked by girls of our group? Both Anni and Channa are working in the administration. They always informed us well. Tonight, I am going to talk to them."

"But they belong to another office. They just have files of Birkenau, Auschwitz and Buna. Where Ilona and Katja are working, there are only Slovakian girls. They came to the Stabsgebaeude after us and knew Hanna and Helga and learned in Birkenau that I am their mother."

"It sounds too good to be true. But who knows? Sometimes miracles happen, even in this hell. Are you going to write this note?"

"Of course. It can't do any harm. I am not too optimistic about receiving an answer or a confirmation."

And so started the devilish game. A week later, Mrs. Litwak received a small scribbled note which supposedly was from Helga. The handwriting was different, but Ilona gave the following explanation:

"The news can travel solely from mouth to mouth. It's only at our end that the message is written down."

Mrs. Litwak blossomed. Her doubts were thrown to the wind. Twice a month she wrote a note, and every week she received a message. And the two girls had to be paid for these greetings. Shamelessly, they exploited Mrs. Litwak. She had to darn socks for Ilona and Katja and knit socks and gloves and bags. We could "organize" as much yarn as we wanted to in the sewing room. All of these items, anyway, were the belongings stolen from the newly arrived victims. Entire suitcases with yarn, thread and other sewing tools were regularly delivered to our work place. Of course, we had no scruples whatsoever to take the best stuff for ourselves. For the SS socks, we took materials we could not use. We darned the gray SS socks with a kaleidoscope of colors. When they complained, we could easily prove that we did not have any gray yarn. Because of this exploitation, Mrs. Litwak did not have time to do other "extra-curricular" work, work where she might have earned a portion of jam or some other edibles. During the little free time she had, she was barely able to fulfill the desires of the two greedy girls.

In the beginning, Mrs. Litwak talked only to me about these pretended signs of life of her daughters, who supposedly lived so well outside in a satellite camp. But gradually, the "resurrection" of the twins became known. Nobody believed that the twins were alive. There were trustworthy witnesses from the former work detail who could confirm that the girls had died. However, no one dared to destroy Mrs. Litwak's illusion. We knew that Mrs. L. was as familiar with conditions in Auschwitz as we were. Perhaps, she just wanted to believe this fairy tale in order to anaesthetize herself.

In the fall of 1946, I visited Mrs. Litwak in Berlin. She was again in possession of her apartment which had remained intact during the bombing. She was very happy to see me and I still did not have the heart to ask her whether she had really believed the lies of those two girls in the Stabsgebaeude. At that time she lived a rather withdrawn life and was hoping to be able to emigrate as fast as possible to the USA in order to join her siblings.

Mine

Mine was already in her late twenties when she was in Neuendorf. She came to us when there was an advertising campaign for San Domingo. Supposedly, it would be easy to immigrate there if one knew something about agriculture. But, unfortunately, it did not work out in her case.

Mine was lucky in Neuendorf. She married a very nice man and lived happily with him until the deportation. Regrettably, he did not survive Auschwitz.

For Mine, our youth group organized a margarine assistance program in the Stabsgebaeude. The Polish woman doctor in our tiny Revier had diagnosed pulmonary tuberculosis and had prescribed a lot of fat since no other medication was available. So, we worked out a plan according to which each one of us would donate her fortnightly margarine ration which was distributed twice a week. For each individual this renunciation was not so difficult—while Mine received her weekly 500g of fat this way, which probably helped her to fight the tuberculosis; because after the war she had licked the disease. Mine never forgot our willingness to help—so common in youth groups—which was eagerly and gladly adhered to by each and everyone of our members—and throughout her life felt a strong sense of belonging to all Neuendorfers.

Frau Eberlein

Mrs. Eberlein was, for us young girls, the epitome of a happy wife. Wives of Gentile husbands were allowed to receive mail twice per month, they could even get packages. When Mrs. Eberlein received a letter, the entire sewing room rejoiced. She always read the letter to us in order to show what a marvelous husband she had.

He wrote touching letters about his yearning for her, about his endeavors to keep the house in tip-top shape, so that she could come back unexpectedly at any time and about the son who was still attending the Gymnasium (high school). He wrote that he often walked through the house caressing those pieces of furniture which she particularly liked.

After the war, I went to see Mrs. Eberlein in her house in Frankfurt/Main and met her husband. He was exactly how I had imagined him to be from the description and the touching letters; a modest, warm-hearted man who was still radiating happiness because his wife had returned intact. And Mrs. Eberlein was thankful for the fact that immediately after liberation she had been able to return to her home and family. She knew that very few of her former comrades had been equally blessed.

Frau Bannert

Mrs. Bannert had been transferred to the Stabsgebaeude because of her Gentile husband. She worked with us in the sewing room entertaining us with fantastic stories about her former life as an opera singer and about her husband, the bank president. Her voice was quite good but, unfortunately, she only sang short songs for us, never any arias. I really could not see her as an opera star.

In addition to story-telling, she was very good at organizing in spite of her age—with her 50 years she was by far the oldest of us all. She always had three times as much soup as we did and double or triple bread rations, all of these she consumed by herself. Nobody knew how she managed to do so.

Only after the war did I find out that she had survived the death march, notwithstanding her 52 years. In 1946, I visited her in her apartment in Berlin, which was not the luxury place she had described, and also met her husband who was already retired and who looked more like a small employee than a bank president, but he seemed to be a nice man. Only the son was missing, since he was still a prisoner of war in America. It was one of those paradox cases in which the mother was leading a dehumanizing life in a concentration camp as "enemy of the people" while the son had been "allowed" to fight at the front for the Fuehrer and the fatherland.

Shulamet

Shulamet sat next to me in the sewing room. She had also belonged to our Zionist group which had resided in a few barracks in Neuendorf, not far from the manor house. Together with her brother, Shulamet had been deported to Auschwitz. After approximately four months we heard that the brother had fallen from a high scaffold, had been admitted to the Revier with very severe injuries and shortly afterward gassed. Since Shulamet had been very attached to her brother and, moreover, was quite hysterical we had kept this news hidden from her, telling her that her brother had been transferred with a men's transport to Warsaw, and that he was doing all right. Shulamet lived with this story for about a year—nobody told her the truth.

In the late summer of 1944, horrible rumors about Warsaw, which was close to the front, circulated. Shulamet listened wide-eyed and began to be terribly troubled about her brother (who was not alive any more). Under these circumstances I felt that further concealment was irresponsible. I could no longer watch how she tormented herself with nightmares which were quite obsolete. I could not do anything by myself, these cases were handled collectively, especially since Shulamet did not belong directly to my group. That's why I talked to Anne with whom I liked to exchange ideas in the sewing room. As our former youth leader, Anne still felt responsible for the few remaining members of our Zionist group. She was in her late twenties, a high school graduate and, contrary to most of the other girls, had a tremendous storehouse of book-learning. Anne tried very hard to share her knowledge with us by telling us instructive stories or by patiently answering our questions, as far as this was possible.

"Don't you think it is crazy not to tell the truth to Shulamet?" I started my conversation with Anne. "Why should she imagine the most dreadful scenario which really can't happen any more. I always feel miserable when I have to listen to her anxiety attacks."

But Anne was still in favor of silence.

"I don't want to take the responsibility. Especially with Shulamet, we have to be very careful. There is the danger that she will do something irrational to herself."

"I believe that she'll get over it like all of us, it might be a little more dramatic and take more time. It makes more sense for her to familiarize herself now with the idea that she is all by herself. Now, at least she has our group to support her."

When I could not take Shulamet's anxiety-filled speeches anymore, I broke the news to her during an evening stroll. We no longer lived in the Stabsgebaeude but in a small, newly constructed camp. The advantage was that we could walk outside a little at night. The daily march to our work place also provided some movement out-of-doors.

Shulamet's reaction was frightful. Before I could comfort her, she left me and ran crying into our block to throw herself on her bed. Some girls of the Zionist group had noticed the incident and asked me for details.

"I told Shulamet the truth because I could not see any more how she was torturing herself," I informed them.

"How could you do this," Channa said. "We had all agreed not to tell her. If Shulamet does something to herself, it will be on your conscience and you will have to suffer the consequences."

All the others nodded consent and deliberately turned away from me. I did not feel too good but the task I had set for myself was neither pleasant nor easy. I even began to doubt whether or not honesty had been the correct policy or whether the majority was right. For three days I suffered from doubts, then everything occurred the way I had expected. Shulamet did not commit any rash acts, but, instead, came to thank me.

"It was good that you told me the truth even if it did hurt a lot, especially now when we can see from our windows the fire from the open pits day and night because the capacity of the crematoria is too small. Now, at least I know and don't have to worry any more. During these last weeks, I was crazy with fear of what he had to go through."

The Transport

After having walked for three days and three nights during the death march in January 1945, when Auschwitz was evacuated, we were put into open freight cars in Loeslau. I had succeeded in obtaining a corner seat for Irene and myself. We had just sat down to rest a little when a big SS man climbed into our car and chased us away from our seats. Furiously, we squeezed together near the wall because the seats in the middle of the car were dreadful. With hostility, we glanced sideways at the guard. Some of the girls who were sitting around tried to flatter him.

"Herr Posten (Mr. SS-man) there is a button missing on your coat, may I sew it on?" Or "Herr Posten, would you like to have a piece of bread?" These were rather dubious offers since they probably had neither needle, nor thread nor a morsel of bread.

The SS-man did not pay any attention to them. He just stared.

Only the lucky ones had food on this transport. It had been planned that everybody receive two loaves of bread, a cube of margarine and a can of meat. We had lined up in long lines since 3 a.m. to receive these treasures. But in the afternoon, not even one half of the line had gotten the items. Abruptly, the distribution was stopped and the march started. I happened to stand in front of the block where the bread had been stored and managed to get a few loaves. Thus we had a little food, whereas most of the others went without anything.

I considered it disgusting to flatter an SS-man. If the girls really had bread, they should rather give it to their starving comrades I thought. Possibly, the SS-man thought the same, he completely disregarded the girls' offers.

The train had been moving for quite some time, the girls had calmed down and Irene and I were munching on a piece of bread.

Suddenly the SS-man approached us, "Give me some bread." We had no choice but to let him have a piece. He was fishing in his pocket and produced a large piece of bacon, cut off a thick slice and handed it to us. That was an excellent exchange, I said to myself. The girls who had previously offered him some bread looked at us silently.

After the SS-man had finished his meal, he started a conversation with me. He told me in broken German that he was from Hungary and that he was impatiently waiting for the war to end so that he could rejoin his family. he showed me photos of his wife and two sons. "By the time they will be 18, the war will be over," he said sarcastically.

"How old are they?"

"The oldest is 14 and the other 12."

We talked about his family, his home, his little village with an unpronounceable name where he had a farm.

The train had stopped at a small station. The SS-man climbed out of the car and went to the railroad building. Soon he was back, and gave us his canteen with hot tea. "Empty it fast, so that I can get more for myself." Irene had a bowl and we emptied the canteen. Slowly we drank the hot liquid. We were still sipping when the SS-man sat down again in his corner. He also shared the food package which he had received at the station with us. This helpful behavior continued throughout the difficult journey. At every larger station there was a Red Cross kitchen from which the SS-man obtained provisions for us.

The closer we came to the interior of the "Reich" the more crowded the railroad stations were. We were not allowed to descend from the cars. The German refugees outside should not be confronted with these starved, dirty, prison-clad figures. This prohibition was, of course, disregarded and from all cars ghost-like creatures emerged begging for bread and water.

I saw how a man threw a large piece of bread into a car. Immediately, a woman grasped his arm energetically and screamed excitedly,

"Are you crazy to give away your precious piece of bread to these people? Don't you know what they did to us? They are our worst enemies and you pity them."

When we descended in Ravensbrueck, we said good-bye to the SS-man like old friends and thanked him. After entering the camp, Irene and I were somehow separated from the rest of the group. We were among the first to be transferred to Neustadt-Glewe after a short stay in Ravensbrueck.

The camp of Neustadt-Glewe was small. It consisted of only ten barracks which were woefully overcrowded. Here we were liberated on May 2, 1945 by Russian troops.

Some Afterthoughts

None of our group had been more convinced that she would survive than I. Often my comrades looked at me as mentally deranged when my conversations became too hopeful.

Like everybody else, I knew that the Nazis wanted to exterminate us, and that it was only a question of time whether or not they would succeéd... I believed that I would belong to those who would survive because of this lack of time.

Now, I am not even sure that it was such a blessing to survive. The disappointments and difficulties that arose after liberation were sometimes so great that I had to ask myself whether it had been worthwhile to withstand all of these horrors.

In camp I had been the big idealist; which is only possible when you are 18 or 19 years old. I had imagined that the post-war years would be very enriching and productive, the whole world would become better and nobler, and that everybody would have learned from the bloody events. Naturally, people did not become nobler and one cannot proclaim that nations have learned form this era. The big settling of accounts and retaliation to which I had been looking forward, with my mania for justice, did not materialize; many of the culprits were able to vanish in the crowd. I had to live among them and needed many years to come to grips with freedom.

I wrote down my memoirs, calling them "The First Years After Holocaust" to demonstrate how difficult it was for a Jewish girl, particularly in post World War II Germany, to find her way and which obstacles she had to overcome to somewhat master the events of the past.

Recently I read a book by Ralph Giordani, *The Second Guilt—or the Burden of Being German.* He himself is half Jewish and survived World War II by living underground in Hamburg together with his family. The book talks about the identical problems from which I still suffer, from liberation to the present.

Everybody has been integrated so smoothly into the Federal Republic; the perpetrators of yesterday are the big shots of today. The United States bears a large part of the responsibility for this state of affairs. After all, the old Nazis are proven and trusted anti-communists, and, therefore, important to American politics.

Ideologically, not much has changed in Germany. We Jews are perhaps some of the more privileged victims. Some people still feel a little ashamed, while only very few remember what the Germans did to other nations, for example, to the Poles and the Russians.

Ralph Giordani states correctly that Hitler's main crime was the war, without which all the other crimes would not have been possible. And it is precisely the war on whose account the majority of Germans are not upset with Hitler. Wars have existed since time immemorial—and that we lost it was just bad luck.

NOTES

Ora Aloni

1   *Hechalutz* was an association of pioneering youth movements aiming to prepare and train for settlement in the land of Israel.

2   Richard von Volkmann (1830-1889) was a German surgeon who wrote fairy tales under the pseudonym of *Leander*.

Jutta Bergt

3   In his chapter on prominent Jewish prisoners, Langbein writes about Slovakian Jewesses with low numbers who advanced to a sort of camp aristocracy. He quotes survivor testimony which asserts that in August 1944 the majority of the block-elders at the women's camp in Birkenau were Jewish girls from Slovakia, often very young, i.e., between 16 and 19 years old, who frequently were extremely cruel and behaved more German than the Germans. But he also points out that the survival rate of some of these first transports of the spring of 1942 was very low and that this should be taken into consideration when passing judgment on their behavior (Langbein, 1972, pp. 75-76, 199-202).

Dr. Irena Bialowna, a Polish, non-Jewish, political prisoner who had worked as physician in the Revier in Birkenau and herself succeeded three times in saving Jewish prisoners from the gas chamber, told this episode: "The patients who waited to be admitted to the hospital had to sit naked in the reception area. When I started working there I obtained a promise from the block-elder that she would procure blankets for the patients. The following day, I again noticed that a part of the sick was naked. I complained to the deputy block-elder, the Slovakian Jewess Manuisza, who replied contemptuously, 'But, Frau Doktor, these are only Jewesses!'" (Bialowna, 1987, p. 177).

Friedel de Wind described the situation in Block 10: "The block secretary and the room elders are all Slovakian Jewesses who were a long time in Birkenau. It was horrible for them there and now they think they have to make it horrible for us. 'If you would have been in Birkenau at that time you would have perished long ago,' they tell us and we have to put up with their brutalities" (de Wind, 1979, p. 177).

CHAPTER 12

Upper Tailoring Studio

The first seamstress who worked in the villa Hoess was Janina Szczurek, a civilian, who lived in the town of Auschwitz. Later, Marta Fuchs, a Jewish prisoner of the first Slovakian transports, together with other inmates, worked for many months for Mrs. Hoess. An attic had been transformed as studio and the yardage most probably came from "Kanada" (i.e., from the Jewish transports that went directly to the gas chambers). Manci, another Jewish prisoner, worked as hairdresser. She induced Mrs. Hoess to request a prisoner to do knitting for the children. Thus, another inmate obtained a good and protected workplace and Mrs. Hoess an additional work slave.

However, there was a lot of talk about the private workers in the commandant's villa. That's why Mrs. Hoess had a tailor shop opened at the Stabsgebaeude so that the wives of other SS-Fuehrer could equally avail themselves of these services.

The seamstresses of "Obere Naehstube," whose Kapo was Marta Fuchs, did sew exclusively for the wives of SS-officers and for the Aufseherinnen (SS women guards), and that at a time when Himmler had repeatedly energetically ordered that as many prisoners as possible should be placed at the disposal of the armament industry and that as few as possible should be used for essential camp work.

Some of the inmates who worked at the upper tailoring studio were the Slovakian Jewish women: Bracha, Baba, Borish, Herta, Irene, Kato, the blond Kato, Lulu, Lenci, Marta, Mimi, Manci, Sari, Hunya, Olga, Renée and Czibi; there were the French political prisoners, Alida and Marilou, as well as Helene, whose nationality is not known.

Hermine (Hunya) Hecht (widowed Volkman, née Storch)
Ramat Gan (Israel)

I was born in Kezmarok, Slovakia, to a family of seven children. Except for me and a younger sister, who survived together with her family in a bunker near the Polish border, all my other five siblings managed to emigrate as Zionists and Halutzim (pioneers) to Palestine. They succeeded in saving my parents at the last moment.

After I graduated from school, I became a seamstress. I then went to Leipzig (Germany), where I had relatives, to learn cutting and worked in this field. At that time I had no inkling of how fateful the choice of this occupation would be for me.

I was married to Nath Volkman, Z.L. He was arrested shortly before our planned emigration and sent to Sachsenhausen concentration camp. After three years, he was transferred to Buna-Monowitz, a satellite camp of Auschwitz. He perished a short time later. In March 1943, the Jewish community in Leipzig received the news that he had died of a heart attack.

Strange as it may sound, thanks to my Czechoslovakian passport, I was still in Leipzig on June 15, 1943. I did forced labor for the Friedrich Rohde factory which furnished furs to the Wehrmacht. Those Jews that had remained in Leipzig after all the resettlements and deportations were lodged in the Jewish Carlebach school. When the class-rooms became empty, we were taken to the Jewish orphanage. A few Mischehen (mixed marriages) were still living here. However, very soon the Jewish partners were also deported.

On June 15, 1943, at 5 a.m., there was a knock at my door: Gestapo. "Today, you won't go to work. Get ready. You are coming with us." I was not unprepared.

I was led to the Leipzig jail in Waechterstrasse, the gathering point of the transport. It was the last fully Jewish transport to leave Leipzig; the employees of the Jewish community and the staff of the Jewish hospital were deported. In Auschwitz, when the men were placed on one side and the women on the other, Dr. Klinger said farewell to his wife, Ruth: "Stick together with Hunya. I have the feeling she'll make it." Already in January 1944, almost none of all these men was alive any longer, and Ruth Klinger and I are the only ones of this Leipzig transport who survived camp.

Before our departure, Friedrich Rohde, my former boss, sent me a food basket which I distributed among the members of the transport. Some "Aryan" acquaintances had offered to hide me. I had firmly rejected the proposal and had told them that I did not want to be the only Jewess to remain alive and was determined to go together with the others.

Two days later, a train took us to the East. Quite a number of Jews from the northern border areas of Czechoslovakia joined the transport.

We arrived relatively fast in Auschwitz-Birkenau. The customary reception was waiting for us: lots of screaming and beatings. Even before we were taken to the Sauna, many from our transport were already missing.

At the Sauna, all our belongings were taken away from us, our hair was shaved from our head and all parts of our body, we received camp clothes and our good shoes were replaced by wooden clogs. Then we were tattooed and sent to Block 9, the quarantine block. It contained 1000 women. A Koje (berth) destined for four persons had to hold fifteen. There was no opportunity to wash and there were no toilets. Everybody had diarrhea. The food was horrible and there was no drinking water.

At 3 A.M., they woke us up. "Make your beds." The toilet was about one kilometer away. There was an endless line, guarded by an SS-woman with a whip in a futile attempt to "keep order." During the long and painful way to work, we were guarded by dogs. We had to march rigorously like soldiers and sing. At noon we received a watery soup, then we had to continue working until early evening. After marching back to camp, we received our scanty daily food ration—a piece of bread with a little slice of margarine or sausage. We were so thirsty that many of us drank from dirty water puddles in the road in spite of the danger of epidemics. Already on our first day, when we marched back from work to Birkenau, we encountered columns of male prisoners carrying their dead on their shoulders. An angel, called Kato Engel from Kezmarok, provided me with a pair of shoes while she went to work barefoot in order to obtain shoes from the men's camp on the way back.

My next work detail was the weaving squad, where we had to pleat whips destined for the inmates. One hundred women worked in a tiny room. The place had to be spick and span, we had to sweep it four times a day—while our food containers were filthy—we had no opportunity to rinse them before the soup was distributed. Our SS-woman, called Weniger, enjoyed hitting each one of us with a rubber truncheon over the head when we entered the building through a low gateway.

Suddenly, I fell ill with phlegmone and was admitted to the Revier (camp hospital). The place was overcrowded, there were no sanitary conditions, no medication, no bandages, no sheets.

The patients lay naked and completely neglected. Otti Itzikson, a colleague of my transport from the Leipzig hospital, who now worked at the Revier, helped me. On the day on which there was a selection, she transferred me temporarily to the "Aryan" Revier.

I stayed in Birkenau from June 16 until October 5, 1943, and then came the lucky turn of my Auschwitz experience. When I returned from the Revier to my block, I was informed that I had been requisitioned by the sewing room of the Stabsgebaeude. A few girls from my hometown, who had good positions in Auschwitz, found my passport in Canada (the clothing warehouse). They made every effort to get me into the sewing room. Since this work detail was located in the Stabsgebaeude where many of the SS-women lived, I had to be cleaned, deloused and examined by a physician before being transferred. Again I was lucky—the nurse knew my family and quickly shook down the thermometer before the physician arrived.

The reception at the Stabsgebaeude, where many girls from Slovakia worked, was quite stormy until Maria Maul, the block elder, asked "What is going on here?" "We haven't seen her for 20 years" was the reply. Some could not hide their horror at the way I looked—shaven head, wardrobe from Birkenau, stockings tied together with rope—the girls who worked in this building already looked a bit more human.

In Auschwitz, the sewing room was a good work detail. It was harmless, in contrast to, for example, the Political Section, where the girls were exposed to interrogations, torture and screams of prisoners and were condemned to remain silent—or to outside work, purposely planned for the extermination of starved, sick and weak inmates. I had the opportunity of working in my chosen field and even of acquiring more knowledge and experience in it. We could take hot showers, had a bed with a quilt (stolen from Jewish arrivals) and were sheltered from heat and cold. It might sound absurd to state that in the sewing room we almost felt "protected." Most of the colleagues came from Slovakia, spoke my language and had a similar background. It was understandable that, under such circumstances, close and cordial relationships developed among the girls which, in most cases, endure until the present.

The purpose of the sewing room was to provide the SS-women and the wives of the SS-officers with decent wardrobes. There was a tremendous supply of yardage and material, all of them expropriated from the Jewish transports.

We were about twenty-three seamstresses. I remember the following names: Bracha, Baba, Borish, Helene, Herta, Irenchen, Kato, the blond Kato, Lulu, Lenci, Martha, Mimi, Manci, Sari, Marilou and Alida (both of the latter were French women), Olga, Renechen, Czibi (nicknamed "der Fratz," the youngest of us) and myself.

Martha Fuchs, from Bratislava, was our kapo. She was capable, intelligent and a wonderful person. She used to relate that she received a prize for Paris but landed in Auschwitz. Borishka Zobel from Poprad, also a very gifted and smart girl, and Martha were our cutters and responsible for the work assignments. Every one of us had to produce two custom-made dresses per week. On Saturday, exactly at noon, the SS big shots appeared to pick up their wives' dresses. Here and there, when we over-completed our quota, and the ladies of the SS were extremely satisfied, we even received some additional food—a piece of bread and a slice of sausage. Generally, the food was similar to that distributed in Birkenau.

It is quite well-known that the SS led a very active social life in Auschwitz, and the sewing room produced not only beautiful everyday wardrobes, but also elegant evening gowns, the kind of which the SS-ladies would probably not have imagined in their wildest dreams. One day, our SS-woman guard told us, "When the war will be over, I am going to open a large dressmaking studio with you in Berlin. I never knew that Jewesses could work, let alone, so beautifully." "Soj a Yur auf Dir" was my instinctive reaction. ("Not on your life!") "What did you say?" she asked. "How nice that will be ..."

Although we had to work very hard and intensely in order to achieve our quota, nevertheless, we often had opportunity to laugh. For example, when the girls told interesting stories about their town or their parents' homes and skillfully portrayed some of the home town folks. Usually, the SS-woman rushed into the room: "I believe things are too good for you here ...!"

Gradually, we became an extended, closely-knit family, united in sorrow and joy by fate. I see each of them, and all together, clearly in front of my eyes—in spite of the fact that some of us, e.g. Lulu Gruenberg, Baba Teichner and Borish Zobel (about whom I am going to speak later) were killed while attempting to escape during the death march.

And thus, month after month passed. It was already the end of 1944, and we still lived in the shadow of Auschwitz. Frequently, we had serious discussions on whether or not we would ever be able to leave camp. Our opinions were divided. Helene Kaufman, who had been jailed as a political prisoner for five years before coming to Auschwitz, was quite optimistic and so was I, while Borish was gesticulating wildly behind my back. "She is fantasizing."

Lulu, who coined the phrase, "Just let me have strapacky (a sort of dumpling made of raw potatoes) before dying," was injured during an air-raid on Auschwitz in September 1944. When she was in the Revier in Birkenau, the girls tried very hard to prepare strapacky for her. She did not die from these injuries but perished, as already mentioned, tragically during the death march.—Incidentally, I recall another incident about Lulu: One day, Mrs. Hoess (the wife of the commandant of Auschwitz) came for a fitting. She always brought her little son along, and he had a good time in the sewing room. Suddenly, Lulu got up, placed the tape measure around the little boy's neck and said in Hungarian: "Nem sokara mindegyik igy fog logni apad, anyad es mindenki." ("Soon you are all going to hang, your father, your mother and all the others.") The next day, Mrs. Hoess came by herself to the fitting and remarked: "I don't know what happened to the boy. Today, he did not want to come with me for anything..."

January 18, 1945 arrived, the day when Auschwitz was evacuated. It was still dark when we had to stand outside in line for the march and it was dark and night when the columns finally started to move. Deep snow, icy frost, days without food and drink—that was the infamous death march. After days, we rested in a big barn. In the morning, we moved on. We arrived in Loeslau and assembled on a large square. Suddenly, we heard Obersturmfuehrer Frank's voice: "A train is waiting for you not far from here." The train consisted of open cattle cars, half covered with snow. We tried to shovel out the snow with our small food dishes in order not to freeze right on the spot. Many persons perished on this train, or arrived with frozen limbs.

Days passed and we continued to travel on the train, until one night at 3 A.M. we reached Ravensbrueck concentration camp. Large flood lights were turned on us. We descended and were counted. Everything around us was snow-white. However, in a few minutes, it turned black. The women from the train, supposedly ten thousand, licked away the snow.

For many endless hours, we waited outside, until they finally announced, "Auschwitz, at attention—you are going to get food." An enormous mass of starved, thirsty, filthy, barely breathing human beings surged forward. When I finally came to the spot where the food was distributed, I noticed that I did not have my food dish. (I shared a dish with my friend, and she was on the other side.) Thus, another one was added to the many days without food.

After waiting several additional hours, we were called again. A giant tent had been erected for eight thousand women. Camp police with rubber truncheons were already inside and the tent was brightly lit all night. Withholding of food and penal roll-calls were the order of the day in Ravensbrueck. It is impossible to describe the inhuman sanitary conditions. Here is an example of a penal roll-call: Some Ukranian prisoners, who had only recently been admitted and did not know camp etiquette, attacked a food detail. As punishment, the entire soup was poured out. "Here, eat from the ground." Because of that incident, 8000 women had to stand for hours at roll-call.

One day, during roll-call, I learned that all work squads of the Stabsgebaeude under the direction of Maria Maul (our former block-elder) would occupy a block in Ravensbrueck. I ran away from the roll-call and re-joined the girls of the sewing-room detail, who were overjoyed to be re-united with me. Even in Ravensbrueck, Maria managed to employ her sense of organization. She saw to it that each one of us at least got a little bit to eat. I was in charge of bread distribution and measured the portions with yardstick and pencil.

Conditions in Ravensbrueck deteriorated from day to day. The pipes burst and refuse was running down the Lagerstrasse (camp street). We were told to report for a transport. Our SS-woman guard from the Stabsgebaeude asked me why I had reported for the transport—she had provided a decent job for me. But, by then, it was too late. She also inquired as to the whereabouts of Martha, Borish, Baba and Lulu. I could not answer; I had not seen them myself.

The transport went to Malchow in Mecklenburg. This time we travelled in a real passenger train, and were given bread and margarine, whose sight caused hysterical laughter in us. We got off in Malchow, and from the horrified expressions of the Germans who saw us, we surmised that we must have looked dreadful. In the camp of Malchow, we first slept on straw on the ground. Later we got beds with straw-mattresses. Some of us received work assignments. I was sent to the ammunition factory which was camouflaged as a forest. I would like to take this opportunity to praise Mr. and Mrs. Mattner from Stettin (the factory owners) who behaved decently toward us. They convincingly claimed that they had not known about the atrocities committed in concentration camps.

On May 1, 1945, Mr. Mattner came to the factory and announced: "Ladies, the Russians are at the gates of Malchow, stay here and don't march again." However, quite a number of the prisoners were afraid that the Russians might harm us. Thus, we decided to return to camp and to join the transport of the other inmates. When the twenty-five of us returned to camp, an SS-man exclaimed: "Who is this bunch of swine?" In the meantime, all the others had received their rations and we were handed only a can of sardines, which we could not even open.

We started to leave camp and marched all night. In the morning, we rested. Everybody ate her pitiful ration of bread; only the twenty-five of the Mattner factory did not have anything to eat. The SS-man looked at us. "You don't have anything," and gave each of us a slice of bread. I would like to mention that shortly before the end, eleven Red Cross trucks with food for the entire camp had arrived. The children and the sick did receive their parcels the same day, and we were supposed to obtain ours the following morning. Maria had promised the person in charge of the Red Cross convoy that a fair distribution would take place. But, even at this late hour, the SS had preferred to keep the food for themselves. The children and the sick had shared their parcels with us, but we never received the items meant for us.

Then we marched on until we reached Criwitz/Mecklenburg. The SS had disappeared. It looked as if the entire German population was retreating, and it was very difficult to get through the crowds. Together with eight of my co-prisoners from Auschwitz, we tried to rest in a barn, but the owner did not allow us to enter. We walked on and sat down in a meadow in Criwitz. Then a very important event took place—three jeeps arrived and stopped in front of us, and that was the place where the Russians, the British and the Americans met.

We witnessed this historic occurrence, and WE WERE FREE!

We returned to the barn. The farmer did not refuse us any longer. We met many persons of different nationalities, and suddenly, Russian officers appeared and asked: "Who are you?" When they found out, they told us in German: "Viel Glueck in der Freiheit" ("lots of luck in freedom").

From Criwitz, we went to Neubrandenburg. There, we lived at first in deserted military barracks and later in a castle. There were former prisoners from many camps, among them a large contingent of Czechs who had been in camp for six years. A representative of the Czech government arrived and later the first president, Mr. Zapototzky, who promised to send buses to take us home. He kept his promise.

When we arrived in Prague, the entire city was in the street rejoicing with us. But, for many there was no home-coming.

The government gave each of us a certain sum of money. Theaters and restaurants were free for us. Charitable organizations distributed food. For two weeks, we stayed in the Masaryk home in a pleasant environment. The Czechs were very hospitable—unfortunately, one could not say the same about the Slovaks.

We left Prague by train. In Slovakia, there were no trains; so we availed ourselves of other means of transportation. Finally, we reached Poprad. My brother-in-law, who had recently returned from hiding with his family to Kesmarok, was at the railroad station with horse and buggy. All the girls from Kesmarok and the surrounding areas—unfortunately, there were not too many—although far too many for the buggy—did not want to miss the opportunity to return home as fast as possible. Was it really home after all that had happened?!?

> Oh Lord, Thou God to whom vengeance belongeth, shine forth!
> Lift up thyself, Thou judge of the earth; render to the proud
> their recompense.
>
> (Psalm 94: 1,2)

> Our Father, our King! avenge before our eyes the blood of thy
> servants that hath been shed.
>
> (Avinu Malkenu)

This report would not be complete without devoting a few lines to Borish Zobel, Baba Teichner and Lulu Gruenberg of the sewing-room work squad.

A few weeks after my return to Kezmarok, I met Martha Fuchs, our former kapo, during a visit to Prague. She told me the following:

Borish, Baba and Lulu, who had left Auschwitz together with us on the death march, felt that they could not walk any more. Somewhere, they discovered a train. They stood in line with other passengers and boarded a passenger compartment. Martha was the last. A Polish inmate next to her warned her not to join the others. She had noticed that the passengers were checked. The three girls who had no identification papers were placed aside. Martha later heard that they had been shot right on the spot.[1] She and the Polish prisoner hid for two days in the woods and then found shelter in a Polish village near the border. Martha offered to sew dresses for the women of the hamlet; they happily accepted. A few other girls from camp joined them and they dressed the entire village. The village was liberated two months later than many of the surrounding areas so that Martha and the girls came home belatedly.

Borish, Lulu and Baba, three young, gifted and happy girls, lost their still un-lived lives after three years of imprisonment in Auschwitz shortly before liberation. They belong to the millions of innocent victims of an inhuman and wicked regime whose evil deeds will be remembered for millennia. The flames they ignited will not be extinguished for a long time.

All of us of the sewing room have not forgotten the three girls. In our minds, they continue to live the way they were in the Stabsgebaeude—young, pretty, witty and helpful.

❖

Alida Vasselin (widowed DeLasalle, née Charbonnier)
Villejuif (France)

My grandparents already lived in the small fishing port of Fécamp (Seine Maritime) in Normandy, midway between Dieppe and Le Havre, where I was born on July 29, 1907. I received the name of Alida Charbonnier, the third member of my family to be so named. My father was a highly qualified mason, and my older brother (born in 1899) was mobilized in World War I in 1917 and later worked for the Parisian fire-brigade, from which he retired in 1960.

After completing my primary studies, I started apprenticeship in a sewing salon in order to become a seamstress. In 1928, I married Robert Delasalle, a baker. We had no children since I had one premature still-birth due to my hemophilia. Both of us were militant syndicalists, members of the French Communist Party and of the Secours Populaire Français. After the outbreak of World War II, we formed groups distributing pamphlets denouncing the collaboration of the government which did a lucrative black market business with its agents. We protested the black-out and the prohibition to go out at night without a special "Ausweis."

I was arrested on February 21, 1942, at 5 p.m. in the salon where I worked as a corset maker and where I had hidden the pamphlets in the finished corsets with the permission of my employer. My husband, Robert Delasalle, was arrested the same day, two hours later when he returned from his job at the confectionery in Colleville, a 5 km. distance from Fécamp. Our apartment was thoroughly searched by French police; the police commissar (inspector) of Fécamp himself was in charge of the operation. But nothing was found because the pamphlets had been hidden at my working place.

Shortly afterward, I discovered the reason for our arrest: A comrade of mine, Suzanne Roze, of the Resistance had been arrested one day earlier in Rouen. In her pockets, the policemen found a letter from her mother, Mme. Clément. The next morning, i.e., February 21, 1942, they were in Fécamp. "So, you are corresponding with your daughter. But not through the mail. Well, how do you do it?"—"Alida Delasalle is our intermediary," Mme. Clément replied. The mother thought her daughter should not be the only one to be arrested. Very simplistic reasoning, indeed. It did not prevent the daughter from dying in Auschwitz on March 1, 1943.

My husband and I denied everything. We were confronted with Mme. Clément, who persisted in her allegation.

From the police commissariat in Fécamp, we were all transferred to the police préfecture in Rouen, the capital of the Seine Maritime province and then, handcuffed, by train to the préfecture of Paris. There we underwent additional interrogation, got beaten up a little, but not very seriously in my case, in comparison to those comrades who held higher positions in our movement. In July 1942, Mme. Clément was set free.

On August 24, 1942, I was transferred to the fortress of Romainville where I found my husband who had been at Cherche Midi prison while I had been incarcerated at the Santé. We were, however, in different blocks. On September 21, 1942, my husband was taken to Mont-Valérien to be executed as a hostage along with a group of 120 Frenchmen in retaliation for the attack on the Rex Cinema which the French Resistance movement had carried out and during which twenty Germans had been killed or seriously wounded. I was able to say good-bye to Robert a few hours before they took him. He left, singing the Marseillaise.

On January 24, 1943, I was deported in a transport of 230 women from Compiègne to Auschwitz. We arrived in Birkenau on approximately January 27, 1943, in freezing temperatures. I was shaved from head to foot and received the tattooed number 31659. For the next two months, I worked outside draining the swamps.

On March 21, 1943, I was transferred from Birkenau to the Stabsgebaeude in Auschwitz to work as a seamstress for the SS-women along with Marielou Colombain, a comrade from my transport. My physical condition was such that I had to go to the hospital five times; for dysentery, typhus, otitis, operation of several abscesses and a cardiac crisis as a result of a beating. I had also developed a natural pneumothorax and some tubercular lesions in the bitter-cold Silesian winter.

We, especially the political prisoners, attempted to practice solidarity—particularly under these extreme conditions—and to help everybody, no matter whether they were Jews, Gypsies, or criminal prisoners, and without regard toward their political affiliations or opinions. Political prisoners had tremendous strength and served as an example in many cases. In comparison, Polish women might kneel and pray to God while they were being massacred, while others were apathetic and let themselves go completely. Like all concentration camp inmates, I also had my moments of discouragements, but I never lost hope due to my deep conviction that we would be liberated by the Soviet Army. This conviction was realized in spite of the fact that the Soviets carried the brunt of the war until the debarkation in Normandie on June 6, 1944.

On August 3, 1943, all of the survivors of our transport of January 24, including myself, were put in quarantine in Birkenau in a barrack situated outside the camp. This was our salvation; there were no more roll-calls, no more work, no more marching. We received a quarter liter of milk per day, had the possibility of washing ourselves, of writing home once a month and of receiving packages and letters.

This quarantine lasted ten months until June 1944. Then we were sent to work in a sewing workshop to mend the clothes left behind by Jews who were gassed. In August 1944, thirty-five of us were transferred to Ravensbrueck where we were all classified as "NN" (Nacht and Nebel [night and fog], signifying that none of us was supposed to leave the camp alive). I also worked in a sewing studio in Ravensbrueck and in spite of the dreadful conditions, the situation was a thousand times better than at Birkenau.

At the beginning of March 1945, thirty-two women of my original transport and I were shipped to Mauthausen. There we worked cleaning the rails at the railroad station. Three of my comrades were killed during an air-raid when the Americans bombarded the station. The three women had danced with joy when they heard the approach of the Allied fighter-planes.

On April 22, 1945, the remaining thirty women were liberated. We were transported by International Red Cross buses to Sankt Gallen in Switzerland, and from there we took the train to Paris where we arrived on April 30, 1945, among tremendous enthusiasm. We were taken to the Hotel Lutetia on the Champs Elysées, thoroughly examined by French physicians, some of whom had been deported themselves, and we slept in real beds with clean white sheets which we had not done in years.

We received a small sum of money, really a pittance, taking into consideration the cost of living in those days. Everything was available but only on the black market at ten times the normal rate. But in addition to all that in this newly regained homeland of mine, taking in the free air of my country, in this crazy environment of the liberation, and experiencing the joy of being alive, I was also filled with sorrow for my executed husband and all of the comrades I would never see again. Of the 230 women of my transport that left Compiègne on January 24, 1943, only 49 returned to France, and today merely some twenty are still alive and most of them are ailing.

▼

I remember the great hope that filled our breasts the day after our return to France, on May 1, 1945. There was the first parade after an absence of five years. It was snowing that day, but we felt warm with fervor and enthusiasm. My people had rediscovered their enjoyment of life, having fought so valiantly for it. We were free without fascism and without Nazism but we also thought of those who did not live to see that day.

The readaptation period was long and difficult; my mental and physical health had been greatly affected by the concentration camp stay and by the emptiness left by the death of both my parents. I spent many months suffering in the hospital: the removal of both ovaries; displacement of the uterus; acute pericarditis; neuritis; general rheumatism; discal hernia; loss of all my teeth; hearing loss due to the repeated ear infections in camp; severe intestinal problems; sclerotic lungs; Parkinson's disease; and loss of memory. All of these ailments handicapped me tremendously in pursuing my career as a seamstress full-time. Consequently, I had very little money to make a living until the degree of my disability was officially recognized.

I returned directly to my former apartment which had been only slightly destroyed; but it was my home where I had once been happy. Max Vasselin, my present husband, was the sole member of my family and friends to meet me at the station when I arrived back in Fécamp. I had already known him before the war since we had both been active in the Syndicate and the Party. He was also the only one who did not believe the rumor spread by Suzanne Roze's mother, the woman who had denounced both my executed husband and myself to the Nazis, that I had been responsible for my husband's death.

Max had been a prisoner of war who had been released in 1942, and as specialist in naval carpentry was a member of the French Interior Forces (F.F.I.). He was also a member of the liberation committee of the town of Fécamp. He was married but on very bad terms with his wife.

We formed a close relationship and supported each other in our misery. He divorced his wife and we lived together in a free union for thirty-two years before we married. Now, we have been married for ten years and we are very happy. We complement each other; help each other since the state of health of both of us is not the best and we hope to remain together for a long time. Max has two sons, four grandchildren and four great-grandchildren. They all consider me their mother, grandmother, and great-grandmother respectively. What a joy!

We belong to many associations, for example: Veterans of the French Communist Party, Old Fighters, Old Resistance members, former deported prisoners, former Concentration Camp inmates of Auschwitz, Ravensbrueck and Mauthausen, Families of Executed Persons; Resistance Museum, Popular French Help and many more.

We co-survivors do not meet too often. At the annual general assembly of former Auschwitz prisoners in January of every year, we come together from all four corners of France. There is an enormously friendly atmosphere, and we all feel tremendous joy and great moral comfort. Unfortunately, we also meet at such occasions to give the last honors to our deceased comrades.

I don't believe there can be any reconciliation with the Hangmen. My heart cannot forgive. We cannot forget our comrades who died under horrible tortures or in the gas chambers. But, of course, one cannot keep today's youth responsible for the horrors perpetrated by their elders. I am also in agreement with Israel in her fight to make those pay who exterminated the Six Million.

No country should ever attempt to exercise hegemony over another. For us, the most beautiful goal will be international peace and indestructible friendship among all people of the world.

❖

Marie-Louise (Marilou) Rosé
(widowed Colombain, née Méchain)
Les Lilacs (France)

I was born on April 12, 1920, in La Courtine, Creuse, the Massif Central, a mountainous area in the center of France. One of my grandfathers was a farmer, the other a blacksmith. After my birth, my parents moved to Paris. My mother worked as a cashier for the subway and my father was a postal employee. A few years later I went to Paris to live with my parents. I attended school until I was thirteen years old and then started an apprenticeship in the Haute Couture (as a dressmaker). I grew up without religion. My paternal grandfather had left the church, but, of course, I had Catholic and Protestant ancestors. We were free-thinkers, which was quite common in France. In 1938 I married Henri Colombain.

Very early on, I was socially active in my union. I was a member of the antifascist movement and participated in several actions against the Nazis and the French fascists who had been united in powerful political parties and spread their doctrine of Nazism and racism (especially anti-semitism). I belonged to a committee that supported the Republicans in Spain. We believed that if the fascists were to triumph in Spain then war in Europe would be inevitable—and that was exactly what happened.

In 1939-40 France was occupied, the French army was behind barbed wire in German camps, the Nazis plundered France and the French were demoralized. That was the sad situation in my fatherland.

After the first shock, my youth group began to act again. On an old Ronéo press we printed tracts in which we called upon the people to defend themselves against the occupiers of our country. We distributed these flyers in the street and ran away before the police arrived. We also wrote little notes by hand which we plastered on the house walls at night. Very soon we were discovered and had to separate, leaving our houses and even our districts. About fifteen young men and women had belonged to our group, all of different nationalities: Poles, Italians, Jews and French, and in 1945 only three girls were alive. The rest had been shot or perished in camp.

In October 1941 my husband was arrested in our house, where the printing press was found. They would have taken me too had I been at home at the time. However, I was warned by a neighbor and changed my residence. It was about this time that my little son died of diphtheria. There had not been enough vaccine at the hospital—because of an epidemic in Germany all anti-diphtheria serum had been requisitioned. I knew that the police were looking for me. That is why I did not even attend the funeral.

Afterwards, I remained in isolation for three or four months before I joined the F.T.P. (the Francs Tireurs et Partisans). I became a fighter, transmitted news, manufactured and transported explosives and arms, and participated in military actions.

I was arrested on December 16, 1942, and was deported one month later to Auschwitz, where I arrived on January 27, 1943, with a transport of 230 women who had been arrested as hostages or for membership in the resistance movement. On the way we suffered from cold, hunger, and especially, thirst.

The arrival in Birkenau was typical: screams, weeping, barking dogs, SS with rifles, confiscation of all goods including clothing, shaving of all hair, tattooing (I received number 31853, which I still have today) and receipt of soiled prison garb full of lice.

We were put into Block 26, which housed approximately one thousand women and there we had our first selection: gray-haired women or those with swollen legs were sent to the gas chamber, the rest were sent to work in the swamps. The water was icy and our shoes had holes. Many died because of frostbite which turned gangrenous, others from exhaustion. A typhus epidemic broke out in approximately March 1943. I fell ill and went to the Revier (camp hospital) which I left toward the end of May, without receiving any medication, cured but very weak and skinny. It was Mala,[2] the Belgian, who took me from the Revier to Block 3. There was no hard work in this block. I was assigned to a work detail where I could sit at a sewing machine.

I stayed in this block for about a month. One day, the block-elder prevented me from marching out to work. I was very scared, since I did not understand any German. On the same day I was transferred to the Stabsgebaeude. I believe that Mala was responsible for this change for the better.

I met Alida again, who had arrived together with me in Auschwitz and both of us worked in the Obere Naehstube, the dressmaking kommando for the SS-women, sewing tailor-made clothes under the direction of our kapo, Martha.

At the beginning of August 1943, something extraordinary happened—all 57 surviving women of my transport were put into quarantine in a barrack in Birkenau outside the camp, exactly opposite the building where the SS-men were lodged. We did not have to work and we got a little more to eat. None of us ever understood this sudden change.

Alida and I remained in quarantine for about two months. Martha requisitioned us and we returned to the Stabsgebaeude to continue working for the Obere Naehstube until August 1944. Then we were transferred, together with the women of our original transport, to Ravensbrueck. We were housed in a multi-national block which was called "Nacht und Nebel" (N.N. night and fog) and we were not allowed to do any outside work. On March 2, 1945, all N.N. prisoners were sent to Mauthausen concentration camp. We were liberated on April 22, 1945, and returned to France by the International Red Cross via Switzerland.

Of course, our return from deportation was celebrated in France, but it was not easy for us. I was unable to either laugh or cry. We had to meet with the families of those who had not come back in order to explain to them how their loved ones had perished. They did not understand anything—and that was very difficult. My husband did not return from Gusen, one of the deadliest satellite camps of Mauthausen. I never found out the date of his death.

I worked again as a dressmaker, remarried and had three sons. Post-war life in impoverished France was not easy.

Now I have three grandchildren, am divorced and live alone. We old resistance fighters have been integrated into the army of the French Republic. I received the rank of sergeant, a medal (which I never wear) and an excellent military pension.

I am active in the organization of ex-deportees and resistance fighters whose task it is to safeguard their moral and material rights and to preserve the memory of the dark period of Nazism. In addition, I belong to a group that works against anti-semitism and racism and to a third one which fights for equal rights on behalf of Third World countries and I participate in peace demonstrations.

In conclusion, I would like to state that I am rather tired. I believe that none of us who survived camp ever did completely regain our health. I am quite worried that there might be another war. I have planted trees on my land. If those trees are still there in 50 or 100 years, then mankind will have avoided the worst. I want to believe in this.

NOTES

Hermine Hecht

1   The escape attempt had been carefully planned before the evacuation (in regards to civilian clothing and other essentials). The group consisted of five Slovakian girls and one Polish woman prisoner chosen especially to facilitate communication. In addition to Borish, Lulu and Baba, there were Martha Fuchs, the kapo of the sewing work squad, and Ella Neugebauer from Bratislava who had worked in the Standesamt (civil registry), a subsection of the Political Department. Ella was shot together with the three women.

Marie Louise Rosé

2   Mala Zimetbaum was a runner in the women's camp. She often accompanied prisoners from Birkenau to Auschwitz. In June 1944 she escaped together with the Polish inmate Edek Galinski. Both of them were re-captured and executed.

CHAPTER 13

Cleaning Squad

Katka Gruenstein (née Feldbauer)
Senica nad Myjavou (Czechoslovakia)

My parents were plain folks who lived in a small town in Western Slovakia where I was born on March 3, 1922. My father was a coachman and my mother assisted neighbors with sewing in order to supplement our income. I had one brother who was apprenticed to a local auto-mechanic. The Jewish community was Orthodox and so were we.

At first, I attended a Jewish school and later the municipal secondary school. I had many Jewish and Gentile girlfriends from school and from our athletic club Sokol (Falcon) to which I belonged as long as it was possible. Until the creation of the so-called Slovakian state in 1939 which promulgated anti-Jewish laws, there was no difference, and nobody cared whether people were Jews or "Aryans." The main thing was that people got along with one another. During the scholastic year 1938-1939, I attended secondary school in Trnava. I was always a straight-A student and had intended to become a teacher. That's why I was deeply stunned when the school principal called me into the office and told me to pack my belongings. As a Jewess, I was not allowed to go to school any more.

1940 was a horrible year in Slovakia; all German legislation, including the Nuernberg laws for Jews, went into effect. My father could not practice his trade any more. I worked illegally, because Jews could no longer be employed officially, sewing for very little wages at a seamstress's who was an "arisator" for Jewish establishments. I toiled, hidden in a back-room, so that nobody would discover me. We could leave our houses only at certain, predetermined times, could only use some streets and were not allowed to use the sidewalks. Shopping was severely restricted, we could do it only at certain times and at certain stores. The Hlinka guards selected us randomly for work if they felt like it. For example, they took my brother to their headquarters, beat him and released him as a bloody mess. The Jews had to hand over all their furs, jewelry, sporting equipment and other valuable items. Everything the Hlinka guards liked, they confiscated. The Jew had no say and no protection, he was just a zero.

On March 27, 1942, two hundred young Jewish adults between the ages of 18 and 30 had to assemble at the Hlinka-house, the former headquarters of the Jewish sport-club of the city and county of Senica nad Myjavou. The men were sent to the camp of Sered and the women to Bratislava-Patronka. My brother and I left on the same day and our parents stayed at home. We were guarded by Hlinka men and German SS who took all our belongings away from us. Everybody tried to acquire as much as possible for his own use. At the Patronka, conditions were horrible. There was complete chaos, extreme overcrowding, no hygiene, insufficient food and we slept on the bare floor. On March 29, 1942, we had to march to Lamac where we were pushed into cattle trains together with young Jewish women from Bratislava and the surrounding areas. We were 1,000 persons altogether. The next day we arrived in Auschwitz.

Auschwitz

The cattle cars were opened and German SS were waiting for us. We heard them shouting and saw their German Shepherd dogs, attack-ready, at their sides. They screamed, "Where is the Jew-doctor?" Dr. Marmorstein from Nitra, a handsome and healthy physician who had accompanied us, stepped forward and stood at attention. One of the Germans pulled out his revolver and shot him point-blank. The doctor fell down dead. The intended message sank in. It was clear to us where we were and what we could expect.

We had to jump from the cattle cars, and we were told to throw down those small belongings we still possessed. They left us only the clothes on our bodies, then chased us to the bath house where we had to undress completely. We were then told to climb up on chairs and German female prisoners had to shave our pubic hair. One SS-man was snickering, "Oh boy, they must be coming from a nunnery. All of them are virgins." The women prisoners from Ravensbrueck were well versed in the procedure. They shaved our heads with a zero shaver and threw us some Russian uniforms full of lice. Then we were registered. Each received a piece of material with a red/yellow star and a prison number. Mine was 2851. The actual tattooing of the number on everybody's lower left arm occurred at a later date.

We had been the second transport of Jewish women from Slovakia; the first one had come from Poprad in Eastern Slovakia. We were led to Block 9. There were so many of us that we did not have room to stretch out. The following morning at 4 a.m., we were chased out for roll-call. We did not yet know how to stand in line properly. Lagerfuehrer Aumeier counted us and screamed, "Pull in your cow breasts!" After the roll-call, Rapportfuehrerin Drechsler assigned us to different work squads. We had to march to the gate; here a kommandofuehrer and SS-men with dogs accompanied us to our work place. My first kommando was "Abbruch Birkenau" (demolition of Birkenau). We had to dismantle the Polish houses that had been bombarded by the Germans, i.e., clean the bricks, level the earth, transport clay, etc. It was very hard work which we performed in the burning summer heat without water and, in the freezing-cold ice and snow, without adequate clothing or food, and always driven on with whiplashes. Our provisions consisted of some watery liquid, called "tea," in the morning, a little soup made of rotten turnips at noon; and in the evening, we received a small piece of bread and either a small spoon of beet jam, margarine or about one centimeter of blood sausage. It was unbelievably frightful because there was no water in Auschwitz and we were dying of thirst. The SS-women made a sport out of having their dogs attack us. These canines were trained to bite and tear prisoners to pieces. SS-woman Runge commanded her dog, "Na, los auf den Haeftling" (to attack me). The dog jumped up on me, but I was not afraid and did not defend myself, but, instead, talked soothingly to the dog. The Aufseherin (SS-woman) approached me and asked me my age and origin. From that day, she liked me. Frequently, she surreptitiously provided me with bread and cookies, without anybody noticing it. I was very grateful.

In May 1942, I was already very weak and exhausted. Out of hunger, I went to the Revier (camp hospital) and asked for some pills so that I would at least have something in my empty stomach. I asked Manci Schwalb (a Slovakian Jewess and former medical student who worked in the Revier) to keep me for 2-3 days so that I could rest a while. She admitted me, and I could at least sleep a little. We were about 15 women in the Revier. One day, a German SS-woman called Oberschwester (head nurse) Erika came to the ward and asked, "Who has to be operated on for appendicitis?" I had no idea of the meaning of the word, but I raised my hand and volunteered. I wanted to put an end to my life. Auschwitz was Golgata for me. The terrain was swampy and muddy all over. We wore wooden clogs which usually were too large for us. I could not walk in them and often lost them in the mire. If an SS-man pushed us, we fell into this sludge. This, combined with everything else, made it clear; I did not want to continue living.

The operations took place in the men's camp. Professor Wasilevski, a Polish prisoner, was the surgeon. We had to undress and lie naked on the operating table. After the operation, we were carried back to the women's camp. In the Revier, there was a German political prisoner, Sister Angela, a former nun.[1] She helped as much as she could and tried to instill the will to live in us. Of the three that had been operated on, two died. I was the only one to survive. Approximately a week after the operation, SS-physician von Bodman came to the Revier and discharged me immediately. Manci Schwalbova advised me to go to SS-woman Weniger and ask to be admitted to the sewing-kommando. I was accepted and worked about two months there. We mended laundry items and dresses. Once, an SS-man appeared and threw out whomever he pleased. I was sent to the peel kitchen. We were standing in water and were very cold, but the work was not difficult. We peeled potatoes and turnips and secretly ate them. In addition, we had a roof over our heads. Our kapo was a German prisoner with a black triangle ("asozial," a prostitute) whose nickname was Bubi.[2] When we worked the night shift, she poured icy water over us. Our dresses had to dry on our bodies since we had only one dress. The kitchen was in the men's camp. Through a little opening in the latrine, we could peep through and see new arrivals in front of the office. We gave them news about the camp and informed them whether or not their wives were in camp, were working and were alive. At that period, there was no mass-gassing. People died from hunger, from being shot at work, from being injected with phenol or other chemicals or by being beaten to death in camp or in the block. Because of the hunger and insufficient hygiene, several epidemics broke out such as infectious meningitis, malaria and typhus among others. At that time, we were not allowed to go to the Revier. Anyway, medication could not be obtained legally, but had to be "organized" (stolen, or provided through connections).

In August 1942, the women's camp was transferred from Auschwitz to Birkenau. Trucks arrived and the SS proclaimed, "Whoever is not feeling well can use the trucks." All those who got on the trucks never arrived in the new camp, but went directly to the gas chambers.

Since human language is almost incapable of conveying conditions of the concentration camp universe of Birkenau, I shall limit myself by describing just a few of its facets.

Birkenau: Metropolis with Gas Chambers

Daily, thousands of Jews came to the extermination camp of Birkenau from all European countries where German boots marched. There were Czechs, Slovaks, Germans, Poles, Bulgarians, Greeks, Rumanians, Hungarians, Yugoslavs, Italians, Frenchmen, Belgians, Dutch, Russians, Norwegians, Ukrainians, et al. Birkenau was a metropolis with four huge gas chambers where the Sonderkommando toiled day and night to gas and burn human beings.

A Few Names

A few names of the many SS-members who worked in Birkenau include: Commandants Hoess and Hoessler; Sturmbannfuehrer Schwarz; Oberaufseherin (chief SS-Woman) Maria Mandel, an Austrian; Rapportfuehrer Anton Tauber; SS-women Weniger and Elisabeth Volkenrath, two sisters; SS-women Opitz, Lotte Klause, Runge, Kraese, Drechsler and Hasse; SS-men Armbruster, Kubasch, Franz Wunsch, Stefan Baretzky, Lauterjung and Koch.

Sleeping Facilities and the "Leichenkommando"

When we arrived in Birkenau in August 1942, the camp consisted of two rows of barracks. The wooden ones were for "Aryan" prisoners, the stone ones for Jews. There was no floor and no insulation, just the muddy soil consisting of clay, urine and feces. Prisoners slept in three-tier "kojen" or berths of small stone cubicles similar to horizontal troughs. If you went to the "koje," you stepped deep into sludge. Approximately 5-7 women slept in one koje, pressed like sardines, on bare wooden boards; only much later did we manage to "organize" some straw.

Washrooms were non-existent. There were only the showers in the sauna, where the Austrian kapo, Muskula, reigned supreme.[3] It was very rare that somebody succeeded in washing herself. Normally, we washed ourselves with the tea we got for breakfast. Eventually, we managed to place some bricks on the floor and, whoever could, tried to organize some blankets to cover herself. We fastened the blankets with nails, but it often happened that the nailed-down blankets were torn off at night.

Dysentery broke out and spread like an epidemic all over camp. The weakened prisoners died in the blocks and in front of the blocks. The only latrine was at a very long distance away from the blocks. In the morning, the corpses had to be piled up one on top of the other, intermittently head to feet and feet to head. Most of the bodies consisted only of skin and bones; they were called "Muselmaenner" in the camp jargon. The Stubendienst (the prisoner in charge of cleaning the blocks) cleaned out about 28-30 on a daily basis. The women from the Leichenkommando (work detail in charge of corpses) arrived and loaded the bodies on their wagons to cart them away to a holding deposit from where they were thrown like boards on trucks to be taken to the crematorium. If the shoes of dead prisoners were still usable, they were "organized."

Young pregnant women who were admitted to the camp gave birth without assistance and threw their newborn babies under the "kojen" (berths), into the ditches or latrines so that they might save themselves.

Block 25

Block 25 in Birkenau was the epitome of barbarity. It was the antechamber to the gas, the terminus of life. The Blockaelteste (prisoner in charge of the block) was Cilka Wechter, a Slovakian girl of about 16.[4] Her function and her position of power went to her head. The Blockfuehrer (SS-man in charge of the block) was Rapportfuehrer Tauber, whose sadism was well-known. The inmate population had been selected by the SS during roll-call, while marching out to work, or from among the sick at the Revier. When a certain quantity was reached, trucks arrived. Whoever could, climbed up by herself. Those who could not were hurled into the trucks by the Stubendienste, one taking the hands, the other the feet. Commandant Hoessler as well as SS-woman Drechsler were in charge together with many other SS-personnel. Since the gas chambers were only a short distance from camp, we heard the screaming and sobbing. The women were chased into the gas, and a short while later we saw the smoke from the chimney of the crematoria.

"General roll-call"

In December 1942, the first general roll-call occurred in the women's camp of Birkenau. At 4 a.m., after the morning roll-call, the entire camp marched outside to the frozen meadows which surrounded the camp. Everybody had to stand at attention all day without food or drink. Any prisoner who sat down was mercilessly beaten. It was already dark when the "at ease" sounded. SS-woman Hasse, Arbeitsdienstfuehrer Stiewitz, Rapportfuehrer Tauber and many other SS-men stood at the gate. They directed each prisoner either to the left or the right. We did not know which side meant life and which one signified death. It turned out that the side of the majority denoted death. Several thousand had stood at attention in the meadows; only one thousand returned to camp. There were quite a number of these general roll-calls. I believe in fate, because I endured thirteen running selections (prisoners had to run past the selecting SS-men) and I survived. I also would like to emphasize that only Jews were subjected to general roll-calls and selections.

Delousing

The Delousing Procedure was a special chicanery that left us with more lice than we had previously. Early in the morning, they routed us out of the blocks. In front of the blocks, there were giant metal tubs filled with water and some chemicals. The chemicals could even have been cyclon-B, originally used as a disinfectant, before serving to gas people. We had to undress completely and wash ourselves, even if it was 30° Celsius below zero and the soil was frozen and covered with snow. They used us for pseudo-medical experiments in order to research the effects of alternate heat and cold on the organism. No normal human brain could have contrived such tortures. Then, Russian male prisoners shaved every part of our body on which hair grows. We could not reenter the blocks then as they had been locked while the interiors were sprayed with disinfectant in order to delouse the blankets and the straw (strohsaecke). Thus, we often remained naked until the following day. At night, we were looking for a spot so that we would not freeze to death. They did not let us enter the "Aryan" blocks, therefore, all that remained were the sauna and the latrine, and since the latter was nothing but a sea of excrement, the sauna was our sole refuge. However, the two Kapos Muskula and Bubi did not allow us to come in and we had to wait until the two fell asleep. Then we stood naked and shivering, glued against each other on the cold cement floor in the icy building and waited for dawn to break. In the early morning, we disappeared so that the Kapos would not beat us, and went searching for our clothes. The clothes had been flung on the roof tops of the blocks. Some girls climbed up on the snow-covered roofs and threw down the totally frozen underwear and clothes. We hastily dressed in these stiff, wet garments and went to work. Since we worked in the kommando Weisskaeppchen, which also was a warehouse of wearing apparel, we could change our underwear and clothing at work. Prisoners who were not as fortunate as we usually had more lice after the delousing than before since, as mentioned beforehand, the entire procedure served only as an experiment.

Weisskaeppchen

In Birkenau, I worked in the Weisskaeppchen kommando #202. Our Kapo was Rita Stoessel, who had a black triangle. The boss was SS-man Armbruster, a Bavarian, but quite decent. The work was relatively easy. We sorted out goods which Jews from many countries had taken with them to Auschwitz: items of value, such as jewelry, money, etc. These articles allowed us to survive. We "organized" them and exchanged them for food: bread, margarine, tea and all those provisions that were available in camp. Our "customers" were prisoners who had certain functions: Kapos, cooks, Blockaelteste and others in charge of alimentation. At the Revier, one could organize medication, white bread and vegetables from civilian workers. Of course, all of this was not easy. It was very difficult to pass the gate where we were checked by the SS. If a woman was caught, she could be dismissed from the kommando, could receive 25 whiplashes on her behind, or could be transferred to the punishment-detail under SS-man Mocruss, which was everybody's nightmare. We had to "organize" in the blocks at night: "Wer will kochedigen haban fuer saccharine?" ("Who wants coffee against sugar?"), "Wer braucht skarpetten?" "Wer will majlkes?" ("Who needs underpants?"), "Will jemand Suppe?" (Does anybody want soup?") Once we went and sold goods to German women prisoners in the Revier. They took everything from us and then created chaos, screaming, "The SS is coming to check." They did it on purpose so that they did not have to pay for the items.

Our kommando worked in the men's camp in a barrack. We often assisted prisoners who were preparing their escape by providing money and valuables. Our boss knew what was going on but pretended not to see or hear anything. He frequently helped us.

Selection in the Men's Camp

The barrack where we worked was situated in the men's camp. One morning when we passed by, there were selections for the gas chamber. Trucks stood waiting, SS-men, Blockaelteste and Stubendienste all were hunting prisoners. The camp streets were full of mud. But in the mud, something in striped uniforms was moving; there were people in the mud, men weakened from hunger and destroyed by heavy work and diseases. They were pursued with whips to the trucks; but they still had the strength to call down from the trucks, "Ihr juedische Majdlech, mir wollen die letzte Gepore fuer Euch sein." There were many events like this during my three years in concentration camp.

16 year old Allegra from Saloniki

I once witnessed a horrible occurrence in front of the kitchen. A giant barrel which had contained jam was standing there, and a young 16 year old Greek girl named Allegra from Saloniki came to scrape at some of the remainder of the jam with a tiny spoon. Rapportfuehrer Tauber appeared and began hitting and pushing her until she fell into the mud. Then he threw the big barrel on top of her and pressed it down for so long that she died. I never saw an SS-man commit atrocities in a drunken state. All such acts were committed while they were sober and fully conscious.

The Stabsgebaeude

One day in the spring of 1944, the Blockaelteste called out my number during roll-call as well as the number of a Greek girl named Esterina. We went to the gate and an SS-woman told a guard, "These two are going to the Stabsgebaeude." I took a deep breath; finally, I could leave behind the hell of Birkenau.

The Stabsgebaeude in Auschwitz was like a rooming-house for all of us from Birkenau. Since we had to work for the SS, everything was clean. There were sinks to wash ourselves, order, tranquility, and even a Revier for the sick. Oberaufseherin was SS-woman Brunner and Blockaelteste was Maria Maul, a German political prisoner who had already been in prison seven years. In the beginning, I worked as Stubendienst together with Baby Tyroler and Fanny Vald. We cleaned up when the kommandos marched out to work. Then I was assigned to the kommando Unterkunftskammer where we had to sort out laundry and linen. Sometimes, we mended the laundry with the aid of sewing machines, on other occasions we went to the houses of the SS to clean, always accompanied by guards. Once, we cleaned the apartment of Obersturmfuehrer Kraetzer, another time we cleaned a huge hall after it had been painted. The SS-man ordered us to pour a lot of water on the hardwood floor. We told him in vain that hardwood cannot take water. It was already late and we had to return to our block. In the morning when we returned, the hardwood floor was flooded and ruined. On these occasions, we encountered male prisoners who worked as artisans. At home they had been engineers, professors or lawyers. They came from many different European countries. By listening to the discussions of the SS, we learned a lot about the political situation, the movement of the front and of the many German defeats. We realized that the Germans were retreating all over and that they would not win the war. This gave us strength to survive at all costs.

Once, in the fall of 1944, we suddenly heard sirens howling. We did not know what had happened, but found out later that the prisoners of the Sonderkommando in Birkenau had revolted and blown up two crematoria. We could see the flames shooting up into the sky. We felt good in our hearts, but the consequences were dreadful. Many male and female prisoners who worked in the ammunition factory "Union" were interrogated. The SS found out that somebody must have smuggled out explosive powder from the factory. Difficult times started in camp. Four girls were arrested and put into Block 11, the Bunker. One day, there was Blocksperre, nobody could enter. Gallows were erected between the two blocks occupied by the women who worked in the Union. We were ordered outside and saw two young Polish Jewesses beneath the nooses. Next to them stood the hangman, Bunker Jakub from Block 11. Commandant Hoessler gave a speech. We all glanced in awe at these young girls who actually had not yet fully lived and who were now sacrificing their lives. All of a sudden, sirens howled announcing an air-raid that sent all of us, including the two girls, underneath the gallows to the basement to wait for the all-clear. It lasted about an hour, then we were all ordered out again. The two girls sang the Polish national anthem and the entire camp sang along. Jakub climbed up and a few moments later the two young women were dead. The two other girls were hung at night so that the kommandos who returned late from work would not miss the spectacle.

After Auschwitz

On January 18 1945, we were evacuated. The front was already very close. At night, at around 7 p.m., we passed the Auschwitz gate for the last time. It was bitter cold. There had been chaos in camp all day but the SS was still in charge. On this death march, they chased us with their rifles all night. Once we rested in the barn of a large farm. Those women who did not find shelter underneath a roof were completely frozen the next morning. We went through snow-covered hamlets and hoped that partisans would liberate us. The next time we made halt in a barn and dug ourselves deep into the straw to hide. The SS checked with dogs and we had to come out. They put us with our faces to the wall, and were about to shoot us, but somebody exclaimed, "Let those women go, it's time to move on." The general confusion saved us. Many weaker prisoners died en route. Finally, we reached Loeslau by foot and were driven into open cattle cars, about 80 persons per car. We were so closely pressed together that we had to take turns sitting down; half of us had to stand while the other half rested, and vice versa. There was no bread and no water, we lived on snow alone. If somebody died, we tossed the body out of the car. At the railroad station of Breslau, we organized some turnips. The train also stopped at the Berlin railway station. A civilian, who carried bread, asked us whether we had any cigarettes. We told him to throw in the bread and we would give him the "papirosy." It was a miracle that we outwitted him since we were not allowed to leave the car. We used an empty tin can to relieve ourselves. Once, we stood in an open field when one woman emptied the can. We suddenly heard screams, "Damn it, who poured shit over me?"

At the end of January 1945, we arrived in Ravensbrueck. There was total disorganization and no space for us. They put us into a huge hall, without beds or water. Again, we had to wash ourselves with snow. I managed to get to the women's camp of Ravensbrueck where I had a Polish acquaintance who was Blockaelteste. She allowed me to sleep in her block, and I could wash myself in the washrooms with icy water, but for the roll call, I had to go somewhere else.

One day I saw an SS-man write down prisoner numbers for women to be transferred. I submitted my number and the ones of my friends. We wanted to get away from Ravensbrueck, regardless of the destination. Our group consisted of about 200 women. We left through the main gate and breathed a sigh of relief. Real railroad carriages were waiting for us at the station, and everybody received a loaf of bread and a cube of margarine. We passed through bombed-out villages, and arrived at a small town called Malchow. They led us to a camp which consisted of wooden barracks, painted green. There was also a Revier for the sick. We met quite a number of Auschwitz prisoners who had arrived with previous transports.

We ate grass and the bark of trees because there was so little food. In the beginning, I worked in the block, then later in an ammunition factory which was surrounded by artificial trees as camouflage. Occasionally, I marched out of camp to clean the houses of the SS. It was in March 1945, and the SS was already quite worried. Air-raids occurred on a daily basis. Many prominent people escaped from the larger cities and tried to hide in Malchow. They came by train, in cars and in buses with the entire family and lots of luggage.

On April 2, 1945, there was a big air-raid. Knowing that prominent Germans were gathered in Malchow, the Allies even bombarded the camp. Some of the SS-men took off their uniforms. We noticed that the end was approaching. Thus, we left the camp in April, removed our prisoner clothes, donned civilian clothing and took to the road ourselves. We saw many evacuees en route in carriages and cars.

On May 9, 1945, the day the Germans capitulated, we arrived in Schwerin. We already knew that the war was over and went straight to the Americans. We showed them our tattooed numbers and explained their meaning. Among the American soldiers were many Jews. They put us up in a villa in Bismarkstrasse. There was no shortage of food. A few days later, we were transported in Red Cross trucks to Luebeck, where we were lodged in the former Hitler barracks. Luebeck was occupied by the British who did nothing to help us. We contacted the International Red Cross and succeeded in sending a message home by radio to Senica in Czechoslovakia. Many former concentration camp inmates, prisoners of war or forced laborers from a multitude of European countries were in these barracks. We received food-stamps as well as ration cards for electricity. Eventually, the Czech artist E. F. Burian, who had been a prisoner in Neuengamme, organized a transport to Czechoslovakia. We traveled in trucks through many German towns and cities, almost entirely destroyed, and arrived in Prague in July. Here, we were provided with repatriation papers, received 500 kcs each and were put into quarantine in the Glass Palace. Again, nobody really looked after us. That's why we took the initiative ourselves and decided to return home as fast as possible in order to re-enter normal life.

Trains went irregularly and were overcrowded. After three days of travel in different directions, we arrived during the night at the station of Senica, about three kilometers away from town. My girl-friends's parents had heard the news on the radio and knew that she was alive. Every day they went to the railroad station with horse and buggy to meet her. My friend's father greeted me and asked me, "To whom are you going? Nobody of your family returned." Indeed, I did not find anybody, my parents had perished at Auschwitz and my brother in Majdanek.

From our district, 739 people were deported, only five people returned; four girls and one boy. All of the others perished in a heinous fashion. I had a cousin in Senica who survived in hiding, while her husband returned from Dachau, and I stayed with them for a year until I got married. I already knew my husband before the war. His entire family had been hidden by peasants and saved.

December 22, 1946 was my wedding day. We had two daughters. The older one, an engineer, died at age 28 in a car accident while on a business trip. Our younger daughter is a dental technician and is married with two sons. My husband and I are living contentedly. We appreciate the fact that we are living in peace, with justice and equality for all citizens. I close with the words of the Czech poet and writer who was killed by the Fascist Germans in Pankrac:

"Lidi bdete. Nikdy viac vojna, nikdy viac fasizmus!" (Never again war, never again Fascism.)

NOTES

Katka Gruenstein

1   The nun Maria Caecilia Autsch, or Sister Angela of the most sacred Heart of Jesus, a member of the Trinitarian order of the convent of Moedlin in Lower Austria, had come with the first transport of 999 German prisoners from Ravensbrueck and had the Auschwitz number of 512. In camp she was generally known as "The Angel of Auschwitz" (Der Dom, 1987).

2   Nomberg-Przytyk describes Bubi in the following way: "One afternoon, Kapo Bubi burst into the room ... she wore men's clothing: pants and a sweater. Her hair was cut short. She had a deep voice and quick, nervous movements. Next to her number she wore a black triangle, which indicated that she was an asocial prisoner ... We feared her as much as we feared the SS-men. She used to come in often to flirt with Orli. She was a lesbian. We all knew about it and we were afraid of her, but we were also repelled by her flirtations. With great relish she described to us all the tragic occurrences in the camp" (Nomberg-Przytyk, 1985, pp. 33, 92).

3   "The all-powerful Puffmutti (Madam), the bathhouse Kapo, whose real name is Musskeller, is the toughest and most brazen creature in the camp. She is a favorite of Oberaufseherin Mandel, since they both come from Austria, and she takes full advantage of this. She does absolutely as she pleases. Perhaps other functionaries, also deprived of any sense of honesty and integrity, do the same things she does, but either from respect for their superiors or from fear of losing their jobs or, maybe, from the remnants of shame that are still left in them, none of them is as beastly and deadly as Musskeller. In her relations with co-prisoners she has no shame whatsoever, no qualms. When, during the delousing, she walks among the nude women, her stout, robust figure inspires more fear than that of the worst SS men. Her picture has become engraved for many long years to come in the memories of the women prisoners of Birkenau, and even today, if any ex-prisoner should happen to come upon Musskeller suddenly and unexpectedly, I am sure she would be startled and run away.

Musskeller gets excited when she beats, her bloodshot eyes grow hazy, the blows from her hand evoke cries not only of humiliation, but also of pain.—There is not a thing or person in the entire camp that Musskeller could not either buy or bribe, with the jewelry or food she steals from the new arrivals who pass through her hands" (Szmaglewska, 1947, pp. 229-230).

4   "Beautiful Cyla," as the blockova of the death block was called, was almost a child when she first came to the camp. She was slim, not too tall, pretty, and came from a well-to-do, middle class Jewish family in Slovakia, religious and highly respected. Up to the moment that Taube took her to step out of the line and stand next to him, she was a normal girl, frightened as the rest of us by what was going on around her.

"Listen to how Taube made a criminal of her", Mancy started telling me. "He picked her out of the Zugaenge. For a few days Cyla was nowhere to be found. We were sure that she was no longer among the living. Then, on that fall day, the day of the first selections, we stood at the roll call and waited for death.

"Taube walked into the roll call area, with Cyla following a short distance behind him. At first I did not recognize her. When finally I realized who she was I was so surprised that my eyes almost popped out. Could it really be Cyla. She looked so elegant and so scrubbed and she smelled so good. She avoided our gaze, looking straight in front of her. She walked behind the Rapportfuehrer, step for step. When he stopped, she stood at his side.

"Taube picked somebody out of the line and Cyla wrote down her number. The number of those standing off to the side began to swell. When the roll call ended, Cyla lined the women up in ranks of five and took the ones that had been selected to the new block. That was how Block 25, the death block, was created, and from that day Cyla was functioning as the blockova there. Today she is eighteen years old and has the heart of a criminal capable of committing murder." That was the story Mancy told me (Nomberg-Przytyk, 1985, pp 53-55).

CHAPTER 14

Grain Warehouse

Cyla Zacharowicz (née Cybulska)
Brooklyn, New York (USA)

I was born on December 28, 1920, in Lomza and lived there until the outbreak of World War II. During the first years of Hitler's occupation I continued living with my parents in the same neighborhood. After the opening of the Lomza ghetto, I had to move in with my family the same as all the other Jews. I don't remember the exact date but at some point I was transferred to a Sammella-ger in Zambrow, from where we were sent to Birkenau on January 19, 1943. My entire family, consisting of my mother Fela, father Mordechaj, older brother Jakub, younger brother Natan and ten-year old sister were brought to the camp.[1]

Immediately upon registration in the camp, I received the prison number 29,558. They assigned us to work details. We did not go through any quarantine. I remember that one of our first work assignments was to demolish the evacuated homes in the region belonging to the Poles. The most primitive tools (hammers, sledge hammers, etc.) were used for this work.

I did not stay in Birkenau for too long. After a few weeks they transferred me, along with other selected prisoners, to Auschwitz. I noticed during the selection process that only young, healthy and attractive girls qualified for this transfer.

Upon our transfer to Auschwitz we were housed in a masonry building called the Stabsgebaeude. We found conditions there completely different from those in

Birkenau. They were incomparably better. These conditions existed for the female prisoners only, because the so-called "aufzierki," or German Aufseherinnen (SS-women) also resided there. Therefore, we could maintain personal hygiene.

I later discovered that they had originally intended to use me as help in a camp office. However, there were not enough openings, and consequently I was assigned to a building where sacks were mended and forwarded to the mill. Ten female prisoners were assigned to the mending detail.

During my stay in Auschwitz I did not have an opportunity to send official letters out of the camp. We Jewesses were not allowed to do this. However, we corresponded illegally with the male prisoners of Auschwitz. These secret notes were called "gryps." They circulated at different occasions between female and male prisoners. All this took place under the most carefully guarded circumstances. Being caught would have had tragic repercussions for each of us.

In the summer of 1943 (it could have been August) I met a Polish prisoner by the name of Jurek Bielecki in the grain warehouse. He was, at that time, working there. Neither the female prisoners nor the male prisoners were allowed contact with each other. We worked in the same building, and therefore there were moments when we met and when it was possible to exchange a few sentences. These moments occurred at specific times, e.g., when we were led to the bathrooms.

My meetings with Jurek Bielecki resulted in sharing our experiences with each other and each encounter was truly moving for both of us. These meetings lasted quite a while, and so the months passed.

One day, during one of our secret rendezvous, Jurek told me of his intentions to organize an escape and of his desire that we should escape together. At first, four people were to have participated in the escape. This conversation took place in the early part of 1944.

When I first heard of his escape plans for both of us, I told him that I thought he was joking and that I was not taking him seriously. He, however, insisted that he was telling the truth and that he was earnestly thinking of our joint escape from the camp. Bielecki figured out everything. He made all necessary preparations, such as arranging for appropriate clothing for me, shoes, etc., and eventually, during the day of escape, for food. For himself he had obtained an SS uniform.

I mentioned that during the initial plans of our escape four people were to have participated. There were the two of us, Jurek and I, and another couple, Tadeusz Srogi, a Pole and Jurek's friend, who also had a girlfriend in our commando, a Jewess. From the beginning it was intended that Jurek would walk us out of the camp in his SS uniform stolen from the warehouse. These plans fell apart and Tadek Srogi did not take part in our escape. However, Jurek did not give up. On a day in July 1944, I was told by him when and at what time he would make his appearance in the Stabsgebaeude in order to get me out of the camp.

Finally, the day of our escape arrived. It was July 21, 1944.[2] If I remember well, I could not, for some time, meet with Jurek in our previously designated workplace. I knew, however, that he would come for me. Having been in Auschwitz for such a long time, I was well aware of the consequences should the escape not be successful. I felt depressed and wanted to back out of the flight. My good friend, Sonia Rotschild, prevented me from doing so. She begged me fervently not to change my mind. "Even if you are free for only a week or two. If you get caught it will be too bad but you must tell the world what goes on here. Let the people know. Let the whole world know what they do to people here." Sonia hugged and kissed me. She did not know at that time that she too, would outlive the nightmare of Auschwitz. After the war she moved to Belgium and presently lives in Brussels.

Finally, the moment arrived when Jerzy Bielecki showed up outside the Stabsgebaeude in his SS uniform.[3] Sonia Rotschild kissed me for the last time and whispered through her tears, "May God lead you." I walked down the stairs and found myself next to Jurek. After some short formalities Jurek walked me out of the Stabsgebaeude.

Jurek wore the SS uniform with a holster at his waist, but I did not know whether it contained a pistol. We moved on. I marched first and Jurek walked behind me as an "escort." When we met I said nothing. After marching for some minutes, we found ourselves in front of a guard house through which a road led to the exterior of the guarded area. As we approached the guard, Jurek took a document from his pocket. The guard said, "Weiter machen," which meant that we could march on. So the guard did not notice anything suspicious. He had no idea that he had escapees from Auschwitz in front of him.

On the day of the escape I wore a dress with a painted red stripe across the back. That was the way civilian clothes were given to prisoners in Auschwitz. I wore sturdy long boots which Jurek had gotten for me. In my backpack which I wore crossing the guard line, there was also a sweater (also "organized" by Jurek) and some food. Those were our total supplies.

After a successful exit from the guarded area, we continued our escape toward the east. We had neither a map nor prepared points of contact, and we tried to walk mostly at night so as to go unnoticed. Walking inland away from the roads was exhausting, especially for me, who was not used to such intensive marching. Bypassing populated areas, we had to cross ponds and rivers. During those moments, especially when the water was deep, Jurek carried me in his arms to the other side.

Finally, a time arrived when I could walk no further. I didn't care whether I got caught any more. I only wanted to rest. I wanted to stop and lie on the ground. I begged and pleaded with Jurek. I told him to leave me because I was only a burden to him. I tried to explain that leaving me would increase his chances of saving himself. But Jurek did not want to hear of it. He kept repeating, "We escaped together and we shall continue together."

The sun directed our escape. I was not at all familiar with these areas, so Jurek had to decide which direction to take. Our food supplies, which Jurek had managed to save before the escape, dwindled quickly. Jurek knocked on some doors of houses on our way. This was obviously very dangerous since we could have run into a trap and fallen into the hands of the Germans.

I am unable to reconstruct the exact route of our escape.[4] I can't even describe closely in which area we crossed the then Reich border and the "Generalgourvernement." We wore the same clothes we had left the camp in. I had on my navy blue camp dress with the red stripe painted on the back from which, at times when we stopped to rest, I tried to remove the paint. However, if we had been stopped and caught by the Germans, we would have been doomed anyway. We each had a tattooed number on our left forearm. The tattoo could not be removed and once caught, we could easily be identified as escapees from Auschwitz.

Our trip took about ten days. Jurek was trying to reach his home area, in the direction of Miechow. I do not recall all the details and adventures we lived through during our escape. The most important fact was that we finally reached a village called Muniakowice, close to Slomniki. Here lived Jan Marus, Jurek's mother's cousin. We were both cordially welcomed by Jurek's aunt and uncle. There we rested after our difficult journey.

For a short period we stayed in the village of Jankowice with the Klimczyk family where Jurek met Leszek, his own brother, a member of the resistance. This meeting was quite coincidental. Later, we also stayed for a while with a certain Banasiek in Przemaczony. Finally, I found a permanent hiding place with a Polish family by the name of Czernik in the village of Przemeczony-Gruszow, 12 kilometers from Raclowie. This family treated me like their daughter. Unfortunately, I had to part with Jurek, who joined the underground resistance movement A.K., and at that time we lost contact.

I received everything necessary from the Czernik family: shelter, food and friendship. Nevertheless, it was dangerous because in case of a routine search or arrest a catastrophe could have occurred. I had no identification papers and my tattooed number could give me away. But everything ended happily and I survived until the liberation.

After the war I began to search for my family living in the U.S.A. In 1945 I received a transit visa which allowed me to travel to Sweden. I spent five years in Sweden and then emigrated to the U.S.A. I went together with my husband.

The reunion with my family was warm but I was soon informed that since we had arrived to settle here we should take the future into our own hands. I must admit that the early years in the U.S.A. were very difficult for me. As an ex-prisoner of Hitler's concentration camp I did not receive any compensation. We had to depend on ourselves and our work. The situation was complicated by the fact that I did not speak English, which diminished my ability to obtain a decent job.

And so the years passed, but my longing for Poland never left me. I was obsessed with seeing my home town and Jurek, since I had lost all contact with him and even did not have the address of the Czernik family any more.

Even without contacts and addresses I did not give up trying. Chance came to my rescue. A few years ago I employed a Polish girl who came from the county of

Krakow where the Czernik family lived. The girl, through a girlfriend who worked at the post office, obtained the address of the Czernik family for me and from them I received the address of Jurek's aunt. I could not understand why she wouldn't give me Jurek's address. After a year of silence, I received a positive reply from her. I finally found out that Jurek was alive and that he lived in Nowy Targ, but I still did not have his exact address. I decided to send a letter to the chief of police in that town. I wrote in the letter that I believed a Mr. Jerzy Bielecki lived in Nowy Targ and that I wished to establish contact with him. I mentioned, of course, briefly our common experience. I received an answer. It was a beautiful letter from the police chief, which really surprised me. He not only sent me Jurek's home address, but also his telephone number. Furthermore, he wished me a pleasant and happy reunion.

After the liberation and immigration to the U.S.A., I shared my experience in Auschwitz with only those closest to me, not wishing to make a martyr of myself. I was often encouraged to write my memoirs in the form of a book. I was not interested in these propositions, despite the fact that my experiences, especially my successful escape from Auschwitz, are of some interest.

I received the first letter from Jurek the day before a trip to Washington to attend a Holocaust gathering. My cousins lived in this city. I called them from the hotel, not intending to meet with them because I wished to devote my stay to the subject of the Holocaust victims. My intentions went astray. My cousin telephoned me to tell me that she must see me. She arrived in my hotel at 11:00 pm. After the initial greeting, I did not omit sharing my happiness over receiving a letter with an enclosed photograph from Jurek. My cousin begged me to read her the entire letter. She found out from the letter of our intended meeting in Poland and what Jurek once meant to me. Long into the night, I told her of those times and of our escape. My cousin was deeply moved, but reacted strongly. She pleaded with me not to go to Poland. She suggested that she and her husband would let me have their house to invite Jurek here for a stay of a week or longer. She just did not want me to go to Poland. Perhaps she was afraid I would stay there. I did not give up my intended trip and in 1983 I saw Jurek again.[5] We went to Auschwitz, which is presently the government Museum Auschwitz-Brzezinka, where a film company assisted us in filming our escape route.

NOTES

Cyla Zacharowicz

1   On January 19, 1943, approximately 2000 Polish Jews—men women and children—arrived in Auschwitz with a RSHA transport from the ghetto of Zambrow. After the selection process, 164 men, receiving numbers 89,845 to 90,008 were admitted into the camp, as well as 134 women, numbers 29,451 to 29, 584. The rest of the group (about 1702 persons) were killed in the gas chambers (Czech, 1989, p. 386).

2   The Polish prisoner Jerzy Bielecki (Nr. 243), born on March 21, 1921, who had been sent to

Auschwitz on June 14, 1940, by the Sipo (Sicherheitspolizei = security police) and the SD (security service) from Tarnow prison and the Polish Jewess Cyla Stawiska (sic) (Nr. 29,558), born on December 29, 1920, who had been sent to Auschwitz by a RSHA transport from Zambrow Ghetto on January 19, 1943, escaped from Auschwitz on July 21, 1944. After a successful escape the two were hiding until the end of the war in the area of Miechow (Czech, 1989, p. 826).

3   It took quite a bit of courage to proceed according to plan, i.e., for Bielecki to accompany Cyla out of the camp in the uniform of an SS-man, exactly the way Edek Galinski and Mala Zimetbaum had done on June 24, 1944. However, by the beginning of July 1944, these two had been caught and were back in the bunker of Block 11. Jurek and Cyla were well aware of this fact. Edek and Mala were executed on September 15, 1944 (Czech, 1989, pp. 303, 805, 879 and Kiela, 1979, pp. 287-343).

4   The escape is described in detail by Jurek (Bielecki, 1990) and by Sobanski in *Auf demselben Pfade* (Sobanski, 1980, pp. 187-193).

5   In 1986 Jerzy Bielecki received the Righteous Gentile Award from Yad Vashem in Jerusalem. His book about the joint escape is entitled, "He Who Saves One Single Life...." corresponding to the inscription on the medal he received

CHAPTER 15

Temporary Stabsgebaeudlerin

Charlotte Tetzner (née Decker)
Gersdorf (East Germany)

I was born on November 20, 1920, in Chemnitz (now Karl Marx Stadt), Saxony. My father had come from Yugoslavia. He had been selected to become an officer in the Austrian Navy. However, his sense of justice did not let him succeed. Several times he was degraded because he spoke up for the "common" troops. After World War I, he settled in Germany, joining his mother who had moved previously.

My mother's maiden name was Dombois. Her ancestors had emigrated from France. She was a dressmaker.

My childhood was protected, as was my youth, until that fateful April 15, 1941.

It was on this day that my parents and I were arrested by the Gestapo. My father, a member of the KPD (the German Communist Party), was Croatian. For this reason, they had not been able to touch him previously. However, as soon as the war with his Yugoslavian homeland started, there was an excellent opportunity to "intern" him. After a two months imprisonment in the main police jail of Chemnitz—where we were still treated decently—my father was transferred to Dachau and my mother and I to Ravensbrueck.

Here, in Ravensbrueck, my first encounter with Jehovah's Witnesses[1] took place. This was a group of people who always attempted to start a dialogue with their fellow-prisoners. Since I had been brought up as an agnostic—hypocritical catholicism, which had spiritually wooed the political rulers from the beginning, had been repugnant to my father and had caused him to become an atheist—I was not inclined to listen to anything connected with faith. I laughed about them like almost all the others.

This soon changed. After having waited in vain for four weeks for a sign, we finally received a letter full of hope from my father. Simultaneously, a telegram from Dachau was handed to us: the notice of his death—Murdered! (Of course, the telegram did not say so.) It was horrible. My mother broke down. I pretended to be the strong one in order to assist my mother. But at night, I silently cried in my bed.

From that moment on, something stirred inside of me. I opened my senses and mind to serious discussions with the Witnesses. I was fascinated to learn about true Christianity, about connections, causes and effects, the coming true of Biblical prophesies in antiquity as well as in the present. More and more I was captured by and filled with real faith which had nothing to do with sentimentality. In addition, I realized how consistently members of this denomination (the only religious assembly one could call a group because there were only sporadic members of other churches or sects) refused, even in the concentration camp, to carry out any work connected with the war effort. Their punishments were cruel: standing outside for days during the ice-cold seasons, bunker, and reduction of their already tiny food rations. Most of them had been in prison or concentration camps for many years. In a Berlin prison, they tried to force them to watch Nazi films and to honor the Nazi flag. When they refused, they were beaten and inundated with water. Nevertheless, they persisted in maintaining their neutral comportment which did not permit any compromise, true to the teachings of Paul the Apostle, "Thou therefore endure hardness, as a good soldier of Jesus Christ. No man that warreth entangleth himself with the affairs of life; that he may please him who hath chosen him to be a soldier." (2 Timothy 2:3,4).Through all of these acts and the clear understanding of the Bible of these women, my mother and I realized the existence of truly alive Christianity similar to primordial Christianity of the first century: Jehovah's Witnesses are not Christians in name only. They do what their name "Jehovah's Witnesses" (adopted in 1931) implies: They bear witness to (attest to the existence of) the master of the universe who had certain designs with the creation of the world and of men and of Jesus Christ.

"Ye are my witnesses" (Isaiah, 43:10/11), Jehovah proclaims, "and my servant whom I have chosen: that ye may know and believe me, and understand that I *am* he: before me there was no God formed, neither shall there be after me. I, even I, *am* Jehovah; and beside me there is no savior."

"For thus saith Jehovah that created the heavens, God himself that formed the earth and made it; he hath established it, he created it not in vain, he formed it to be inhabited." (Isaiah, 45:18)

On December 15, 1941, my mother and I were to be released. To our surprise, SS-woman-in-chief Langefeld[2] presented us with the same document which all witnesses of Jehovah could have signed, but did not, in order to be discharged. I read the entire document. They required us to subordinate ourselves body and soul to the state. Furthermore, we were obliged to report anybody to the police who would approach us in matters of faith. If we would not act in accordance with these requirements, we would be arrested immediately—I did not sign. In addition, this procedure was entirely unfair since we had been admitted as political prisoners.—My mother signed without reading the paper.—And I had to give back my civilian clothes which I had already donned and return to the camp "marsch, marsch" (on the double).

What followed was a test of strength. However, my faith had become so strong during the course of the preceding six months that I could withstand the pressure. Now I was called to the Kommandatur (commandant's office), now to the Political Section, now to the SS-woman-in-chief, now to the work-allocation leader. They tried enticements, threats, mockery. When Himmler visited Ravensbrueck, I had to appear in front of him. Probably, they believed they could achieve a change of mind with these means. My standard reply was that as long as they could not offer me anything better, I would keep my faith.

The (mostly older) political women prisoners were the worst. They would have liked to lynch me when I returned to the block. This reaction only reinforced my determination to continue on my path because now I realized through these communists that politics only engenders hatred. John the Apostle's words are true: "Whosoever hateth his brother is a murderer." (1 John, 3:15)

Unfortunately, one does also encounter this hatred in Christian religions which certainly does not contribute to stamping them as true churches. A blood-debt of many centuries lies on their shoulders. In Revelations, they speak about the (world-) kingdom of false religion comparing it to an unclean woman: "Baby-lon the Great, the Mother of Harlots and Abominations of the Earth. And I saw the woman drunken with the blood of saints, and with the blood of the martyrs of Jesus." (Revelations, 17:5/6)

The first transfer of prisoners from Ravensbrueck to Auschwitz occurred in March 1942. My transport left in the fall of 1942. I remember the trip vaguely as nothing extraordinary occurred en route. But my first impression of our arrival is very distinct. We had barely descended from the train (naturally far away from the town of Auschwitz), when we saw a group of male prisoners, who were working close by, very quickly, of course. Those who could not keep up the pace were beaten mercilessly with thick sticks. Horrible! I thought of my father, wondering if he had been treated in the same way, and my heart contracted convulsively—I wanted to scream.

And then the camp of Birkenau! Upon arrival, we had to stay close to the barbed wire in front of the rather deep and wide ditch until we were allowed to enter the barrack. My senses were paralyzed by that which my eyes perceived. The entire area was nothing but a muddy desert, devoid of a single tree, bush, or even a tiny blade of grass. The barracks lacked windows. And the prisoners; you could hardly call them human beings. They were walking skeletons. An all-pervasive, loathsome stench hung in the air.

Then we received our numbers; mine is indelibly engraved in my mind: 21962. Finally, I was taken with a small group to the Stabsgebaeude in Auschwitz and assigned to the secretariat (to do office work). Here, at long last, I again had contact with like-minded prisoners (co-religionists), which was very important to me.

In order to show my sense of belonging in an outward manner, I embroidered my number and the purple triangle. They had again classified me as "political" prisoner, which was incorrect. The next morning, the SS-woman on duty discovered my purple triangle. Her name was Hasse—and she was a sadistic creature. She started to scream and rage and threatened to send me to the penal camp in Budy (one of the worst satellite camps). If I still would not give up my crazy idea, they would send me to Birkenau and finally to Block 25 (the station before the Crematorium).

I stood silently and let her pour out her venom. But deep inside me everything turned upside down. It was an indescribable feeling because one never knew whether or not her threats would be realized. They were capable of everything. *They* were the real "Untermenschen" (subhumans).

In my distress I could only do one thing, entrust myself to Him for whose name I wanted to stand...and implore Him in my prayers to give me strength. I did not change anything on my triangle. Some time passed by, and one day I actually was transferred to Birkenau, not to Block 25 but to the office.

I suppose it is not necessary to write much about Birkenau. Others have described it in detail. Nevertheless, I would like to add a little.

Catastrophic hygienical conditions reigned. Typhus raged. There were up to 120 deaths daily. However, according to the death certificates, people were dying of everything except typhus. The camp was full of vermin: fleas, bugs (roaches) and lice; head-lice as well as clothes-lice; the latter being responsible for transmitting typhus.

One had to invest tremendous energy in order to wash oneself. First, one had to walk quite a distance to reach the water. There was only one faucet in the latrine building which was located at the end of the camp. The liquid that dripped out of this faucet was of a rusty reddish color. After a long time the rust settled into the soil and one could finally use the water. This was a long procedure. Most of the women, especially the tortured Jewesses and Slavs, did not have the strength to do it.

Especially in Auschwitz and Birkenau, the difference between these two groups and so called "Aryans" was much more acute than in Ravensbrueck, at least during the time I was there. Later it supposedly also changed. That which was done to Jews, Poles and Russians is indescribable. I saw Aussenkommandos (outside working details) of Jews in January/February who marched into camp without shoes or stockings, their feet wrapped in rags. The legs of these tormented women displayed a kaleidoscope of frost bites, in many cases pus was running out of open wounds.

When new transports arrived, I had to be present together with the SS-woman. Some of these persons struck you particulary because of their intelligence or beauty. I could save a few by assigning them to work in the camp office. But these possibilities were very limited. When I met some of these women after three or four weeks, I was shocked to see the short period of time it took to transform a human being into a physical and psychological wreck. The selection for the gas chamber was usually only a question of time.

During my "free time," sometimes also during working hours (the long walks to the latrine could not be precisely checked), I visited sick co-religionists in the camp hospital. One was a young Dutch woman. She was a delicate and sensitive person and suffered under those conditions to such an extent that she got attacks. I comforted her, caressed her and held her hands. She liked my company and calmed down. But I could not be with her all the time. One day, when I visited her, I learned that they had put her on the walled-in heating which ran through the entire length of the horse-stable barrack in order to subdue her. As a result, she had suffered serious burns on her legs. Shortly afterward, she died.

Another co-religionist had severe stomach problems. She was in very bad condition and had lost a tremendous amount of weight. They released her from the Revier (camp hospital) although she was still very weak. In the meantime, a punishment sentence had been passed against her. A co-prisoner had accused her slanderously of having stolen some detergent (she, herself, had probably done it). The punishment took place a day after her release from the Revier: 25 whiplashes. And *how* the SS-women could hit! In many cases, the entire camp had to watch these tortures.

In the beginning, I worked in the sewing room under SS-woman Massar. The prisoners of the kommando confided that they were supposed to watch me. Probably, they had the task of observing my contacts. Since they were obviously on my side, nothing actually happened.

I suffered a lot from constipation and, since nothing helped, had to go the Revier to get a laxative. There were strict rules in the sewing room: we could only go to the latrines at certain pre-determined times. When I felt the result of the laxative, I asked the SS-woman to be allowed to relieve myself. She did not permit me. So I said, "Thank you!" As if stung by a tarantula, she turned around. "Why are you thanking me?" "For your human kindness," I replied. The prisoners of the cutting-room (that's where this incident took place) told me afterward that their hearts almost stopped beating out of fright of what might happen next.

Nothing happened, however. SS-woman Massar went through the entire section of the sewing room and delivered a speech (almost in form of an apology) stressing the fact that everything was our fault.

Then I was commandeered for work in the office of Maria Mandel,[3] the new SS-woman-in-chief, which was located in the Blockfuehrerstube, a barrack outside the barbed wire where everybody who entered or left the camp had to pass by.

One day, the commandant came to the office. I was so absorbed in my work that I noticed him only when the other prisoners were already standing at attention. He did not say anything, but when he left and I assumed the door had closed and returned to my work, he suddenly re-opened the door abruptly (he must have observed me through a tiny slit) screaming that I should be transferred at once to the punishment block. There I stayed for several weeks. (I do not remember whether it was five or six weeks.) Together, with Asozialen and BVern (prostitutes and criminals), I had to carry bricks. The contact with this type of persons (not to mention the hard labor) was very unpleasant. Eventually, the SS-woman-in-chief let me come back. This event had greatly amused her.

In 1943, I don't remember whether it was spring or summer, I succumbed to the typhus epidemic. My blood agglutination was positive for spotted fever as well as typhoid. I was very seriously ill and had extremely high fever for many days. Dr. Rhode, the SS camp physician on duty, who had already tried to have me transferred to his house as house-hold help before I fell ill, came to the hospital every day. Normally, he would appear at the utmost once a week (the nurses told me afterward). Only weeks later, after the liberation, did I learn that an ambulance driver who came, like me, from the Erzgebirge, had "organized" medication for me and handed it over to the prison doctor (a Jewess). The help I received was a big exception!.

The SS ambulance driver, whose name was Martin Boehm, knew from the index card that was sent to the hospital for every prisoner-patient, from which part in Germany I came. It might have been, in his case, a sort of "Heimatverbundenheit" (nostalgic connectivity with one's native place). After my recovery, I met him in camp. He asked me whether he should give greetings at home since he was going on leave.

By the way, the hospital I was sent to was not one of those dirty horse-stable barracks, but a newly constructed small wooden building with real windows meant only for inmate nurses who had fallen ill. For example, there was a special room where amputations (e.g., of frozen toes) were performed by the Jewish female doctor.

After liberation, I had contact with Mr. Boehm. One evening his brother, with whom he was staying, came from Glauchau and asked me to come and see him. We had a long conversation until the early morning hours. I found out that toward the end, he had also been arrested because of "Haeftlingsbeguenstigung" (favoring prisoners). In spite of this, he was understandably afraid and asked me if I would be willing, if necessary, to appear as "Kronzeugin" (chief witness). But it did not come to this. My mother and I were invited to his house a few times. Later, he left his family. One day I received a letter from Konstanz (West Germany). And then: finis.

To counter the loss of hair after my illness, and the infestation of head-lice as a result of the long stay in the Revier, I had my head shaved. It did not really matter here where the majority ran around with bald heads.

After my recovery, I again worked in the office of SS-supervisor-in-chief Maria Mandel. Frequently, SS-officers came and many of them wanted to have me in their households, but I was not released. Yet, a few weeks later, I had to pack my few belongings. I was taken to Auschwitz, not as household-aid, but as secretary for the SS-Lazarett of whom SS-physician Dr. Kitt was in charge.[4]

I had contact with the patients, mostly soldiers, in the hospital. Dr. Kitt took me along on his rounds so that he could dictate the notes for the file directly at the sick bed; the same applied for radiology (the x-ray department). I had to type the diagnoses and anamneses, and had to keep lists and statistics. In addition, I had to copy Dr. Kitt's doctoral dissertation. The topic was silicosis. Dr. Kitt was friendly with the other prisoners who worked in the hospital and to me; yet another side of him existed.

The eight other women prisoners in the Lazarett had red triangles; among them was a Russian professor who worked in the laboratory. A red triangle was not always an indication that the person was in camp for political reasons. For example, women who had befriended Poles also had red triangles.

One of my activities consisted of going to the SS-Revier, either to fetch medication from the pharmacy or to deliver something to the office of Dr. Wirths, the Standortarzt (SS physician-in-chief of the camp). There I met Hermann Langbein, who was Dr. Wirth's secretary.

Like all Jehovah's Witnesses, I could move freely within the large sentry chain. This way I met other co-religionists, also Mrs. Elsa Abt. Since the liberation, she lives in Poland and I am still in touch with her.

This freedom of movement was granted only to very few prisoners. It concerned mostly those witnesses of Jehovah who worked outside the barbed wire (i.e., the small sentry chain). The large sentry chain covered the entire huge area with all the numerous satellite camps, such as Buna, Monowitz, Budy, etc.

In 1944, a newly constructed SS-hospital, consisting of five barracks, was inaugurated. Since it was located closer to Birkenau, we had to move back to camp. Back to the horror and the dirt. In the old hospital, we nine women prisoners had had a room with three three-tier beds. We had been able to take a shower every evening and did not have to see the misery and torment of the tortured inmates.

Anybody who has not experienced it will not be able to understand what it means to live in the midst of this inferno. Even if we received better treatment as "Aryans." After all, nobody was safe. None of us knew how all of this would end; or whether it would end at all. We could not ponder this question without going mad.

But the end did come. In January 1945, a single bomb fell on the hospital. A few days later there was a regular air raid, and the hospital was destroyed. There were also a few dead. After the air raid, we had to return to camp immediately.[5]

Hectic activities started at once. The evacuation of the camp was prepared.

It was already evening when we marched out of Birkenau. It was bitter cold but the sky was clear. Pretty soon we saw the corpses on both sides of the road in the pale moonlight. It was gruesome.

We marched a long time and our feet were hurting. Suddenly we heard, "Halt, we'll rest awhile." No sooner had we fallen to the floor of a barn dead-tired, there came a new command, "All up, we continue." The march lasted 75 km. until we were finally put into cattle cars and shipped to the concentration camp of Gross-Rosen in Upper-Silesia. I only remember that we received an awful soup made of sugar beets, without salt. It was inedible, inducing one to vomit. Soon we left Gross-Rosen.

The trip in open cattle cars continued until we arrived in Mauthausen in Austria. The journey was dreadful. We were penned in closely together, freezing and had standing-room only. It lasted several days. One young woman died of diphtheria. But having nothing to drink caused the worst suffering. I remember that, after our arrival in Mauthausen and having climbed the steep path to the concentration camp, I bent down with my last strength to eat some dirty snow just to have something moist in my mouth. In addition, both my big toes were frozen. For three days, I made compresses out of urine, a little more stench did not matter. It helped a lot, and seemed to have taken care of the problem (I did not have any serious consequences or side-effects).

We went on transport again. This time we landed in Bergen-Belsen in Northern Germany. I hardly remember anything about this camp in which we stayed approximately two weeks.

One day, all Jehovah's Witnesses prisoners had to stand at attention. A few SS officers—some of whom we knew from Auschwitz/Birkenau—came and selected twenty-five women, among these were Else Abt and I. We were taken to the concentration camp Mittelbau/Dora, located near Nordhausen/Harz. After the destruction of the town, the camp had to be evacuated. We twenty-five women (the only ones in Dora, since it was a men's camp where subterraneously the V1 and V2 had been manufactured) were sent out guarded by two SS-men. But this time it was a march to freedom. We spent one single night, together with our two guards, in the haystack of a barn. It was impossible to sleep with the tremendous tension in the air. We could hear shooting not very far from us and a thundering noise. Early the next morning our two SS-men led us off the main highway into a small forest. They declared that we were free and disappeared. It was April 14, 1945.

We remained three months in the beautiful Harz Mountains to recuperate. As soon as trains were running again, each of us went home.

After I had "re-acclimatized" myself sufficiently, I worked together with my mother and passed the journeyman board as a seamstress.

In the beginning of 1949, I met Heinz Tetzner. We married in 1951. One year later our daughter Gabriele was born, and in 1954, our son Matthias.

My husband is a painter and a graphic artist. He was also born in 1920, but, because of the war, he commenced his studies at the University of Weimar only in the fall of 1945. In 1949, he received his diploma. Subsequently, he was assistant to Professor Herbig who had been his teacher. In 1953, the Academy of Arts was closed. Since this time, my husband has been an independent artist.

We had difficult years because the road toward becoming known and recognized is a toilsome and painful one. On top of that, I did not receive any type of Wiedergutmachung (indemnification payments). On the contrary, I received a letter stating that I was unrecognized as a victim of Fascism because I did not participate in elections (which are not compulsory here). In this manner, I would assist Neo-Fascist endeavors!! This document is carefully preserved (see Appendix C, page 274).

In the beginning, when the children were small, we did not need much money. I sewed their entire wardrobe out of old clothes, undid old sweaters and knitted new ones. Later, I did dressmaking at home. The last thirteen years before I was eligible for Social Security (which women receive here at age 60), I had a good job as secretary for an attorney.

In the meantime, my husband is more and more recognized owing to his artistic achievements. He also received several art prizes (which are more valuable to him than money). Nevertheless, it is nice not to have any more financial worries.

We live in the little house which used to belong to my husband's parents all by ourselves; no, Newfoundland Barry, Elfi the cat and the two tom cats, Mohrle and Kunibert, keep us company.

For the last two years, we have been able to travel to the other part of Germany to visit our children. Matthias and his young wife had left four years ago. Until now, they have not received permission to visit us.

I have always felt the need to speak about the horrible events of those times; however, I could do this only privately. I was also never asked to do so by national groups or governmental agencies. I am, therefore, happy to now have an opportunity of making a modest contribution to our collective publication.[6]

NOTES

Charlotte Tetzner

1   The Jehovah's Witnesses' faith is based on eschatological doctrine; in every generation they expect the "end of days" which will be inaugurated by a great trial of all people who do not belong to the sect. The "end of days" will be preceded by political catastrophe, such as war, revolution or economic crisis. Obviously, the Nazi policy of persecution and war could be interpreted as heralding the approach of the "end of days."

There is no evidence of concrete action on the part of the Witnesses against the Nazi regime in its early period. It is only when the Witnesses refused to make the "Heil Hitler" salute, and, beginning in 1935, to serve in the army, that the sect adopted a clear posture of opposition to the regime. This led to the first wave of arrests of Witnesses in 1936 and 1937, which in many cases resulted in imprisonment in concentration camps.

As a rule, the Witnesses imprisoned in the camps refused to renounce their convictions. Even though they could obtain their release, or could have escaped imprisonment in the first place by signing a declaration that they would no longer be active on behalf of their organization, most of the Witnesses refused to do this.

Inside the concentration camps, the Witnesses were a relatively compact group, supporting one another and conspicuous by the order, cleanliness and discipline they maintained. Their helpfulness also benefitted other groups. However, their behavior was determined by their religious beliefs. They did not cooperate with the illegal political groups and refused to try to escape from the camps or to offer active resistance to the SS (Gutman, 1990, pp. 742-743).

2   Margarete Buber-Neumann, who as prisoner in Ravensbrueck was secretary of SS-woman Langefeld, wrote: "In the course of my five years of confinement I came across quite a few overseers who tried to remain human. One of these was Senior Overseer Langefeld ... This woman still had a sense of good and evil, which her colleagues in the SS had long since thrown overboard" (Buber-Neumann, 1988, pp. 180, 183).

This humaneness was probably the reason that Auschwitz commandant Hoess did not get along with Langefeld. "The chief female supervisor of the period, Frau Langefeld, was in no way capable of coping with the situation, yet she refused to accept any instructions given her by the commander of the protective custody camp" (Hoess, 1959, p. 152). (See also Note 3.)

3   On October 8, 1942, the SS-women-in-chief of KL Auschwitz and KL Ravensbrueck were exchanged. Johanna Langefeld, the former SS-woman-in-chief, returned to Ravensbrueck because of a dispute with commandant Hoess and received her old position. SS-woman-in-chief Marie Mandel, born on January 10, 1919, in Muenzkirchen, Upper Austria, took over the job in Auschwitz-Birkenau. Mandel was experienced in this field—since October 15, 1938, she had been a guard in KL-Lichtenburg and since May 1939 she had been working in Ravensbrueck (Czech, 1989, pp. 316-317).

4   The SS Revier was located outside the camp of Auschwitz I, next to the Administration Building and across from the old, half-submerged Crematorium I and the barrack of the Political Section. It was the hospital for the SS. Only nine women prisoners worked here, all of them non-Jewish. Among them was a political prisoner number 512, Maria Autsch, a nun belonging to the discalced order of Trinitarians, imprisoned for Fuehrerbeleidigung (insulting of the Fuehrer), who as Sister Angela was known as the "Angel of Auschwitz." She died of a heart attack in December 1944 when the SS Revier—which by then had been moved to Birkenau—was hit during an air raid.

The men's prison work detail of the SS Revier contained many members of the Auschwitz underground movement, such as the political prisoners Hermann Langbein and Karl Lill, as well as the Poles Zbigniew Raynoch and Czeslaw Duzel. The latter two were betrayed during the ill-fated attempt of five prominent prisoners in October 1944 and when caught committed suicide before they could be tortured.

The civilian nurse Maria Stromberger, from Austria, also worked at the SS Revier. She helped prisoners wherever she could, smuggled letters for the resistance and served as a courier for them.

5   On December 26, 1944, during a renewed American air raid on the I.G. Farben factory in Dwory near Auschwitz, a few bombs fell on the SS hospital, located near KL-Auschwitz-Birkenau. Five SS men were killed (Czech, 1989, p. 950).

6   This report was written before the German reunification.

APPENDIX A

Biographical Notes on the SS

Ackermann, Fred
Unterscharfuehrer in the Kommandantur. On April 20, 1943, he received a medal in Auschwitz, the Kriegsverdienstmedaille.

Armbruester, Michael (Ludwig?)
Born on August 4, 1914, in Radautz. SS-Unterscharfuehrer in the adminstration of prisoners' possessions. He died on September 7, 1974, in Stuttgart.

Aumeier, Hans
Born August 20, 1906, in Amberg. Since 1938 Hauptsturmfuehrer, Lagerfuehrer in Auschwitz. He came from Sachsenhausen and was transferred in August 1943 as commandant to Riga concentration camp. He received a death sentence in Cracow on December 22, 1947.

Baer, Richard
Sturmbannfuehrer, born on September 9, 1911, in Floss/Oberpfalz. Worked in 1933 in Dachau and was later adjutant of Pohl in Oranienburg. Since May 11, 1944, he was commandant in Auschwitz. His wife reported him deceased after the war. He lived as Karl Neumann in Dassendorf. In December 1960 he was arrested and died in prison in Frankfurt on June 17, 1963.

Baretsky, Stefan
Unterscharfuehrer, born March 24, 1919, in Czernowitz. Blockfuehrer 1942-1945 in Birkenau. Lived in Plaidt (Eifel) after the war. Was arrested in 1960 and sentenced in the Frankfurt Auschwitz trial.

Becker, Dorothea (married name Pritzkoleit)
Born October 10, 1912, in Saarbruecken. She was first Aufseherin in Ravensbrueck and from fall 1942 onwards in Auschwitz. At the Cracow trial she was sentenced to five years in prison. She lived (or lives) in Hamburg-Bergedorf.

Berger
Unterscharfuehrer in the office of the Landwirtschaft.

Bischoff, Karl
Sturmbannfuehrer. Born August 9, 1897, in Neuhausbach/Saarpfalz. From October 1941 until autumn 1944 he was the second in command at the Bauleitung in Auschwitz. Afterwards, he became director of construction of the Waffen SS and police in Silesia with headquarters in Kochlowice. He died on October 2, 1950, in Bremen.

Bodmann, Dr. Franz von

Born March 23, 1908, in Munich. SS-Standortarzt in Auschwitz, fell ill in August 1942 and was transferred. Died on May 25, 1945, in a military hospital in Pongau (Salzburg) as per death certificate, presumably suicide.

Boehm, Martin

From the Erzgebirge. Rottenfuehrer and ambulance driver.

Boehme

Dr. Boehme was director of the botanical laboratory in Rajsko. He died in Poland after the war.

Boger, Wilhelm

Oberscharfuehrer, born on December 19, 1906, in Stuttgart. In 1922 he was already a member of the Nazi youth movement. "Ich war ein alter Hase in der nationalsozialistischen Bewegung." After business training, a few apprenticeships, unemployment, service as an auxiliary policeman and attendance at the police academy, he worked for the criminal police and later for the Gestapo.

In Auschwitz he was in charge of the escape detail and excelled in barbarism and sadism beyond anybody's imagination. The prisoners were terrified of him. It was Boger who introduced the torture instrument, called the Boger-Schaukel after him, which he used during his interrogations. His specialty was to torture recaptured prisoners who had attempted to escape.

Boger participated eagerly in the shooting of prisoners with small caliber weapons in the death block. He took part in the mass gassing of Jews. He also organized informers among the prisoners.

In June 1945, he was arrested by American military police and in November 1946 was supposed to be handed over to Poland. However, Boger escaped and for three years lived underground near Crailsheim, not far from Stuttgart. "Da zeigte sich noch, dass die Deutschen zusammenhielten, denn sie kannten mich alle." (This shows that the Germans did stick together, because all of them knew me.)

In 1958 he was arrested once more and was sentenced to a prison term in the Frankfurt Auschwitz trial of 1964-65. He died in the prison hospital of Ziegenhain on March 4, 1977.

Boger had been married twice and was the father of five children, three daughters from his second marriage and two sons from his first.

Bormann, Juana (Hanna)

Born September 10, 1893, in Birkenfelde, Eastern Prussia. From May 5, 1943, onward, she was in Auschwitz, also in Babitz and Budy. On November 17, 1945, she was sentenced to death in the Bergen-Belsen trial and was executed on December 13, 1945.

Broad, Pery

Rottenfuehrer, born on April 25, 1921, in Rio de Janeiro, son of a Brazilian businessman father and a German mother. Shortly after his birth his mother took him to Germany while the father remained in Brazil. Broad attended school in Berlin and, because of his early membership in that organization, received the gold medal of the Hitler Jugend. After graduation from high school he studied at the Technische Hochschule in Berlin. In 1941 he volunteered for service in the Waffen-SS.

In June 1942, Broad came to the Politische Abteilung in Auschwitz. He did general interrogations and was in charge of selecting women for the camp bordello. "Bei uns arbeitet jeder in seinem Beruf, d.h. ein Musterlager." (Here everybody works according to his calling; that's what I call a model camp), he was fond of saying.

Later he was responsible for the Gypsy camp in Birkenau until its liquidation in the summer of 1944. He was one of the most cultured SS-men of the Politische, spoke German, French and English, and studied Polish and Russian in camp. He loved to read classical authors and was a fine musician. In Birkenau he had organized what he used to call "the finest Gypsy orchestra in the world" and afterwards participated in the mass gassing of the entire Gypsy camp.

In May 1945, he was taken prisoner by the British. While in prison he wrote his reminiscences of Auschwitz, highly critical of the camp and the atrocities committed there. However, as a defendant in the Frankfurt Auschwitz trial, solidarity with his old cronies prevailed. He was sentenced to a prison term and now lives in Kaarst. He was married twice. Both marriages were childless.

Brose, Anton
Born September 26, 1909, in Braunsberg, Eastern Prussia. Before and after his activity at the Political Section in Auschwitz, he worked for the Gestapo of Kattowitz. After the war he worked for Kieserling and Albrecht in Solingen. His address was (or is) Drosselstrasse 2, Solingen. Hermann Langbein's request of August 2, 1965, for criminal investigation was not acted upon.

Brunner, Luise (née Kalb)
Born August 25, 1908, in Aidhausen/Unterfranken. Aufseherin since October 1, 1942, in the Stabsgebaeude in Auschwitz. She was formerly in Ravensbrueck and returned there in October 1944.
On July 28, 1948, she was sentenced by a British court to three years in prison. On September 15, 1960, she was arrested by German authorities. On October 10, 1960, she tried to commit suicide. On December 27, 1960, she was released.

Buehning
SS-Unterscharfuehrer and SDG. A former barber, who performed sterilizations on Clauberg's orders in Block 10 in Auschwitz.

Burger, Wilhelm
Born April 19, 1904, in Dachau. From June 1942 until May 1943 he was in charge of administration in Auschwitz. On April 9, 1952, he was sentenced in Poland and released on May 21, 1955. He lives in Munich, Hilblerstrasse 31.

Caesar, Dr. Joachim
Born May 30, 1901, in Boppard. SS-Obersturmbannfuehrer. An agronomist who worked for the SS-Rassen-Siedlungshauptamt. From March 1942 until the evacuation in January 1945, he was the director of the agricultural enterprises in Auschwitz. He was a witness at the Nuernberg trial and was imprisoned until January 30, 1949. He was equally a witness ad the Frankfurt Auschwitz trial. He died in Kiel on January 25, 1974.

Christophersen, Thies
He came from Schleswig-Holstein. SS-Sonderfuehrer at the Pflanzenzucht in Rajsko from January to December 1944.
For many years he has been active in the neo-Nazi movement. After having been sentenced by the German Federal Republic, he escaped to Denmark, from where he was not extradited.
Author of *Auschwitz...Truth or Lie*, An Eyewitness Report (in German, *Die Auschwitz Luege*).

Cichon, Flora
SS-Aufseherin in Rajsko.

Clauberg, Carl, M.D., Professor of Gynecology.
Born September 28, 1898, in Wupperhof, near Solingen. Honorary SS-Brigadefuehrer. Conducted criminal experiments on women prisoners in Auschwitz on orders of Himmler to find a method for mass sterilization. After the war he was a prisoner of war in the Soviet Union. In 1956 he returned to Kiel. Soon afterwards he was arrested and died in custody on August 9, 1957.

Dejaco, Walter
Untersturmfuehrer. Born September 16, 1909. From 1940 until the evacuation he worked in the

Central Construction Company in Auschwitz. The still-existing plan of the large crematorium carries his signature.

In 1950 he was released as a prisoner of war and worked as a master builder in Reutte/Tyrol. At the initiation of Hermann Langbein there was a trial in Vienna from January 18 to March 10, 1972. He was acquitted.

Delmotte, Dr. Hans

Born in 1917 in the Alsace. Camp physician in Auschwitz. Worked in the Institute of Hygiene under Dr. Bruno Weber. In 1945 he committed suicide.

Draser, Hans Andreas

Unterscharfuehrer and an attorney, he was in charge of the Fuersorgeabteilung (welfare section) of the Politische Abteilung. He was a Volksdeutscher from Rumania, spoke German, French and English, and studied Russian in camp. He handled inquiries from the International Red Cross. If an inquiry concerned a non-Jewish inmate, it was answered, after verification of the card file with a statement that X was in camp, was feeling fine and worked in his/her profession. If it concerned a non-Jewish prisoner who had died, or had been hanged or shot, the reply was that X was not in camp. Inquiries for Jews just went into the waste paper basket. All letters and incoming packages also went through Draser's office. He interrogated prisoners and participated in gassings.

In 1947 Draser was in a sanatorium in Schleswig. On February 8, 1965, Hermann Langbein requested a judicial investigation of his activities. However, the German authorities said they could not locate him.

Drechsler, Margot

Born May 17, 1908, in Nengersdorf (Saxony). Oberaufseherin. She was sentenced to death in the Cracow trial and executed in Poland after the war.

Egersdoerfer, Karl

Born July 20, 1902 in Rosenbach/Bavaria. SS-Unterscharfuehrer, member of the NSDAP since 1934. Membership number in the SS, #289457.

Worked since March 1941 in Auschwitz. From July 1941 he was in charge of the prison kitchen in Auschwitz I. He was acquitted in the trial of the British Military Tribunal in Lueneburg on November 17, 1945, against the crew of the Bergen-Belsen concentration camp. He lives (or lived) in Erlangen, Schillerstrasse 8.

Emmerich, Wilhelm

Born July 2, 1916, in Tiefenbach. SS-Unterscharfuehrer. He supposedly died of typhus in the military hospital of Schwarmstedt.

Erber, Josef (formerly Hustek)

Born October 16, 1897, in Ottendorf, Czechoslovakia. From autumn 1940 until the evacuation he worked in reception of the Political Section of Auschwitz. On February 1, 1944, he became Oberscharfuehrer. Later he worked in Mauthausen. In Frankfurt he was sentenced to life in prison.

Frank, Dr. Willy

Born February 9, 1903, in Regensburg. He worked from March 1943 until August 1944 as dentist in Auschwitz and later, in Dachau. After the war he was in private practice in Stuttgart, Bad Cannstadt. He was sentenced in the Frankfurt Auschwitz trial.

Franz, Anneliese (née Hasse)

Born December 28, 1913, in Goerlitz. She was SS-Aufseherin in the kitchen of the women's camp in Birkenau. After Auschwitz she went to Muehldorf. She died on August 29, 1956.

Fugger, Franz (or Andreas)

Born November 18, 1920, in Mettnitz, Austria. Unterscharfueher. He worked in the Institute of Hygiene. After the war he changed his name to Creigher and lived (or lives) in Friesnach (Kaernten).

Gierisch, Martin

Architect of the Central Construction Company in Auschwitz. He was acquitted in Poland. He died on November 11, 1965.

Glaue (or Claue), Bernhard

SS-Oberscharfuehrer. Came from Pomerania. He was Kommandofuehrer in Harmense. He is said to have fallen during the war.

Goebel, Dr. Johannes

Born October 29, 1891, in Berlin. A chemist (or pharmacologist) who worked for the Schering Company. He was the assistant of Prof. Clauberg in Block 10 in Auschwitz. He died on November 8, 1952, in Bremen.

Grabner, Maximilian

Untersturmfuehrer. A Viennese, he was the director of the Politische Abteilung. He was of medium height and spoke unclearly, as if he had something in his mouth. He loved sports and gymnastics and jogged every morning in a dark blue outfit. Scruples did not exist for him. He participated in the Sondergerichte (special court proceedings which took place in Block 13, and later in Block 11. These sessions occurred every so often at the initiative of the Gestapo in the death block (the name given to the aforementioned blocks) and were parodies of justice administered by the Politische Abteilung. For example, in early spring 1943, when the secret resistance movement was discovered in camp, Grabner randomly selected prisoners from many kommandos, and most of them lost their lives. He especially pursued members of the intelligentsia.

Grabner's abhorrence of the intelligentsia and his lack of education are corroborated by former SS-man Pery Broad: "Grabner's hatred for the intelligentsia, to which he could not be said to belong, not even by the greatest optimist, was limitless" (*Reminiscences of Pery Broad*, p. 84). "The disconnected sentences of his oration and his vulgar German betrayed his complete lack of education. Nevertheless, he had silver stripes on his uniform. The initiated knew that in his civilian past he used to be a cowherd in the mountains. Now he proudly wore the uniform of the S.D. and was criminal investigator in the Gestapo" (Ibid., p. 16).

Furthermore Grabner was active in the mass gassings of Jews. He himself ordered the shooting of prisoners with small caliber weapons and afterwards faked the causes of death. In the fall of 1943 he was arrested on orders of the SS in Berlin and supposedly sentenced to a twelve-year prison term in Weimar.

After the war, Grabner wrote his memoirs while in a Polish prison. However, these are of questionable value. Not only did he gloss over his own activities, he exaggerated those of his colleagues who had denounced him in Auschwitz during the SS-trial.

He was sentenced to death in the big Auschwitz trial in Cracow and was executed by hanging on December 12, 1947.

Grell, Hermann

Born January 20, 1910, in Siebenbaeumen, County Lauenburg. SS-Rottenfuehrer. Kommandofuehrer in the gardening work squad in Rajsko. He was in Auschwitz from March 1941 until the evacuation in January 1945. He lived (or lives) in Luebeck.

Grese, Irma

Born July 10, 1923, in Wrechen (Mecklenburg). From March 1943 until the evacuation she was Rapportfuehrerin in Auschwitz. Later she came to Bergen-Belsen.

At the British trial in Lueneburg she was sentenced to death on December 12, 1945, and executed.

Hasse, Lisl
Born September 17, 1925, in Goerlitz. Aufseherin in the Arbeitseinsatz in the women's camp in Birkenau. At the end of 1944 she became pregnant through a liaison with SS-man Schippel. Supposedly she has been in custody by the British.

Herpel, Christoph
Born in 1905 in Seeheim an der Bergstrasse. SS-Unterscharfuehrer in the office of the Kommandantur from the beginning of 1943 until the evacuation.

Herpel, Friedrich
Born January 4, 1912, in the Rhineland. SS-Unterscharfuehrer in the kitchen.

Hoess, Rudolf
Born in 1900 in Baden-Baden, SS-Obersturmbannfuehrer. He was the first commandant of Auschwitz from 1940 to 1943. In December 1943, Hoess was appointed chief of Section ID of the SS WVHA. In late June of 1944, he was sent back to Auschwitz, on a temporary assignment, to preside over the murder of the Jews of Hungary. In the operation…Aktion Hoess, as it was named…430,000 Jews were brought to Auschwitz in 56 days to be annihilated there. The Supreme Court in Warsaw, Poland, sentenced Hoess to death and he was hanged in Auschwitz on April 16, 1947.

Hoessler, Franz
Born April 2, 1906, in Kempen. SS-Obersturmfuehrer. He was at first Arbeitsdienstfuehrer and later Lagerfuehrer in Auschwitz. On November 17, 1945, he was sentenced to death by a British tribunal and executed on December 13, 1945.

Hoffman, Hans
Born December 2, 1919, in Yugoslavia. SS-Unterscharfuehrer at the Political Section in Birkenau until the evacuation. At the Cracow trial he was sentenced to 15 years. He was released on July 28, 1956, and lives in Stuttgart-Muffenhausen, working as a locksmith. He was a witness at the Frankfurt Auschwitz trial.

Josten, Heinrich
Born December 11, 1893, in Malmedy.
SS-Obersturmfuehrer. He was second Lagerfuehrer and Arbeitseinsatzfuehrer in Auschwitz I. On December 22, 1947, he was sentenced to death in the Cracow Auschwitz trial and executed.

Jothan, Werner
SS-Obersturmfuehrer. Deputy of Bischoff at the Central Construction Company. He was a witness at the Frankfurt Auschwitz trial.

Kapper, Hans
Born May 4, 1920, in Trachenberg. SS-Unterscharfuehrer in the work allocation center (Arbeitseinsatz). On June 11, 1954, he was declared dead at the request of the Frankfurt District Attorney's office.

Kampmaier, Philipp
Born in 1924 in Uivydek, Hungary. SS-Rottenfuehrer.

Kiefer, Gwendolyn
Came from the Suedsteiermark or Slovenia. He worked in the Kommandantur. His post-war whereabouts are unknown.

Kirschner, Herbert

Oberscharfuehrer, he came from Dresden, was Grabner's right hand man and chief administrator of the Politische Abteilung from 1940 to 1945. On Grabner's orders he shot prisoners in the death block with 5-6 mm. small caliber weapons. He fabricated false documents and fictitious death certificates. The S.B. lists of those prisoners who were gassed immediately upon arrival at the ramp were handled by him. Kirschner participated in the special gassings which took place in the small "farmhouses" and in the mass gassings in the Stammlager in Auschwitz as well as in Birkenau. He sent goods which had belonged to the murdered Jews to his wife, Jesse Kirschner in Dresden, although he had signed an agreement (required of all SS-men) not to touch the property of Jews. Feliks Mylyk packed and dispatched the packages.

Kirschner also participated in the liquidation of the ghetto of Bedzin. After the war, Kirschner could not be located.

Kitt, Dr. Bruno

Born September 8, 1906, in Hamm. From June 1942 until the evacuation he was camp physician in Auschwitz. Then he came to Neuengamme. In May 1946 he was sentenced to death by a British tribunal for crimes committed in Neuengamme. He was executed on August 10, 1946.

Klein, Dr. Fritz

Born November 24, 1888, in Zeiden, near Kronstadt (Rumania). SS-Untersturmfuehrer. From December 1943 until December 1944 he was camp physician in Auschwitz and later in Bergen-Belsen. On November 17, 1945, he was sentenced to death by a British tribunal in Lueneburg and was executed on December 13, 1945.

Klein, Marianne (married name Rendel)

Director of the poultry farm in Harmense.

Kleindienst, Karl

Born February 26, 1903, in Austria. SS-Unterscharfuehrer. He worked in the bookkeeping section of the agricultural offices. After the war he was interned in Glassenbach (Salzburg). He died in Graz on September 2, 1958.

Koch, Hans

Born August 13, 1912, in Tangelhuette. SS-Unterscharfuehrer. SDG (medical orderly) and disinfector (Cyclone-B operator). On December 12, 1947, he received a life sentence in Cracow. He died in prison on July 14, 1955.

Koenig, Dr. Hans Wilhelm

Born May 13, 1912, in Stuttgart. SS-Untersturmfuehrer. He was camp physician in Auschwitz. His last known residence was in Holt-Colnrade. On May 4, 1945, his wife, Mrs. Dagmar Kalling-Koenig, reported him dead. Dagmar is Swedish and lives in Uppsala.

All inquiries as to whether Dr. Koenig is living in Sweden have been unsuccessful, although the likelihood of his living there is very great.

Kopotinski, Josef

SS-Rottenfuehrer, had received an honorary military medal during World War I.

Kramer, Josef

Born November 10, 1906, in Munich. SS-Hauptsturmfuehrer. Worked in Dachau, Struthof-Natzweiler, and in May 1944 as commandant of Auschwitz II...later in Bergen-Belsen.

On November 17, 1945, he was sentenced to death by a British tribunal and on December 13, 1945, he was executed.

Kremer, Dr. Joachim Paul

SS-Obersturmfuehrer, born in 1884. Professor of Anatomy at the University of Muenster. He was camp physician in 1942 in Auschwitz for three months. At the Cracow trial he was condemned to death, but because of his age his sentence was commuted to a prison term. After ten years, he was released in 1958 and returned to West Germany, where he died in the 1960s.

Langefeld, Johanna, née May

Born February 5, 1900, in Essen-Kupferdreh. She was Aufseherin in the first women's camp in Nohringen (county Nordheim). From 1941 unti April 1942 she was Oberaufseherin in KL Ravensbrueck and from April 1942 to October 1942 she was SS woman-in-chief in Auschwitz. In Auschwitz she was sentenced by the SS because of "organizing."

After the war she was extradited to Poland from where she escaped. She is said to have become mentally ill and became very religious. She died in Augsburg on January 26, 1974.

Lettmann

SS-Rottenfuehrer. Born approximately 1923. He worked as a guard in Rajsko.

Liebehenschel, Arthur

Born November 25, 1901. SS-Obersturmbannfuehrer. He worked in the Gestapo headquarters in Oranienburg and was commandant of Majdanek. From November 1943 until May 1944 he was commandant of Auschwitz I. On December 22, 1947, he was sentenced to death in Cracow and executed.

Lolling, Dr. Enno

Born July 19, 1888, in Cologne. SS-Standartenfuehrer. Chief of the Section D III in the WVHA (Wirtschaftsverwaltungshauptamt) in Oranienburg since March 3, 1942. He committed suicide on May 27, 1945, in the military hospital in Flensburg.

Mandel, Maria

Born January 10, 1912, in Muenzkirchen, Upper Austria. She worked at first in Ravensbrueck and later became SS-woman-in-chief of the women's camp in Birkenau. On December 12, 1947, she was sentenced to death in Cracow.

Manger, Herbert

SS-Unterscharfuehrer, born December 12, 1904. He worked in purchasing in the agricultural offices of Auschwitz.

Martin, Rudolf

Born in Burg, near Magdeburg, June 23, 1904. SS-Unterscharfuehrer. He was in charge of the ponds in Harmense. After the war he had been indicted in Poland. The sentence is not known. He lives in East Germany.

Mayer, Dr. Georg Franz

Born September 5, 1917, in Vienna. SS-Obersturmfuehrer. Camp physician in Auschwitz since the middle of July 1942.

In spite of information against him he was not investigated by the Austrian judiciary. He is mentioned in Dr. Kremer's diary. He practices medicine in Vienna 5, Reinprechtsdorfer Strasse 57.

Mengele, Dr. Josef

Born March 16, 1911, in Guenzburg. SS-Hauptsturmfuehrer. Since May 30, 1943, camp physician in Auschwitz.

He escaped to Argentina after the war and later went to Paraguay. Through intervention of Herman Langbein he was deprived of his M.D. and Ph.D. degrees from the Universities of Munich and Frankfurt. On March 23, 1954, he divorced his wife in Duesseldorf. All attempts by the Federal

Republic of Germany to have him extradited have been unsuccessful. The mysterious report about his death is rather doubtful in the light of new information.

Moeckel, Ernst Karl
Born January 9, 1901. Obersturmbannfuehrer, director of the SS-Standortverwaltung. On April 20, 1943, he was transferred to Burger. He was sentenced to death in Cracow on December 22, 1947, and executed.

Mokrus, J.
Came from Upper Silesia. SS-Oberscharfuehrer. He was the head of the penal squad in the women's camp and later Kommandofuehrer in Plawy.

Moll, Otto Wilhelm
Born March 4, 1915, in Hohenschoenberg, county Greuesmuehlen. SS-Oberscharfuehrer. He worked in Sachsenhausen and became the chief of the crematoria in Auschwitz. After the war he was sentenced to death by an American military tribunal for killings that occurred during the evacuation of a satellite camp of Dachau. On May 28, 1946, he was executed in Landsberg.

Mrugowsky, Prof. Joachim
SS-Oberfuehrer and chief of the Hygienic Institute of the Waffen-SS. He was sentenced to death during the Nuremberg trial of physicians by an American military tribunal on August 20, 1947, and was executed.

Muelsow
SS-Untersturmfuehrer. Meteorologist in Rajsko.

Muench, Dr. Hans
Born May 14, 1911, in Freiburg/Breisgau. SS-Untersturmfuehrer. From summer 1943 until the evacuation of Auschwitz he worked in the Institute of Hygiene. He was acquitted in the Cracow Auschwitz trial on December 22, 1947. He lives in Rosshaupten, county Fuessen, Allgaeu.

Nebbe, Detlev
Born June 20, 1912. SS-Stabscharfuehrer. From 1941-1944 he worked in the Kommandantur in Auschwitz. Later he worked for the Wehrmachts-Leitstelle in Cracow. On December 12, 1947, he received a life sentence in Cracow. On October 23, 1956, he was pardoned. He lived in Husum and died on April 17, 1972.

Nestroy, Edith
SS-Aufseherin. She was sentenced to three years in prison after the war in Poland. Later she lived in Kaiserslautern.

Opitz, Erna
SS-Aufseherin, born on October 6, 1910. She died on May 16, 1945.

Orlowska, Alice (or Alicia)
Born September 30, 1903. SS-Aufseherin in Auschwitz. She was sentenced to fifteen years in prison in the Cracow Auschwitz trial.

Pach, Josef (or Ludwig)
Rottenfuehrer, he came from Silesia and spoke Polish well. From 1943 he was a guard in the Politische Abteilung. He was cruel and especially hated Poles. He was present as interpreter when prisoners were interrogated and tortured. He also participated in the mass gassings of Jews and appropriated Jewish belongings.

Palitzsch, Gerhard Arno Max
Born June 16, 1913, in Grosspitz nr. Tharandt. SS-Hauptscharfuehrer, member of the SS since

March 1933. He worked at first in Sachsenhausen as Arbeitsdienstfuehrer. From May 20, 1940, onward, he was Rapportfuehrer in Auschwitz. On October 1, 1943, he was transferred as Kommandofuehrer to the satellite camp of Brno.

Because of a liaison with the Slovakian Jewish Rapportschreiberin of the women's camp, Katja Singer, he was first put into the bunker, then was court-martialed by the SS and sent to the penal camp in Matzkau and later to the front for probation. He fell in Hungary on December 7, 1944.

Pargner, Karl

Born August 6, 1921, in Kutterschitz, Czechoslovakia. Administrative Unterscharfuehrer in the Institute of Hygiene from June 1943 until the evacuation in January 1945.

On August 31, 1948, he was sentenced to fifteen years in prison in Poland. On June 16, 1956, he was pardoned. He lives in Conweiler, county Calw.

Rohde, Dr. Werner

Born June 11, 1904, in Marburg/Lahn. SS-Untersturmfuehrer and camp physician in Auschwitz. At the end of June 1944 he became SS-Standortarzt (physician-in-chief) in Natzweiler.

On June 1, 1946, he was sentenced to death in the Natzweiler trial by a British tribunal. He was executed on October 11, 1946.

Rosenthal, Guenther

SS-Unterscharfuehrer. He worked in the Landwirtschaft. He fell in February 1945.

Runge

SS-Aufseherin. Kommandofuehrer in the shoe detail and in the penal camp at Budy.

Sauer

SS-Obersturmfuehrer from Ingolstadt. Director of the DAW in Auschwitz.

Schlachter, August

Born January 25, 1901, in Barabein, county Biberach. SS-Hauptsturmfuehrer, director of the Construction Company before Bischoff, i.e., until 1941. He was later in Oranienburg, Natzweiler and Dora. As architect, in 1941 he installed the gas chamber in Crematory I in Auschwitz. After the war he lived as an architect in Biberach, Remminger Str. 17.

Schmidt, Otto

Born March 9, 1906, in Saarbruecken. SS-Oberscharfuehrer. Worked in the Political Section, also in the satellite camps of Blechhammer and Janinagrube.

Schulz, Wilhelm

SS-Scharfuehrer. Worked in the office of the Landwirtschaft.

Schumann, Dr. Horst

Born May 1, 1906, in Halle/Saale. Air Force physician and SS-Sturmbannfuehrer. Director of "Euthanasia" Institutions. In Auschwitz he selected prisoners in 1941 for "Euthanasia" Institutions. He later did sterilization experiments in Birkenau and Block 10 in Auschwitz.

Until 1951 he lived undisturbed under his name in Gladbeck. Then he went to Africa. After long endeavors he was finally arrested in Ghana and extradited to Germany on November 16, 1966. His trial in Frankfurt for having murdered 13,720 mental patients in the "Euthanasia" Institutions of Grafeneck and Sonnestein was discontinued in April 1971 for health reasons. In a separate indictment he was accused of having conducted sterilization experiments on male and female prisoners at Auschwitz. Before the start of the trial, 54 out of 115 witnesses had died.

Schumann died in Frankfurt in September 1983.

Schurz, Hans

Untersturmfuehrer, he came from Vienna and belonged to the S.D., the Sicherheitsdienst. He was Grabner's successor and headed the Politische Abteilung from the fall of 1943 until its liquidation in January 1945. It was during the directorship of Schurz that the mass transports from Hungary arrived. He frequently was present and assisted at the gassings. It was Schurz who gave a premium of two liters of liquor and 150 cigarettes to each SS-man of the Politische Abteilung in reward for the smooth operation in the crematoria.

He has been missing since December 1944 and been legally declared dead.

Schwarz, Heinrich
Born June 14, 1906, in Munich. SS-Haupsturmfuehrer. At first Arbeitseinsatzfuehrer and since November 1943 commandant of Auschwitz III. He later came to Natzweiler. In 1947 he was sentenced to death by a French tribunal and was executed on March 20, 1947.

Sell, Max
Born January 8, 1893, in Kiel. SS-Obersturmfuehrer. Director of the Arbeitseinsatz in Auschwitz. Beforehand he had been in Ravensbrueck and after Auschwitz he was in Dora-Mittelbau. On October 2, 1950, he was officially declared deceased.

Stiwitz, Friedrich
Born May 15, 1910, in Sobernheim, county Kreuznach. SS-Unterscharfuehrer. Rapportfuehrer and Arbeitsdienstfuehrer. In February 1944 he was transferred to Riga. He is said to have fallen during the last months of the war.

Swoboda
From Vienna. SS-Untersturmfuehrer in the Construction Company.

Tauber, Anton
Born February 13, 1922, in Grein (Sudeten). SS-Unterscharfuehrer, Blockfuehrer and Rapportfuehrer in the women's camp of Birkenau. Later he was Lagerfuehrer in Laurahuette. His post-war whereabouts are unknown.

Thilo, Dr. Heinz
Born October 8, 1911. In October 1942 he became camp physician in Auschwitz II. Toward the end of 1944 he was transferred to Gross-Rosen. He died either in May 1945 or in November 1947.

Thomsen, Reinhard
Born February 7, 1901, in Eckernfoerde. SS-Obersturmfuehrer since November 1943. From May 28, 1940, until the evacuation he was in Auschwitz. He worked as Caesar's deputy in the agricultural office. He lived as a farmer in Schleswig-Holstein after the war.

Tietz (or Teitze), Richard
SS-Rottenfuehrer, born February 12, 1902). Secretary of Caesar in the agricultural office. He had a glass eye.

Vetter, Dr. Helmut
SS-Obersturmfuehrer, born March 21, 1910, in Rastenburg. Camp physician in Auschwitz. He had been in Dachau before and was later transferred to Mauthausen. He was sentenced to death by an American military tribunal and was executed on February 2, 1949.

Volkenrath, Elisabeth (née Muehlan)
Born September 5, 1919, in Schoenau nr. Bad Landeck. Originally a beautician. She came to Auschwitz in March 1942 and worked in the distribution of bread and parcels. On November 17, 1945, she was sentenced to death by a British tribunal and on December 13, 1945, she was executed.

Wagner, Rudolf
SS-Haupsturmfuehrer at the Administration. He fell at the front in July 1944.

Weber, Dr. Bruno Nikolaus
Born on May 21, 1915, in Koblenz. SS-Hauptsturmfuehrer. Director of the Institute of Hygiene. He died in Homburg an der Saar on September 23, 1956.

Weimann-Caesar, Ruth
Civilian worker, director of the laboratories in Rajsko.

Wilk
SS-Hauptscharfuehrer from Upper Silesia. He worked as bookkeeper at the Construction Company.

Wirths, Dr. Eduard
Born September 4, 1909, in Wuerzburg. SS-Sturm-bannfuehrer. He was SS-physician in Dachau, Neuengamme, and from September 1942 until the evacuation, SS-Standortarzt in Auschwitz. He was arrested by the British and on September 20, 1945, he committed suicide in the camp of Neuengamme.

Wunsch, Franz
Born March 21, 1922, in Drasenhofen (Lower Austria). SS-Unterscharfuehrer. He worked in the Effektenkammer (Kanada). At the end of August 1971, he was denounced and arrested in Austria. On June 27, 1972, he was acquitted in Vienna.

Zabel
SS-Scharfuehrer. He worked in the Institute of Hygiene. He probably fell at the end of the war.

Ziemssen, Wilhelm
SS-Hauptsturmfuehrer, born February 21, 1910. Caesar's deputy in the agricultural offices.

Zimmer, Emma
SS-Aufseherin in Auschwitz. The Frankfurt Court of Justice halted the proceedings against her on August 25, 1961.

Zoller, Viktor
Born June 22, 1912. SS-Obersturmfuehrer and adjutant of camp commandant Hoess. He was sentenced to death by an American tribunal and was executed in Landsberg on July 28, 1947.

APPENDIX B

Synopsis of Major Dates and Events

Referred to by Participants

March 26, 1942 The women's concentration camp of Auschwitz came into being with the arrival of a transport of 999 German non-Jewish prisoners from Ravensbrueck and 999 Jewish women from Eastern Slovakia receiving prison numbers 1-1998

August 1942 The women's camp of Auschwitz was moved to camp BIa in Birkenau.

September 1942 A section of the basement of the Stabsgebaeude was used as living quarters for some women prisoners working in Auschwitz-based squads.

November 1942 Dr. Horst Schumann started sterilization experiments of male and female Jewish prisoners in Block 30 of the women's camp in Birkenau.

December 1942 The "Big Selection" took place in the women's camp in Birkenau.

January 1943 Prof. Carl Clauberg commenced sterilization experiments of Jewish women in Block 30 of the women's camp in Birkenau.

January 27, 1943 The only transport of French political women prisoners arrived in Birkenau.

March 1943 Block 10 in the men's camp of Auschwitz, having been remodeled to Prof. Clauberg's specifications, was opened as the experimental block for sterilization experiments.

April 20, 1943 The Neuendorf transport arrived in Auschwitz.

June 1943 Living quarters for the kok-saghyz women prisoners were completed and the Pflanzenzucht (plant cultivation) work detail left the Stabsgebaeude and moved to Rajsko.

August 1943 Thirty women prisoners from Block 10 and 85 men prisoners from

Auschwitz were gassed in the Struthof-Natzweiler concentration camp. Their bodies were delivered to the anatomy laboratory at Strassburg University for Prof. Hirt's skeleton collection.

November 10, 1943   Ten oophorectomies were performed in record time by prisoner physician Dr. Wladyslaw Dering on Dr. Schumann's teenage Greek guinea pigs of Block 10.

Summer 1944   The women prisoners of the Stabsgebaeude and of the experimental Block 10 were transferred to the newly constructed camp extension in Auschwitz.

September 1944   One SS block adjacent to the camp extension was destroyed by an air raid and Block 1, housing the former Stabsgebaeude prisoners, was damaged.

October 7, 1944   Uprising of the Jewish prisoners of the Sonderkommando in Birkenau.

January 6, 1945   Four Jewish women prisoners: Alla Gartner, Roza Robota, Regina Saphirstein, and Esther Wajcblum, who had smuggled gunpowder out of the Union factory for the resistance movement, were hanged in the camp extension in front of the prisoners.

January 18, 1945   Auschwitz was evacuated. Approximately 60,000 prisoners started the death march towards the West.

January 27, 1945   The Soviet Army reached Auschwitz and liberated about 7000 prisoners who had been left in camp.

APPENDIX C

Das Auschwitzlied

von
Aranka Heitlinger und
Margit Grossberg-Bachner

Zwischen Weichsel und der Sola schoen verstaut
zwischen Suempfen Postenketten, Drahtverhau
liegt das KL-Auschwitz, das verfluchte Nest,
das der Haeftling hasset, wie die boese Pest.

Wo Malaria, Typhus und auch andres ist,
wo dir grosse Seelennot am Herzen frisst,
wo so viele Tausend hier gefangen sind
fern von ihrer Heimat, fern von Weib und Kind.

Haeuserreihen steh'n gebaut von Haeftlingshand,
bei Sturm und Regen musst du tragen Ziegeln, Sand,
Block um Block entstehen fuer viele tausend Mann,
Alles ist fuer diese, die noch kommen dran.

Ausser Floehen, Laeusen, plaget Fieber Dich,
viele tausend mussten sterben kuemmerlich,
ja du wirst gequaelet hier bei Tag und Nacht
und bei jedem Schritte ein Posten dich bewacht.

Traurig siehst Kolonnen du vorueberzieh'n,
Vater, Bruder kannst du oft dazwischen seh'n
darfst sie nicht mal gruessen, es braechte dir den Tod,
vergroesserst unwillkuerlich dadurch nur ihre Not.

Traurig ziehn die Reihen nun an dir vorbei,
schallend hoerst Befehle du, wie "Links, zwei, drei!"
Hier etwas zu sagen hast Du gar kein Recht,
Wenn Dein Mund auch gerne um Hilfe schreien
    moecht'.

Vater, Mutter! Ob ihr noch zuhause seid?
Niemand weiss von unsrem grossen Herzeleid,
traeumen darfst Du hier nur von dem Elternhaus
aus dem das Schicksal jagte so schnoede dich hinaus.

Sollte ich dich Heimat nicht mehr wiederseh'n
und wie viele andere durch den Schornstein geh'n
seid gegruesst ihr Lieben am unbekannten Ort
gedenket manchmal meiner, die ich musste fort.

The Auschwitz Song

by
Aranka Heitlinger and
Margit Grossberg-Bachner

Hidden between the Weichel and the Sola
Amid swamps, sentry chains and barbed wire fences,
Lies the camp of Auschwitz, that stinking hole
Hated by its inmates like the plague.

Here there's malaria, typhus, and a whole lot else,
Here the soul's deepest anguish gnaws at one's heart.
Here are imprisoned so many thousands,
Far from their home, their wives and children.

You see rows and rows of houses built by prisoners.
Through rain and storm you must lug bricks and sand,
Barracks after barracks for thousands of people,
All this is for those yet to come.

Not only fleas and lice, but fever plague you,
Many thousands had to die wretchedly.
Yes, here you're tortured day and night
And guards watch your every step.

Sadly you watch columns marching past,
Often you see a father or brother in their ranks.
You can't even say hello, it would mean your death
Only adding needlessly to their suffering.

Sadly the rows file past you now,
You hear orders ringing out, like "Left-two-three!"
Here you have no right to say a word,
Even if you ache to scream for help.

Father, mother, are you still at home?
No one knows about our great agony.
Here you can only dream of the home
From which fate cast you out so cruelly.

If I should never see my home again
And like so many others, go up in smoke,
I send my greetings to you, my dears,
Think of me sometimes—who had to leave you.

Melody of the Auschwitz Song

(from a German folk tune)

Ministerium für Wirtschaft und Arbeit
des Landes Sachsen
Hauptabteilung Arbeit und Sozialfürsorge
VdN-Landesdienststelle
IV/3542:   D/52 - Oe.

Dresden, den ......28.7.1952......
Hausapparat 456, Zimmer H 17
Rückwirkende Versagung /
Zurücknahme der Anerkennung
bedeutet nicht Erstattung von
inzwischen erfolgten Leistungen.

~~XX~~/Frl./~~Herrn~~ ..... Charlotte Decker, Gersdorf, Badstr. 11

Betr.: ~~Zurücknahme~~/ Versagung der Anerkennung als Verfolgter des Naziregimes ~~(Hinterbliebener)~~ X

Auf Grund der Überprüfung gem. der Anordnung zur Sicherung der rechtlichen Stellung der anerkannten Verfolgten des Naziregimes vom 5. 10. 1949 wurden Ihre Unterlagen vom Rat des ~~Stadt~~ Landkreises - Sozialamt, VdN

.... Glauchau .... nach hier eingereicht.

Nach Durchsicht derselben wird die Anerkennung nach den Richtlinien für die Anerkennung als Verfolgter des Naziregimes vom 10. 2. 1950 (Gesetzblatt der DDR Nr. 14 vom 18. 2. 1950) lt. § ..5 Abs. b u. d)..

...(mit Wirkung vom 29.6.1951)...

versagt / ~~zurückgenommen~~

Mit der Versagung der Anerkennung als Verfolgter des Naziregimes ~~(Hinterbliebener)~~ wird zugleich die bisherige Anerkennung als Opfer des Faschismus ~~(Hinterbliebener)~~ zurückgenommen.

Begründung:

Sie haben durch Ihr Verhalten (Nichtbeteiligen an Wahlen, an
der Volksbefragung) die politische Bedeutung der VDN herab-
gesetzt und neofaschistischen Bestrebungen Vorschub geleistet,
so dass eine Anerkennung als VDN nicht erfolgen kann.

Ihnen steht das Recht der Beschwerde gegen diesen Beschluß innerhalb von 4 Wochen nach Erhalt dieses Schreibens spätestens jedoch bis zum ...30.8.1952...................... beim Landesprüfungsausschuß, Ministerium für Wirtschaft und Arbeit, VdN-Landesdienststelle, in Dresden A 50, August-Bebel-Straße 19, zu. Die Beschwerde muß eine zwar kurz gefaßte, aber eingehende Begründung enthalten.

Diese Begründung muß durch die entsprechenden Unterlagen belegt sein. Allgemeine Angaben in der Beschwerde versprechen keinen Erfolg.

Sie werden aufgefordert, Ihren OdF/VdN-Ausweis bis spätestens ...15.8.52...... bei Ihrer zuständigen Kreisdienststelle abzugeben, andernfalls er zwangsweise eingezogen werden muß.

VdN-Landesdienststelle

i. a. Berger

112 III/21/19 B 1,5 R 338

Notice of Abjudication as Victim of Facism

GLOSSARY

Abbruchkommando	*(German)* Work squad that destroyed houses
Abitur	*(German)* High school certificate
Ahnenpass	*(German)* Genealogical record to prove "Aryan" descent
AK	*(Polish)* Armja Krajowa, a Polish partisan organization
Aliya	*(Hebrew)* Immigration to Israel
Altweibermuehle	*(German)* Literally old women's mill, legendary rejuvenation process
Amie des Juifs	*(French)* Friend of the Jews
Am Yisrael Chay	*(Hebrew)* The people of Israel will live
Antreten	*(German)* To line up (for roll call or for marching out to work)
Appell	*(German)* Roll call
Arbeit Macht Frei	*(German)* Work liberates—notorious inscription at the entrance gate of Auschwitz
Arbeitsbaracke	*(German)* Work barrack
Arbeitsdienst	*(German)* Labor allocation office
Arbeitsdienstfuehrer	*(German)* SS-man in charge of the division of labor in camp
Arbeitseinsatzkommando	*(German)* Prisoner kommando which worked in the labor allocation office
Arbeitslager	*(German)* Labor camp
Arisierung	*(German)* Confiscation of Jewish property and business by "Aryans"
Askarah	*(Hebrew)* Memorial service or ceremony
Asozial	*(German)* Anti-social. The term used in camp for the black-triangled prisoners, mostly prostitutes and Gypsies
Auf der Flucht erschossen	*(German)* Shot while escaping
Aufnahmegebaeude	*(German)* Building of the reception
Aufseherin	*(German)* SS-woman
Aufstehen	*(German)* To get up
Auschwitz-Luege	*(German)* Auschwitz-lie, signifying the denial of the extermination process, punishable by law in Germany
Aussenkommando	*(German)* Work squad which labored in the outdoors
Austreten	*(German)* To relieve oneself
Ausweis	*(German)* Identity card
Autobahn	*(German)* Freeway
Baccalauréat	*(French)* High school diploma
Bauleitung	*(German)* Building section
Berufskartei	*(German)* Index file according to occupations

Beth Noar	*(Hebrew)* Youth movement
Bezaubernd	*(German)* Charming
Bibelforscher/in	*(German)* Jehovah's Witnesses
Bituach Leumi	*(Hebrew)* National Insurance
Blockaelteste/r	*(German)* Block senior (an inmate)
Blockfuehrer/in	*(German)* SS-man (or woman) in charge of a block
Blockfuehrerstube	*(German)* The office of a Blockfuehrer, usually near the entrance of camp
Blockova	*(Polish)* Female block senior (inmate)
Blocksperre	*(German)* Curfew during which no prisoner was allowed to leave the block
Buegelstube	*(German)* Ironing room
Buero	*(German)* Office
Bunker	*(German)* The prison block in a concentration camp. In Auschwitz I it was Block 11
Burgenland	Most easterly portion of the Austrian Republic bordering on Hungary
BV-er	*(German)* Befristete Vorbeugungshaft (limited preventive custody); in camp jargon, Berufsverbrecher (professional criminal), i.e., a criminal prisoner with a green triangle
C'est fini	*(French)* It's finished. It's all over
Chaluz/im	*(Hebrew)* Pioneer/s
Chacham	*(Hebrew)* Wise man
Chanoine	*(French)* Canon
Chanukah	*(Hebrew)* Festival commemorating defeat of Syrian Greeks by Maccabees, 165 B.C.E.
Chaver/a/im/ot	*(Hebrew)* Friend, comrade
Chevrah	*(Hebrew)* Group, community, commune
CNRS	*(French)* Centre national de la recherche scientifique, i.e., National Center for Scientific Research
Colposcopy	*(Greek)* Examination of vagina and uterus by means of an apparatus with strong optical lenses
Damenorchester	*(German)* Ladies' orchestra
DAW	*(German)* Deutsche Ausruestungs-werke, i.e., German Armament Works
DEST	*(German)* Deutsche Erd und Steinwerke, i.e., German Mineral and Stone Works
Deutsche Gruendlichkeit	*(German)* German thoroughness
Deutsche Staatsbuerger	*(German)* German citizens
Dienstverpflichtet	*(German)* Obliged to serve
DP	Displaced person
Durchfall	*(German)* Diarrhea
Effektenkammer	*(German)* Storehouse, section of camp where incoming goods were sorted out and stored
Einbrenne	*(Yiddish)* Basic stock for sauces, roux
Entlausung	*(German)* Delousing
Entzueckend	*(German)* Exquisite
Erez Israel	*(Hebrew)* The land of Israel
Erweiterung	*(German)* Enlargement, extension
Extraordinarius	*(Latin, used in German)* Extraordinary professor
Fahrbereitschaft	*(German)* SS motorized vehicle corps in camp

FFI	*(French)* Forces francais de l'interieur, i.e., French Forces of the Interior
FFL	Forces français libres, i.e., French Free Forces
FIPO	*(German)* Acronym for Finanzpolizei, i.e., financial police
FKL	*(German)* Frauen-KL signified the Birkenau women's camp
Fleckfieber	*(German)* Spotted fever
Flickstube	*(German)* Mending room
Forsteinsatzlager	*(German)* Forestry labor camp
Frauenlager	*(German)* Women's camp
FTPF	*(French)* Francs-Tireurs et Partisans Francais, i.e., French Freearchers and Partisans
Fuehrer	*(German)* Hitler's title. In camp everything was based on the Fuehrer principle, i.e., each Kommandofuehrer or Blockfuehrer and even Kapo and Blockova was a Fuehrer en miniature.
Fuehrerheim	*(German)* Officers' club in Auschwitz
Funktionshaeftling	*(German)* Prisoner occupying a prominent position
Gaertnerei	*(German)* Gardening, nursery
Gartenbau	*(German)* Horticulture
Gauleiter	*(German)* Nazi district commandant or governor
Gefahr	*(German)* Danger
Geheimnistraeger/in	*(German)* Bearer of secrets
Geist	*(German)* Spirit
Geltungsjude	*(German)* Considered a Jew according to the Nuremberg laws
Generalgouvernement	*(German)* Part of central Poland placed under German control in 1939
Geraetehaus	*(German)* Tool shed
Gestapo	*(German)* Geheime Staatspolizei, i.e., Secret State Police
Gryps	(Polish slang) Illegal, smuggled notes
Gut	*(German)* Manor, large farm
Gymnasium	(Greek) High school in Germany
Hachsharah	*(Hebrew)* Preparatory agricultural education for chalutzim (Israeli pioneers)
Haeftling	*(German)* Prisoner
Haeftlingsbeguenstigung	*(German)* Favoritism toward prisoners
Haeftlingsbekleindungs-kammer	*(German)* Clothing storehouse for prisoners
Haeftlingsschreibstube	*(German)* Inmate secretariat
Halt Deine Schnauze!	*(German)* Shut up!
Haute Couture	*(French)* High fashion
Hazkarah	*(Hebrew)* Memorial ceremony or service
Heimatgefuehl or Heimatverbundenheit	*(German)* Feeling of connectivity and alliance with home
Heim ins Reich	*(German)* Back to the Reich
Herrenmensch	*(German)* Master race specimen
HIAS	Hebrew Immigrant Aid Society, formed in the USA to assist immigrants
Hitlerjugend	*(German)* Nazi youth movement
Horah	*(Hebrew)* Modern Jewish Folk Dance
Hundestaffel	*(German)* SS canine corps in Auschwitz
HWL	*(German)* Hauptwirtschaftslager, previous term for TWL (q.v.)
Hygieneinstitut	*(German)* Hygienic Institute

Interessengebiet	*(German)* The blocked and sequestered area around the camp complex of Auschwitz, a region of approximately forty square kilometers.
Jahrzeitlicht	(German) Candle to be lit on the anniversary of the death of close relatives
Jude	*(German)* Jew
Judengasse	*(German)* Ghetto
Judenrein	*(German)* Free of Jews
Juedische Gemeinde	*(German)* Jewish community
Jugendlager	*(German)* One of the areas in Ravensbrueck concentration camp where women prisoners who arrived from Auschwitz in January 1945 were housed
Kaernten	*(German)* Carinthia, Austrian province
Kalfaktor	*(Latin)* Cleaner, heater
Kanada	*(Camp jargon)* Auschwitz kommando in charge of sorting out the belongings of the Jewish arrivals
Kapelusz	*(Polish)* Hat
Karpele	*(Yiddish)* Term for the camp soup in Birkenau
Kapo	(Camp jargon) Prisoner in charge of a work detail
Kartei	*(German)* Card file
Kashern	*(Yiddish)* Verb signifying process of rendering foods and utentils Kosher according to ritual law
Kassiber	*(Hebrew)* Clandestine communication between prisoners, or letters smuggled into or out of camp
KB	*(German)* Krankenbau, i.e., sick bay
Kennkarte	*(German)* Identification card
KL or KZ	*(German)* Konzentrationslager, i.e., concentration camp
Kochanyi	*(Polish)* Boyfriend
Kogel Mogel	(Slang) Food mixture
Koje	*(German)* Berth, three tier mass stone beds in Birkenau
Kol Nidre	*(Hebrew)* Beginning prayer on the Day of Atonement
Kommandantur	*(German)* Command building
Kommando	*(German)* Word squad
Kommandofuehrer	*(German)* SS-man in charge of a kommando
Kommandoruf	*(German)* Order, command
KPD	*(German)* Kommunistische Partei Deutschland, i.e., German Communist Party
Kraeuterkommando	*(German)* Work detail to collect herbs
Kriegswichtiges Unternehmen	*(German)* Enterprise important for the war effort
Kristallnacht	*(German)* The Night of Broken Glass, the pogrom of November 1938
Kronzeuge/in	*(German)* Star witness
Kurhaus	*(German)* Spa hotel, casino, health resort, restaurant
Kvutzah	*(Hebrew)* Group, especially in kibbutzim
Lager	*(German)* Camp, concentration camp
Lageraelteste	*(German)* Camp senior, the highest position a prisoner could occupy in camp
Lagererweiterung	*(German)* Camp extension
Lagerfuehrer/in	*(German)* SS-officer, deputy of the commandant
Lagerkleidung	*(German)* Prisoner clothing, the striped uniform
Lagerkommandant	*(German)* Camp commandant

Lagerstrasse	*(German)* Camp street
Landwirtschaft	*(German)* Agriculture
Lazarett	*(German)* Military hospital
Lehrgut	*(German)* Training farm
Leichenkommando	*(German)* Work squad charged with removing corpses
Libérez!	*(French)* Imperative: Free! Liberate!
Los, los	*(German)* Fast, quickly
Madrich/a	*(Hebrew)* Youth leader
Maquis	*(French)* Resistance movement in France during World War II
Marketenderei	*(German)* Sutlery, dealing with peddlers (sutlers) who sell goods and food to an army
Maslow, Abraham (1908–1968)	Professor of psychology at Brandeis University. He posited a need hierarchy from most to least powerful (see figure below). Only when the basic needs have been sufficiently satisfied can the needs for growth and cognitive understanding become salient.

Self-actualization needs
Esteem needs
Belongingness and love needs
Safety needs
Physiological needs

Meldung	*(German)* Short for Strafmeldung, penal report
Messtruppe	*(German)* Term for land surveyor work squad in Auschwitz
Mischehe	*(German)* Mixed marriage (here usually between a Jew and a Gentile
Mischling	*(German)* Offspring of one Jewish and one Gentile parent
Mishpoche	*(Yiddish from Hebrew Mishpaha)* Relatives
Mittlere Maedchen	*(German)* Intermediate girls, age group category in Gross Breesen
Mittlere Reife	*(German)* Diploma below the level of a high school certificate. Roughly equivalent to 0 level certificate in the United Kingdom
Mitleid	*(German)* Compassion
Mitmenschen	*(German)* Fellow creatures or human beings
Moorsoldaten	*(German)* Moor soldiers; title of first concentration camp song that circulated in Central Europe in the thirties
Muede bin ich geh' zur Ruh'	*(German)* Sleepily, I go to bed; first line of a German children's evening prayer
Muselmann(er)	*(German, inmate slang)* Literally, Moslems, extremely emaciated prisoners, walking corpses
Musterlager	*(German)* Model camp
Mutti	*(German)* Mommie
Nach vorn	*(German)* To the front—refers to prisoners being summond to the camp commandant, Blockfuehrer, SS-woman-in-chief, etc.
Nacht und Nebel or N.N.	*(German)* Night and fog, code word for particular treatment of prisoners; often it signified that the inmates were not supposed to leave the camp alive.
Naehstube	*(German)* Sewing room
Noar Agudati	*(Hebrew)* Religious Jewish youth group
NSDAP	*(German)* Nationalsozialistische Deutsche Arbeiterpartei, movement founded by Hitler

Nuremberg Laws	*(German)* In September 1935, Hitler promulgated discriminatory measures against all German Jews at the annual party congress in Nuremberg
Nummernbuch	*(German)* Book of numbers, prisoner records according to inmates' numbers kept by the work allocation office in Auschwitz
Obere Maedchen	*(German)* Older girls, age group category in Gross Breesen
Obere Naehstube	*(German)* Upstairs fashion studio or tailoring workshop in the Stabsgebaeude
Oberaufseherin or O	*(German)* SS-woman-in-chief
Oberlyzeum	(Germ. from the Greek) High school
Oberschlesische Zeitung	*(German)* Upper Silesian newspaper
Oberschwester	*(German)* Head nurse, matron
Oberwachtmeister	*(German)* Squadron sergeant, German police rank; also in the Schupo
Oneg Shabbat	*(Hebrew)* Social gathering in honor of the Sabbath
Ordensburg	*(German)* SS cadet training school
Ordnungsdienst	*(German)* Privileged prisoners in the Slovakian transports
Organisieren	*(German, inmate slang)* Obtaining a thing or things by some kind of sharp practice
Ostjuden	*(German)* Jews from Eastern European countries
Panzerfaust	*(German)* Rocket used in World War II to fight enemy tanks
Papirosy	*(Polish)* Cigarettes
Pechvogel und Glueckskind	*(German)* The lucky and the unlucky person, a fairy tale by Volkmann Leander
Perennierender Roggen	*(German)* Perennial rye
Personalkartei	*(German)* Card file of inmates by name
Pflanzenzucht	*(German)* Plant cultivation
Pfleger/in	*(German)* Practical nurse
Pflegestube	*(German)* Sick bay
Pfoertner/in	*(German)* Gate keeper
Pilpel	*(Inmate slang)* Young inmate boy who performed various services— including in many cases sexual favors—for a kapo, block elder or other camp functionary
Politische Abteilung	*(German)* Camp Gestapo of Auschwitz
Posten	*(German)* SS-guard
Postenkette	*(German)* Sentry chain. Auschwitz had a kleine (small) and grosse (large) Postenkette.
Primus	Small portable petroleum cooking stove
Protektorat	In 1939, Germany established a protectorate over parts of Czechoslovakia, i.e., over Bohemia and Moravia.
Protektorats-angehoerige	*(German)* German designation of the inhabitants of Bohemia and Moravia between 1939 and 1945
Quaddel	*(German)* Swelling of the skin
Raeder muessen rollen fuer den Sieg	*(German)* War slogan: wheels have to run for victory
Rampe	*(German)* Ramp, platform in Auschwitz where the Jewish transports arrived and the selection for the gas chambers took place
Rapportfuehrer	*(German)* The SS-man underneath the Schutzhaftlagerfuehrer and in charge of all the Blockfuehrers.
Rapportschreiber/in	*(German)* Inmate functionary helping with the administrative work of the Rapportfuehrer

Rashomon	*(Japanese)* A Japanese film produced in 1950, based on two short stories by Akutagawa Ryunosuke. It recounts a crime—rape and murder—from four different points of view: the rapist-murderer bandit's, the raped wife's, her murdered husband's, and that of a witness to the crime. Each story is creditable and the truth, always elusive, is never established.
Rassenforschung	*(German)* Race research
Rassenlehre	*(German)* Racial theory
Rassenschande	*(German)* Disgracing one's race
Rasse-Siedlungsamt	*(German)* Government office for settlement and racial affairs
Raus! Raus!	*(German)* Get out!
Realschule	*(German)* School stressing the teaching of mathematics and natural science
Rechtsabteilung	*(German)* Legal section
Registratur	*(German)* Registration office
Reichsprotektor	*(German)* Official title of Heydrich
Revier	*(German, inmate slang)* Hospital
Revieraelteste/r	*(German)* Revier senior
Rittergut	*(German)* Manor belonging to titled gentry
Rosh-ha-Shanah	*(Hebrew)* The Jewish New Year
Rotkaeppchen	*(German, inmate slang)* Women prisoners who worked in Kanada and wore red headkerchiefs
RSHA	*(German)* Reichssicherheitshauptamt, Nazi Department of Security, organized in 1939 and headed first by Heydrich and later by Kaltenbrunner
Rusznikarnia	*(Polish)* Weapons arsenal
S.A.	*(German)* Sturmabteilung, i.e., storm troop, Nazi brownshirt organization
Sachsen	*(German)* Saxony, province in Germany
Sammellager	*(German)* Collection point from which Jews were deported to extermination camps
Sammelplatz	*(German)* Square which served as gathering point for deportations
Saujuden	*(German)* Jewish pigs
S.B.	*(German)* Sonderbehandlung, i.e., extermination of Jews
Schloss	*(German)* Castle
Schnell, schnell	*(German)* Fast, hurry
Schreibstube	*(German)* Office
Schroepfkoepfchen	*(German)* Cupping glasses
Schuettelmaschine	*(German)* Shaking machine
Schutzhaftlagerfuehrer	*(German)* SS-man in charge of the camp, directly under the commandant
Schutzpolizei	*(German)* Protective police
S.D.	*(German)* Sicherheitsdienst, i.e., Security Service
SDG	*(German)* Sanitaetsdienstgrad, an SS-man who had received training as disinfector and practical nurse
Seder	*(Hebrew)* Ritual around the table in the home on the first two nights of Passover
Shabat-ha-Gadol	*(Hebrew)* The Great Sabbath preceding Passover
Sheitl	*(Yiddish)* Wig worn by Orthodox women
Siddur	*(Hebrew)* Daily prayer book
Schneidermeister	*(German)* Master tailor

Sonderhaeftling	*(German)* Special prisoner
Sonderaktion	*(German)* Euphemism for murdering Jews
Sonderkommando	*(German)* Special squad working in the gas chambers
Sortierung	*(German)* Selection for gassing
Sperre	*(German)* a) In camp: prohibition of leaving a certain block or area; b) In Holland: being put on a list to delay deportation
Spitzmaeuschen	*(German)* Literally, little shrew-mouse. May be used as a term of endearment.
Spritze	*(German)* Injection, shot. In Block 10 "die Spritze" usually referred to Clauberg's sterilization.

SS-Ranks

Army Equivalent	SS
Private	SS-Mann
Lance Corporal	Sturmmann
—	Rottenfuehrer
Corporal	Unterscharfuehrer
—	Scharfuehrer
Sergeant	Standartenjunker
Staff Sergeant	Oberscharfuehrer
Warrant Off. Cl. II	—
Warrant Off. Cl. I	Hauptscharfuehrer
—	Standartenoberjunker
Second Lieutenant	Sturmscharfuehrer
—	Untersturmfuehrer
Lieutenant	Obersturmfuehrer
Captain	Hauptsturmfuehrer
Major	Sturmbannfuehrer
Lt. Colonel	Obersturmbannfuehrer
Colonel	Standartenfuehrer
Brigadier General	Oberfuehrer
Major General	Brigadefuehrer
Lieutenant General	Gruppenfuehrer
General	Obergruppenfuehrer
—	Oberstgruppenfuehrer

Staatsoberrealgymnasium	*(German)* State-run high school with emphasis on mathematics and natural sciences
Stabsgebaeude	*(German)* Staff building
Stammlager	*(German)* Base camp or the mother camp, e.g., the men's camp in Auschwitz I
Standesamt	*(German)* Recorder's office or civil registry
Standortarzt	*(German)* The SS physician-in-chief of the camp
Standortverwaltung	*(German)* Camp administration
Stichtag	*(German)* Key date
Stinkjuden	*(German)* Stinking Jews
Strafgefangene	*(German)* Prisoner
Strafkolonne or Strafkommando	*(German)* Penal squad
Strohsack	*(German)* Straw mattress
Stubenaelteste or Stubendienst	*(German)* Inmate who cleaned the block and distributed the food
Sudetendeutscher	*(German)* Ethnic German from the Sudetenland
Sztubowa	*(Polish)* Room senior
Talmud	*(Hebrew)* Comprehensive term for the Mishnah, next to the Bible

	the main teachings of Judaism
Teichwirtschaft	*(German)* Pool management
Tenach	*(Hebrew)* Acronym for trilogy of Torah, Prophets and Writings (Hagiographa) formed from the initial letters Torah, Neviim, Ketuvim.
Tochus	*(Yiddish, from Hebrew Tahat)* Behind, posterior, arse
Todesmarsch	*(German)* Death march
Torwache	*(German)* Gate keeper
Totenkartei	*(German)* Card file of the dead
Triangles	A prisoner was identified not only by his or her camp number but also by the triangle which preceded it. The colors revealed the reason for imprisonment—red stood for political prisoner, green for criminal, pink for homosexual, purple for Jehovah's Witness, black for prostitute, black with the letter "Z" for gypsy (i.e., Zigeuner), yellow for Jew. However, the Jews wore a double triangle which formed a Star of David. All the RSHA Jews (those sent to Auschwitz for the "Final Solution") had a yellow and red Mogen David. Those admitted for "crimes" wore yellow and green on their number sign. A German non-Jewish inmate accused of Rassenschande (miscegenation) had a yellow and black Star of David.
Trockenboden	*(German)* Loft for drying clothes or laundry
Truppenwaesche	*(German)* Laundry for the troops
TWL	*(German)* Truppenwirtschaftslager, i.e., supply storage for the troops
Uebersicht	*(German)* Survey, review
Unter den Linden	*(German)* Boulevard in Berlin
Unterkunft	*(German)* Storage facility in Auschwitz
Unterkunftskammer	*(German)* Specific area in the Unterkunft
Untermencsh	*(German)* The counterpart to Nietzche's Superman
Verfuegbar	*(German)* Available
Vernichtungslager	*(German)* Extermination camp
Versippt	*(German)* Related
Verwaltung	*(German)* Administration
Volksdeutscher	*(German)* Ethnic German
Volkssturm	*(German)* German military units toward the end of World War II consisting of adolescent boys and old men
Vorzugshaeftling	*(German)* Privileged prisoner
Waescherei or Waschkueche	*(German)* Wash-house, laundry detail
Waffen-SS	*(German)* Armed SS
Wandervogel	*(German)* German youth movement
Wasserpolacken	*(German)* Poles living near the German border
Wegerich	*(German)* Plantain
Wehrmacht	*(German)* All German military forces from 1933-1945
Weisskaeppchen	*(German)* Women who worked in the Weissen Effekten squad in the men's camp in Birkenau, sorting out incoming goods. They wore white headkerchiefs.
Weltanschauung	*(German)* Philosophy of life
Wiedergutmachung	*(German)* Popular term for the German legislation concerning individual reparation payments under the German Indemnification Law
Wirtschaftsbetriebe	*(German)* Economic enterprises

Wirtschaftskueche	*(German)* Designation for the kitchen in Malchow camp
WVHA	*(German)* Wirtschafts-Verwaltungshauptamt (Economic-Administrative Main Office). The central administration for SS economic activities, based in Berlin. Obergruppenfuehrer Oswald Pohl was head of the WVHA.
Zaehlappell	*(German)* Roll call
Zehnfingersystem	*(German)* Typing with ten fingers
Zentralbauleitung or ZB	*(German)* Central Construction Co.
Z.L.	*(Hebrew)* Of blessed memory
Zugangsliste	*(German)* List of new arrivals
Zurueck!	*(German)* Go back! (imperative)

Bibliography

Adelsberger, Lucie. *Auschwitz, Ein Tatsachenbericht.* Berlin: Lettner, 1960

Adler, H.G.; Langbein, Hermann; and Lingens-Reiner, Ella (Eds.). *Auschwitz, Zeugnisse und Berichte.* Koeln & Frankfurt/M: Europaeische Verlagsanstalt, 1979.

Allainmat, Henri. *Auschwitz en France.* Paris: Presse de la Cite, 1974.

Augé, Claude & Augé, Paul (Publ.). *Nouveau Petit Larousse.* Paris: Librairie Larousse, 1947.

Bailer-Galanda, Brigitte. "Der Leuchter Bericht," in *Information der Gesellschaft fuer Politische Aufklaerung,* Nr. 29, Juni 1991, pp. 1-2.

Bauer, Yehuda. "Danger Signals." *London Jewish Chronicle,* pp. 34-35. July 8, 1988.

Bauer, Yehuda. "The Danger of Distortion." *The Jerusalem Post,* International Ed., Sept. 30, 1989, p. 7.

Berger, Karin; Holzinger, Elizabeth; Podgornik, Lotte; and Trallori, Lisbeth (Eds.). *Ich geb Dir einen Mantel, dass Du ihn noch in Freiheit tragen Kannst.* Vienna: Promedia, 1987.

Bettelheim, Bruno. *The Informed Heart* (Autonomy in a Mass Age). New York: Avon, 1979.

Bezwinska, Jadwiga; and Czech, Danuta (Eds.). *KL Auschwitz in den Augen der SS.* Katowice, Poland: Krajowa Agencja Wydawnicza, 1981.

Bialowna, Irena. "Aus der Geschichte des Reviers im Frauenlager in Birkenau." In *Die Auschwitz-Hefte,* Band I. Weinheim & Basel: Beltz, 1987, pp. 173-184.

Bielecki, Jerzy. *Kto Ratuje Jedno Zycie...* Ludowa Spoldzielnia Wydawnicza, 1990.

Borowski, Tadeusz. *Bei Uns In Auschwitz.* Muenchen: Piper, 1987.

Brewster, Eva. *Vanished in Darkness.* Edmonton, Alberta: NeWest Publishers, 1984.

Broad, Pery. *Reminiscences of Pery Broad, SS-Man in the Auschwitz Concentration Camp.* Oswiecim: Panstwowe Museum, 1965.

Buber-Neumann, Margarete. *Milena.* New York: Seaver Books, 1988.

Christophersen, Thies. *Auschwitz: Truth or Lie?* P.O. Box 156, Verdun 19, Quebec, Canada.

Czech, Danuta. "Kalendarium der Ereiguisse im KL Auschwitz-Birkenau." In *Hefte von Auschwitz 4,* 1961, p. 4.

Czech, Danuta. "Die Rolle Des Haeftlings Krankenbaulagers im KL Auschwitz II." In *Hefte von Auschwitz 15,* pp. 5-112. Auschwitz, Staatliches Museum, 1975.

Czech, Danuta. *Kalendarium der Ereignisse im Konzentrationslager Auschwitz-Birkenau 1939-1945.* Reinbek bei Hamburg, Rohwolt, 1989.

Delbo, Charlotte. *Aucun De Nous Ne Reviendra.* Paris: Les Editions de Minuit, 1970.

Delbo, Charlotte. *Le Convoi du 24 Janvier.* Paris: Les Editions de Minuit, 1965.

De Wind, Eduard. "Der Experimentierblock." In *Auschwitz, Zeugnisse und Berichte,* M.G. Adler, Hermann Langbein and Ella Lingens-Reiner (Eds.). Cologne: Europaeische Verlagsanstalt, 1979.

Fejkiel, Wladyslaw. "Ethisch-Rechtliche Grenzen Bei Experimenten In Der Medizin—Und Der Fall Prof. Clauberg." In *Hefte von Auschwitz 2*, pp. 33-87. Wydawnictwo Panstwowego Muzeum W Oswiecimiu, 1959.

Friedmann-Vesela, Sylvia. Depositions in the case against Dr. Horst Schumann made before Judge Vojtech Majoros at the Hall of Justice in Presov, Czechoslovakia on July 1, 1968.

Garlinski, Josef. *Fighting Auschwitz: The Resistance Movement in the Concentration Camp*. Glasgow: Fontana/Collins, 1975.

Gutman, Israel (Ed.). *Encyclopedia of the Holocaust*. New York: Macmillan, 1990.

Hamburger Institut fuer Sozialforschung (Eds.). *Die Auschwitz Hefte*. Weinheim: Beltz, 1987.

Hartman, Geoffrey H. "Learning From Survivors." In *Remembering for the Future*, Theme II, pp. 1713-1717. Oxford: Pergamon Press, 1988.

Hautval, Dr. Adelaïde. *Médecine et Crimes contre L'Humanité*. Arles: Actes Sud, 1991.

"Heroes of the Jewish Resistance Honored for the First Time in Germany." *The Voice*, 1985, 31: 9-10, July/August.

Hill, Mavis M.; and Williams, L. Norman. *Auschwitz in England*. New York: Ballantine, 1966.

Hoess, Rudolf. *Commandant of Auschwitz*. Cleveland: The World Publishing Co., 1959.

International Auschwitz Committee. *Nazi Medicine, Doctors, Victims and Medicine in Auschwitz*. New York: Howard Fertig, 1986.

Jagoda, Zenon; Klodzinski, Stanislaw; and Maslowski, Jan. "Bauernfuss, goldzupa, himmelautostrada." Zum "Krematoriumsesperanto, der Sprache polnischer KZ-Haeftlinge." In *Die Auschwitz Hefte*, Band II. Weinheim und Basel: Beltz, 1987.

Jagoda, Zenon; Klodzinski, Stanislaw; and Maslowski, Jan. "Das Ueberleben im Lager aus der Sicht ehemaliger Haeftlinge von Auschwitz Birkenau." In *Die Auschwitz Hefte*, Band I. Weinheim und Basel: Beltz, 1987.

Kagan, Raya. *Nashim B' lishkat Na 'Gehennom*. Sifrat Poalim, Palestine, 1947.

Keesling's *Reference Publications*. "The Radical Right." London: 1987.

Kielar, Wieslaw. *Anus Mundi: Fuenf Jahre Auschwitz*. Frankfurt (Main): S. Fischer, 1979.

Kieta, Mieczyslaw. "Das Hygiene-Institut der Waffen-SS und Polizei in Auschwitz." In *Die Auschwitz Hefte*, Band I, pp. 213-217. Weinheim and Basel: Beltz, 1987.

Klodzinski, Stanislaw. "Laboratorium Instytutu Hiegieny SS w Oswiecimiu, Bulion z miesa ludzkiego." In *Przeglad Lekarski*, Nr. 1, 1969, pp. 67-71.

Koelbl, Herlinde. *Juedische Portraits*. Frankfurt/M: S. Fischer, 1989.

Kogon, Eugen. *Der SS-Staat*. Muenchen: Kindler, 1974.

Langbein, Hermann. *Menschen in Auschwitz*. Vienna: Europaverlag, 1972.

Laska, Vera (Ed.). *Women in the Resistance and in the Holocaust: The Voices of Eyewitnesses*. Westport: Greenwood Press.

Lengyel, Olga. *Five Chimneys*. Chicago: Ziff-Davis, 1947.

Levi, Primo. *The Drowned and the Saved*. New York: Summit, 1988.

Lewinska, Pelagia. *Vingt Mois a Auschwitz*. Paris: Editions Nagel, 1945.

Lifton, Robert Jay. *The Nazi Doctors*. New York: Basic Books, 1986.

Lill, Karl. "Erinnerungen." In *Hefte von Auschwitz 16*, pp. 137-157. Auschwitz: Staatliches Museum, 1978.

Lorska, Dorota. "Block 10 in Auschwitz." In *Die Auschwitz-Hefte*, Band I, pp. 209-212. Weinheim und Basel: Beltz, 1987.

Michalak, Wanda. *Auschwitz, Faschistisches Vernichtungslager*. Warsaw: Verlag Interpress, 1981.

Micheels, Louis J. *Doctor #117641, an Auschwitz Memoir*. New Haven: Yale University Press, 1989.

Minney, R.J. *I Shall Fear No Evil*. London: William Kimber, 1966.

Mitscherlich, Alexander; and Mielke, Fred. *Medizin Ohne Menschlichkeit*. Frankfurt a. M.: Fischer, 1981.

Muller, Filip. *Eyewitness Auschwitz*. New York: Stein and Day, 1979.

Naumann, Bernd. *Auschwitz: Bericht ueber die Strafsache Mulka und andere vor dem Schwurgericht Frankfurt*. Frankfurt/M: Athenaeum, 1965.

Nomberg-Przytyk, Sara. *Auschwitz, True Tales From a Grotesque Land*. Chapel Hill: University of North Carolina Press, 1985.

Nyiszli, Dr. Miklos. *Auschwitz, A Doctor's Eyewitness Account*. Geneva: Ferni Publishing House, 1979.

Ourisson, Dounia. *Les Secrets du Bureau Politique d'Auschwitz*. Paris: Amicale d'Auschwitz, 1947.

Perl, Dr. Gisella. *I Was a Doctor in Auschwitz*. New York: International University Press, 1948.

Piper, Franciszek. *Zatrudnienie Wiezniow KL Auschwitz*. Oswiecim, Poland: Panstwowe Museum, 1981.

Poliakov, Leon; and Wulf, Joseph. *Das Dritte Reich Und Die Juden*. Berlin: Verlags GmbH, 1955.

Pozner, Vladimir. *Descente Aux Enfers*. Paris: Juillard, 1980.

Rotmensch, Siegfried; Avigad, Itamar; Soffer, Eddy; Horowitz, Ada; Bar-Meir, Simon; Confino, Ronit; Czerniak, Abraham; and Wolfstein, Isidor. "Carcinoma of the Large Bowel After a Single Massive Dosis of Radiation in Healthy Teenagers." *Cancer*, 57:728-731, 1986.

"Schwester Angela—Der Engel von Auschwitz." In *Der Dom*. Kirchenzeitung fuer das Erzbistum Paderborn. 42 Jahrgang, Sept. 27, 1987, Nr. 39.

Sehn, Jan. "Carl Claubergs Verbrecherische Unfruchtbarmachungsversuche An Haeftlings-Frauen In Den Nazi-Konzentrationslagern." In *Hefte von Auschwitz 2*, pp. 3-32. Wydawnictwo Panstwowego Muzeum W Oswiecimiu, 1959.

Shelley, Lore. *Criminal Experiments on Humans in Auschwitz*. Lewiston: Mellon Research University, 1991.

Shelley, Lore. *Jewish Holocaust Survivors' Attitudes Toward Contemporary Beliefs About Themselves*. Ann Arbor, MI: University Microfilms, 1983.

Shelley, Lore. *Secretaries of Death*. New York: Shengold, 1986.

Sherwin, Byron. "Primo Levi and Arnost Lustig on Moral Implications of the Holocaust." *Shoah I*, No. 4, 1979, pp. 24-29.

Skodova, Julia. *Tri Roky Bez Mena*. Bratislava, Czechoslovakia: Osveta, 1962.

Smolen, Kazimierz (Ed.). *Problemes Choisis de l'Histoire du KL Auschwitz*. Oswiecim, Poland: Edition du Museé d'Etat, 1979.

Smolen, Kazimierz; Bezwinska, Jadwiga; Brandhuber, Jerzy and Czech, Danuta (Eds.). *Reminiscences of Pery Broad, SS-Man in the Auschwitz Concentration Camp*. Auschwitz: Panstwowe Muzeum Oswiecim, 1965.

Sobanski, Tomasz. *Fluchtwege aus Auschwitz*. Warszawa: Sport i Turystika, 1980.

Steger, Bernd & Thiele, Guenther. *Der Dunkle Schatten, Leben mit Auschwitz, Erinnerungen an Orli Reichert-Wald*. Marburg: SP Verlag Norbert Schueren, 1989.

Svalbova, Margita. *Vyhasnute Oci*. Bratislava, Czechoslovakia: Nakladatelstvo Pravda, 1948.

Szmaglewska, Seweryna. *Smoke Over Birkenau*. New York: Henry Holt, 1947.

The Leuchter Report, Decatur, Alabama: Samisdat Publishers, 1988.

Tichauer, Eva. *J' etais le numero 20832 a Auschwitz.* Paris: L'Harmattan, 1988.

Uris, Leon. *Exodus.* New York: Bantam, 1986.

Uris, Leon. *QBVII.* New York: Bantam, 1989.

Wellers, Georges. "A propos 'Rapport Leuchter' und die Gaskammern von Auschwitz." In *Informationen der Gesellschaft fuer Politische Aufklaerung.* Innsbruck: Nr. 24, Maerz 1990.

Wistrich, Robert. *Who's Who in Nazi Germany.* New York: Bonanza Books, 1982.

Zatuchni, Gerald I.; Shelton, James D.; Goldsmith, Alfredo & Sciarra, John J. *Female Transcervical Sterilization.* Proceedings of an International Workshop on Non-Surgical Methods for Female Tubal Occlusion, held June 1982 at Northwestern University, Chicago. Philadelphia: Harper & Row, 1983.

Zieba, Anna. "Das Nebenlager Rajsko," *Hefte von Auschwitz,* 1966, Verlag Staatliches Museum, Auschwitz, #9, pp. 73-108.

Zieba, Anna. "Die Gefluegelfarm Harmense," *Hefte von Auschwitz,* 1970, Verlag Staatliches Museum, Auschwitz, #11, pp. 39-72.

Index